STAYED ON
FREEDOM

STAYED ON
FREEDOM

The Long History of Black Power
through One Family's Journey

DAN BERGER

BASIC BOOKS
New York

Basic Books
Hachette Book Group
1290 Avenue of the Americas, New York, NY 10104
www.basicbooks.com

Printed in the United States of America
First Edition: January 2023

Published by Basic Books, an imprint of Perseus Books, LLC, a subsidiary of Hachette Book Group, Inc. The Basic Books name and logo is a trademark of the Hachette Book Group.

The Hachette Speakers Bureau provides a wide range of authors for speaking events. To find out more, go to www.hachettespeakersbureau.com or call (866) 376-6591.

The publisher is not responsible for websites (or their content) that are not owned by the publisher.

Print book interior design by Linda Mark.

Library of Congress Cataloging-in-Publication Data
Names: Berger, Dan, 1981- author.
Title: Stayed on freedom: the long history of black power through one family's journey / Dan Berger.
Description: New York: Basic Books, 2023. | Includes bibliographical references and index.
Identifiers: LCCN 2022037502 | ISBN 9781541675360 (hardcover) | ISBN 9781541675377 (ebook)
Subjects: LCSH: Black power—United States—History—20th century. | African Americans—Politics and government—20th century. | Simmons, Zoharah, 1944- | Simmons, Michael, 1945- | Simmons family. | African American political activists—Biography. | African American civil rights workers—Biography. | Civil rights movements—United States—History—20th century. | African Americans—Civil rights—History—20th century.
Classification: LCC E185.615 .B455 2023 | DDC 323.1196/073—dc23/eng/20220823
LC record available at https://lccn.loc.gov/2022037502

ISBNs: 9781541675360 (hardcover), 9781541675377 (ebook)

LSC-C

Printing 1, 2022

For Aishah and Julian, catalysts of
an ever-expanding freedom journey

Look. How lovely it is, this thing we have done—together.

—TONI MORRISON

Contents

PART III: **THE KEY OF LIFE**

Photo section appears after page 196

EVERYDAY PEOPLE

2000

Every student loves a guest speaker. And the history class I took my freshman year of college had some great ones. There was the Vietnam War veteran who became an anti-war leader, spied on and shot at by the government he once served. There was the folk singer who performed ballads of strife and struggle. It was the only class I looked forward to that semester.

The guest speaker who would most change my life was a professor. She was a new instructor at the University of Florida, having started there that year. She was not a history professor. In fact, she didn't even speak about her scholarship. Faith and marriage had given her the name Zoharah Simmons, though she was born Gwen Robinson. And thirty-five years previously, she had been a member of the Student Nonviolent Coordinating Committee (SNCC). Her involvement in the civil rights movement had led her to put a two-and-a-half-decade pause on her college studies.

Her hair braided and pulled back, bright red lipstick visible from halfway back in the lecture hall, she began to speak. I cannot, in all honesty, remember what she said that day. She probably mentioned that she had been raised by her grandmother, who had been raised by her grandmother, an enslaved woman. She might have mentioned her first political act: an unplanned sit-in on a Memphis bus she did as a teenager after white employers refused to hire her for the middle-class jobs she was raised to desire. Regardless of the specifics, more than twenty years later, I remember feeling enthralled. To my surprise, she was teaching in the Religion Department—a field far removed from my interests at the time. Nevertheless, the following year, I enrolled in her Race, Religion, and Rebellion class. We read about the ways messianic faith and political protest comingled in African American history, from the nineteenth-century prophecies of abolitionists Nat Turner and David Walker to the ecumenical liberation theology of Martin Luther King, Malcolm X, and the larger civil rights movement. Along the way, Dr. Simmons revealed tidbits of her Baptist upbringing, her time in the Nation of Islam, and her embrace of Islamic mysticism.

Outside of class, Zoharah—as she invited me to call her—drew on her movement history as a faculty advisor to the campus activism I was doing against racism and for worker rights. Zoharah introduced me to the concept of Black Power. Pointing to her time as one of the only woman project directors of Mississippi Freedom Summer, she described Black Power as a response to the feeling of inferiority and helplessness Black people expressed under segregation. She described the motivations plainly: Black people needed to see one another as leaders, thinkers, and doers. Such self-assured affirmations of power were necessary to do away with decades of segregation and terrorism. What's more, she said in her lilting Tennessee accent, Black Power was a call for white people to confront racism at its source in institutions created and led by white people. Rather than division, Black Power pursued a coalitional strategy of organized constituencies pursuing social change.

I was shook. As she explained it, Black Power offered a plan of action—even for a white kid from the suburbs. I rushed to read what I could on the civil rights movement, disappointed to find that many historians associated Black Power with Stokely Carmichael or the Black Panther Party but dismissed the Atlanta Project of SNCC that Zoharah had codirected, where the call for Black Power originated, as an aberration. If her story was true, their story was at best incomplete.

That summer, I drove with several friends to Philadelphia to protest the Republican National Convention. We went to meetings at the American Friends Service Committee (AFSC), a Quaker peace and justice organization whose headquarters was blocks from city hall. Before coming to the University of Florida, Zoharah had spent two decades on staff at the AFSC doing everything from investigating government surveillance to leading international human rights delegations. Her ex-husband, Michael, whom I would meet a few years later, still worked there. They came to the AFSC as part of a cohort of 1960s radicals who looked to make social change their avocation—Black Power's long march through various institutions and across the planet.

2010

Dan, what are you doing here? The smooth baritone voice inquired behind me. I was surprised, for I was coming out of my own apartment building, where I had lived for almost two years, so none of the residents would be startled by my presence. And my surprise grew when I saw who was asking. *Michael?!* I half-yelled, in bewildered delight. *You live in Hungary! What are* you *doing here?* We moved to the porch and began to catch up, Michael with a backward Kangol hat and unflappable soul aesthetic, puffing on a cigarillo.

Michael Simmons grew up in a two-bedroom house about four miles from my two-bedroom apartment in West Philadelphia, in a part of the city that some called Brewerytown but that he lovingly called Norf Philly. Michael's stepfather had recently passed away, and Michael was staying in the family home, as he always did when he was in town from Budapest. But today he was in West Philly paying a social visit: it turns out that my downstairs neighbors were his niece and nephew. Their Arabic names owed to the fact that their parents, Michael's brother and former sister-in-law, had been in the Nation of Islam. My ongoing connection to the Simmons family was larger than I realized.

I had met Michael in 2005, a year after I moved to Philadelphia. He was a featured speaker at an event at the American Friends Service Committee presenting about Black resistance to the Vietnam War. He knew the subject intimately: he had refused induction into the US military in 1966, for which he spent almost three years in prison, and he organized a Black draft resistance network. We hit it off immediately. His face broke into a wide smile when I introduced myself as Zoharah's former student. (*Look, the marriage didn't work out*, Zoharah told me when I described our meeting, *but there's still a lot of love between us.*) I learned that he had grown up in Philadelphia, a bookish student in underfunded but integrated schools who narrowly avoided expulsion in his senior year of high school after he refused to stand for the Pledge of Allegiance. He left college in 1965 to join the Southern civil rights movement, a decision he described, despite seeing himself as *a born-again heathen*, with almost religious devotion. The freedom movement was his only aspiration. *I just knew I had to be there*, he would say. *There* began in the US South but would encompass a Black radical foreign policy that would take him to Cuba, the Soviet Union, Yugoslavia, and beyond. To him, Black Power was a plank of a universal freedom struggle—because there are no issues that are not "Black issues."

In prison Michael was a bridge between white pacifists and Black radicals—a connection that led him to three decades of work with the AFSC and ultimately to relocate to Hungary, a country I had only associated with my grandmother's deportation to Auschwitz. Coincidentally, I was participating in a conference in Budapest that fall. Michael met me at the airport, and I nursed my jetlag at a café patio in the Budapest sun near his apartment. The highlight of my trip was the "Ráday Salon," a monthly gathering of artists, activists, and others interested in human rights that Michael and his partner, human rights attorney and American expat of Costa Rican heritage Linda Carranza, hosted at their flat on Ráday Street. About seventy people of all ages crammed into the apartment for a delightful blend of food, music, and conversation.

Michael returned to Philly every year or two. If we didn't see each other in person, we might talk on the phone. Now, chatting on my porch in 2010, I asked if he would join me for a panel discussion I was moderating on Philadelphia activism in the 1970s, to be held at Robin's Books, which had, once upon a time, provided meeting space for the Black Panthers and Students for a Democratic Society.

It was a packed house and, to this day, one of the most generative public conversations I've been part of. As part of his remarks, Michael offered his own Zen meditation question on the erasure of Black Power's internationalism: *If a group of Black people organized an anti-war demonstration and no white people showed up, did it really happen?* Not according to many journalists and historians, he said, turning the punch line into a pointed barb. Michael had spent the 1970s working on two fronts: using affirmative action law to organize workers and fighting apartheid and colonialism in southern Africa. He applied both efforts within the AFSC, too, pushing the organization to adopt an affirmative action policy and divest from businesses that did business in South Africa. It was a matter of principle, for, as he saw it, daily actions determine political mettle. *I don't care who you are or what you've done in the past*, he told the crowd. *You've got to earn your wings every day.*

2011

As a newly minted PhD, I invited Aishah Shahidah Simmons to give a lecture on Black cinema to my class. Michael and Zoharah's only child, Aishah was also a celebrated filmmaker. She had spent more than a decade making *NO!*, the first documentary about sexual violence in Black communities. Zoharah had mentioned the project to our class in 2001, five years before its release. The film screened internationally and earned several awards. I first saw it at a Philadelphia art house.

I met Aishah at the AFSC event where Michael spoke in 2005 and would see her around infrequently. In 2009 a conference brought me to Chicago when she was a distinguished visiting professor at the University of Chicago. My visit overlapped with one from Zoharah, and the three of us had a sweet reunion in a different city.

Gregarious and quick with a smile, Aishah had a suffer-no-fools attitude that perfectly combined both of her parents into something all her own. She had grown up at the AFSC, first as a child and later as an employee. Now she devoted her energies to her advocacy filmmaking as AfroLez Productions. I didn't know it then, but she was beginning to devote increasing attention to addressing the sexual abuse she had suffered as a child from Michael's stepfather. Proudly committed to Black community media, Aishah was a big hit with my students. And when she mentioned that her brother, Michael's son from another relationship, was Tyree Simmons—better known as DJ Drama—several students gasped. And then their eyes turned to me, visibly reconsidering their sense of who I was. After Aishah left, when one brave student raised his hand to ask *How do* you *know* her?, I tried to explain the serendipitous influence of a good guest speaker.

2016

For years, as I read histories of activism and then as I started to write my own, I thought often of Michael and Zoharah. They seemed representative of the rich messiness of social movements. Their particular stories, rife with drama and excitement, raised several questions about the easy assumptions animating conceptions of the past. If the peace movement has been so white, how does one explain Michael's incarceration for draft resistance and transcontinental anti-militarism organizing? If Christianity is the foundation of Black activism, how can we understand Zoharah's journey from Baptist to Sufism, working alongside Quakers and communists? If Black Power developed in the North and contrary to the Southern civil rights movement, how could two civil rights organizers—one from the South, one from the North—have helped develop the concept in Atlanta as part of the premier Southern civil rights organization and then bring it with them to Philadelphia and points beyond? Their stories raised other questions too. How did Black Power converse with social movements around the world, from the fight against apartheid in South Africa or Palestine to the ongoing civil rights struggles of Roma people in eastern Europe? What are the personal costs of such full-time commitment to radical social change?

Two years earlier, I had published a book about the central role incarcerated people played in the Black Power movement, an extension of both my doctoral research and activism for prison abolition. That story ended in the early 1980s, with the entrenchment of mass incarceration and the death of several key participants in the anti-prison movement. It was a depressing story, and I longed to tell a hopeful story. Above all, as I promised my toddler that he would grow up in a better world—despite so much evidence to the contrary—I wanted to know how long-distance freedom fighters persevered through fear, panic, and the humdrum responsibilities of daily life.

So, in 2016, on International Women's Day, I asked Zoharah and Michael if we could collaborate on a joint biography. I knew they both had teased the idea of writing memoirs, yet their ongoing organizing often prevented them from the solitary discipline of writing. They agreed to the project. In discussing the process, we agreed that our interviews are their intellectual property, that I would be the book's author and bear the responsibility for gathering and interpreting the facts, and that any royalties the book may earn will be split evenly among us. What follows is their story, told to the best of my ability.

We spoke often over the next six years. In addition to the research I conducted in several archival collections, I spent hundreds of hours with Michael and Zoharah recording their stories. I went with Zoharah to Memphis, where the shotgun house she had shared with her grandparents and father is now an empty lot, surrounded on either side by replicas of the structure she once lived in. The neighborhood that had once joined well-to-do Black people with their working-class neighbors is now run-down, abandoned people living next to abandoned houses. The church she grew up in still stands, though, and we attended a Sunday service together.

During a weekend of interviews, Michael showed me the Philadelphia neighborhood he was raised in—now more integrated between Black and Brown than Black and white. Its working-class imprimatur persists. Michael's roots in Philadelphia are unshakable. The house where he spent his teenage years, the house where his stepfather molested his daughter, is his home whenever he is in the United States. (A friend of his lives in it year-round.) I stayed there for two nights in February 2019, filling up a whole legal pad with notes as Michael and I chatted until my wrists ached and my eyes drooped in the early morning hours.

The research for this book also took me to several archives around the country, where I sought to verify, contextualize, and expand Michael's and Zoharah's stories. It took me to many living rooms, too, some in person and many more over the phone or Zoom. In addition to Michael and Zoharah themselves, I interviewed dozens of people who have worked with them over the years, including their daughter, Aishah. Most of those I spoke with, like Michael and Zoharah, have rich histories of activism but little acclaim. These first-person testimonials capture the beating heart of the fight for freedom as can be recalled decades later. Even the memory of true events can be fungible and open to other interpretations, however, so I have opted to render remembered quotations in italics. Unless otherwise noted, passages in italics or other personal reflections shared here come from my interviews with Michael and Zoharah. A full list of interviews appears at the end of the book.

Two of many foot soldiers in the movement, both then and now, Zoharah and Michael show the multitudes of Black Power—a philosophy, an orientation, a social movement—as lived in one family. Their story is the story of a larger freedom movement that connects South and North in the age of Jim Crow, East and West in the Cold War era, and the world in a time of increased globalization. It links dorm rooms and jail cells, union halls and nonprofit offices, the church and the mosque, the study group and the classroom as laboratories of political participation. Black Power is the worldmaking pursuit of global justice, one that reaches well past the 1960s and into our own day and age, where the distribution of power continues to uphold profound inequalities that are often realized through racist violence and national exclusion. Seen from the lives of Michael and Zoharah, from the grassroots, such questions of power come sharply into focus. In their lives, Black Power drives a global struggle for freedom.

What follows is a story of love and hope, despair and persistence in pursuit of justice. This book is two people's stories, as those stories intersect, divide, and parallel each other. It is neither only their story nor all of their story. Rather, it encapsulates how people made through social movements remain, as the gospel song reworked to be a civil rights movement anthem puts it, stayed on freedom. The story unfolds largely in real time, thrills and heartbreaks alike. The past is a foreign country that we still live in, and this record of Black Power's evolution is undoubtedly shaped by the deep injustices and urgent mobilizations of our contemporary context. I hope that readers, like the subjects of this book, use each deepening revelation to ask new questions of themselves and each other about the world we live in and the one we would like to inhabit.

A LOVE SUPREME

THE MODERN BLACK STRUGGLE FOR FREEDOM IS A GLOBAL SYM-
bol of the pursuit of justice. Its glories can be found in print and in
song, on screen and on streets. Its details have been told through famous people, through major organizations, through signature places.
We have gotten to know Martin Luther King, Malcolm X, and Rosa
Parks more intimately than their famous speeches or dramatic actions
have revealed. We have gotten front-row seats to the hyper-democracy
of the Student Nonviolent Coordinating Committee, the patriarchal
charisma of the Nation of Islam, the inner workings of the Black
Panther Party. We have ridden the buses of Montgomery, faced the
snarling dogs of Birmingham, visited the homes of the "local people"
who welcomed movement organizers into rural Mississippi, stepped
inside the factories of Detroit, walked the Oakland streets. In each,
we learned something of the divergent goals, strategies, and philoso-
phies of the freedom fight.[1]

The story most of us have been told is already a riveting one. Yet
it is an incomplete one. Politicians crib its slogans—"We are the ones
we've been waiting for," Barack Obama averred in his 2008 presidential run—while both proponents and detractors cherry-pick the past,

describing Black Lives Matter as "not your grandfather's civil rights movement." Whether in plagiarism, disavowal, or genuflection, the civil rights movement continues to be the mother tongue of American protest. Every effort at transformational change speaks its language. Or at least tries to. Yet in cleaving civil rights from Black Power, politicians, pundits, and partisans slur the movement's collective spirit—its demand for jobs, housing, democracy, an end to police violence: for freedom. Juxtaposing the civil rights movement with contemporary efforts treats the former as either weak-kneed or too pure and the past as antagonistic rather than intimately connected to the present.

Black Power is the bridge connecting the twentieth-century battles against Jim Crow to the ongoing fights against war, racism, patriarchy, and capitalism. For the Black struggle for freedom has always exceeded the boundaries of person, place, and thing, of time and place, that have been put on it. The divides often used to interpret the movement—between North and South, self-defense and nonviolence, faith and secularism, the local and the global, the past and the future—were blurred in practice. Every movement produces a rich archive of strategic and tactical debates. But in the lives of people who bring the movement to life, those debates are not so easily partitioned. Because, as historian Robin Kelley has said, social movements "generate new knowledge, new theories, new questions," they count among them a curious and reflective lot. The needs of one era are not the same in the next, and the practices needed to change the world often shift accordingly. Yet the people persist.[2]

These transformations in activism are best seen over the duration of long political lives. Limiting the freedom fight to a time ("the sixties") or even a set of campaigns ("the civil rights movement") creates a distance greater than that lived by its partisans and participants. The children who grew up in segregated cities and towns, raised by people who bore the scars of Jim Crow's origins, became the foot soldiers in a battle against the ugly persistence of racism in housing, education, employment, and the legal system. Swept into action decades ago, many of those who survived struggle still. They did not cease their efforts because the 1960s became the 1970s, the 1990s became the 2000s, or because pundits and commentators proclaimed the movement dead and gone.

What keeps them going is fury that violence still haunts the land, that their children and grandchildren, their unknown fellow citizens of the world, live in a world of injustices made by race and class as well as gender, sexuality, ability, and nation. What keeps them going is the hard-fought realization that, even if change is difficult, the status quo is only guaranteed through apathy and indecision.

What keeps them going is love.

LOVE HAS LONG been associated with Christian pacifist tradition, an unquestionably large influence on the Southern civil rights movement of the mid-twentieth century. But the love I speak of here is not turn-the-other-cheek endurance. I mean something both more basic and more expansive. Love—for people, for struggle, for possibility—is where we seek to unify what we believe with what we do, to bring our best selves in service of an other. Love is an experiment and a leap of faith, a mixture of beliefs and practices, and in that process, it becomes a potent way to understand the long-haul commitments of those who join, and sustain, the fight for freedom.[3]

Inveterate organizer Ella Baker captured this spirit. Baker began her fight against racism and capitalism in the 1930s, at the height of the Great Depression. She worked for the Southern Christian Leadership Conference (SCLC) in the 1950s, until she could no longer stomach its patriarchal structure. Preferring to stay in the background, she served as an advisor and mentor to the Student Nonviolent Coordinating Committee (SNCC), the organization whose youthful members comprised the front lines of the battle against Jim Crow. In a 1964 speech, the sixty-year-old Baker described the object of her commitment. "Because as far as I'm concerned, I was never working for an organization, I have always tried to work for a cause. And the cause to me is bigger than any organization, bigger than any group of people, and it is the cause of humanity. The cause is the cause that brings us together. The drive of the *human* spirit for freedom."[4]

When Baker talked of the human spirit for freedom, she was speaking of the love that animates the heart of the organizer. Freedom is a love story. It is cacophonous and seamless, beautiful and tedious. Both felt and enacted, the practice of freedom is full of excitement and heartbreak. The thrill of discovery, of recognizing yourself and your aspirations in someone, something, beyond yourself. The joy and the anxiety, the exploration and the endurance that guide a loving human relationship can be found in the political realm as well, where the dream of possibility leads people to take big risks on the gamble that love might reward them their dreams.

Love clouds as well as inspires. It sharpens our appreciation of unnoticed features and blinds us to imperfections. It constricts attention while it expands our sense of the world. Love is not a zero-sum phenomenon: it is not something won or lost, good or bad. It is an encompassing relation. Love is the process through which people battle with the family that raised them and choose the family that sustains them. No less than the fight for freedom itself, love can be a source of hardship and exhaustion, of pain and loss, of sacrifice and redress. Love regenerates. It is the impulse to keep going.

OBSERVERS OFTEN LIMIT the emotional register of social action to naivete, or to anger. Yet grassroots organizing resembles life's other great creative pursuits. As in music so with grassroots politics: experimentation and improvisation reign. John Coltrane offers insight into the emotional complexity. During a UK tour in 1961, the jazz saxophonist explained his approach. "I've been told my playing is 'angry,'" Coltrane said of his exuberant style. "Well, you know musicians have many moods, angry, happy, sad." Coltrane rejected what he saw as the projection of critics. "Change is inevitable in our music—things change," the celebrated auteur of the Black avant-garde explained.

Coltrane himself had changed, having recently headed up his own quartet after playing a supporting role for jazz greats Miles Davis and Thelonious Monk. "I used to plan routines like mad," he said of shifting from ensemble to lead, "now I don't have to plan so much, as I learn and get freer." Experimentation was the linkage between education and freedom. "Sometimes we start from nothing. . . . I know how it's going to end—but sometimes not what might happen in between!"[5]

A leading figure of what was called free jazz, Coltrane's experimental style also describes how people make a life out of the pursuit of social justice. Movements are often remembered for their recognized leaders and organizations. But they are made by the mostly unheralded figures who act, learn, and act again. The story of social movements is a story of ordinary people doing extraordinary things, of changing and being changed by a changing world. Rather than limit focus to dramatic events—a march or a murder—the story of movements is one of polyphonic experimentation. It is a practice "of collaboration and improvisation" made primarily by those scholar Saidiya Hartman has called the chorus: "The chorus is the vehicle for another kind of story, not of the great man or the tragic hero, but one in which all modalities play a part, where the headless group incites change, where mutual aid provides the resource for collective action, not leader and mass where the untranslatable songs and seeming nonsense make good the promise of revolution. . . . So everything depends on them and not the hero occupying center stage, preening and sovereign."[6]

The chorus drives social change. Their individual voices leave fewer traces in the archives than the lead singer's. But the accumulation of harmonies makes the music. The accumulation, the gathering, draws attention to the practices of freedom. In naming the Black struggle for freedom, the historian Vincent Harding focuses our attention on the process itself. "Beyond protest, resistance, and rebellion," he asks, "what was the freedom they sought? What were the sources of their vision and hope?" These questions linger still, and in moving members of the chorus to center stage, we can begin to see how people labored to answer them—and how those answers deepened and evolved amid new challenges both intimate and existential.[7]

IN FOLLOWING THE experiments of two workaday organizers over sixty years of activism, *Stayed on Freedom* is a love story about the long history of Black Power as it developed across a variegated set of organizations, temporalities, and even continents. Though Michael Simmons and Zoharah Simmons (formerly Gwen Robinson) have scantly appeared in the pages of other published histories of the civil rights movement and its aftermath, the story of their lives stretches how—and what and when and where and who—we understand Black Power to be. It is a love story, not *between* two people but *of* two people, lifelong friends who shared a brief romance, united in pursuit of an evolving and global notion of freedom. The story takes us between South and North, West and East, the head and the heart, in a marathon race toward freedom. It is a human story, not a heroic one, although readers will find a great deal of heroism alongside fear, excitement, confusion, and even painful inaction.

Black Power was both a paradigm and a movement. *Stayed on Freedom* finds the origins of Black Power in the insights and strategies developed by the descendants of enslaved people—both those, like Zoharah's grandmother, who stayed in the South and those, like Michael's parents, who migrated north. Yet in both places, Black Americans developed networks of mutual aid, determination, education, and love to withstand the virulence of white supremacy. In what became the Black national anthem, James Weldon Johnson honored this approach in a song "full of faith that the dark past has taught us" and "full of the hope at what the present has brought us." That foundation enabled Michael and Zoharah each to lift their voice and take both planned and spontaneous steps toward becoming activists.[8]

Zoharah and Michael drew upon their experiences battling segregation and paternalism in both the South and the North when they helped voice a paradigm of Black Power in 1966. They did so as members of the Student Nonviolent Coordinating Committee, one of the premier civil rights organizations of the era. Yet from its beginning, Black Power was bigger than any one organization or geography. Indeed, as they transitioned from friends to lovers and back again, Michael and Zoharah remained stayed on freedom across an ever-expanding set of both organizations and geographies. At the height of the Black Power movement, Michael and Zoharah went from SNCC to the Nation of Islam, the National Council of Negro Women, and organizing both college students and prisoners. When James Brown sang "say it loud / I'm Black and I'm proud," he put to music the bold determination that Black Power organizers such as Michael and Zoharah brought to a slew of organizations in the late 1960s and early 1970s.

For many of those heeding its siren song, Black Power guided their focus as they made their way through what Stevie Wonder's 1976 album memorialized as "the key of life"—the work of parenting, aging, and maintaining hope in dark times. Although the Black Power *movement* receded in the mid-1970s along with Michael and Zoharah's romantic relationship, Black Power itself had a life that outlasted the movement's heyday. With intertwined lives, they plied the lessons of Black Power to shifting terrain as partisans of an ongoing fight for freedom. Black Power was a coalitional politics of self-determination, collective empowerment, and transnational solidarity. They brought those ideas, and the skills they developed pursuing them, into the Quaker social justice organization, the American Friends Service Committee (AFSC). For a time, their freedom journeys also prompted attempts to organize insurgent political parties. When those failed, they leaned into Black Power's global affinities. Throughout the late twentieth century and into the present, they have supported human rights movements in Africa, Asia, the Middle East, and Europe. Their journeys across borders fueled their endurance across time as they remained stayed on freedom into the new century.

To TAKE ON the possibility and suffering of other people—to stay on freedom—is an intimate project of solidarity. Although Black Power has been seen as a male-dominated movement, it was led and shaped by women and others able to embrace the intimacy freedom requires. Yet intimacy is no prophylactic against harm, and those who take on the awesome task of saving the world can also miss the violations that happen between those we love. To stay on freedom is a constant, if uneven, process of reflection and reckoning. As Black Power reaped global decolonization, it sowed the seeds of Black feminism—as much a continuity with the past as a departure from it. Perhaps the most harrowing step of the freedom journey, as for Zoharah and Michael, addressing the abuse their daughter experienced involves confronting intimate harm.[9]

Freedom beckons. Its ideal calls us forth, pulling at the heart, tugging after the mind. Freedom is not given, not legislated. It is taken, desired, pursued, studied, and learned. It is practiced. Its makers are workers and students, farmers and prisoners. This story focuses on two partisans of the Black struggle for freedom. Their stories are unique, yet the worldmaking talents of otherwise unknown people could be gleaned through the stories of countless others who, dissatisfied with injustice and alive to the possibility of freedom, chose to act and learn and keep acting still. And in doing so, they choose love.

PART I

LIFT EVERY VOICE

CHAPTER ONE

A MEMPHIS EDUCATION

From her grandmother, Zoharah learned America's political inheritance.

Rhoda Bell Temple moved to Memphis a widow. Born in 1898 in Earle, Arkansas, Rhoda was one of nine children of two sharecroppers. She was among the seven who survived into adulthood and grew up picking cotton. By the time she was twelve, both of her parents had died, their lives cut short by the toil of unending labor under the severities of Jim Crow. Her brother came home from Memphis to care for her and her siblings. He picked up the plow that he had abandoned so that his siblings could stay together instead of being sent to an orphanage. As with other Black children, Rhoda left school after sixth grade to work full-time. She pled with him to send her to boarding school so she could continue her education. But there was never the money.

At eighteen, Rhoda married Zebedee Robinson and gave birth to Major Lewis Robinson the next year. But Zebedee died of pneumonia in 1919, when Major was just two, and Rhoda moved thirty miles east, to Memphis, to live with her older sister. Black people, concentrated on the north and south sides, made up 40 percent of the Memphis population at the time.

She remarried there. The rocky relationship produced a daughter in 1923 and lasted two decades before they divorced. In her fifties, she met and married Henry Douglas, a World War I veteran and union member who worked at a local whiskey distillery. They bought a three-room shotgun house at 865 McComb Avenue, on a small street in an area of North Memphis called "the bottom." Each room in the house was connected to another, offering little privacy. In its cozy environs, Rhoda assisted her daughter-in-law, Juanita Cranford, in giving birth to a child she would raise.

Gwendolyn Delores Robinson was born on August 9, 1944. Though Juanita had a child from a previous marriage, Gwen was the only child born to Juanita and Major. She was Rhoda's only grandchild, and Rhoda would watch over this child from the beginning. Henry's job paid enough that Rhoda no longer needed to work outside the home, while Gwen's parents labored long hours—Juanita at the laundry where Rhoda had once worked, Major at a wood processing plant. Gwen's mom was the first Black woman at Loeb's Laundry to interact directly with customers, giving them the tickets for their dirty clothes.

Gwen was born into a segregated world. The library, the zoo, the pool, the lunch counter—all of Memphis's public institutions and most private ones either excluded Black use altogether or granted access just once a week, month, or year. Although there were three all-Black theaters, Black people had to climb three flights of an external fire escape to sit in the balcony in order to see first-run movies. Most Black workers chopped wood, picked cotton, or tended to white households for limited wages.

Routine incidents of police violence reinforced the city's hierarchies. Black suffrage was a privilege in Memphis. The city incorporated the small number of Black elites into its political machine in exchange for votes. When it seemed that Black Republicans and others might challenge the status quo in 1940, the Memphis police department began a campaign of harassment against Black Memphis that would come to be known as a "reign of terror." It was the latest in a series of pogroms that afflicted the city in the decades after the Civil War. "Psychologically," the eminent sociologist C. Eric Lincoln would say of the city where he earned two degrees, "Memphis has always been in Mississippi. Its presence in Tennessee is a geographical accident."[1]

When Gwen's parents separated when she was almost four, Rhoda took on full-time care. Gwen moved into the house on Mc-Comb, where she would live for the next fourteen years. Her bed was a fold-out couch in the living room. Her mother and half-brother lived a few blocks away, and she spent weekends with them. Her cousin Gloria, the same age as Gwen, lived within walking distance too. Gwen and Gloria were inseparable. When Gwen was about ten, Major moved into Rhoda and Henry's house. Juanita and her son joined family dinners on Sundays. At the center of it all was Rhoda, who relished her role as primary caregiver.

While gardening, canning vegetables, or quilting, Rhoda spoke of her own grandmother, Lucy Goldsby, who had helped raise her, much as she was now helping raise her own granddaughter. Lucy was a blond-haired, blue-eyed, light-skinned Black woman who was enslaved in Arkansas. Rhoda told Gwen that, as a teenager, Lucy was given as a gift to her half-sister. The white woman hated having a Black relation. She took that resentment out not on their father, the plantation owner, but on Lucy herself. Rhoda would cry as she recounted stories of Lucy's ordeal, of how Lucy was lashed with a buggy whip, of how she had a darning needle jammed between her fingernails and nail beds while she begged for mercy. Gwen would cry, too, as they quilted blankets huddled around the stove to keep warm in their uninsulated home. Solemnly, Rhoda would remind her, *White people are low down and dirty; they'll kill a Negro just as soon as look at them.*[2]

Gwen's mother feared white people; Rhoda taught Gwen to avoid white violence as best she could. The invisible marker dividing white from Black disappeared suddenly in the middle of Pearce Street, the road Gwen had to walk down to catch the bus connecting North Memphis to downtown. And when Rhoda determined that Gwen could ride the bus by herself, she advised her how to cross this treacherous terrain. *Don't stop*, Rhoda warned Gwen about the two-block walk to the bus. *If somebody tries to stop you or to talk to you, don't stop, don't look around.* At issue was not just safety but also justice. *If they do anything to you, nothing is going to be done about it*, Rhoda advised. *If need be, run.* And so Gwen ran. When white kids younger than her called her "nigger," she ran. When white teenagers threw rocks, she ran. When an older white man got out of his car, unzipped his trousers, and said, *Girl, look*, she ran.

Gwen's grandmother, however, did not run. Nor would she tolerate the diminutives of white elites who darkened her door. *I am not your "auntie,"* Gwen once heard her tell a condescending insurance salesman, there to collect his due on a predatory policy: *My sister didn't have any bastards.* Rhoda's brusque demeanor nearly resulted in bloodshed when her dogs caught a white man rustling among the fruit trees in their backyard. Rhoda grabbed her shotgun and put Gwen behind her as she opened the door and demanded to know who was there. Turned out to be a police officer. But Rhoda would not back down. *What are you doing in my yard? Oh, auntie*, the officer tut-tutted, *put that gun away before you hurt somebody. We're looking for somebody.* Rhoda told the officer to knock first next time.

Rhoda belonged to the International Order of Twelve Knights and Daughters of Tabor, a benevolent organization founded in 1871 by Moses Dickson. A barber and abolitionist who fought for the Union Army and later became a prominent clergyman in the African Methodist Episcopal (AME) Church, Dickson formed the Knights and Daughters of Tabor after the Civil War. One of many benevolent organizations formed in the late nineteenth century, the Knights and Daughters of Tabor claimed a membership of more than one hundred thousand people by the twentieth century. Its chapters stretched from Memphis to Maine to Michigan. There were even branches in England and the West Indies.[3]

Like other Black mutual aid societies at the time, the Knights and Daughters of Tabor stressed self-help, racial pride, and collective care of Black communities. Members received cash payments when ill, and their tithing offset burial expenses. Dickson encouraged members to "acquire real estate" and live moral and dignified lives. The Taborian Order preached ownership, nondenominational religion, "worldwide brotherhood and sisterhood," communal solidarity, and celebration "of black heroes who fought and fell for our freedom."[4] Even more than the church, benevolence organizations facilitated women's leadership. Tabor's close proximity to organized religion provided an easy pathway for women like Rhoda to participate. And like the church, Tabor was highly structured. It had formal roles and ran meetings using Robert's Rules of Order. Rhoda enrolled Gwen in the youth auxiliary committee, where she would raise money for the Taborian Hospital, which had opened its doors in the all-Black town of Mound Bayou, Mississippi, in 1942.[5]

Rhoda's commitment to citizenship rights exceeded her involvement in the Taborian Order. She had registered to vote in 1920—as soon as women were granted access. Whenever a white candidate deigned to speak about his platform at a nearby church, Gwen watched Rhoda and Henry ask him questions and debate with the congregation about whom to endorse. *We have to vote*, Rhoda would explain to neighbors, Gwen by her side. *This is our only voice.* The right to vote was about power, not candidates. When Willa McWilliams, Gwen's second-grade teacher, ran for school board, death threats poured in, and some neighborhood men took up armed posts outside her house.

And yet, Rhoda did not raise Gwen to be a political activist. She raised Gwen on family, church, and education. Sitting around the potbellied stove, Rhoda held class. She had loved school and resented that Jim Crow economics had forced her to forsake her own education. Gwen knew that she was to get as much education as she could. And she wanted to. She could see that her neighbors who had gone to college—her teacher, the family doctor, the pastor—all had nicer houses. Their floors were made of marble, not wood. They had gas stoves and space between the bedrooms.

At the center of Rhoda's and Gwen's lives was the church. Gospel Temple Missionary Baptist Church, a red brick building on North Manassas Street, first opened its doors in 1904. By the 1950s, it boasted a thriving membership. Blues musician W. C. Handy, the child of former slaves, performed an annual concert for the church. Even Rhoda, who inherited the religious suspicion of popular music, attended. The first time Gwen heard opera was when Alpha Brawner, her doctor's daughter, who had studied at Julliard and performed across Europe, gave an annual concert at Gospel Temple in full operatic regalia.[6]

The pastor, Rev. Dr. Charles Epps, would tell the congregation, *How we are being made to live is a sin.* Yet it was faith in God that would eradicate sin. Their obligation was to endure and to better themselves as best they could. Every week, Gwen would join parishioners in reciting 1 Corinthians, verse 13, which concludes, "And now these three remain: faith, hope and love. But the greatest of these is love." Gwen was deeply involved in the church: she sang in the choir and participated in church functions. It was at church that she learned how to participate in meetings, take minutes, and complete a task. And church wasn't just at church. Wednesday night Bible study met often at her school principal's house.

A stone's throw from the church was Manassas School. Originally a two-room schoolhouse built at the turn of the twentieth century on Memphis's north side, Manassas School served grades 1 through 12 and was a fixture of Black excellence. Both of Gwen's parents had attended, as had much of her extended family. Several of her teachers had been her parents' teachers, a fact they were keen to remind her of if ever she seemed derelict in her assignments. Whether as a pupil or a member of the staff, to be at Manassas was to be an emissary of Black uplift. They were committed to each other. The school boasted a proud tradition, in academics and in culture. Wearing his Phi Beta Kappa key, the principal would remind Manassas students of their school's accomplishments. Some of them, like jazz musician Hank

Crawford, had graduated from Manassas a decade earlier. Others, like the kid who had a perfect score on the SATs and was now at Harvard College, were recent alums.[7]

Gwen was as much a joiner at school as she was at church. She was editor of the high school newspaper, member of the Glee Club, and president of the Double Tenors, a social club for upwardly mobile young women at Manassas. She helped the school chorus raise money so that one of its stars, a broad-shouldered young man with a booming voice named Isaac Hayes, could afford to buy a suit for their performances. And that dedication was not just to classmates: it was to Black people.[8]

Such determination helped Gwen navigate her first social encounter with white people. Gwen had been a Girl Scout since she was a child; the troop operated out of Gospel Temple. And Girl Scout troops across the city were coming together for a sleepover. Standing at attention, Gwen watched as her troop's two leaders carefully inspected what each girl had packed. There would be no dirty or torn clothes in the group. The troop leaders even bought new underwear, just in case any girl needed them. Everyone had to look their very best. Gwen felt anxious. It was the first time any of them would be in such close quarters with white people, the first time they would set foot in the downtown Girl Scouts headquarters, and they were eager to make a good impression. But the white girls mainly ignored them. Segregation would not be so easily overcome.

Gwen was leery of white people. The pages of *Jet* magazine showed her why. The September 1955 issue arrived in her mailbox shortly after her eleventh birthday. In it, she saw the gruesome photographs of Emmett Till's disfigured body. Weeks earlier, fourteen-year-old Till had taken a train from Chicago to Mississippi to visit his family. A white woman there alleged that he had whistled at her—a fatal violation of segregation's color line. Her husband and his half-brother kidnapped Till from his grandfather's house. They tortured him, shot him, tied him to a cotton gin, and threw him into the Tallahatchie River. Three days later, his bloated corpse was pulled from the water and, with the help of Pullman porters and his mother's tenacity, shipped back to Chicago. His mother, Mamie Till, demanded an open casket funeral. "Let them see what they did to my boy," she insisted. *Jet* brought the pictures to Black communities nationwide. An all-white jury took less than an hour to find both men, who had bragged of the murder, not guilty.[9]

Gwen's immediate world, though, was full of love, people who nurtured Black excellence. But the world beyond that was too cruel to comprehend. While the news sang of American prosperity, why did some kids in her neighborhood lack shoes? Why couldn't she sit anywhere on the bus? Why were there limits on when she could use the library, watch a movie, or go to the bathroom? Her family, her teachers, and her pastor all agreed it was wrong. They assured her that Black people were being given a raw deal, and they cheered on Martin Luther King. Many counseled patience and self-regard, but what good had that done Emmett Till? The adults in her life lived with segregation. More and more, she could not.

Comic books and radio serials told of aliens and spaceships and far-away galaxies. As Gwen sat on her porch, overwhelmed by the vast expanse of the galaxy and the immeasurable meanness of her immediate surroundings, she felt out of place. Maybe, she tried to convince herself, she was from outer space. Looking at the night sky, she prayed for a flying saucer to return her to her home planet, somewhere away from all this suffering.

GWEN NEVER MADE it to outer space, but she did leave Memphis. A year after Till's funeral, Gwen and her cousin Gloria, both twelve, took the train north to Chicago to visit Gwen's aunt Jessie, Rhoda's daughter. A fun-loving spirit with a keen sense of style, Jessie chafed at Rhoda's strictness. She had graduated high school early and left Memphis as soon as possible. Jessie wore fur coats, beautiful clothes, and strong perfume. Gwen thought she looked like a movie star. On visits home to Memphis, she had taught Gwen and Gloria to dance, something Gwen loved despite her grandmother's warnings about the devil's corrupting influence. And now Gwen was on a train headed north to see her! The excitement began well before they reached Chicago. As soon as the train crossed the Mason-Dixon Line, the Black passengers stirred. *Little girls, c'mon! C'mon!* they encouraged Gwen and Gloria. *We don't have to sit back here anymore!* Swept up in the excitement, the two preteens moved into what, moments ago, had been white train cars. Some of the white passengers glared at them, others moved to avoid having to sit next to them. Didn't matter to Gwen: everyone could sit where they pleased now.

Chicago dazzled Gwen. Jessie wanted Gwen to see everything the South denied her. She worked styling mannequins at an upscale clothing store, perhaps the only Black woman window trimmer in a store catering to whites. Yet Jessie took off work for the week to show them around. They ate at the Woolworth's lunch counter, something they could never do in Memphis. They went to the museum and the movies, and they rode the subway.

Lake Michigan may have been the highlight. Gwen had been to the Black swimming pool in North Memphis but had never been in fresh water. *Is this the ocean?* she asked upon seeing the vast beach. And, seeing large groups of white people lounging in the sun, she wondered, *Are we allowed to be here?* It was all okay, Jessie affirmed, not mentioning that Lake Michigan once had been so segregated as to prompt a pogrom when a Black teenager was drowned after swimming into the ostensibly "white beach" in 1919. By 1956, the beach was integrated. Gwen splashed in the water, delighted to be ignored by the white people all around.

The two weeks raced by, and Gwen didn't want to return home. She pleaded to stay with Aunt Jessie. But when Rhoda threatened to come up and get her, Gwen and Gloria made the journey south.

AT SIXTEEN, FOCUSED on how she would support herself in college, Gwen needed a job. Her friends spent summers chopping or picking cotton. But Rhoda wouldn't have it. *You're not picking one boll of cotton,* she told Gwen. *I have picked enough cotton for you and anybody in our family.* Gwen would have to find another way.[10]

Looking to utilize the clerical training she received in high school, she clipped ads for several secretarial jobs from the *Commercial Appeal*. She caught the Number 31 cross-town bus to the commercial district. At each office, she was received with the same callous impatience: *Yes, girl? What do you want?* When she showed them the job ad, they showed her the door with a stern admonishment: *Who do you think you are? Those jobs are for white women.* First one, then two. Then another. All day. It was humiliating. It was enraging. And, when she got outside, it was pouring rain. *I do not belong here,* she told herself, as much in reference to the world of Jim Crow as to the business district. Her tears mixed with the rain as she, for the first time, felt like she understood what it meant to be Black in the South.[11]

When the bus came to bring her back across town, she was still crying. Without thinking, she sat in the front seat of the segregated Memphis bus.

Girl, you better get up from there and go on back where you belong, the driver snarled. Gwen just glared at him. No white passengers had boarded yet, but the Black passengers pleaded with her and prayed for her. *Oh, God! Please!* they pleaded. *You're gonna get yourself killed!* Gwen thought they were more upset than the bus driver. No white person could sit behind a Black person. So as white passengers boarded, they filled the aisles behind Gwen's front-row seat. The driver grew more upset. *Have you lost your mind, girl?* The white passengers hurled their curses, the Black ones their prayers. But as the bus wound its way from the white part of town to the Black, she would not be moved.

When Rhoda found out, she threatened to beat Gwen. *Are you crazy?* Rhoda shouted. *You can't do what them people down there in Montgomery did. You're never going to do that again.* Gwen had never seen Rhoda so scared. She asked a neighbor to help Gwen get a job at Harlem House, a Black-owned chain of hamburger joints. Gwen worked as a dishwasher until she went away to college.

After defying Jim Crow, Gwen felt something stir inside her. She pressed her grandmother for permission to join the National Association for the Advancement of Colored People (NAACP) youth group. Ultimately, Rhoda relented. They hadn't talked much about the NAACP or other activist groups at home, but a lot was happening in Memphis by that time. In 1959, a strong electoral effort brought 64 percent of Black voters to the polls in an attempt to integrate the city commission, the school board, and the juvenile court. It was an impressive turnout, even if it could not stop the election of mayoral candidate Henry Loeb, the racist former commissioner of public works and owner of the commercial laundry company where Gwen's mother worked.

That year, Black sanitation workers launched a unionization effort, and growing campaigns for desegregation linked access to public services with broader political power. In 1960, the year of Gwen's refusal to abide segregation on the bus, Black college students in Memphis staged a sit-in at the public library. All of this led to skyrocketing membership in the NAACP, local members of which had supported a number of these efforts. After years of dormancy, the Memphis NAACP reached almost six thousand members—an impressive feat given that the organization was still banned in Alabama at the time. It was the biggest branch of the national civil rights organization in the South.[12]

Gwen didn't participate in these dramatic actions; she didn't even know about most of them. She was still in high school, and much of the action was planned by college students, both in Memphis and in Nashville, Tennessee's other major city. There, Black college students had built a nonviolent army committed to toppling Jim Crow. In 1960, the Nashville Group began sitting in to protest segregation locally. The following year, they joined the Freedom Rides, integrated groups of activists challenging segregated facilities on an interstate bus trip through the South. After an initial batch of Freedom Riders had been badly beaten in Alabama, the Nashville students hurried themselves onto Alabama buses and into Alabama jails. Their bravery earned them a leading role in establishing the Student Nonviolent Coordinating Committee. Gwen had not heard of SNCC when she staged her impromptu sit-in. Three years later she would be elected to its leadership body.[13]

Gwen was on track to graduate third in her class as college acceptance letters arrived. She had been accepted to Howard University, Bennett College, and some of the primarily white institutions her teachers at Manassas had encouraged her to apply to. But she knew where she was going: Spelman College. Not only had Spelman offered her a full scholarship, but also many of the women Gwen most admired had attended the school, including the pastor's wife as well as the daughters of her family doctor. The first private college for Black women, Spelman had a long list of notable alumnae. Stepping out of the shadows of slavery and sharecropping, Gwen was headed to college. It was hard to tell who was more elated, Gwen or her grandmother.[14]

Gwen and her family drove to Atlanta while on the train came classmates from Manassas who were attending either Spelman or Morehouse College, both pillars of the historically Black colleges that comprised the Atlanta University Center (AUC). No doubt seeing her own dream of a college education fulfilled through her granddaughter, Rhoda reminded Gwen of her rules: *Join the first Baptist church that you find, don't get into any trouble with boys, and stay away from those people causing all that mess*—meaning the burgeoning civil rights movement.[15]

The church part was easy. *Come with me to my sister's church,* one of her new friends said. They walked past two churches, bending but not yet breaking Rhoda's instruction, before they got to a big brick building on the corner of Fair and West Hunter Streets. Gwen walked in and sat down, happy to be getting settled in her new city. Her friend waved to her sister, Juanita Abernathy, who turned out to be the pastor's wife.

Gwen was used to hearing sermons about the power of faith to heal the wounds of racism. Black churches nationwide criticized

racism's evils, and congregants prayed to God to ease their suffering. But this Atlanta pastor was different. A barrel-chested man
with a round face and a passionate sense of urgency, he still prayed
to God, but he also told the parishioners that they had the power to
effect change. *It's time for us to bring down Jim Crow*, Ralph David
Abernathy told his congregants. Gwen had no idea that Abernathy
was second in line at the Southern Christian Leadership Conference.
Before too long, his boss—the man Gwen had admired from afar in
Ebony and *Jet*, on the radio, and eventually on the television—Martin
Luther King Jr., preached to the church as well.

I joined a church, Gwen dutifully if partially reported in a call home
to her eager grandmother. *It's the West Hunter Baptist Church*, she said.
And I'm thinking of joining the choir. The whole family was delighted.
But the Robinson family's middle-class dream was soon disrupted.
For Gwen had joined not just a church but a movement.

CHAPTER TWO

WORLDMAKING IN PHILADELPHIA

MICHAEL'S PARENTS TAUGHT HIM THE POWER OF MOVEMENT through their separate journeys out of the South. His father, John William Simmons, and his mother, Rebecca White, were two of almost four hundred thousand Black people who left the South in the 1930s. Luck, family, and train lines would send them both to Philadelphia.

John left a farm in Avera, Georgia. John's father, six years old when slavery ended, couldn't read, but, as family lore had it, he could count. A successful farmer, he owned seventy-five acres of land in the small town between Macon and Augusta. That wealth spared the family some of the indignities of Jim Crow life. That bit of independence also provided his son John enough resources to head north with his first wife and two young sons. When he divorced, John retained custody of the kids.

For twelve-year-old Rebecca White, ingenuity more than money fueled her journey north. In 1933, the year unemployment skyrocketed to 25 percent and Franklin Roosevelt took office for the first of four terms, a determined young Rebecca left Rock Hill, South Carolina, and headed to her sister's house in Philadelphia. Rebecca supported herself through the only labor beyond agriculture routinely open to Black girls and women: domestic work for white households.[1]

John and Rebecca both settled in North Central Philadelphia, where almost a hundred thousand Black people lived by 1940. They found a city hardened by segregation and battered by the Great Depression. North Philly's bustling manufacturing industries received the new migrants with half-closed arms. To identify whether to finance mortgages and at what rates, the federal government's Home Owners' Loan Corporation drew red lines around and avoided the "hazardous" neighborhoods where Black migrants and their families lived in parts of North, South, and West Philadelphia. The housing stock was overpriced and poorly maintained.

Still, a house was only part of making a home, and there was a richness to Black life even amid the enforced poverty. As in the South, mutual aid and communal self-help provided what the law denied. In the eighteenth and nineteenth centuries, Black Philadelphians founded several prominent churches and benevolent associations, starting with the African Methodist Episcopal Church (1793) and the African Friendly Society (1795) and its women auxiliary, the Female Benevolent Society (1796). By the mid-1800s, the city had become a prominent stop on the Underground Railroad, aided in part by the Quakers' embrace of abolitionist sentiment. Philadelphia also hosted several meetings of a national "Black Conventions Movement" in the mid-1800s to plot a freedom course.[2] According to the Reverend Paul M. Washington, who would become pastor of the famed Church of the Advocate and a doyen of the city's civil rights movement in the twentieth century, North Philadelphia "contained every ingredient necessary to make a world."[3]

REBECCA AND JOHN tried to make a world of their own. They married in 1942, a year after the United States entered World War II. As thousands of soldiers headed overseas, labor shortages and the reorientation of the economy toward the war effort opened up the segregated employment market. John and Rebecca both benefited from this cracked ceiling of Black employment options: John took up work at the Philadelphia Naval Shipyard, and Rebecca made train cars at the Budd metal factory. Like their migration, their wartime jobs were part of a historic sea change. An estimated 40 percent of women provided manufacturing labor during the war, while more than forty thousand Black Philadelphians moved into industrial labor in just three years. This rapid transformation, along with the large number of Black soldiers fighting overseas, led Black Philadelphians to demand an end to segregated employment across the city. Yet, on August 1, 1944—less than two months after Allied troops stormed the beaches of Normandy in the war against fascism—white workers at a series of factories walked off the job to protest Black employment in the city's public transit system. The strike ended only after President Roosevelt sent five thousand troops to Philadelphia and threatened to send any strikers to the front lines in Europe.[4]

As the war raged on, both in Europe and on the streets of Philadelphia, John and Rebecca focused on their homelife. In June 1943, they welcomed their first child, Reginald, into the world. And at two o'clock in the afternoon on August 5, 1945, the day before the United States dropped an atomic bomb on Hiroshima, Rebecca gave birth to their second child: Michael Waldo Simmons. It was quite the full house then: in addition to Michael and two-year-old Reginald, John's two teenaged sons from his first marriage lived with them in the modest two-bedroom home.[5]

The war ended soon after baby Michael arrived, and labor segregation returned. John worked as a maintenance man at a local dairy and Rebecca at a clothing company. The family lived on a small alley at 2506 Stewart Street, a few blocks north of Girard Avenue, the dividing line separating poor Blacks from poor whites, and much of Michael's upbringing was characterized by this blend of proximity and distance. His elementary school was integrated and uniformly poor, yet social life remained segregated and unremarked upon. Many of his teachers were European immigrants passionate about

education, his doctor a Black woman. When his family gathered do-
nations for the even less fortunate, they delivered care packages to
as many white families as they did Black. Life at home echoed this
dynamic of proximate distance. Twenty years separated his parents'
ages, and his two oldest brothers, John and Nate—from his father's
first marriage—were nineteen and seventeen years older than Mike.
His other brother, Reginald, just two years his senior, seemed a to-
tally different person, reserved and into uniforms, athletics, and routine, whereas Mike delighted in books, music, and exploration.

Though Mike had a pronounced stammer, he would talk to anybody who would listen and read anything he could. Rebecca enrolled
her kids in the Boy Scouts and the church choir, both of which Reginald loved and Mike hated. Mike's third-grade teacher told Rebecca
to get Mike a library card: he had already read all of the books the
school library had to offer. He devoured every book about baseball
he could find, adopting his father's love of the Negro Leagues and
Jackie Robinson, who became the first Black person to play in Major
League Baseball when he joined the Brooklyn Dodgers in 1947. Next
to an encyclopedia set and his nightly prayer for straight hair, Mike's
biggest ambition was to have box seats at a baseball game. He read
baseball novels, memorized baseball statistics. He watched dramas
on television or at the neighborhood theater, but never cartoons. He
hated the four hours he had to spend at the AME Church every Sunday, restless and bored, while his parents enjoyed the only spare time
they had all week.

Mrs. Simmons ran a tight ship. Though Mike and Reggie played
with kids in the neighborhood, Rebecca always knew where her kids
were—and she made sure they knew that she was watching. *There's no
such place as "out,"* she would tell them: they were not free to roam, and
they were in bed by seven. Rebecca's formal education had stopped at
third grade, though she told everyone sixth. She guided her children
by a series of truisms. *There's no such word as "can't"*; she prodded her
children against making excuses or taking shortcuts. More affirma-
tively: *Good deeds are their own rewards.* As their coach: *Be willing to*

challenge any authority if you believe you are right. And, most importantly to her, *it's so easy to be nice.*[6]

The family read *Jet* and Chester Himes; they boasted of Jackie Robinson and "the Brown Bomber," prizefighter Joe Louis. On Election Day, John would join their city councilman neighbor in serving as a committeeman for the burgeoning Democratic Party machine, which was making inroads in this tightly knit community. Rebecca would soon become a shop steward of her union. Every few years, they went to Georgia, and sometimes South Carolina, to visit family. Mike was struck that his maternal grandmother's house had no indoor plumbing, that his cousins often went barefoot, that there were few places his family could eat or sleep on the journey south from Philadelphia.

SHORTLY BEFORE HIS eighth birthday, the same year he got his library card, the government executed suspected communist spies Julius and Ethel Rosenberg. On the radio, Mike heard that the Rosenbergs left behind two kids, ages six and ten, and he wondered what it was like to lose your parents. Two years later, he saw the bloated corpse of Emmett Till in *Jet* magazine. Mike saw himself in Till, a precocious Northern Black boy of Southern heritage. Yet when he tried to talk about it, his teachers, all white, scolded him for being disruptive.[7]

Around this time, Mike noticed a change in his oldest brothers. Although John and Nate had both served in the military—Nate fought in Korea—they were as different as two brothers could be. Regal and ambitious, John surrounded himself with upwardly mobile strivers. He went to college on the GI Bill and completed four years of study in two years' time. He earned a degree in accounting and even interviewed for a position with the FBI. Instead, he became the CPA for a local Black real estate firm. Nate, however, lived for the street. His gambling and promiscuity earned him a reputation in the neighborhood.[8]

Then, Nate stopped gambling and chasing women and started wearing a suit and bowtie. Intrigued, John followed Nate into a new

faith. Along with other friends and family members, the two brothers were among the initial recruits to the Philadelphia branch of the
Nation of Islam (NOI). Originally called the Lost-Found Nation of
Islam, the NOI had formed in Detroit in 1930. Like its predecessor
in the Moorish Science Temple, the NOI was Black popular religion
born of the Great Migration that blended an eschatology of Eastern mysticism, patriarchal self-reliance, and separatist anti-racism. Its
enigmatic founder, a man known as Wallace D. Fard, cheered the
people of Asia, preached that Black people were of "Asiatic" ancestry, and defined white people as a devil race created by an evil Black
scientist named Yacub. Within three years of founding the religion,
Fard disappeared mysteriously and his lieutenant, a slender transplant
from Georgia with a timid voice who declared himself the messenger
of Allah, had taken over. His name was Elijah (Poole) Muhammad.[9]

During World War II, Muhammad served three years in federal prison for sedition for encouraging NOI followers to refuse service in the US military and to not register for the draft. His prison
experience, together with the fact that many recruits to the NOI
were working-class Black people well acquainted with the criminal
legal system, led the NOI to recruit converts—"fishing among the
dead," they called it—from prison. And that is how a petty hustler
named Malcolm Little learned of the NOI while in a Massachusetts
prison. Several of Malcolm's siblings had joined the Nation, and his
own communication with Elijah Muhammad sealed his conversion.
Adopting the NOI naming convention that recognized that chattel
slavery had stolen his true surname, he became Malcolm X. Elijah
Muhammad, recognizing Malcolm's talent and energy, sent him to
organize congregations on the East Coast.

After opening a mosque in Boston, Malcolm was tasked with establishing NOI Temple 12 in Philadelphia. It opened at 1643 North
Bailey Street, four blocks from the Simmons family home.[10]

Mike didn't know any of these things when Malcolm walked into
the family house in the spring of 1954, a guest of his older brothers.
He regarded this wiry, well-dressed man with interest. Malcolm was

serious, respectful. Mike saw how courteously he treated Rebecca, despite her obvious suspicions of these men and their religion. They didn't talk much about Islam—Rebecca wouldn't allow it. But at dinnertime, Mike could not resist voicing his most urgent question: *How come y'all don't eat pork?*

He couldn't follow the answer, nor could he understand the god who would prohibit pork. But he knew it must be serious when John decided to move to New York City to be Malcolm's secretary.

MIKE EXCELLED AT school. His teachers praised him as "friendly to all" and "well-liked by his classmates." He was "an outstanding citizen and worker," a "leader in the classroom," with a special talent for social studies (even if, midyear, a teacher lamented that "he has been quite playful").[11] No doubt he was trying to understand his social world. On the news he saw President Eisenhower send federal troops to Little Rock in 1957. Their mission was to escort Black children to high school, after the state's governor sent in the National Guard and local white racists to block their admission three years after the Supreme Court had ruled segregated schools unconstitutional.

Mike couldn't believe it took the military to accomplish something as simple as letting Black and white kids attend the same school. At the same time, he could not yet know that white flight was deepening segregation in Philadelphia, and no federal intervention was forthcoming. As more Black people made Philadelphia their home, whites fled the city in growing numbers, taking up residence in segregated suburbs. Throughout the 1950s, with talk of segregation focused on Montgomery and Little Rock, white Philadelphia developers built more than 150,000 new houses. Barely 1,000 of them were available for Black families to rent or own.[12]

In Mike's home, the events in Little Rock were overshadowed by a more intimate tragedy. Weeks after troops were sent to Arkansas, his father died. He had had a stroke over the summer and never recovered. Mike took solace in baseball, making a scrapbook of the

newspaper clippings his dad had asked him to keep on the World Series when he was in the hospital. But reality soon knocked him off
the baseball diamond. With the family and close friends gathered at
his house after John's funeral, Mike was surprised when the idle chat-
ter turned serious. *Islam is the Black man's religion*, he heard someone
say, maybe his uncle or maybe it was Minister Malcolm, who had accompanied his brothers in their time of grief. *Christianity kept us enslaved*. Mike couldn't follow the heated remarks between his uncle, his
brothers, and their friends and his God-fearing Christian family, who
didn't know much about Islam other than that they didn't like it. But
he marveled at the repartee, the way his Muslim family kept talking
about slavery and its afterlife. Mike was intrigued but confused. He
knew that he liked pork chops and was bored by church. He wondered
what slavery had to do with the stolen childhood of Emmett Till.

WITH JOHN GONE, Rebecca eased some of her rules. Mike ate his
first hoagie, got a job delivering newspapers, and started going to
dances. So, too, did Rebecca. Two years later, Rebecca married Willie
Chapman, a gas company worker. The family moved a mile and a half
away to another squat rowhouse, and though it had a third bedroom,
Reginald and Mike still shared a room. At least now they each had
their own bed. Whereas their old house had been in an all-Black
neighborhood, now they were one of the first Black families to live
on the block.

With more freedom to explore the city, Mike stumbled across
New World Book Fair, a Marxist bookstore operated by a communist stalwart named Bill Crawford. Located in West Philadelphia,
the bookstore opened in 1961, the year when groups of multiracial
nonviolent activists braved racist mobs in Freedom Rides throughout
the South and a coalition of civil rights groups in Georgia faced mass
arrests in trying to desegregate the town of Albany.

Mike devoured the titles Crawford supplied him with, books by
communists Harry Haywood and Herbert Aptheker, and delighted

at Crawford's stories of Paul Robeson and the Scottsboro Boys. At sixteen, he was reading three newspapers a day, along with books by Howard Fast and Sinclair Lewis, George Orwell and Richard Wright. He didn't understand it all, but everyone he liked seemed to fit under the label of "rebel."

He rooted for rebels everywhere he saw them: the heroes he saw on television challenging Jim Crow in the South, the local NAACP members protesting employment segregation, and even Howard Roark, the protagonist of Ayn Rand's libertarian opus *The Fountainhead*. Watching the movie version, Mike cheered when Roark blew up a public housing project. *This is the baddest motherfucker to ever lace up shoes*, he thought of Roark's boldness. He read the book with enthusiasm and quickly joined the Nathaniel Branden Institute, the eponymous club established by Rand and her lover.

The rebels in his immediate midst were Black radicals. A flyer on a street pole led him to a debate about Black nationalism and communism. The two participants were Debbie Amos, who had been purged from the Student Nonviolent Coordinating Committee because of her membership in the Communist Party, and Max Stanford, co-founder of a semisecret organization called the Revolutionary Action Movement (RAM).

Any association with the Communist Party was risky because racists had long tarnished Black activists with the corrupting influence of communism. RAM, meanwhile, was a Black nationalist organization that launched its Philadelphia branch in 1963. RAM encouraged self-defense and self-reliance as foundations for Black political power. Its program included a plan to "propagandize the black community constantly by utilizing all forces of indoctrination" and staging "controversial public meetings" and demonstrations. Like the Communist Party, RAM was highly class conscious. And, similar to the NOI, RAM advocated Black people organizing apart from whites. RAM urged "Afro-American college youth to unite with black working class youth" in study groups and collective protest, north and south.[13]

The particulars of the debate were lost on him, but Mike was eager to learn from Stanford, who talked about Marcus Garvey and the Universal Negro Improvement Association, which had garnered upward of six million members at the height of Jim Crow with its message of pan-African internationalism. Confident of his studies, Mike was adamant: *Man, there is no way in hell that that could be true and I am just hearing about it for the first time.* But he dutifully asked his teachers. When they didn't know either, he hit the books.[14]

He kept seeking out Stanford, who told him about the case of Robert Williams, the head of the Monroe, North Carolina, NAACP who was run out of town for practicing armed self-defense against white terrorism. Williams took up refuge in Cuba and China; later he would go to Tanzania. He was a model for RAM, Stanford said. Mike wanted to know more and read anything he could find about the present cohort of civil rights activists garnering national attention, a small cross section of the larger movement he so desperately wanted to join. Williams published a newsletter, *The Crusader*, that Mike began to read.[15]

Mike spent Friday nights discussing philosophy and politics with a collection of polymaths and autodidacts at a North Philadelphia community center called the Heritage House. Part of the Philadelphia Cotillion Society, the Heritage House was founded in 1954 by Dr. Eugene Waymon Jones, a patrician man of arts and letters. The building was located in a mansion on Broad and Master Streets, a busy intersection near Temple University. Jones was on the board of the local NAACP and Dra-Mu Opera Company and had started the Philadelphia Cotillion Society. Heritage House was the "educational wing" of the Cotillion Society, and it hosted the lavish annual fundraising gala. Heritage House provided educational and cultural opportunities for Black youth. It held classes and performances in dance, theater, and music.[16]

The Heritage House tutors were serious about preparing the teenagers for the annual cotillion, a step toward the middle-class life many Heritage House parents imagined for their children. The youth spent three months learning the dances and adjusting to the formal wear. But for curious youth like Mike, Heritage House was also a space to hang out. In the welcoming environment provided by Dr. Jones, Black teens could talk about the world outside away from the prying eyes of teachers and parents. Mike made fast friends. He earned a reputation as a curious but affable young man, contrarian without being annoying. Mike relished the heady environment, surrounded by people asking big questions of the world. There was no form to it, just exploration. People shared book recommendations as they discussed cybernetics and Sartre, Camus and the Algerian Revolution. Through John Churchville, who played piano at Heritage House and had traveled south as an activist, Mike learned of Friends of SNCC, a Northern support organization to the front lines of the Southern movement.[17]

In June 1963, when Malcolm X visited nearby Camden, New Jersey, to give a talk, Mike recruited several Heritage House friends to accompany him. It was hard to reconcile the fiery speaker in front of him with the reserved man who had visited his house a decade earlier, but here he was. With the news focused on the upcoming March on Washington for Jobs and Freedom, Malcolm outlined an even more provocative vision for change. "The government has failed us, you can't deny that," Malcolm roared. "Any time you are living in the twentieth century and you're walking around singing 'We Shall Overcome'—the government has failed us. This is part of what's wrong with you: you do too much singing. Today it's time to stop singing and start swinging." Mike joined the boisterous crowd in laughter and applause. Afterward, he reintroduced himself to Malcolm.[18]

MIKE'S GOOD GRADES and gregarious personality landed him as the senior class president. But all that was jeopardized when he refused to participate in the daily recitation of the Lord's Prayer and the Pledge of Allegiance. *I'll stand outside the classroom, but I'm not doing that no more*, Mike told his teachers. Much as Gwen did on that Memphis bus, Mike no longer wished to abide by the rules of a country he now found hypocritical. His stance cost him a spot in a class field trip to Greece. When a teacher complained about Mike and his friends to the principal, Mike called him a fool. The school devised a strange punishment. For a week Mike and two of his friends were required to go to school every day but were prevented from attending class. Not even teachers were allowed to talk to them. They sat alone in a room, denied even the chance to complete the required school work in their last semester. After a week, the trio was officially suspended.

Mike was ready to fight. Max Stanford encouraged him to escalate, with protests and a lawsuit. But after Rebecca met the principal and sobbed about his lost potential, Mike caved. He apologized to the teacher he had insulted and signed a paper pledging to be good. *They won the battle*, he stewed, *but I ain't never going to back up again*. And he reminded his mother: *You taught me never to back down if I think I'm right*. It would not be the last time he gave her cause to regret that instruction.

This was just the beginning. Only weeks until graduation, he skipped school to join a rolling protest against a bulwark of Jim Crow North: the segregated construction trade. The Philadelphia NAACP had staged a series of boycott campaigns in attempting to weaken racism. But in May 1963 they embraced more direct action when they protested the all-white work crew that was building a new middle school in Strawberry Mansion, a Black neighborhood adjacent to where Mike lived.

When the construction workers attacked the protestors, police joined the melee. Mike saw Stanford's bloodied face in the newspaper and resolved to attend the next day's protest. It was his first time at a protest, and it was peaceful. Marching in a circle, carrying a sign, Mike was exhilarated.[19]

REBECCA WAS ADAMANT that Mike go to college and earn the education that had been denied her. Mike wanted to go to Lincoln

University, the historically Black university an hour outside of Philadelphia. The first degree-granting Black university in the country, Lincoln had graduated a long list of distinguished alumni, including poet Langston Hughes; Kwame Nkrumah, who in 1960 had become the first president of independent Ghana; musician Cab Calloway; and educator Horace Mann Bond. Mike was elated when a Pennsylvania state senator sponsored him for a one-year scholarship to Lincoln.[20]

But his suspension canceled the scholarship and jeopardized his admission to Lincoln. Scrambling for a second option, he applied late to Temple University and was accepted. Not yet a public university, Temple was at least close to home. Monitoring events down South, Mike would start college that fall right there in Philadelphia.

CHAPTER THREE

SNEAKING TO SNCC

Gwen loved Spelman at first sight. She had been assigned to a room in the esteemed Packard Hall, one of the oldest buildings on campus. Spelman wore its age with prestige. The buildings were hallowed and beautiful. The nine-acre campus had almost two dozen buildings, devoted to teaching Black women how to be teachers, missionaries, nurses, and wives in the service of uplifting the race. That dorm room in the fall of 1962 was Gwen's first time having her own bedroom (albeit one she shared with another student), and the first time that she had white teachers.

In teaching its students how to be respectable ladies, Spelman had a lot of rules. A network of deans and older Black women known as "house mothers," enforced them. The house mother at Packard Hall was a stern woman in her sixties named Miss Gordon. Ever the disciplinarian, Miss Gordon reminded Gwen and her peers of what it meant to be a Spelman Lady. Though the campus was just two miles southwest of downtown Atlanta, Spelman students were not allowed into the city. They were not even allowed inside of a car. Additionally, Spelman students had a nine p.m. curfew, had the cleanliness of their rooms subject to inspection, and could only wear pants at

Sunday breakfast. The administration determined the dress code for class ("simple tailored dresses, skirts, sweaters, or blouses" with "low-heeled, comfortable shoes"), for "teas, concerts, and informal dances" ("dressy date dresses"), and for formal functions (an evening gown or a white dress and gloves). Many social gatherings required a faculty chaperone, and students were required to attend chapel service six days a week. Violating the rules could result in expulsion.[1]

Gwen's initial encounters with the civil rights movement were serendipitous. She had already stumbled across the West Hunter Baptist Church, where Rev. Ralph Abernathy intoned his parishioners to action against white supremacy. Blocks from that church—and less than a mile from Gwen's dorm room—at 8½ Raymond Street, the Student Nonviolent Coordinating Committee had its offices.

Few at Spelman participated in the freedom movement. Spelman officials feared it, even though the administration was proud of Martin Luther King Jr., a Morehouse alum. Spelman's president was an erudite and elite man named Albert E. Manley, the first African American and the first man to hold that position. He saw college as the site "to develop thinkers who can identify facts, who can state truths and who are motivated by Christian principles." To Manley, the Black college should be a place to nurture prudence, faith, responsibility, and hard work. And the Black *women's* college was a place to make women into ladies, respectable in demeanor and upwardly mobile in status. To his mind and to those of the college's benefactors, this required a rigid environment. Black women's comportment and mobility had to be strictly controlled. When the sit-ins erupted in February 1960, Manley joined others in Atlanta's Black middle class—including Martin Luther King Sr., who made his son promise not to stage protests in the city—in encouraging students to challenge segregation through lawsuits and the NAACP rather than through protest. Manley hoped to enlist students' families in quieting youthful urgency, telling Spelman parents that "the institution cannot accept responsibility for your daughter's participation in any of these demonstrations and the possible consequences." Spelman's rules aligned with Rhoda's—Gwen was to stay focused on her studies and her faith.[2]

Yet even if the movement was far away, its concerns were ever present. Her first semester, Gwen enrolled in a history and literature class co-taught by Staughton Lynd, a Quaker-Marxist and pacifist. Lynd and his co-instructor, another white progressive Northerner named Esther Seaton, were well acquainted with the Black struggle for freedom. For all the pride that Manassas had instilled in her, Gwen had learned little of Black political aspirations—either in the United States or in Africa.

At Spelman, Gwen learned that African countries were beginning to achieve independence from decades of European colonialism. She learned that slaves sometimes revolted, that Black people had a rich literary and intellectual tradition. She was riveted to learn of Nat Turner's and Denmark Vesey's rebellions, to learn of labor strikes and Black protest before she was born, to read books by James Baldwin and W. E. B. Du Bois, by Ralph Ellison and Richard Wright. She also attended lectures by the head of Spelman's History Department, another radical pacifist by the name of Howard Zinn, whose lectures on the history of American protest were frequently held off campus to avoid Manley's scrutiny.

Later Gwen would hear *Invisible Man* author Ralph Ellison call in to a literature class. She would discuss what she was learning with her dorm RA, a woman from north-central Georgia named Alice Walker who showed great interest in literature. And every Sunday Gwen would be at West Hunter Baptist Church to hear fiery sermons from Reverend Abernathy. She heard Martin Luther King Jr. preach at Abernathy's pulpit and had accompanied the West Hunter choir to hear him at his own pulpit at Ebenezer Baptist Church.

She also spent a lot of time at Canterbury House, a co-ed social club for AUC students that was run by the local Episcopal church. It was a meeting place for overachievers, the eggheads and misfits. Canterbury had a bustling café, where students could be heard debating Albert Camus and existentialism alongside current events. One

of few women who frequented Canterbury, Gwen loved its passionate intellectualism, its blend of the abstract and the immediate. The
Committee on Appeal for Human Rights, the AUC's primary activist group, met there, and Gwen observed their meetings from an
ever-shrinking distance.[3]

Spelman offered only a morning meal on Sundays. After chapel
services, students were otherwise on their own. Hunger of the stomach more than of the spirit led Gwen to the Mennonite House, the
congregation's first interracial fellowship house, which offered free
dinner along with its Sunday evening fellowship. Led by Vincent
and Rosemarie Harding, Mennonite House was located just a block
away from where Martin Luther King Jr. and his family lived. Close
with the King family and with the Southern Christian Leadership
Conference, the Hardings ministered a social justice theology. Gwen
was surprised to see several white people respond to the Hardings'
blend of faith and freedom, and she admired Vincent Harding's
erudite spirit.[4]

Yet Gwen was determined to follow the rules that Spelman
and, especially, her grandmother had laid out. She still wanted the
middle-class life she had been raised to achieve. She was staying
away from the movement. But the movement wasn't staying away
from her.[5]

HEY, SISTER, CAN I talk to you? the man asked. Gwen knew who
he was. He, or someone like him, was on campus every day, trying
to recruit Spelman students to this demonstration or that meeting.
He was part of the Student Nonviolent Coordinating Committee
(SNCC). "Snick," as everyone called it, had formed in April 1960 out
of that year's rush of sit-ins. A founding conference drew three hundred students to Raleigh, North Carolina—about "200 more than we
expected," Ella Baker would later say of the effort. The conference
provided structure and strategy to advance what had been a spontaneous sit-in movement.[6]

SNCC was not the only freedom organization based in Atlanta or trying to recruit among AUC students. So too was Martin Luther King's organization, the Southern Christian Leadership Conference (SCLC). Though they shared a home city, both the SCLC and SNCC focused their on-the-ground organizing elsewhere in the South. The SCLC had, by 1962, seven years of experience contesting segregation through mass marches and a willingness to meet racist violence with Christian grace. SNCC's approach channeled youthful energy into both direct action and developing the leadership of local organizers—with the goal of upending white supremacy. Their propensity for charging headlong into sites of danger had earned SNCC the reputation of being the "shock troops" of the Black freedom movement. SNCC organizers had participated heavily in the Freedom Rides that contested segregated interstate bus travel the year before Gwen started college, and they were developing long-term struggles in southwest Georgia and in Mississippi. Their advisors included veteran organizer Ella Baker, who had left SCLC to support SNCC's grassroots initiative over the preacher-led SCLC, as well as Spelman's own Howard Zinn.[7]

Both SCLC and SNCC recruited among the four campuses at the Atlanta University Center. Even though Gwen attended an SCLC-aligned church, she was never moved to join. Her friends at the Canterbury House mocked the SCLC's bourgeois approach, calling them *the American Boys*. Wearing the deliberately proletarian denim overalls, SNCC recruiters mocked such respectability. *Sister, can I talk to you?* they'd ask. At first, she offered a resolute no. But their heckling wore on Gwen. *Don't be the next generation of handkerchief head Negroes!* they'd chide. *What do white folks call a Black man with a PhD?* a SNCC organizer would ask, the prelude to insisting that racism did not respect individual Black success.[8]

While Gwen's in-class studies opened her eyes to the deep history of Black struggle, SNCC's barbs began to tear away at her middle-class dreams. Maybe, she began to think, she could visit the SNCC office. Just to check it out.

GWEN DID NOT tell anyone that she was going to SNCC's office. The office was on the second floor above a beauty shop, crowded with people and papers. It was dirty. Cigarette butts spilled onto the floor. SNCC staff wore denim, not the respectable fashion required at Spelman, and the women wore their hair naturally. She was also shocked to find two Asian American men participating in the meetings. She found SNCC mysterious, chaotic, and exhilarating. She needed to come back.

She could return without getting involved, she told herself. But she needed a reason to be there. Every time she went, she noticed a broad-shouldered man a decade older than the rest cleaning up even as he participated in the political debates raging around him. *I could just help him clean*, she thought, as she started emptying ashtrays and taking out the garbage. He turned out to be James Forman, SNCC's disciplined executive secretary and a man who would mentor new members, handle the organization's finances, and scrub the office floors with equal enthusiasm. He welcomed her help and gave her a role. She kept coming back. And one day, someone asked if she could type. Suddenly, she had a new job, typing press releases and brochures for SNCC.

As she became a regular at the office, she worked up the courage to ask the two Asian Americans an indelicate question: *What are you Chinese people doing here?* She couldn't believe it when the men, Ed Nakawatase and Tamio Wakayama, said that they were Japanese— and on the staff. *But why?* she asked. *It's our fight too*, they said. Both of them had been born in concentration camps, where their families were among 120,000 Japanese Americans who had been incarcerated in one of ten US prisons during World War II.[9]

Spelman made no distinction between being around the freedom movement and being in the freedom movement, and the lines increasingly blurred for Gwen too. She enlisted her roommate to covertly sign Gwen's name to the sign-in sheet so Miss Gordon wouldn't know that Gwen was still out. Coming back from a late-night meeting, Gwen would throw pebbles at her dorm window so that her roommate or other friends would know to let her in the back entrance. College wasn't the only place to learn.

THE SUMMER AFTER her freshman year, Gwen was back in Memphis washing dishes at the Harlem House. As the summer drew to a close, she dreamed of boarding the bus to Washington, DC, for the 1963 March for Jobs and Freedom. For two decades, Black activists had threatened to indict the whole social order of white supremacy by marching on Washington. Now, on August 28, it was finally happening. Fearful it would be a violent melee, Gwen's grandmother forbade her from going.[10]

Planned to coincide with the centennial of the Emancipation Proclamation, and to remind the nation of how elusive emancipation remained, the march was organized by a coalition of civil rights organizations. The speakers roster included Brotherhood of Sleeping Car Porters union leader A. Philip Randolph, who had planned a March on Washington Movement in 1941; Mississippi activist Myrlie Evers, whose husband, Medgar, was the NAACP field secretary for Mississippi when a white supremacist had gunned him down two months earlier; and SNCC's chairman, John Lewis; along with several prominent labor and faith leaders. Morehouse president Benjamin Mays would give the closing benediction. The keynote address was to be delivered by Martin Luther King Jr.

As 250,000 people crowded the National Mall to hear King deliver his famous "I Have a Dream" speech, Gwen crowded her living room with friends and family to watch the event. Her house was one of the few in the neighborhood with a television. Much as she had done when Ray Charles was going to be on the *Ed Sullivan Show*, Gwen roused the neighbors to hear Dr. King address the nation.

Before Dr. King took the stage, SNCC chairman John Lewis delivered his remarks. Gwen was excited to see her new friend, and the organization he—and now she—represented, enjoy pride of place on the dais. She did not yet know that in his speech, SNCC's chairman had planned to pan Kennedy's civil rights bill as "too little, and too late" for its refusal to address police violence, safeguard the right to vote, or provide the full measure of equality. Lewis's initial draft promised a nonviolent "'scorched earth' policy" to "burn Jim Crow to the ground." But the civil rights old guard bristled at this insurgent call and edited Lewis's speech, which had been collectively drafted by several SNCC organizers.

Watching from home, Gwen did not pick up on Lewis's anger at this last-minute shift. Instead, she nodded at the inspiration he drew from the wider Black world: "'One man, one vote' is the African cry," Lewis railed. "It is ours too. It must be ours!" Gwen didn't tell her friends that she knew John Lewis, but she bragged to her friends that she had met Dr. King at her new church and had even heard him speak at his own church. Her secret still more or less safe, her heart buoyed: things were changing.[11]

WHEN SHE RETURNED to Atlanta that fall, Gwen was more excited to reconnect with SNCC than with Spelman. Even before the fall term began, the college had made its distaste for the freedom movement known by firing History Department chair, and SNCC advisor, Howard Zinn. With the students gone for summer break, Dr. Manley had written to Zinn that "your services will not be required in the 1963–1964 academic year." Several Spelman students condemned the administration's actions with letters to Dr. Manley or in the school newspaper.[12]

Gwen chose to follow in Zinn's activist footsteps. She had already joined the Atlanta University Center's Committee on Appeal for Human Rights. Then she was elected as one of two representatives from the committee to serve on SNCC's leadership body, the "coordinating committee" of campus-based organizers from which SNCC drew its name. *Oh, Lord, I'm getting into leadership now!* she marveled with equal parts fear and excitement.

Gwen wasn't alone in hoping to seize the momentum of the March on Washington. The Committee on Appeal for Human Rights turned their attention to Atlanta's persistent segregation. They called their efforts an "Open City" campaign, and it was a broad challenge to white Atlanta's moderate self-image. With Ivan Allen's election as mayor in 1962, Atlanta boosters proclaimed the city a beacon of a new postracial South: Atlanta was "the city too busy to hate." Yet many in the city still made the time. The former head of the Chamber of Commerce, Allen became mayor after besting avowed segregationist Lester Maddox. Maddox owned a string of fast-food restaurants called the Pickrick, and he encouraged his employees to accost any demonstrators who came in. Though Allen won the election, many of the downtown businesses, hotels, and eateries remained segregated, as did the city's schools.[13]

The Open City campaign endeavored to bring justice to Atlanta through sheer force of will. Almost two dozen SNCC activists spent Christmas 1963 in jail after trying to integrate downtown restaurants while Kenya's minister of home affairs, Oginga Odinga, visited the city. The sit-ins accelerated in the new year, and more than 150 people were arrested throughout January in demonstrations against Atlanta's segregated downtown business district.[14]

Gwen was still trying to hold on to her scholarship at Spelman and the future it portended. But she had also become comfortable walking "the line," as SNCC called pickets. As the protests continued, she could not keep leaving the demonstrations early. She soon found herself in back of a paddy wagon, singing with her comrades *Oh Freedom, Oh Freedom, Oh Freedom over me / And before I'll be a slave, I'll be buried in my grave / and go home to my Lord and be free.* The singing quieted her nerves at the thought of being the first in her family to go to jail, after being the first in her family to go to college. One of the cops threatened the group, *Keep it down back there before we give you something to shout about.* Already under arrest, they sang louder and louder. The group found communion in the segregated jail, singing songs, telling jokes, smoking cigarettes, and awaiting bail.[15]

Their release brought new terror for Gwen. The dean of students chastised her for leaving campus without permission, lying on the sign-out sheet, and participating in forbidden activism. Worse, the dean had told Gwen's grandmother of her transgression. When Gwen called her, Rhoda repeated many of the same threats of expulsion the dean had made, but in a far more menacing manner.

Devastated, Gwen retreated to her room and cried in bed until her roommate persuaded her to come to dinner. Many of her classmates cheered her entrance with a round of "For She's a Jolly Good Fellow" and calls for her to give a speech. That response no doubt helped persuade Spelman officials not to place her on academic probation. It certainly steadied her hand for the fights ahead.

GWEN'S ARREST WASN'T the only reason she wound up in the dean's office. She also landed there for violating a more pedestrian Spelman rule: hair style. *What have you done with your hair?* the dean demanded when she switched from straightening her hair to wearing it naturally. *I washed it*, Gwen responded coolly. *It's called a natural or an Afro*, she added. *Don't get smart with me*, the dean replied. *It's a disgrace*, she said, adding that Gwen would never land a man with her hair like that. What she meant, though, was that Gwen would never get a Morehouse man. But Gwen wasn't too concerned about that since a set of classed and colored assumptions that favored light-skinned Black women from well-to-do families over working-class women with darker complexions seemed to diminish her access to AUC's social life anyway. At the formal dance, Gwen flouted Spelman norms further by inviting a friend from Georgia Tech—a white man she had met through the Mennonite House—to be her date.[16]

Gwen felt herself growing more daring. Her time with SNCC had taught her how to be at a demonstration. Sit-in protests always included "spotters," people who would observe the action from a safe distance in order to alert the demonstrators when police arrived and serve as reliable witnesses for the media and the court. She knew how to respond nonviolently to the pageantry of attack, the almost scripted violence with which white customers had often responded to Black patrons ordering food at a diner. She knew that putting your body on the line was not solely an act of bravery but also the manifestation of the movement's demand for freedom. More than any individual lesson, however, the accumulation of these lessons bolstered her self-confidence to enter potentially dangerous situations with a feeling that she would survive them.

And so Gwen told Rhoda that she was going to spend spring break visiting with one of her college friends. In actuality, she slept on John Lewis's couch while planning a wave of sit-ins with her friend and fellow Spelman student Barbara Simon. The goal was to either integrate or shut down a popular burger joint called Krystal. Segregated restaurants had grown accustomed to closing for the day when protestors came. The students' plan was to go from one Krystal location to another, forcing them all to shut down if they wouldn't serve the interracial group. If not an end to segregation, Gwen wanted to cost them money. With several friends from SNCC and Spelman, including some white exchange students from the North, she did just that.

The first two days went well, as the group shut down three restaurants at lunchtime. Day three seemed to be more of the same. But as the manager flipped the sign to Closed, Gwen noticed that the windows had been steamed so that no one could see in or out. Before she had time to register the change, a group of young white men came charging in from the back of the restaurant, armed with sticks and clubs. Gwen jumped over the counter but was attacked by a waitress, who clawed Gwen's arm with her nails. Bleeding, Gwen punched her and pushed her away. She and Barbara began throwing dishes at their assailants. She hoped that noise in the background was SNCC spotters fighting their way in to assist. Soon the police arrived and arrested all of the demonstrators, none of the attackers.

Gwen and her comrades spent three days in jail, eating half-rotten bologna and drinking Kool-Aid while she pondered her expulsion. And sure enough, upon her release, the dean informed her that her scholarship had been revoked. Dr. Manley asked Gwen if she was a communist agent sent to disrupt campus. Yet, once again, her classmates rallied to her defense. Though few of them joined SNCC, many of them recognized the movement's importance. After several marches on the president's lawn, the administration agreed to let Gwen and the others remain enrolled and with their scholarships intact—albeit on strict probation.[17]

GWEN SPENT AS much time at the SNCC office as she could, burying herself in its frenetic urgency. As a member of SNCC's executive body, she attended national meetings as well. There were lots of familiar faces at these meetings, including Ella Baker and Staughton Lynd, plus everyone from the SNCC office. Anyone coming from Mississippi, the site of her worst nightmares, earned Gwen's utmost respect. Bob Moses, the Harlem-born, Harvard-educated SNCC leader who first went to Mississippi in 1960 had, by 1964, amassed a small army of organizers to support local people in contesting white supremacist rule. An inveterate teacher and skilled organizer, Moses had a wise and enduring determination that seemed to fit both his biblical surname and the hefty purpose of eradicating bondage in the Sunflower State. With him were people like Fannie Lou Hamer, the forty-six-year-old sharecropper from Mississippi whose singing voice and fighting spirit inspired Gwen beyond words.

She watched them at the national meetings, these nonviolent soldiers from the front lines in the war against white supremacy. She observed as they interacted with other SNCC leaders, like twenty-four-year-old John Lewis, who left Fisk University to become SNCC's chairman and had been arrested twenty-seven times, and Ruby Doris Robinson Smith, two years Gwen's senior, who had left Spelman to work full-time for SNCC. She watched these tireless freedom fighters, and she knew: she needed to be where they were, to do what they were doing.[18]

What they were doing was planning to launch an ambitious assault on Mississippi. The plan had been developing for months, and by spring it was official: SNCC would anchor a coalition of civil rights organizations to engage in voter registration and citizenship education efforts in Mississippi. To prompt federal intervention against the state's racist authoritarianism, SNCC would call upon a vast network of volunteers—mostly white, mostly from the North. The sons and daughters of white America, the children of politicians and executives and laborers, would force the country to act in concert with Black mobilization. This was Mississippi Freedom Summer.[19]

Gwen had to be there. She knew her family would never grant permission. So she didn't ask. She applied to go to Mississippi, a foot soldier in the ambitious summer project to tackle the most viciously racist state in the union. She was one of a thousand volunteers to be accepted; only about 10 percent were Black. Though she knew in her heart that she wouldn't be returning to Spelman afterward, she still managed to align her political commitment with her academics by partnering with Staughton Lynd on an independent study to develop the curriculum for the summer's "Freedom Schools," the citizenship education classes at the heart of how the project aimed to organize, educate, and mobilize.[20]

At six a.m. the day after final exams, Gwen awoke to Miss Gordon pounding at her door. *You have guests*, she boomed. *Your grandmother, your mother, and your stepfather are here to take you home.* Gwen's mother and grandmother—no men were allowed in the dorms—marched in. *Thank God the dean told me you were going to do something stupid*, Rhoda scolded. *You think I'm going to let you get yourself killed?* As her family packed her things, Gwen jotted a note to her roommate: *Tell Dr. Lynd to tell Jim Forman what happened.* And just like that, Gwen and her things were headed four hundred miles back to Memphis.

Gwen felt like a hostage. As scared as she was of Mississippi, she was determined to be part of Freedom Summer. She called the SNCC office. Forman offered to send bus fare if Gwen could leave.

They can't make me stay, Gwen boldly affirmed. But Rhoda could check the mail, which is how she found the wire transfer from SNCC. She tore it up. *Two years of college have turned her into a fool*, Gwen's father proclaimed.

She called the SNCC office again, asking this time that Forman send the money to a friend of hers. It worked. Gwen packed her bag for the trip. *I'm grown!* Gwen insisted with the certainty of all her nineteen years. *You cannot keep me here against my will.*

Rhoda and Gwen's father insisted that they could keep her there—and that they would, for her own good. They argued back and forth until Gwen threatened to call the police to report her own kidnapping.

Rhoda gave up. *You'd call the police on me?* she said, bewildered and outraged. *I give up. Those people have brainwashed you.* Rhoda relented. But she wouldn't let Gwen go without a parting shot: *If you leave, don't ever come back.*

Gwen was still crying when the bus reached Atlanta.

STAUGHTON AND ALICE Lynd met Gwen at the bus station, their young children trying to cheer her up. *She didn't mean it*, they told Gwen about her grandmother's admonition. Soon enough, she and Staughton headed to Ohio with all of the curriculum and materials for the Freedom Schools neatly packed in his trunk. Gwen would now help the Lynds in two weeklong training sessions at the Western College for Women in Oxford, Ohio, for Freedom Summer volunteers. On the way, they stopped in Yellow Springs so that Gwen could tour Antioch College. Earlier that year, Lynd had encouraged her to apply there in case Spelman expelled her. At Lynd's encouragement, Gwen met with Antioch alumna Coretta Scott King, who wrote her a letter of recommendation. Gwen had been accepted months earlier, but this was her first time seeing the school. Being on a predominantly white campus for the first time was a small shock. Still, the daylong tour left an impression on her. She could see herself at Antioch—one day. For now, she knew that she wouldn't be at any college that fall.[21]

SNCC had divided the Freedom Summer volunteers into two groups. The first week of training was dedicated to voter registration efforts, the second to teaching Freedom Schools. Gwen had been accepted to Freedom Summer as a volunteer. But unlike many of the white volunteers, Gwen had no money—and now, no family—to her name. SNCC put her on staff as soon as she had left Memphis, so she was technically no longer a volunteer but staff, earning ten dollars a week. That also meant that she stayed for the full two weeks of training. She was especially eager for that second week. She felt excited about the curriculum she had helped develop and still dreamed of being a teacher one day.

The training was weighty but fun. Gwen sublimated her fears of what was to come, as well as her sadness at what she may have given up to get there, by reveling in the training. Lynd, Vincent and Rosemarie Harding, Jim Forman, Ruby Doris Robinson, SNCC staff—they were her family now. She enjoyed meeting the volunteers. They spent their days learning about Mississippi and how to organize. Some people paid close attention to security protocols while others scoffed at SNCC's self-seriousness. *This is America, isn't it?* one of the white volunteers naively assumed his invincibility. *Exactly*, Gwen thought. She worried that some of the volunteers just wanted to shock their segregationist parents. Still, she felt that together they would topple Jim Crow. They passed the night singing and dancing and getting to know each other. *I'm going to be okay*, Gwen reassured herself, *until those people in Mississippi kill me.*[22]

The Freedom Summer training was only Gwen's second time out of the South, and she soon discovered how dangerous the North could be. For weeks leading up to the Freedom Summer training, the local white press had touted lurid tales of the interracial group descending upon small-town Ohio. Coverage had ginned up reaction with the old canard that civil rights was nothing but Black men preying on white women. Gwen paid scant attention to it until a group of white men surrounded her and a white Freedom Summer volunteer at a local convenience store. The two women ran out of the store and hopped in their car. But the men surrounded the car, yelling and pounding on the doors, trying to either pull them out or tip the car over. They had just about given up hope when another group of SNCC comrades drove up and chased the assailants away. *We haven't even gotten to Mississippi*, Gwen thought, *and they're trying to kill us.*[23]

THERE WERE DANGERS within the movement as well. One night in Ohio, Gwen was talking with a prominent SNCC leader after the workshop ended. He was one of her heroes, and Gwen was elated that he had taken an interest in her, a relative newbie. They had grown closer during the training, and now he asked to walk her back to her room. *Can I come in?* he asked when they got back to her dorm. Gwen hesitated, remembering her grandmother's warnings about being alone with a man. But her grandmother had kicked her out—this was her family now. She opened the door, and it wasn't long before he started kissing her. *No*, she protested. *No! I don't want to do that. You need to leave.* But he didn't stop. Not for the first time, she began to fight back against a man's sexual predation. She pushed, scratched, and writhed against his force. He was stronger than her, though, and Gwen was relieved when her roommate came in. Seeing a man present, the roommate began to excuse herself. *Don't leave!* Gwen pleaded. *I want him to leave!* Her roommate stayed, the man departed.

Later she commiserated with another woman who had experienced her own sexual assault by a different man volunteering for the project. That woman, who was white, did not know how to raise the issue with SNCC leadership that a Black man was her assailant. The taboo of interracial sexual contact was already too overwhelming. There were whispers among women volunteers of other such abuses. Through the dorm walls, Gwen had even heard another woman protest unwanted sexual contact. Gwen could not stay silent. She told

Jim Forman, SNCC's executive secretary and her trusted friend, what had happened to her. *We don't have time to deal with that*, he told her. Worse, he said: *You should've given him some.*

She did not how to process this dismissal. She thought of telling her family, but she didn't want them to think anyone in SNCC was capable of such violence. Gwen didn't want to think that herself.

And then the news out of Mississippi renewed her terror heading south. Two days into the second week of training, SNCC leaders informed the volunteers that three men, two white and one Black, who had left Ohio for Mississippi days before were missing. Gwen remembered waving good-bye to Andrew Goodman, one of the three. Freedom Summer had a detailed reporting system to keep track of everyone: if people were missing, SNCC leaders reported to those gathered in Ohio, it could only mean that they were dead. *Oh my God*, Gwen thought in disbelief. *You mean they will kill white men?* At that moment, she thought none of them would survive the summer. *But it's too late to turn back.*[24]

CHAPTER FOUR

MISSISSIPPI AMAZON

THE MISSISSIPPI SUMMER PROJECT WAS A COORDINATED EFFORT among four civil rights organizations—SNCC, the Congress of Racial Equality, the NAACP, and the Southern Christian Leadership Conference—working together as the Council of Federated Organizations (COFO). But mostly it was SNCC. It placed volunteers at the knife's edge of jail, beatings, and death. Volunteers, college-aged youth, were asked to bring at least $500 in bond money with them. As SNCC staff, Gwen was spared this request. It was irrelevant anyway, since the only money to her name was her $10 weekly salary. SNCC had dubbed the initiative the Mississippi Challenge: the frontal assault on racism in what seemed to be the most racist state. Gwen viewed Mississippi as hell on earth—the most terrifying place she could imagine.[1]

As the Freedom Summer training wrapped up in Ohio, SNCC staff informed Gwen that she would be working on a project in a town called Laurel. They introduced her to the two men she would be working with, Lester McKinnie and Jimmy Garrett. While both men had been Freedom Riders, Lester had worked in Laurel as SNCC's field secretary in 1962 and was selected as project director.

Gwen was glad to be paired with someone who knew the area, and she was eager to begin teaching the Freedom School curriculum she helped develop.

But she was shocked that the other project staff were both Black. To her, the whole point of Freedom Summer was to leverage the possible protection that *white* Northern volunteers might bring with them to Mississippi. Black suffering had long failed to force federal intervention against the segregationist state government. In building support for the project, SNCC had made it plain that a "large number of students from the North making the necessary sacrifices to go South would make abundantly clear to the government and the public that this is not a situation which can be ignored any longer, and would project an image of cooperation between Northern and white people and Southern Negro people to the nation." Yet Gwen observed that her group included neither white nor Northern students (Jimmy was from Los Angeles, by way of Texas and Louisiana). She protested: *Why create an all-Black project?*[2]

The answer from SNCC staff was not encouraging: *It's too dangerous to send any white people there.* To make matters worse, Laurel had little movement infrastructure. They would have to create it from scratch. She wished, in that moment, that she still had a home to return to.

GWEN LISTENED INTENTLY as Lester explained how to stay safe in Mississippi. Mostly, though, she tried to sleep off her fears on the drive from Ohio. It was only when they crossed into the state that her comrades woke her. Gwen expected the worst. Stories of slavery and lynching rang in her ears. But there were no monsters or goblins waiting for them on the tree-lined road. The landscape reminded her of Memphis. The fear of Mississippi had so overwhelmed her imagination that she was surprised to find the sweet smell of verbena, the bright blue and purple hydrangea, the quiet grace of cedar and oak trees.

Freedom Summer volunteers had to maintain a low profile as they got established in Southern communities. Her team started out in Hattiesburg, the closest city to Laurel where SNCC supporters could house them. One of the largest Freedom Summer projects, Hattiesburg was bustling with activity. The trio spent about a week there, learning from that project while driving thirty miles north to Laurel every day.[3]

Laurel was far away from the Mississippi Delta, the eighteen-county region that garnered much of the national attention that summer. The town sits in Mississippi's Fifth Congressional District, the heart of Jones County, in the southeastern part of the state. During the Civil War, Jones County was home to a group of Confederate deserters who pledged fealty to the United States, sabotaging some Confederate supplies. The rebellion's leader created a family with a woman enslaved by his own grandfather, and they all lived together after the Civil War. A century later, however, this radical past was hard to find. The Klan was known to have its headquarters near Laurel, and most Black people were scared of the movement that Gwen, Jimmy, and Lester represented.[4]

An internal assessment drafted before Freedom Summer held that Laurel was "one of the more moderate areas in the state, and harassment should be minimal." At the same time, SNCC estimated that the local Black leadership was "conservative" and that "receptiveness to the COFO program has varied from lukewarm to cold." There was no easy assignment in Mississippi.[5]

Day after day, Gwen and her two compatriots walked up and down the town's hot, dusty streets knocking on people's doors. They hung out in barbershops and anywhere Black people were, talking to them about their lives and about the summer project. Wearing the SNCC uniform of blue jeans and a work shirt, the trio worked to blend in to the working-class Mississippi aesthetic.

Three local NAACP activists gave them the names of residents they thought might be receptive to the project. But the trio had suffered enough fearful rejection to keep their hopes modest. When

Gwen stepped on the porch of a wooden house and knocked on the door, a fifty-year-old woman named Eberta Spinks answered. *Are you one of those Freedom Riders?* Mrs. Spinks demanded. Hesitantly, Gwen said, *Yes, ma'am*, unsure whether that would be welcome news. Fortunately, it was. *Come in*, she said. *I've been waiting on you all my life.*[6]

Eberta Spinks was the kind of person who made Mississippi Freedom Summer possible. One of eighteen children, she grew up taking care of friends and neighbors. She was a native Mississippian, ebullient and well known in her community, and committed to bettering the state. She had two biological children and was the foster mother to eight others. Mrs. Spinks had just retired from working at a meat packing plant, and her husband, a union man, worked at the Masonite plant making insulation board and doors.

Mrs. Spinks brought Gwen into her household, which she shared with her husband and fourteen-year-old son. She gave Gwen a bed. She also gave Gwen a curfew, expected her to report her comings and goings, and required her frequent attendance at church. And when she found out that Gwen wasn't alone, Mrs. Spinks convinced her neighbors, Carrie Clayton and Susie Ruffin, to open their homes too. *She has a bigger house*, Mrs. Spinks said of Ms. Clayton, *and white folks consider Ms. Ruffin "crazy."* The Laurel Project had finally established a beachhead in Laurel.[7]

With their living quarters established, the three SNCC staffers set up an office—initially, on Mrs. Clayton's back porch. When it rained, the SNCC workers would hurry to get their typewriters, papers, and mimeograph machine inside. Soon they rented another place, a trailer without a bathroom. From there, they would coordinate their voter registration efforts and build the Freedom School. Voter registration would challenge white supremacist political power, while the Freedom School would equip Black Mississippians with the intellectual resources and collective self-confidence of citizenship. The schools would make up for the education the state denied Black people and provide a communal experiment in freedom. Gwen was excited to teach. Even if she had disobeyed her family by coming here, she might still honor the spirit of their wishes for her by becoming a teacher.

Then Lester McKinnie disappeared.

It was just after July 4, and the group had been in Mississippi for less than two weeks, in Laurel for an even shorter time than that. Gwen feared the worst. Lester had firsthand experience in the state that she lacked. And the bodies of three Freedom Summer volunteers kidnapped weeks before remained missing.

McKinnie's disappearance left the fledging project in Laurel without a director. When she wasn't calling local jails to track down Lester, Gwen phoned SNCC offices in Mississippi and its national office in Atlanta. *Who can you send to take over as project director?* she inquired. *And how soon can they get here?* Instead, they told her to do it. She pleaded for someone else, anyone else. *Listen,* SNCC's executive secretary Jim Forman told her, *You can do this. You've got to step up. I'm trying to find somebody to send, but we don't have anybody right now. Everybody's tied up. So we need you to become the project director.* Forman tried to reassure her. *You're from the South. You've been to jail. Don't worry.*[8]

Not for the last time, Gwen's determination overshadowed her fear. What else could she do? She had sacrificed her family to be there, and she wasn't going to abandon the effort. She was now the project director.

Luckily, the project had already developed strong momentum in that short time. With Lester's fate still uncertain, on July 9 Gwen led a mass meeting of eighty-five people, the majority of them teenagers, at the New Bethel Baptist Church. The town's youth were eager to challenge segregation—"they have nothing to lose," Gwen told a reporter—and the next day more than fifty kids signed up for the Freedom School. Lyndon Johnson had signed the Civil Rights Act a week prior, outlawing discrimination by race, sex, color, or creed. Yet segregation was so deeply entrenched in Mississippi's social, political, and economic relationships that no one, Black or white, thought national law applied in the state. When the teenagers, many of them members of the local NAACP, pledged to test the Civil Rights Act by visiting downtown businesses, Gwen secured legal funds and public support from SNCC. But hospital funds were equally necessary: Within forty-eight hours of the mass meeting she had organized, ten whites surrounded six Black youth inside a five-and-dime. The mob threw an eight-year-old to the ground, hit a twelve-year-old with a baseball bat, and slashed a fourteen-year-old while local police watched. Racists cut another fourteen-year-old in the face, neck, and arm later that day. These attacks came days after another racist mob had used razors to slash two Black youth seeking service at a local hamburger stand.[9]

While tending to the wounded youth, Gwen found Lester. It took two days of panicked phone calls—including to the FBI agent in Laurel, a man discomfortingly named Robert E. Lee—to discover that he was in jail. Unbeknownst to anyone, McKinnie had missed a court appearance for a sit-in he did in Jackson two years earlier, and there was a warrant for his arrest. Officials were threatening to send him to Parchman, the state penitentiary, for five years. SNCC's lawyers negotiated a compromise: let him go and he would agree not to set foot in the state for at least five years. He accepted the deal. Besides, Laurel already had a new project director.

On July 21, white supremacists burned down a Black nightclub in Laurel, threw a rock—signed "KKK"—through a window of the home belonging to a local NAACP leader, and successfully pressured the landlord to evict the Laurel Project from its office. But all was not hopeless. The project continued to grow. It gained enough support among the locals to finally quell the fears of one of the town's few Black property owners. He made a boarded-up nightclub available to SNCC as an office—at a high price. Gwen balked at the rent, but the landlord remained a landlord. *It's just business*, he said over Gwen's protests. *After all, I'm taking a real chance renting to you folks. Suppose crackers decide to burn the place down? I'll lose everything.* Gwen accepted his terms so that the project could have its own space.[10]

Members of the community banded together to install windows, shellac the floor, and make the space safe enough to be used; they helped SNCC pay the rent, too. Soon, that dance hall was buzzing with activity. It housed not only the SNCC office but also a voter registration project, where people would learn about overcoming the state's racist barriers to voting and where they could practice democracy itself. The project held mock debates and elections. It was there that participants learned of the Mississippi Freedom Democratic Party (MFDP), the COFO-backed effort to unseat the state's racist Democratic Party. They would select delegates to represent Laurel at the MFDP State Convention later that summer, some of whom would in turn represent the MFDP in its challenge to the Democratic National Convention in Atlantic City that August. It was the first time that most Black people in Laurel participated in the formal political process.

Then there was the Freedom School. During the day, the school taught kids from elementary school to high school. In the evenings, it held literacy classes for adults. The Laurel Freedom School, with its sixty-five students, was one of forty-one such schools providing education to more than two thousand students across the state. Connecting the written word to the wider world, the curriculum included everything from Black history to math and science. The former nightclub that the Laurel Project operated out of was bigger than most other project offices in Freedom Summer, and Gwen put it to good use. They built a Freedom Library to accompany the Freedom School, and they ultimately gathered 1,500 books to lend to a community that had been denied access to the local "public" library. And some young women in the community set up a day care center nearby to provide communal childcare for children too young to participate in the Freedom School classes.

As she had done for Manassas and Gospel Temple, Gwen established a fundraising initiative for the Laurel Project. Among other things, funds helped pay for a visit from the Free Southern Theater. When the SNCC-affiliated cultural project performed *Purlie Victorious* and *Waiting for Godot*, it was the first time many Laurel residents—and SNCC staff, for that matter—ever saw live theater. Gwen brimmed with pride days later when she heard some youth in her Freedom School say they were going to be actors when they grew up. Freedom Summer, this radical rewriting of social relationships, was working.[11]

Through dependability as much as courage, the Laurel Project earned the support of the community. The personal relationships Gwen and other project staff built made SNCC's politics real. When a child fell out of a tree or a resident's wood stove caught fire in a poorly ventilated house, it was to the Laurel Project office that people ran. The town's fire trucks wouldn't be found on the Black side of town, so Gwen and other Freedom Summer volunteers filled buckets full of water to douse the flames.[12]

Gwen felt this to be a spiritual success as well as a practical one. The freedom fight taught everyone, SNCC worker and Mississippi resident alike, to reach beyond materialistic values. Of the movement's relationship to the locals, Gwen told a reporter: "We want to learn with them new values. This is a struggle for *me* to get away from this [materialism], and while I'm struggling, I help them struggle." Not everyone in SNCC had such transcendent aims, she acknowledged. But the movement was giving her a glimpse of heaven on earth, of a future without racism. "This is religion to me," she said.[13]

FREEDOM SUMMER WAS a seven-day-a-week job. SNCC workers would start early, doing what they could before it got too hot. They'd spend the morning talking to people and trying to encourage people to register to vote. The volunteers would eat lunch together at a local church, a feast prepared by Laurelites who, in food as in housing, shared what little they had. They spent afternoons registering voters, teaching freedom classes, or holding a protest before the mass meeting that night. Gwen gave the volunteers directives, pressured reluctant ministers—and all the ministers in Laurel were reluctant—to support the movement, taught Freedom School, supported local leaders, and led the mass meetings. Everyone expected men to lead the meetings; Mrs. Spinks refused Gwen's efforts to get her to speak. So Gwen, adopting a preacherly affect, had to lead them herself.[14]

Gwen asked SNCC to send more volunteers to staff the programs. Before long, the Laurel Project had a staff of twenty-three people, all but four of them white. Most were college students from well-heeled families in the North or West. For Gwen, as for most participants in Freedom Summer, this was her first experience in sustained interracial organizing. The project structure emphasized developing local Black leadership, but old hierarchies were not so easily sundered.

As project director, Gwen took it as her responsibility to enforce the communal norms of Laurel's Black community. More than once, she told a white volunteer to put on a longer skirt and to never wear shorts or halter tops no matter how hot it got. This was a matter of collective safety as much as local respect: white people stood out in the Black community, and the racist fiction of protecting white women's sexual purity from Black male intrusion necessitated extreme precaution. In no uncertain terms, Gwen stressed, what white volunteers wore could get someone killed. When project staff Jimmy Garrett's white girlfriend joined the Laurel Project, Gwen wouldn't allow them to stay in the same household.[15]

Gwen ran a tight ship, but keeping so many young adults in line amid the terrifying thrill of upending an entire social order was no easy task. When a pair of volunteers begged her to let them throw a party when their host family was out of town, Gwen reluctantly allowed it to happen so long as no one got drunk or too loud. But with the moonshine flowing, the festivities soon spilled out of the house and into plain view of the neighbors. Gwen was mortified. And sure enough, when the family returned and learned of what happened, they gathered Mrs. Spinks and the project volunteers for a difficult meeting. As project director, Gwen bore the brunt of the blame. The Laurel residents threatened to kick the volunteers out of town and close up the project. Many apologies and stern warnings later, local people allowed them to stay. But never again would they violate the moral code of the community.[16]

Still outraged from her experience in Ohio, where she was nearly raped and got no support from the organization, Gwen was also resolute that there would be no sexual harassment in the Laurel Project. While she generally discouraged project staff from dating anyone in Laurel, whether staff or resident, she forbade any man from dating a local girl under the age of eighteen. Male volunteers would be given only one warning. If there was a repeated offense, she would kick them out of the project.

She might not have technically had the power to dismiss staff over sexual impropriety. SNCC hadn't discussed sexual relationships within the project, consensual or otherwise, and many movement men were inattentive to women's desires. But no man who violated this rule would be allowed to stay in the project, Gwen was certain.

Some men in SNCC ridiculed her for it. Talk swirled: *She don't take no shit, especially off of men.* By the end of the summer, some men avoided Laurel altogether. Fearful of woman warriors, some called it the Amazon Project. Gwen wore their derision with pride. And she enforced her policy.[17]

GWEN HAD AN additional challenge: she had to learn to drive. Growing up, her family had always walked or taken the bus. Even when her family kidnapped her from Spelman in a failed attempt to stop her from going to Freedom Summer, she was never behind the wheel. If she was going to be project director, she needed to drive herself. SNCC staff had to get around town quickly. Frequent arrests and demonstrations meant that they were being constantly pulled to other parts of the region as well. And the threat of Klan violence meant being prepared for a quick departure. Gwen also viewed it as a point of pride. She needed both volunteers and locals to respect her authority. And that meant driving a car.

Cars were a constant challenge in SNCC. In preparation for Freedom Summer, SNCC established the Sojourner Motor Fleet, assuming payment for a stable of vehicles, including twenty-three cars purchased at cost from the United Auto Workers. SNCC's Atlanta office determined access to the cars. Most of the fleet consisted of used, often worn-down cars, and there was no obvious process for who got which car. Though some longtime SNCC staff had nice cars, most projects—certainly Laurel's—had clunkers.[18]

To learn to drive, Gwen got behind the wheel of the Laurel Project car, a 1953 Chevy sedan with the gear shift below the giant steering wheel, and set to work grinding away the gear box. Once the car was moving, it wasn't long before she wound up in a ditch. SNCC men had to push the car out. *You can't drive*, they mocked. *It's dangerous.* And then, more politely: *Let us drive you.* But she was resolute. *Everything is dangerous! Just being here is dangerous*, she said. Being a project director means driving a car, she told herself as she got behind the wheel again. Soon enough, she earned her driver's license from the state of Mississippi.

VIOLENCE WAS A constant companion in Mississippi. A new driver, Gwen had to learn quickly to drive at speeds of over a hundred miles per hour to escape threatening racists. Luckily, one of the summer volunteers drove race cars, and his tutoring improved her skills fast. But not all threats could be escaped by car. In addition to attacking demonstrations, the Klan regularly threw Molotov cocktails and other incendiary devices at the homes of known activists. As the threat level accelerated and young white men drove back and forth in front of her house, Mrs. Spinks would keep vigil on her porch with a shotgun. *They might get me*, she chuckled, *but I'm going to get one or two of them first. You all can sleep, because I'm watchin'*, she reassured them. A group of young Black men in the neighborhood also kept watch over the houses where movement activists lived, and at times they, too, chased off the Klan. As early as June, SNCC staff recognized that the armed self-defense philosophy of the Northern Black nationalist group Revolutionary Action Movement (RAM) "has exerted a great deal of influence" in Mississippi.[19]

Gwen took to keeping a pistol under the seat in her car. Many Black Southerners had guns—including Gwen's grandparents—and though SNCC was committed to nonviolence, guns were everywhere in Mississippi. That included in some COFO offices. A local man involved in the Laurel Project gave the gun to Gwen, hoping that if it came to it, she could at least take out some racists before they got her. Outwardly, it made her feel safer, like maybe she would have a fighting chance against the Klan, even though she had minimal training in firearms. Inwardly, her nerves began to fray as anger and resentment swirled with fear and determination.[20]

In an organization of tough people, Gwen earned a reputation for being tough. Privately, she was often scared. Publicly, she learned that she had to project authority. Leading a demonstration to desegregate a diner, Gwen found herself staring at the sheriff's gun, pointed right at her. He ordered her to turn around. The demonstrators were mostly kids, though, and Gwen felt that they needed to see that together Black people had the power to stand up to white violence. She kept walking toward the sheriff, silently praying but outwardly confident. The sheriff let them through, smiling at Gwen and saying, *You gonna git your damn self kilt one of these days.*

It was a prophecy her mother had issued as a warning. After a month without contact, her mother had finally written her a letter in Mississippi: *Try not to get killed.* Gwen had not yet heard from her grandmother.[21]

GWEN WAS ON her way across the state to rescue a car. One of the newer cars in SNCC's fleet, a 1964 Plymouth Valiant, had been impounded in Holly Springs when the local project director was arrested. The Jackson COFO office called Laurel: if she could get the car, it was hers. At that point, she would've done anything for the movement—and most anything for a good car. She convinced someone to drive her to the SNCC office in Jackson to pick up the paperwork and then to the sheriff's office in Holly Springs. Once there, Gwen insisted on going in alone. She had a plan.

Gwen announced her presence with an exaggerated drawl. *'xcuse me, suh*, she said to the sheriff. *I'ma he'h to pick up a car.*

The officer looked her over. *Girl, how did you get hooked up with these people?*

I don' know, suh, Gwen pantomimed. *They just told me to come up he'h and get this car.*

You're not involved in that mess, are you, girl? the sheriff asked.

Nossir, nossir, I'm not, she replied. *I'm jus' deliverin' this car to some people.*

Not quite satisfied, the officer asked where Gwen was from. She produced her Mississippi driver's license, proof that she was no outside agitator.

You know that Nigras don't know nothing 'bout votin' and runnin' for office, the sheriff offered, reassured he was speaking with someone who knew the ways of the state.

Yessir, Gwen replied.

The sheriff persisted in ignorance, as did Gwen in dissemblance, both playing their parts in this Southern drama, until he relented and released the car to her. Behind the wheel, she exhaled and headed back to Laurel.

When Cleve Sellers, the assistant project director in Holly Springs who would soon be elected SNCC's program secretary, got out of lockup, he demanded the car back. They argued about it, Gwen recounting the litany of problems with the cars in Laurel and the offer of wheels that sent her to Holly Springs to begin with.

Sellers was adamant. So was Gwen.

No, you're not taking this car from me, Gwen said at last, flashing the pistol she kept in the car for protection against the Klan. *No way.* Gwen would drive that car until she left Mississippi fourteen months later.

As THE SUMMER ended, all the local projects geared up for a state-wide convention of the MFDP. In Jones County, 2,709 people voted for Aaron Henry and the MFDP. That number was more than the number of registered members of the Democratic Party in the county, a sign of the hard work done by Freedom Summer volunteers.[22] The next step was to challenge the Mississippi delegation at the Democratic National Convention in Atlantic City. They hoped a summer of bravery, suffering, and diligence exposing the racist hostility to democracy in Mississippi would convince the national Democratic Party to seat instead the only delegation that was chosen by free and fair elections—the Mississippi Freedom Democrats.

While SNCC and its allies headed to Atlantic City in August 1964 to make their case to a national audience, Gwen headed to California with comrades from the Laurel Project. Jimmy Garrett had already gone back to Los Angeles after suffering a vicious beating by Mississippi police. He headed up the LA SNCC office, and though his formal role was fundraising, he saw it as an organizing vehicle and a site of rejuvenation for war-weary Southerners. Two other Freedom Summer volunteers in Laurel—one of whom had taken refuge in Laurel after being badly beaten in Hattiesburg—also had connections in California. They were joined by the latest recruits to the Laurel Project: two Black teenage boys, Ulysses Everett and Charles "Ben" Hartfield, natives of Mississippi, who had staffed the Laurel Project after fleeing Hattiesburg to avoid imprisonment, or worse, when their civil rights agitation got them expelled from high school.[23]

Gwen piled into the car with five other people, two up front and four in the back. To avoid the indignities of segregation, the group wouldn't risk stopping at a motel. They drove day and night for four days. With no air-conditioning, the heat remained constant. But their mood grew more boisterous the farther they got from Mississippi. The trip to California offered a much-needed rest before Gwen returned to the Laurel Project. The summer's work was too urgent, too fundamentally unfinished to abandon. She felt committed to the people of Laurel and their cause. She would stay in Mississippi, the state that months ago had been her worst nightmare and whose routine violence pushed her to new depths of resourcefulness and panic.[24]

Gwen put her fundraising skills, honed through years as a Girl Scout and in the church, to use in the freedom project. In a note to project supporters, she explained that the project was squatting in Mrs. Clayton's house while they regrouped in search of a new office space. She also intimated that the work of voter registration remained as difficult as ever. Noting that much of the local Black leadership opposed their decidedly activist approach to voter registration and political organizing, Gwen vowed to carry on with the COFO model. "In one devious way or another, I will turn this into a Freedom Democratic Party," she told supporters of the project. She also outlined her plan to continue a Freedom School to focus on "college preparatory work," establish a community center for adults in the area, and provide "classes in Birth Control, Diet, Budgets, Sewing and other things that help poor people to live better healthier lives. (whew)."[25]

Freedom Summer was over. But the work of freedom was just beginning. Gwen now led a small team of five dedicated workers, together with Laurel's indigenous leadership. In addition to herself and the two teenagers from Hattiesburg, there were two white women from California, Marion Davidson and Linnell Barrett. The three women stayed at Mrs. Spinks's house. Two of them shared a bed while the third slept on a cot. In the interest of fairness, each week the trio would rotate who slept on the cot.

Six months earlier, Gwen was a sophomore in college who had never heard of Laurel, Mississippi. She didn't know Mrs. Spinks or Mrs. Clayton existed, never imagined that she would be sharing a bed and a cot with two white women she had just met, wouldn't have guessed that she—at twenty years old—would take on a sense of protection for two teenagers restless at injustice or that outrunning the Klan would become a regular feature of her life. She couldn't have imagined then that she would become who she was now: the Mississippi Amazon.

CHAPTER FIVE

FREEDOM NORTH

WHILE GWEN WAS ESTABLISHING HERSELF AS A LEADER IN THE freedom movement, Mike's time as an activist was just beginning. Mike was restless as the car sped to Atlantic City, lost in thought as the radio blared Otis Redding and Marvin Gaye. Like other Philadelphians, Mike had spent many summer days at the New Jersey shore with his family, weathering the broken glass of its segregated beaches to enjoy the refreshing ocean waters. It was a welcome break from the oppressive summertime of a landlocked city. But it was not the ocean waters that beckoned him this August 1964 day. Rather, he and his friend Dwight Williams were going to Atlantic City to join a protest against the Democratic Party.

Party leaders had hoped that the Democratic National Convention in 1964 would coronate Lyndon Johnson for a full term as president. The DNC had been planning for a glitzy Atlantic City gala since before Johnson had assumed the presidency after John F. Kennedy's assassination in 1963. The 1964 election would be his first time at the top of the ticket. His opponent was Arizona Republican Barry Goldwater, a staunch conservative senator who openly opposed the civil rights movement. Johnson mocked Goldwater as an extremist threatening the United States. Yet, on his way to winning one of the biggest landslides in American history, Johnson sought to sideline the moral clarity of the civil rights movement.

Battle-tested veterans of Mississippi had come to New Jersey to defenestrate Southern Democrats in the interests of genuine democracy. Mike had diligently followed Mississippi Freedom Summer in the newspaper and on the radio, longing to be part of the action. Now it had come north. Gathered on the Jersey shore, the civil rights coalition urged the national party to seat the Mississippi Freedom Democratic Party over the segregationist state delegation that had been the Democratic Party standard bearer. And Mike, still frustrated at not having gone south himself, came to support that objective. His brother Reginald had joined the military in June, and Mike was eager to enlist in the freedom fight.

The MFDP, which brought together several prominent organizations of the civil rights movement, was negotiating with Democratic Party officials to be seated on the convention floor. In bitter backdoor meetings as in the public square, activists and their allies stated the obvious truth: the MFDP included the only democratically elected delegates from Mississippi. They should be the ones to formally nominate the Democratic presidential candidate. Johnson, however, refused to consider it. Though he no longer endorsed segregation, the Texas-born Johnson did not want to lose the support of the segregationist Southern Democrats.

As MFDP's lawyer and allies pleaded their case behind closed doors, the Freedom Democrats made their case to the party's credentials committee two days before the convention officially began. The credentials committee formally authorized state delegations to nominate the presidential candidate. Their imprimatur was a formality to gain entrance. And so, on the one-year anniversary of the March on Washington, the Freedom Democrats marched in and took their seats opposite the segregationist delegation. Several Freedom Democrats testified. The most searing testimony was offered by Fannie Lou Hamer, the forty-six-year-old sharecropper who exemplified the indigenous leadership and bravery of Black rural communities. Mrs. Hamer recounted the arrest and torture she experienced two years earlier when she tried to vote in her home state. Her poignant testimony was broadcast nationwide—until Lyndon Johnson recognized its damning power and held an impromptu press conference to cut her off.

The stalemate grew more rancorous over days of heated negotiations between two visions of what America should be and who should decide. Ultimately, Democratic officials offered two spots on the convention floor to MFDP representatives as "at large delegates" and a promise not to seat any openly segregated state delegation at the following convention, four years later. More insultingly, the party specified that the two MFDP representatives needed to be the male leaders present, not Mrs. Hamer. They would be invited guests of the party, present to observe the segregationist Democrats cast their vote, without a say in the process. "We didn't come all this way for no two seats," Mrs. Hamer replied. And the protests continued to swarm Atlantic City. Members of the Congress of Racial Equality (CORE) and SNCC staged a sit-in on the boardwalk outside the Convention Center the day after Hamer's testimony.[1]

Mike wasn't privy to the backroom dealings and didn't hear Hamer's testimony. He had met the Philadelphia Friends of SNCC organizers earlier, slowly beginning his initiation into the Northern Student Movement that attempted to bring the strategy of the Southern freedom movement to the segregated urban North. He came to Atlantic City bearing supplies Friends of SNCC had raised to donate to the efforts down South, to people like Gwen, who didn't come north, and the Mississippians who couldn't. He was awed when Jim Forman, whose organizing career he had followed as diligently as he had once tracked baseball statistics, addressed the crowd. But returning to Philadelphia, Mike was once again reminded of his frustration at not being more involved. He didn't know how to do something as dramatic as join the Southern freedom movement.[2]

Weeks later, he returned to Temple to start his sophomore year. He had largely left the world of Heritage House and didn't join a fraternity, which was then the only identifiable Black social presence on campus. He had a small group of friends to discuss politics with, including a serious girlfriend with whom he shared an apartment. But they were all white. He was struggling to find his place. His heart was with the freedom movement down South, his head was in his books, and his body was at a predominantly white university in his hometown.

He was struggling to find his footing in other ways, as well. As a freshman, he had worked in the periodical division at the campus library and pulled a twelve-hour shift at a local pharmacy on weekends. Despite his high marks in high school, he had never written a term paper and was ill prepared for college. The B in English and D in History saved him from flunking his first semester. The difficulty balancing work and school landed him on academic probation. He planned to devote this year to his studies.[3]

MIKE HAD SPENT the previous academic year volunteering with the Northern Student Movement (NSM), a SNCC-associated effort across northeastern campuses. The NSM began at Yale in 1961, an attempt to leverage student energy to not only support the Southern civil rights movement but also apply its aims in the urban North. Similar efforts had been carried out by Friends of SNCC groups throughout the North as their attempts to aid anti-racism in the South clashed with local racism in the North. By the time Mike had begun college in 1963, the "NSM had 50 full-time staff and 2,500 volunteers." NSM projects blended the youthful energy of college students with the efforts of church and civic group affiliates serving underresourced Black neighborhoods. Philadelphia was home to the NSM's perhaps most ambitious effort: a tutoring program, shaped by Black educators and clergy, under the slogan "Make education a living experience." At its height, five hundred NSM volunteers tutored more than eight hundred high school students twice a week at forty-two neighborhood sites. Most of the tutoring centers were in North Philly, in neighborhoods where 60 percent of the residents didn't finish high school. Mike became a tutor. So did his friends Dwight and Max Stanford of RAM.[4]

John Churchville, Mike's old friend from the Heritage House who had served as a SNCC field organizer in Georgia and Mississippi in 1962, created the Freedom Library, aiming to "have books by and about black people." Modeled after the Freedom Schools Gwen helped develop in the South, the library aimed to provide a positive sense of Black history that extended before and beyond slavery. The library could be "a program that would instill racial pride in the community and hence create a positive identity" in neighborhoods that "revealed a tremendous sense of worthlessness and self-hatred." Ultimately, it gathered more than two thousand titles and connected them to lectures on Black history. Nation of Islam leader Jeremiah Shabazz, whom Mike had known since childhood, donated a raft of books from Mohammed's Mosque. Other books came from the Anti-Defamation League, B'nai Brith, and the city library system.[5]

Education was rewarding. Mike liked giving back. But he wanted to push back, to confront the power of Jim Crow. That was why he was so excited by the Freedom Democratic Party challenge—and so outraged by the party's bowing to white supremacy. The capitulation in Atlantic City showed him and so many others that the existing system would not accommodate democracy. And tutoring wasn't going to change the system.

TRAGEDY WOULD HELP give Mike purpose. SNCC and the Southern Christian Leadership Conference had opened the year of 1965 with an expanded voting rights campaign in Selma, Alabama. The effort spread to neighboring counties, building on the work SNCC had done throughout the Black belt. As demonstrations proliferated, police arrested 3,400 people over the course of four weeks—and killed two voting rights activists in the span of one week, including Jimmie Lee Jackson, a deacon and military veteran. Civil rights activists planned a march to the state capitol for March 7. As demonstrators reached the Edmund Pettus Bridge, local and state police attacked with batons and tear gas. Those at the front of the line, including Hosea Williams of SCLC and SNCC's John Lewis, bore the initial brunt of the fury. But police attacked people indiscriminately as they chased marchers back to the housing projects where the march had begun. (Once there, residents fought back with bricks and bottles.) Scenes of the police violence carried the news nationwide: Bloody Sunday. Martin Luther King called for others to join the effort. Two days later a crowd of two thousand people marched to, but not across, the bridge. That night, a racist mob beat demonstrator James Reeb, a white Unitarian minister. He died in the hospital from his injuries.[6]

The violence in Selma catalyzed demonstrations nationwide, including in Philadelphia, where Reeb had earned his master's degree in theology. The NAACP led a march that ringed city hall with twelve thousand people, one of the largest demonstrations in Philadelphia's history. The only elected representative present was a Black city councilor. The city hall march was just one of the demonstrations that day. Mike and Dwight, working with anti-war professor Herb Simons and some other white leftists they had befriended, organized a march that began on Temple's campus and walked to Independence Hall downtown, before meeting up with the rally at city hall. It was Mike's first time directly organizing anything, but everything was so urgent that he felt as if it almost organized itself. All they had to do was put the word out about when and where to meet. More than a thousand people from Temple participated.[7]

Though catalyzed by events in Selma, the march took aim at the totality of American priorities. Many of the campus leftists had been brought into action by the US war in Vietnam, which accelerated alongside the violence in Selma. The United States conducted aerial bombings throughout February 1965, and on March 8, the day after Alabama troopers attacked demonstrators on the Edmund Pettus Bridge, more than three thousand Marines landed in Da Nang, marking the official beginning of the US ground war in Vietnam.

Several of the professors who assisted Mike in organizing the Selma solidarity demonstration had recently formed University Faculty for Peace in Viet Nam and linked the anti-communism driving the war with the racism upholding segregation. Of the march, Herb Simons urged students to fight locally: "We must erase the image of the 'closed gates' of Temple University—An image of a white island in the black ghetto." The simultaneous escalation of war and racism, of war abroad and war at home, led Mike to reject Cold War doublespeak. *America is not a liberated zone* became his mantra.[8]

Thrilled at the success of the demonstration, Mike and Dwight helped form a group called Conscience. Continuing the NSM's community service in North Philadelphia, Conscience created an after-school program for neighborhood kids, did a neighborhood cleanup event, and would soon launch a summer camp. The group was also friendly with the burgeoning anti-war organizing on campus. The effort complemented Mike's growing involvement in the intellectual life of campus. Mike attended any lecture he could: novelist Ralph Ellison, activist James Meredith, Communist Party intellectual Herbert Aptheker. His mind was expanding, but he still wanted for a formal outlet to direct his energies.

In his freshman year, he had read *Reveille for Radicals*, a 1945 tome on community organizing by Saul Alinsky, who stressed that radicalism is a persistent battle for fairness that proceeds through the leadership of organized communities. "It is apparent that the primary and most difficult job confronting an organizer is the actual identification of the local leadership," Alinsky wrote. "With few exceptions, the real local leaders are completely unknown outside of the community." Mike knew that SNCC's model corresponded with his own developing theory of change. He recognized, too, that SNCC would train him to do what he wanted to do.[9]

A MONTH AFTER the Selma march, Mike and Dwight were once again in the car. It was spring break, and they were headed to Atlanta—

home of SNCC. The journey took over thirty hours, more than twice
what it should have because they had to stop often to put water in
the overheating radiator. But their excitement propelled them deeper
and deeper into Dixie. Mike was thrilled to meet John Lewis, whose
savage beating on the Edmund Pettus Bridge on March 7, 1965, had
driven Mike and so many others to the streets in protest. He wondered how anyone's skull could be hard enough to withstand so many
blows, wondered, too, whether he could withstand such abuse. Much
as Gwen had done when organizing protests in Atlanta a year earlier,
Mike and Dwight stayed with Lewis.

Chatting with SNCC field staff, Mike was single-minded. *How
do I go to Mississippi this summer?* That seemed to be the toughest place
in the country, and he was convinced it would be the place to teach
him the most. But Jimmy Travis told him otherwise. Travis was a
Mississippi native who had become a full-time SNCC worker at
twenty. A patient agitator, he had been arrested numerous times in
voter registration drives. And in 1963, as he and Bob Moses tried to
escape an unmarked vehicle that had been following them from the
SNCC office, Travis was shot in the head and shoulder. SNCC responded to the near assassination by increasing its presence in Mississippi and demanding federal intervention against such racist attacks.[10]

Travis knew something about where the action was. And he encouraged Mike and Dwight to go to Arkansas instead of Mississippi.
People in Mississippi were still recovering from the previous year's intense activity and national attention, he said, while the SNCC effort
in neighboring Arkansas had developed a little-noticed but tightly
run campaign. They would learn a lot in Arkansas, Travis assured
Mike and Dwight. Here were people who had demonstrated the kind
of fearless commitment Mike wanted to emulate. If Travis said Arkansas was the place to be, that was where they would go.

MIKE RETURNED TO Philadelphia determined to leave as soon as his
semester ended. His friends in the NSM tried to persuade him to stay

in Philadelphia, where there was ample work to be done. That May, a rolling picket began outside Girard College, a walled boarding school for fatherless children. Located in the heart of North Philadelphia, blocks from where Mike grew up, Girard College remained segregated. The NAACP called for the school to be integrated, and much of the daily picketing was helmed by young men connected to street organizations: the explosive energy of the 1964 uprising was being channeled in a more coordinated fashion.[11]

But Mike was resolute. He finally knew how to do what he had been wanting to do since 1961. Mississippi Freedom Summer had given SNCC a vast network of volunteers, which it used subsequently to screen potential recruits before they headed South. So Mike submitted his application and had a screening interview with a white educational sociologist from Temple University. Mike was caught off guard by having to prove himself to her. *You mean to tell me that* you *can determine if I go down South to work with Black people*, he fumed. She asked him to demonstrate his commitment to nonviolence. Their meeting only soured from there. *Are you an angry Black male?* she asked. *Let's hope so!* Mike said, thinking of what awaited him in Arkansas.[12]

Mike wasn't sure who she reported to, but by the time it was over he didn't care. He was determined to go South regardless, and he finally had a mechanism to guide him. It didn't matter anyway. He was approved to join the Arkansas Project of SNCC. Friends committed to supporting him financially for three months.

When the semester ended, Mike dropped out of school. He threw some clothes and supplies in a bag. As he headed for the door, he ran into the immovable object that was his mother. Blocking his path, Rebecca then began unpacking his bag. *You're not taking this with you*, she said as she removed something from his bag. *This isn't yours*, she said of a towel but meant of his life. Her oldest was already in Vietnam, now Mike was heading to battle segregationists in the land she had fled as a child. Rebecca didn't even know how much time she had left. Three years earlier doctors had diagnosed her with multiple myeloma and gave her five years to live. One by one she emptied his bag, hoping to sap his will to do what they both knew he was going to do.

I tell you what, he told her at last. *You can have it all. I'm going.* They both knew it. After all, she was the one who had raised him to believe *If you think you're right, I don't care who it is, you stand up. You never back down.*

PART II

SAY IT LOUD

CHAPTER SIX

FREEDOM IS NOT ENOUGH

WHILE MIKE PREPARED TO HEAD TO ARKANSAS, GWEN WAS hard at work in Laurel. Mississippi was still run by segregationists. Like so many other places, Laurel remained dangerously volatile as white supremacists sought to thwart the growing assertiveness of the long-suppressed Black population.

President Lyndon Johnson wasn't paying much attention to either Arkansas or Mississippi when he traveled two and a half miles from the White House to deliver the commencement address at Howard University on June 4, 1965. Several SNCC staffers—including Stokely Carmichael, Cleve Sellers, and Muriel Tillinghast, one of the only women project directors in Freedom Summer besides Gwen—had studied at the historically Black university. On the precipice of passing the Voting Rights Act, Johnson chose Howard as the site to declare that "freedom is not enough." Claiming the defeat of segregation, Johnson said the goal was "not just freedom but opportunity."

But for Black people, both freedom and opportunity remained elusive.

THOUGH JOHNSON WAS ready to proclaim a new day in America, conditions in Mississippi remained dangerously similar to before the passage of landmark legislation. After most of the civil rights volunteers had left the state, Mississippi segregationists tried to get back to normal. Two days before Christmas 1964, Laurel police arrested twenty people for "breach of peace" after the group tried, on three different occasions, to order food at a coffee shop attached to the Travel Inn hotel. It was the second time in a month that SNCC members had been arrested there. On Christmas, Gwen was one of a dozen civil rights activists at the city jail singing Christmas carols and freedom songs for their incarcerated kin when police attacked them and warned "the Klan is coming." The NAACP sent $1,700 to Gwen to bail everyone out, and the group was out in time to participate in mass meetings on December 29 and 30.[1]

Things only worsened in the new year as the Mississippi Freedom Democratic Party launched its "Congressional Challenge" in an attempt to unseat the state's congressional representatives. The segregationist congressmen had been elected in an apartheid election. On January 14, which MFDP had dubbed "Freedom Day," supporters in Washington, DC, picketed the House of Representatives to block seating the five white congressmen from Mississippi. Gwen celebrated Freedom Day by bringing thirty residents to Laurel's courthouse to register to vote. But the county registrar allowed only one member of the group to take the restrictive literacy test before closing the office. Police attacked the would-be registrants, including the fifty-six-year-old Mrs. Ruffin, who had housed the SNCC workers when Gwen first arrived the previous summer. She was seen being dragged from the courthouse by her leg. "This violent element in law officers was in some kind of unholy alliance with the local racists," Gwen later testified. "We were in real fear."[2]

In support of the Congressional Challenge, the Laurel COFO office began gathering testimony from residents about the humiliations and barriers that greeted their attempts to vote. Residents patiently described poll taxes, literacy tests, arbitrary and capricious dismissals by the registrar—and chains, pistols, knives, and clubs wielded by local whites, some of them in police uniform. Word soon got out that the MFDP was recording these depositions. The office telephone line rang constantly with threats of gruesome violence.

Some of those callers tried to deliver. First, there was the shot fired at the office one Tuesday night. Then, around three a.m. on February 17, persons unknown entered the COFO office, smashed the mimeograph machine, stole the typewriters, and set fire to the building. The attackers had already burned a restaurant and hotel owned by Cleveland Golden, who had rented COFO the building. Now the expansive office Gwen had built—which included work space, a community center, and the Freedom Library of more than two thousand titles—had gone up in flames. So had Golden's confidence. He refused to rent to SNCC again. "He was the only person in town who would rent to us," Gwen said. "After this fire, I don't know where we'll go." She was devastated.[3]

Two weeks later, racists targeted the home of another local activist with a firebomb—this time thrown from a speeding vehicle.[4]

EVEN WHILE LIVING under such constant threat of violence, Gwen stayed on freedom. Her overarching mission was to bolster the self-confidence, determination, and skill of Black Mississippians to end white minority rule over the state's political, economic, and social order. Throughout the spring, she investigated the possibility of union organizing in Laurel—another challenge to the economic order upheld by racism. The Mississippi Freedom Democratic Party had created the Mississippi Freedom Labor Union in the hopes that Black workers could better their lot relative to both the often-brutal employers and the small and frequently segregated labor movement that existed in the state.

As summer neared, the Freedom Democratic Party (FDP) planned a smaller summer project for 1965. That summer, fewer than two hundred people traveled to the Sunflower State to participate in voter registration, Freedom Schools, and other community-organizing efforts. But even without the national spotlight, the FDP remained focused on ousting racists from power, and Gwen focused on the MFDP political campaign.[5]

Those in power wouldn't go willingly. On June 9, Mississippi governor Paul Johnson called a special session of the state legislature with the surprising task of scrapping the state's voting restrictions and aligning its voting requirements with those of Northern states. Johnson's decision was strategy, not benevolence. The US Senate had passed the Voting Rights Act weeks earlier. The bill—which would repeal the Southern states' use of literacy tests, poll taxes, public advertisement of new registered voters—was being debated in Congress as President Johnson eagerly awaited its arrival on his desk. The Mississippi governor wagered that formally eliminating the barriers to Black suffrage would obviate the need for a bill focused on the South. Johnson wagered that if the state legislature acted first, Mississippi would be in a stronger position to mount a successful legal challenge to overturn any voting rights laws—and restrict Black political fortunes—in the future.[6]

The Freedom Democrats saw through the governor's cynical ploy, itself the product of an illegitimate electoral system. For Gwen and the FDP, the special legislative session was not just a ruse but a fraud; it did not represent the democratic will of the people. Once again, the FDP took to the streets to shut down the authoritarian legislature and its bad-faith policies. Even before the governor convened the special legislative session, the FDP's goal was to unseat the Mississippi state legislature as well as its national representatives.

The FDP mobilized for a march on June 14. As she had done many times before, Gwen made the trek from Laurel to Jackson. Other SNCC staff had come in from around the state. This was to be a big show of strength. Gwen was fired up in the early summer heat, excited to be joined by so many people, as the group set off on a one-mile march from Morning Star Baptist Church to the state capitol. The march was boisterous, exuberant. As the FDP headed through local neighborhoods en route to the capitol, people spontaneously joined in. Nearly half of the marchers were teenagers. Gwen's enthusiasm swelled with the crowd's size.

Whereas the legislature had tried a new tactic, the police stuck with a familiar one. Halfway into the march, state police cordoned off the demonstrators and began beating and arresting them for marching without a permit. Almost five hundred people were arrested. Undeterred, FDP kept coming back for the rest of the week, with activists traveling from across the region to participate. The police kept arresting people—eventually detaining more than nine hundred people in demonstrations in Jackson that week.[7]

Gwen had been arrested before, but never like this. Police loaded her, along with demonstrators by the dozens, into their wagons. Gwen saw that they were being taken not to the jail but to the state fairgrounds.

Thick white arms pulled her into a livestock pen, cursing all the way. She was overcome by the smell of shit and hay, overcome, too, with panic at the arrests of so many people, some still in house slippers, who clearly did not expect to join a demonstration much less be arrested. Mothers, who had come with their young kids, were now terrified to find themselves caged in barns at the segregated fairgrounds. Children were crying, some soiling themselves in despair. There was no food, no beds, not even a blanket.

Gwen joined other experienced organizers in trying to boost morale. They began singing freedom songs. *Ain't gonna let nobody turn me around*, their voices echoing in the cavernous space. *I'm gonna keep on a-walkin', keep on a-talkin', marchin' into freedom land.* Louder and louder they sang, determination starting to conquer fear as their songs carried them into nightfall.

Then the barn doors cracked open to allow in a slew of white men, armed with sticks but no uniforms. These men attacked the prisoners indiscriminately until they got bored, only to return again a few hours later or the following day. Gwen saw one Black woman dragged by her legs and then beat about her breasts and groin. Two visibly pregnant women were beaten, one so badly that she miscarried. Pools of blood gathered beside the white activist guards beat unconscious. Police then doused the prisoners in water and sprayed them with disinfectant, the chemical burning their eyes. Gwen thought her anonymous tormentors took special delight in hitting people who had fallen asleep, waking them in terror. *Move!* they'd demand, only to bark *Sit down.* Thwack. *Get up!* Jab. *Sit down!* Repeat.[8]

Gwen tried to steel her resolve. She saw some of the guards approach a group of teenage girls in the makeshift prison. *You want to get out?* one of the men menaced. *Well, you need to come go with me.* (None did.) Other assailants violated women with their clubs. The conditions wore on the prisoners, who were well acquainted with white men's sexual violence against Black women. Winson Hudson, a forty-eight-year-old NAACP activist and local leader of the nascent Head Start program in Harmony, Mississippi, sat down and refused to get up. When a particularly brutal cop went to drag her away, she grabbed his testicles as hard as she could. As he howled in pain, his face bright red, a gang of police beat her unconscious. Gwen, fearing Hudson had been killed, saw them drag her out.[9]

At first, everyone was held together on the fairgrounds without regard to sex or race—a rarity in Mississippi. After a couple of days, convention kicked in, and the white demonstrators were brought down to the city jail to be properly contained, while Black men and Black women were separated between the two buildings on the fairgrounds lot—animal stockades. The beatings lessened once the quotidian forms of segregation were in place. Prisoners received grits, bread, and something resembling beans for breakfast. Lunch and dinner consisted of just corn and peas, sometimes served in garbage bins. Gwen tried to keep her spirits up. At least, with so many people having been bailed out, she finally had a mattress to sleep on. She spent two weeks at the fairground prison before the Fifth Circuit court ordered everyone released.[10]

Gwen was out of jail but far from free. Shortly after the fairground was cleared of its captives, the Klan made a show of its macabre strength.

Starting on July 1, they staged cross burnings in nearly every county in the state. Arsonists turned Laurel into pyrotechnics of white supremacy, with six attacks that destroyed thirteen homes. The most fearsome came at one thirty in the morning at the house that now served as the local FDP office. It was a duplex, with FDP office and Freedom School on one side—and a family of five sleeping soundly on the other. Ben and Ulysses, the teenagers who had come to Laurel under Gwen's protection to escape racist violence in their native Hattiesburg, slept in the office. When one of them heard what he thought was a car backfiring, he went out to investigate. He found a smoldering fire set right under the gas line of the house. He tried to call the fire department, but the phone lines had been cut. He was able to douse the flames before the gas line exploded. Two weeks later, armed men tried to abduct an MFDP activist. In September, arsonists blew up a COFO truck in Laurel.[11]

GWEN WAS EXHAUSTED. It had been a long two weeks in that makeshift jail, a long summer, a long three years fighting for the freedom that the Constitution, and now ostensibly the law, guaranteed. She had sacrificed her relationship with her family to be arrested, insulted, assaulted, and threatened with death on more than one occasion. She tried to focus on the local work. But she couldn't shake the sight of petrified children wetting themselves in the fairground jail, the sound of clubs cracking bone and flesh. She closed her eyes and saw flames—the flames that had destroyed the first MFDP office, the second MFDP office, and now nearly a third. She thought of the library she had painstakingly built smoldering in ashes, of the people she loved just narrowly escaping inferno. She thought of the men chasing her in cars and on the street, calling her names and threatening her harm. How much longer, she thought, before one of those bombs exploded as it was designed, before the bullets hit their mark?

She thought about everything but the traffic light and the car in front of her. Nerves frayed, she ran a red light and hit another car.

A few days later, she got into another car accident—minor, like the first one, but revealing of her mental state. Jim Forman called from the national office to tell her what she could not yet admit to herself: she needed a break from Mississippi.

At first she refused. She felt a deep responsibility to the project workers and local community she had both mentored and learned from. But Forman persisted. *You're no good to anyone if you have a nervous breakdown,* he told her. Plus, he assured her, he needed her help in the Friends of SNCC office raising money for the organization. She had proven herself a talented fundraiser. She would still work in the movement full-time. Tearfully, Gwen said good-bye to Mrs. Spinks and the two remaining volunteers of the Laurel Project, Linell and Marion, who wished her well as they packed their own bags.

Shortly before heading to New York, she opened a package of materials that had been donated to the Laurel Project library after the last firebomb attack. Among the food and clothes was a record album—not music but a lecture. She placed the needle on the vinyl to hear a booming voice declare, "The government has failed us. You can't deny that. Any time you're living in the twentieth century and you walking around here singing 'We Shall Overcome,' the government has failed you." Gwen was as shocked as she was thrilled. Who was this man, with such a strident critique of both the government and the prominent civil rights organizations? Thinking of her own brushes with death, she wondered how so bold and powerful a speaker could survive this dangerous country. Gwen looked at the record sleeve to see who it was. His name was Malcolm X, and he had been assassinated a few months earlier.

THE DAY GWEN was arrested in Jackson, Mike stepped off a bus in Little Rock, Arkansas. After a thirty-three-hour trip from Philadelphia, he headed to the local SNCC office for an orientation. Members of the Arkansas SNCC project called it "Arsnick" and hoped that their efforts could end the white supremacy poisoning the state. It wouldn't be easy. Mike had watched on television when Orval Faubus, the state's governor, had deployed the National Guard in 1957 to prevent the integration of Little Rock's Central High School. Almost a decade later, less than half of the voting-age Black population was registered to vote. Some state legislators hoped to reduce that number further. Black Arkansas had a median income less than half that of whites but an infant mortality rate double that of white counterparts. More than half of Black households in the state lacked a flush toilet; nearly three-quarters had no shower, tub, or bathing facility. Largely ignored, even within SNCC, Arkansas would be a true test of desegregation.[12]

Arsnick began in 1962, when members of the Arkansas Council on Human Relations invited SNCC to the state. The council was a cautious effort to pursue civil rights, and members hoped that SNCC's direct-action energy would convince local elites to desegregate faster. The project's initial director was Bill Hansen, a white man from Cincinnati who had had, among other things, his jaw and ribs broken by a mob of racist whites following a civil rights demonstration in Albany, Georgia. In 1964, Hansen recognized that the project needed local Black leadership to thrive, and he stepped aside. The project had a staff of eight people, evenly divided between white and Black. It retained that even split in its summer project of 1965, welcoming upward of seventy volunteers from around the country to conduct "voter registration, anti-discrimination, and community organizing drives." Anchoring it all was a network of community centers that would serve as sites of education, socializing, and convergence.[13]

Eager for action but ignorant of Arkansas, Mike showed up ready to work. The volunteers gathered in Little Rock for two days of orientation, which included a one-hour discussion, "What Is Arkansas," together with the geography of Arsnick projects. The central item was how to stay safe. Recalling the history of Emmett Till and the Scottsboro Boys, the racist specter of Black men attacking white women, Mike had one idea: *I do not want to ride in a car alone with a white woman,* he declared. And if he had to, he certainly would not sit next to her. A white volunteer took umbrage at his position. *It's not about you*, Mike thought in annoyance, and this policy would become the norm throughout the state. Mike even joked that he did not want to ride in a car with Hansen, whose marriage to a Black woman had made him a hated target of local racists.[14]

Mike was assigned to the Helena Project, in the eastern part of the state where most Black Arkansans lived. Located in Phillips County, Helena lay in the Arkansas Delta and bordered Mississippi. (Novelist Richard Wright had lived there for several years as a child.) The Mississippi River, with its history of cotton production and chattel slavery, ran through town.

Arkansas had contributed one of the grimmest episodes in establishing the Jim Crow order when, during the bloody summer of 1919, the state's governor ordered five hundred soldiers to join local vigilantes in a pogrom of the Black population of Elaine, a town less than thirty miles from Helena. The vigilantes and soldiers were trying to stop Black sharecroppers from organizing. More than two hundred people—men, women, and children—were slaughtered in Elaine. No whites were ever prosecuted for their participation, yet twelve Black men were charged for killing the five white men who died in the assault. The NAACP defended the men, ultimately earning a ruling from the Supreme Court that expanded civil rights protections in jury selection, trial location, and from coerced confessions.[15]

The massacre had a chilling effect on Black political participation. "The people of Helena are afraid of work, starvation, and death," an Arsnick newspaper affirmed. "Since the white man usually causes these situations, they are most afraid of him." Arsnick's first attempt to start a project in Helena fell flat in 1963 as a result of police harassment and insufficient staff. SNCC returned in 1964, still weathering routine police pressure; on one occasion, police arrested an Arsnick member inside his own home for "vagrancy."

The summer project gave them enough people to be more proactive. Segregation remained routine, and as Mike went door to door trying to register voters in West Helena, he found the routine severity of racist violence terrified many people. State officials used patronage for those Black people willing to endorse the status quo, something many had learned to accommodate already. The town sheriff even convinced the Phillips County NAACP leader to encourage Helena Blacks to vote "absentee."[16]

SNCC had another resource at its disposal, for Arkansas also had a proud radical tradition. The Southern Tenant Farmers Union (STFU) formed in the Arkansas Delta in 1934; a survivor of the Elaine massacre participated in its founding. It would soon, though briefly, boast a biracial membership of more than thirty thousand people. Though its star had faded by the time SNCC arose to challenge Jim Crow's ongoing stranglehold, its legacy of a socialist critique of the New Deal now inspired Arsnick's anti-racist challenges to the Great Society, President Johnson's set of anti-poverty programs. Many of those who took in Arsnick workers had been STFU members in their youth, and they were eager to support the youthful militancy that Mike and others brought with them. Not since his days at the New World Bookshop had Mike heard communism discussed as positively as he did among Arkansas sharecroppers.[17]

White intransigence was everywhere. On a Tuesday afternoon in the middle of July, Mike brought a group of kids to the Helena Pool. Arsnick had already sent two white volunteers to the pool to see if it was privately owned. After the white volunteers were assured it was public, Mike arrived with nine children. When an employee informed them that the pool was off-limits, the white civil rights activist reminded her that she had assured him otherwise and that he had in fact gone swimming without a membership card. She soon called the police, who asked them all to leave. By the time they did, the once-crowded pool had emptied. When Mike and the children returned another day, he informed the security guard that the 1964 Civil Rights Act prohibited segregated public facilities. The staff then drained the pool and said it was closed for repairs.[18]

About two months into his stay in Arkansas, Mike went to get a minor repair on one of the project's cars. *Ain't that Hansen's car?* the owner asked, unleashing a string of expletives while reaching for a gun under the counter. Three other white men converged on Mike, whose survival instincts sent him scurrying to the door. He ran from the shop and jumped into the car. He was almost in the passenger seat as he started the engine from a low crouch. As he peeled out of the parking lot, through the rearview mirror he could see the owner with gun in hand.

He headed back to the SNCC office, where, when his nerves had settled enough to do so, his comrades told him to file a police report. Mike dutifully reported the incident to the local sheriff. Within seconds, police arrested him for disorderly conduct, disturbing the peace, and resisting arrest. It was his first arrest. At trial, the auto repair shop owner testified against Mike and once again threatened to kill him. Mike was convicted, given a thirty-day suspended sentence, and told to leave the county. But he wasn't going anywhere, not yet.[19]

As an added precaution, Mike had reported the episode to the local FBI agent, a man with the improbable last name of Smart. The bureau had agents stationed throughout the South to monitor the status of civil rights workers. *I need to report a violation of my civil rights*, Mike told Agent Smart. The affable agent had reassured him that nothing would come of the incident and offered to help Mike in any way he could. Glad for the powerful new friend, Mike hoped that Agent Smart might be an ally against the excesses of local state officials.

Yet police remained a threat, and not just in Phillips County. Later in the summer, Mike and another SNCC worker were sent to a neighboring county to see about setting up a project there. Lacking local contacts, they visited the sites of economic power in segregated Black communities: the church, the barber shop, and the funeral parlor. The funeral director proved to be a valuable resource in connecting Mike to local residents. Not long after Mike arrived, the funeral director also set up a meeting with the local sheriff. *I've got a peace-*

ful town, the sheriff informed them. *There's no need for y'all to be here.* Though his point was already clear, the sheriff continued. *If there's any trouble, I'll have to deputize men off the soda trucks*—and, of course, *I can't be responsible for what they might do.*[20]

MIKE RETURNED TO Philadelphia to visit his family in September 1965. He had to break the news to his mother that he would not be returning to college. She had suspected as much. The movement would be his life, they both knew. He was not in Philadelphia long. Though the summer project was over, the Arkansas freedom movement continued. Hundreds of students in Forrest City had elevated the fight against segregated schools to a new level by boycotting classes and picketing the school board. More than two hundred young people had been arrested, SNCC National staffers Cleve Sellers and Julian Bond visited the state to lend support, and Arkansas officials were trying to send one of the Arsnick organizers to prison for a decade. When they heard all this, Mike and Dwight drove south.[21]

Mike was at the Forrest City SNCC office when the police banged on the door. Fearing the police response to this multiracial meeting, the one white woman present hid in a closet before anyone let the police in. Gripping clubs and heavy flashlights, a parade of officers entered and ordered everyone against the wall. Police threatened to kill the men if they did not share the location of SNCC leaders Julian Bond and Cleve Sellers. Mike breathed a sigh of relief when he saw Agent Smart, the FBI gumshoe who had taken Mike's civil rights complaint earlier in the summer, at the end of the police line. *Agent Smart*, he called, thinking he had a way out. *Shut the fuck up you black sonofabitch and get up against the wall*, Smart replied.[22]

And then Mike knew: The federal government would not be shamed, cajoled, or convinced into doing the right thing. The movement could not rely upon those in charge. No amount of moral appeals or playing by the rules would create change. They needed power.

A SUMMER OF knocking on doors and taking risks had endeared Mike to some in SNCC's national office. In October, Cleve Sellers asked if he would be a campus traveler. Mike agreed immediately, hoping it would give him a bird's-eye view of the movement throughout the region. The job took him between Virginia, North Carolina, and the SNCC national office in Atlanta. He was one of four campus travelers working across six Southern states. He partnered with Willie Ricks, who was among the SNCC staffers whose jeremiads at the Atlanta University Center pushed Gwen to the SNCC office two years earlier.

Long accustomed to recruiting people off campuses, SNCC would bring to historically Black colleges its strategy of developing local leaders to amplify their efforts as part of a broad anti-racist movement. Campus travelers brought with them the SNCC philosophy of political education, democratic deliberation, and popular agitation.[23]

Mike liked the lack of a fixed address, working full-time in support of and alongside local organizers. At Saint Paul's College in Lawrenceville, Virginia, he helped students protest the restrictive policies on their campus. Students in Petersburg were setting up their own civil rights conference. In Richmond, he supported students at Virginia Union who wanted to take on the state's still segregated educational system.

It was exciting work, but he grew frustrated by what he saw as the lack of fight that existed among many Black people in the South. "In a Negro community in the South you find people accepting laws which they don't like and didn't have a part in making," he reported back to SNCC. "Although they dislike the laws, there is fear and/or apathy that stop them from doing anything about that." The relative economic comfort of Black college graduates in the South reinforced this learned helplessness. "They get accustomed to accepting rules and laws while in college and carry this into their lives after graduation," he observed.[24]

Mike saw his job as helping more people feel confident enough to break the rules.

CHAPTER SEVEN

THE MONSTER WE LIVE IN

GWEN WAS BURSTING WITH ENERGY AS SHE RETURNED TO Atlanta for a five-day SNCC retreat at the end of November 1965. She had spent the last three months living in New York City, where Jim Forman, her beloved mentor, had sent her to recuperate from the terrors of Mississippi. She spent her days lecturing about the Mississippi freedom movement at high schools and colleges throughout the Northeast to raise funds for SNCC. While in New York, she also accompanied Forman on fundraising trips to large donors. Gwen thrilled at going to the house of legendary singer and movement supporter Harry Belafonte, who had paid for eleven SNCC leaders to visit Guinea for a much-needed break after Freedom Summer. Forman also brought her to raise money from a group of liberal lawyers in midtown Manhattan. Gwen seethed as the attorneys, who had defended movement organizers but were not activists themselves, deigned to tell Forman what SNCC should do. Her anger became devastation as she realized Forman would not challenge their haughty lecturing. *This is what he goes through to keep SNCC afloat*, she realized. *This is the problem with begging the enemy for money.* Black people, she felt, needed to fund their own movements.[1]

A belief in Black self-reliance led her to the newly opened Black Arts Repertory Theatre/School (BARTS), a performance and social space led by the charismatic polyglot poet Amiri Baraka. BARTS was born in the wake of Malcolm X's assassination as an effort to build institutions devoted to Black people loving and learning from each other. Gwen found in BARTS a communion familiar to what she had felt at church concerts of her youth and Free Southern Theater performances in Mississippi. She also found a scathing denunciation of white people as devils. She had to agree. Still processing the terror and dashed hope that exiled her from Mississippi, Gwen had come to believe that whites hated Black people too much and that integration had been a foolish goal. Between BARTS and the Nation of Islam street speakers she heard, Gwen became a Black nationalist.[2]

Like Malcolm X and countless other Black nationalists before her, she rejected the US nation-state. Her loyalties now included Black and colonized people worldwide. She brought her newfound faith to the SNCC meeting in Atlanta. In 1965, SNCC was bigger than ever. Its size and stature, together with changes to federal law, unmoored the organization from the strategies that had anchored its first four years. Gwen felt certain that the plight of rural Black communities was part of a world problem that SNCC needed to address. Every day brought grim reminders that US interests abroad were connected to racism at home. The same Democratic Party that seated segregationist members at its national convention had sent US troops to invade the Dominican Republic in April 1965 and daily extended the war in Vietnam. By the time SNCC gathered, almost two hundred thousand American troops were stationed in Vietnam. Gwen didn't know much about either place, except that the United States was using its military might to undermine the self-determination of nonwhite people. But she saw her fortunes tied up with theirs more than with white elites, whether they hated SNCC or funded it.[3]

Others in SNCC shared Gwen's internationalism. In March, SNCC had already joined the Congress of Racial Equality (CORE) and Students for a Democratic Society (SDS) outside Chase Manhattan

Bank to protest its financing of South African apartheid. In July, the SNCC project in McComb, Mississippi, issued a statement opposing the war after a local resident was killed in Vietnam. Fannie Lou Hamer spoke out against the war as well. Gwen was excited by the opportunity for SNCC to build political power for Black people. Recent redistricting in Georgia had created three Black-majority districts, and SNCC decided to back one of its members, communications secretary Julian Bond, in a run for a seat in the state legislature. Representing an overwhelmingly impoverished Black district, Bond won the seat handily after defeating a Black Republican by a four-to-one margin.[4]

Gwen also wanted to address power imbalances within SNCC. The previous year, she had participated in a SNCC women's workshop that sparked ongoing conversation about gendered division of labor within the movement. From experience Gwen knew that women were tasked with secretarial duties while men took on the visible leadership. But, despite SNCC's egalitarianism, even her work as project director had been slighted. Gwen winced when she heard a SNCC leader apologize for appointing a woman as interim project director or when she saw a SNCC report on Mississippi organizing dismiss the Laurel Project as just "three girls." And at some of the organization's informal parties, some men in SNCC treated women with greater disregard.

Gwen endorsed the position paper that was drafted out of the women's workshop, which observed that "just as Negroes were the crucial factor in the economy of the cotton South, so too in SNCC, women are the crucial factor that keeps the movement running on a day-to-day basis." She was more cautious about the "kind of memo" that two white SNCC women, Casey Hayden and Mary King, subsequently drafted on "Sex and Caste" that claimed parallels "between treatment of Negroes and treatment of women." She agreed that women in the movement "seem to be caught up in a common-law caste system that operates sometimes subtly, forcing them to work around or outside hierarchical structures of power which may exclude them." But she hesitated at aligning with a statement written by white women, addressing their criticisms to primarily Black men, when Black women suffered by race as well as sex.[5]

As she saw it, the critique of male domination needed to be latticed with a rejection of white paternalism. Women were the bedrock of far-reaching Black collective action. Bond's victory opened a new front in its battle for democracy, but Jim Crow's strong grip was undeniable—and seemed to circle the globe. New York had broadened her horizons, giving her a new clarity. As Mike felt after his confrontations in Arkansas, Gwen arrived in Atlanta with a focus on how the organization could pursue what was most needed: power. As they each traveled across and between the North and the South, Gwen and Mike both learned that racism, no less than Black radicalism, was everywhere.

GWEN'S AND MIKE'S journeys finally converged on November 24, 1965—the day before Thanksgiving. While many young people headed home for the holidays, they were among a band of survivors to assemble at the SNCC national office for five days of meetings. It was the third staff meeting that year, this one dedicated to the "projects and programs that the whole staff needs to know about." It being SNCC, even the menu was political. The Thanksgiving banquet featured Nonviolent (turkey), Freedom Fighting (dressing), Justice (green beans), the FDP (hot rolls), Equality (ice tea), and plenty of Voter Registration (pumpkin pie).[6]

Meeting for the first time, Gwen and Mike regarded each other as survivors. They had been through a lot—everyone there had: arrested and attacked, abandoned by the political system, estranged from their families of origin. SNCC gave them a venue through which to imagine a future together.

Surviving the fires of battle made everyone a veteran, whether they had been in SNCC a few months, as in Mike's case, or a few years, as in Gwen's. But the difference mattered. Mike looked up to Gwen immediately. She was strong-willed, determined. Most of all, she had been in Mississippi—the front lines. As the meeting got underway, he saw quickly that he wanted to be where she was going.

A running theme of the meeting was whether SNCC should come out against the US war in Vietnam. In theory, this was not a controversial position for an organization whose sympathies lay with the oppressed and a rejection of state violence. Everyone was opposed to the war in Vietnam. Many in SNCC already saw their fight as a global one; the 1964 trip to Guinea that Harry Belafonte funded was the stuff of legend, and the organization's motto—"one man, one vote"—was adopted from Zambia as an early expression of solidarity with anti-apartheid and anti-colonial movements in southern Africa. Yet decades of Cold War repression had stifled public civil rights commentary on foreign policy.

Debate about whether SNCC should denounce the war came to a head on November 29, the fifth and final day. Mike bristled when he heard Jim Forman and SNCC's first chairman, Marion Barry, fret that discussing the war would harm the organization's funding and public support. He was glad to see Gwen lead the charge against US empire, an organizing challenge as much as an ideological one.

"We have to talk to the people about how rotten the country is that we live in," she implored her comrades. "The MONSTER we live in." Black men and poor whites are being sent to kill and die, she said, so that the United States could "keep the world in its pocket." The war would weaken the movement, too, she argued, since the draft would steal many would-be recruits, while the threat of conscription would keep students ensconced in the safety of college deferment and away from the freedom fight.[7]

Mike agreed with her instantly. But he saw that the room was split—not morally but strategically. One member made a motion to change SNCC's slogan from "One man, one vote" to "self-determination." (The motion failed to be seconded.) Without making a formal motion, another suggested changing the name to the Student Nonviolent Anti-Colonial Committee. Another member cautioned against taking a stand on the draft unless the organization was willing to embrace draft resistance—but then offered that he would personally fight alongside the Vietnamese if they came to the United States. Several people wished the Vietnamese victory over the United States. But how could they organize against the war? Should they work to ensure the draft was racially integrated in implementation or oppose it outright? How would ending the war contribute to ending the system that produced the war? And how would this affect SNCC's relationship with white funders? Mike looked to Gwen for next steps.

Gwen agreed that anything SNCC did needed to be action oriented. She suggested the organization set up committees to conduct public education. And it was not just Vietnam. "We must come out against South Africa and Rhodesia," she said, referencing the two white supremacist regimes of southern Africa. Led by a racist minority government of white settlers, Rhodesia had recently severed its links with England in order to be an independent settler colony in what was once (and would be again) Zimbabwe. Being ruled by a racist minority government was a condition that Black Southerners would well understand. "We have basis in the South," Gwen said. "We must have research" on world affairs. She asked that SNCC commit to doing workshops for both staff and community on Vietnam, South Africa, and Rhodesia. She volunteered to work on it. And the organization agreed to issue a statement on Vietnam and to begin organizing against the draft.

Mike was ecstatic: SNCC could move beyond the moralizing of the mostly white peace movement that wanted to end the war to critiquing the system that made the war possible to begin with—US imperialism. In his mind he had already drafted the statement, short and to the point: *Vietnam is a continuation, you dirty motherfuckers, of what you all have been doing forever.* And he was similarly taken by the quiet rage of the person who had pushed the motion so eloquently. Though he didn't speak much in the meeting, he agreed with Gwen completely. He wanted to follow her into battle.

Besides Gwen, the most support for pushing SNCC to adopt an anti-war statement was from those who had been working in Lowndes

County, Alabama. In the heart of Alabama's cotton-rich Black belt, Lowndes County was as fiercely contested an area as any in Mississippi. The SNCC project there was as deeply rooted as any in Mississippi, too. Its members were as frayed and fired up as Gwen was. Their disgust at white supremacy had been sharpened months earlier when a sheriff murdered white SNCC volunteer and seminary student Jonathan Daniels when the group tried to visit a local store. When the meeting ended, Gloria House, a Lowndes County SNCC organizer who had taken leave from a comp lit program at UC Berkeley to go south, committed to putting the statement together. She took the ideas from the conversation and drafted it by hand, typed it up when she got to the SNCC office, and left it there for someone in the national office to circulate.[8]

SNCC hadn't decided when it would actually release the statement. And some of those concerned about issuing a statement had secured a promise of review before anything was circulated. Gwen and Mike and the Lowndes County organizers were confident that the statement would be released—SNCC was ready to broaden its scope. But there was no clear timeline for its release, given the seemingly endless list of tasks for their existing projects. Sure, opposing the war was the right thing to do morally, but some still saw it as separate from the urgency civil rights workers faced in the South.

Then a young SNCC organizer named Sammy Younge was murdered, and the war wasn't so far away anymore.

A TWENTY-ONE-YEAR-OLD NAVY veteran and college junior, Sammy Younge was in Tuskegee, Alabama, trying to register people to vote. When Younge attempted to use the bathroom at a service station on January 3, 1966, the sixty-eight-year-old gas station attendant shot him in the face, leaving his lifeless body slumped in the alleyway. The monster Gwen had spoken of in pushing SNCC to adopt an anti-war plank had claimed another victim—a veteran of both the war and the freedom struggle. It was a grim reminder that, no less than the war in Vietnam, Jim Crow was a form of US aggression.

Gathered with others once again at the SNCC national office, Gwen knew what to do. *We've got to get the statement out, and we've got to organize Tuskegee.*

Released on January 6, three days after Younge's murder, SNCC's statement on the US war in Vietnam was as unequivocal as Gwen and Mike had advocated for two months earlier. The statement called Younge's murder "no different than the murder of peasants in Vietnam, for both Younge and the Vietnamese sought, and are seeking, to secure the rights guaranteed them by law." Labeling the "country's cry of 'preserve freedom in the world' . . . a hypocritical mask behind which it squashes liberation movements," the statement encouraged Americans to join the civil rights movement instead of the US military. Expressing its solidarity with "the men in this country who are unwilling to respond to a military draft," the statement concluded with a bold rhetorical question: "We ask, where is the draft for the freedom fight in the United States?"[9]

Even for an organization as bold as SNCC, this was an incendiary call. Although an anti-war movement had gathered force since a national march the previous spring, its representatives had not yet promoted draft resistance. And SNCC had indicted all of US foreign policy outside of Europe, naming its duplicitous actions in "the Dominican Republic, the Congo, South Africa, Rhodesia, and in the United States itself." It was a blistering denunciation.

Privately, the Johnson administration urged other Black organizations, together with the six Black congressmen, to issue a statement opposing SNCC. Several white legislators branded SNCC's statement "disloyal" and treasonous. The *Atlanta Constitution* predicted SNCC's ruin: "From now on, when Snick speaks, the Negro suffers." The NAACP, an ally of SNCC in the Mississippi fight, distanced itself from the organization's anti-war stance. So did the prominent Southern white writer Lillian Smith, who denounced SNCC as sharply as she once had segregation. "In Snick, there is almost no one of erudition, of philosophical depth, of historical sophistication," she wrote in response to its Vietnam statement.[10]

Mike observed the harsh response with bemused confusion. *Damn*, he pondered, *you'd have thought we had burned something down!* And in a way they had. Two decades of repressing left-wing organizations had muted critique of American foreign policy among civil rights organizations, which had long been maligned as communist fronts. A previous generation of Black radicals had faced censure for challenging US foreign policy: the scholar W. E. B. Du Bois and the entertainer Paul Robeson had their passports confiscated, and Trinidadian-born communist Claudia Jones was deported to England. Since the mid-1950s, when the current upsurge in civil rights activity had begun, most of the major organizations had purposefully focused on the urgencies of the home front, where just trying to vote or access public services was hard enough. They either avoided discussing US foreign policy or endorsed it openly.[11]

Now, at the exact moment when it had pierced the invincibility of Jim Crow political power, SNCC had crossed another line. When Lyndon Johnson signed the Voting Rights Act in 1965, the civil rights movement had won a victory as major as it was rudimentary: the act removed the poll taxes, literacy tests, and other barriers to voting common across the Southern states, and it pledged the federal government would "enforce the guarantee of the fifteenth amendment" that, though it guaranteed the right to vote without regard to "race, color, or previous condition of servitude," had been widely ignored, especially in the South, since its ratification in 1870.[12] This expansion of the vote followed a 1962 Supreme Court case that reapportioned districts on the basis of population rather than partisan desire. Together, these developments held out the possibility of accruing political power in the neighborhoods segregation had made.

That was the hope that prompted SNCC's twenty-five-year-old communications secretary Julian Bond to run for election to the Georgia state legislature. Bond's run to represent Atlanta's 136th district was, like everything SNCC did, a collective decision. The organization had long debated how to translate its community-organizing model into formal political power, and the shifts in law and apportionment suddenly made Georgia—the state SNCC called home—an open contest. Lanky and light-skinned, Bond was both a veteran of SNCC and a scion of Black Atlanta. His father was dean of the School of Education at Atlanta University and a well-regarded sociologist whose research was cited in the *Brown v. Board of Education* case outlawing school segregation. Bond had high name recognition, and his savvy grassroots campaign propelled him to victory. Under the slogan "A vote for Bond is a vote out of bondage," Bond's campaign called for a two-dollar minimum wage to include the domestic and service work many in his district did, and for an end to Georgia's anti-union "right-to-work" laws. He won the Democratic primary with 82 percent of the vote and easily trounced his Republican opponent in the general election that summer.[13]

Asked about the Vietnam statement on the eve of his inauguration, the congressman-elect said he supported it. Hell broke loose. By a vote of 184–12, the Georgia state legislature refused to seat the duly elected congressman on January 10 and again on January 19. Yet current events would reinforce the connection between war and racism highlighted in SNCC's statement. The same day Bond was denied his seat, racists murdered Vernon Dahmer, an NAACP leader in Hattiesburg, Mississippi, whose four sons were then fighting in Vietnam. With leaders being killed or denied the elections they had fairly won, the passage of the Civil Rights and Voting Rights Acts seemed a Pyrrhic victory that called to mind the brutal end of Reconstruction a century earlier.[14]

Bond had no campaign infrastructure left when he was denied his seat, not so much as a chief of staff, and he now faced a special election to keep his seat. James Forman asked Gwen to codirect a new SNCC project, the first one to be based in Atlanta, in Bond's district. She and Mike had been in Tuskegee helping to organize demonstrations after Younge's murder. Now they returned to Atlanta, Gwen to build a new project and Mike hoping to develop SNCC's anti-war organizing. What happened next would change not only their lives but also the entire civil rights movement.

CHAPTER EIGHT

BLACK CONSCIOUSNESS

GWEN WAS NAMED AS CODIRECTOR OF THE SPECIAL COMMITTEE to Re-Elect Julian Bond. But, adopting the vernacular common to SNCC organizing efforts, it was quickly nicknamed the Atlanta Project. Her codirector was Bill Ware, a Mississippi native raised by sharecroppers who had been a brave and dedicated SNCC worker for three years. Ware was a decade older than most of the SNCC staff and, through the Peace Corps, had spent time in Ghana shortly after its independence. He wore African clothing, not yet common among Black Americans, studied African social movements, and saw US racism through the prism of European colonialism. The only white member of the project was Mendy Samstein, a SNCC staffer who had worked in Mississippi since 1963.[1]

Gwen went back to the Canterbury House, the social club for bookish students at Atlanta University Center, to recruit her friend Al Pertilla—not just to the Atlanta Project (which, like other SNCC projects, recruited local volunteers who might not have joined the national organization) but also to SNCC, which he had been around but never joined. He was concerned that the large number of whites who had joined SNCC since Freedom Summer would overwhelm its Black leadership. Gwen skillfully used that to aid her case: *That's why we need you to join*, she told him. He did. Mike recruited his friend Dwight Williams, with whom he had first joined SNCC. Others came organically. Donald Stone quit his job at the post office to join the movement full-time. At thirty, Stone was among the oldest members of the group, and he brought more than the wisdom of age. Stone's grandfather had studied under Booker T. Washington and operated an "industrial school" based on Washington's self-help philosophy. When Spelman student Margaret Mills joined the project, she saw in it the message of self-determination her Garveyite parents had instilled in her.[2]

The Atlanta Project established its office in a neighborhood called Vine City. Located west of Atlanta's business district, the neighborhood was desperately poor. It barely had paved streets. A report by the city's Community Relations Commission described the area's housing as "dilapidated," and the neighborhood had neither recreation centers nor parks. Its residents seemed beaten down to the point of hopelessness. Drug use and homelessness were common in Vine City, more so than Gwen or Mike had ever seen elsewhere. The project office was an aging three-room shotgun house at 142 Vine Street.[3]

Although Bill Ware stayed with a family in Vine City, Gwen, Mike, and other project staff initially stayed with SNCC comrades in an apartment complex in southwest Atlanta. On bus rides to Vine City, Gwen and Mike's friendship deepened into something more. Mike saw in Gwen a fearless veteran from the front lines, a person with indomitable courage. To Gwen, Mike was shy and sweet. She appreciated that he seemed to take her ideas seriously, that he was open-minded and funny. The romance was slow boiling, at least compared to the speed with which their lives were otherwise moving. Yet as they filled their nights dancing, their mornings smoking cigarettes and talking politics at Pascal's diner, and their days canvassing the neighborhood, they embraced each other as companions. Their snug connection was more than a friendship.

Gwen waited for Mike to ask her out—though her leadership in the project was uncontested, some conventions proved too hard to shake. Before long, Mike regarded himself as *Mr. Gwen Robinson*. Being next to her, fierce and beautiful, boosted his confidence. Gwen laughed at his iconoclastic jokes over walks through Atlanta's Sweet Auburn neighborhood or barbeque dinners near the SNCC office. They imagined not only their future but also *the* future—the world they were creating together.

THE ATLANTA PROJECT was SNCC's first sustained foray into organizing in an urban context. Yet the dire conditions Black people faced in American cities, together with the ongoing patterns of Black migration to urban areas, necessitated attention to the Black urban condition. Confronting the particular desperation of urban poverty caused by white racist divestment would test Gwen and Mike as it would Martin Luther King, who announced his own plans to desegregate Chicago just as Bond risked being refused his seat.[4]

As in other SNCC efforts, Atlanta Project staff wanted to live in the community. Gwen found a house for Atlanta Project staff at 69 Electric Avenue, not far from their Vine City office. She and Mike shared one of the two bedrooms in the new freedom house.

Their primary focus was on shoring up support for Julian Bond in his district, but the project staff also hoped to confront the problems that Bond had raised in his campaign. Because Bond had maintained his strong "moral conviction" in refusing to disavow SNCC's anti-war position, the Atlanta Project could inaugurate a "program of political organization and education." Many Black people in Atlanta were registered to vote; what they lacked was "human dignity and economic justice." The Atlanta Project would build support for Bond by helping the neighborhood get its needs met—just as SNCC had always done.[5]

Gwen organized a project to canvass the neighborhood, soon joined by a fleet of student volunteers from Spelman. The most immediate concern was the blighted state of housing. Old shacks that often lacked plumbing and heat sat on cinder blocks to prevent flood-ing. One of the biggest slumlords was Joe Shaffer, who operated what the Atlanta Project described as a "plantation-like system in which he acts as landlord, employer, grocer, creditor, sheriff, judge and jury over the people who live on his property." Shaffer overcharged and under-served his tenants in violation of the city's already weak housing laws. At the suggestion of SNCC attorney Howard Moore, the Atlanta Project began collecting affidavits from residents about the problems with their landlords. A thirteen-year-old who lived in an apartment without so much as an icebox reported that the "rats are almost bigger than my doll." In a two-room apartment occupied by eight people, a twenty-three-year-old man "had to kill a snake." "The floor has holes and it is partly rotten," he reported. "I'm afraid it will fall in."[6]

When Shaffer evicted several residents for failure to pay rent that January, the Atlanta Project—only weeks into existence but already with strong ties in the neighborhood—organized a protest. Gwen borrowed a truck from SNCC's headquarters to help one of the fam-ilies move to another house while other project staff brought blankets to those without heat. Days later, the project held a rally against Shaf-fer, demanding, "Slumlords must go!" This maelstrom helped catalyze a rent strike among the residents. All winter, the project kept pushing. With a paneled van and a loudspeaker, project staff drove through the neighborhood blaring The Impressions ("You've been cheating," ded-icated to Shaffer) and Bobby Bland ("Too far gone to turn around," dedicated to the tenants) while residents placed furniture in the street. With the streets blocked, Atlanta Project members helped residents charge a toll to anyone who wanted to cross. The unauthorized tax collection garnered $180, including ten cents from a police officer, to help bail out tenants and SNCC activists who had been arrested in the protest. All the while, they coordinated a sophisticated get-out-the-vote operation—providing childcare for voting mothers, calling constituents, taking people to the polls, and knocking on doors, al-ways knocking on doors. On February 23, Julian Bond was easily reelected to a seat he had yet to occupy.[7]

Mike was delighted. This was the kind of bold action he had hoped to be part of in moving to Atlanta. The police, who had assigned an officer to monitor the irksome Atlanta Project, were less pleased. In early March they arrested Bill Ware and another SNCC activist for leading an unsanctioned tax collection. Dispatched to bail them out, Mike walked into the police station with self-assurance. Before he could announce himself, an officer walking in the opposite direction knocked into him. *Some people are just rude*, Mike said sarcastically. The cop dared Mike to repeat himself. *Man, you just bumped into me*, Mike said—and then, more calmly, *You could have said "excuse me."* Instead, the cop threw him against the wall at the police station and arrested him.

Next thing he knew, Mike was in a cell with the comrades he had come to rescue. *What the fuck are you doing here?* they asked in surprise. Gesturing to the money that had been in his pocket, Mike informed them, *I came to bail you out, man.*

MIKE WAS NOT in jail long before someone bailed all three of them out. They returned to their work in Vine City. The project was not just securing Julian Bond's base—it was doing what SNCC workers always did: mobilizing local people to address their own needs. They had to find some new ways to do it. Vine City had the density of urban life but lacked the central gathering impetus that churches and social clubs had provided in rural Mississippi and Arkansas—and, for that matter, in urban Memphis and Philadelphia.

The maxim of organizing still held true: meet people where they were at. And where they were, bright and early every weekday, was at Five Points. Segregation had kept Black from white when it came to housing but bonded through labor. Almost half of Atlanta's population in 1966 was Black, and the majority of them worked as laborers. Five Points was the transportation hub connecting Vine City to other parts of Atlanta. It resembled the area in the Bronx that SNCC advisor Ella Baker had, decades earlier, described as a "slave market."

From Five Points, Black women would catch buses to the northeast-ern suburbs to get white children to school on time and tend house as domestics, while Black men headed downtown to the military induc-tion center or low-level work. Five days a week, Gwen, Mike, and the nucleus of the Atlanta Project would get to Five Points by six a.m. to pass out flyers in the rush-hour foot traffic and rail against slumlords and war and the other threats poor Black people faced.[8]

Experienced organizers, the Atlanta Project staff approached the city as a riddle whose solution held great promise. If they could create an apparatus to empower the demoralized locals of Vine City, they perhaps would have a means to channel the outrage that had exploded in Watts the previous summer, as it had in Harlem in 1964. The At-lanta Project proposed a wide array of tools: a community store and a radio station in addition to campaigns for the rights of tenants and people on welfare. The project proposed to "develop among the ur-ban masses an intense pride, dignity and self-respect" in the "beauty, strength and resourcefulness" of Black people working toward free-dom, power. Atlanta, where Black people had a median income half that of whites, was the perfect site for this experiment.[9]

As part of their outreach in the Five Points neighborhood, the Atlanta Project began a newspaper. They hoped it would be some-thing the community might identify with. Gwen's friend Al was the editor; Mike and Dwight served as assistant editors. SNCC had its own printing press, so the paper would be easy to produce regularly. It would not be a movement paper, aimed at other organizers, but a com-munity paper, shaped by the idioms of Black working-class life in Vine City. They decided to call it the *Nitty Gritty*. The phrase "nitty gritty" was common parlance among Atlanta's Black working class, for whom it meant straight talk. But it had sexual connotations too. When Shir-ley Ellis sang "now let's get right on down to the nitty gritty" in her hit 1963 song of the same name, she didn't mean rent strikes.

Members of the SNCC national office found the title unbecom-ing. Some offered alternatives: "The Torch" or "The Truth"; something that channeled heavenly righteousness? Or a return to the student movement origins with "The Atlanta Voice"? The head of SNCC's research department, Jack Minnis, was particularly opposed to the name *Nitty Gritty*. Minnis, a brusque former attorney, had a knack for following the money behind segregationist rule and was one of the most influential white members of SNCC. His work mapping the Mississippi power structure was of inestimable value to Freedom Summer, and he had discovered the obscure Alabama statute that allowed for the formation of the SNCC-affiliated Lowndes County Freedom Organization. His studies of Arkansas formed the backbone of Mike's orientation to the state. But Minnis seemed less keen about Black Power emerging within his own organization. In a meeting about the newspaper, Minnis sarcastically offered, *Why not just call it "the motherfucker"?*[10]

Without thinking, Gwen grabbed a steel folding chair and lunged at him. Mike stopped her before she could crack it over Minnis's head. The relationship between the Atlanta Project and the SNCC national office was not going to be an easy one.

DESPITE OPPOSITION FROM Minnis and SNCC's national office, the *Nitty Gritty* made its appearance at the end of February, promising "we tell it like it is." While Atlanta's elite boosters claimed that the city was "too busy to hate," the *Nitty Gritty* wrote that the conditions of Vine City meant that Atlanta was "the city too busy to care." The paper embraced the anti-imperialist politics that had caused such outrage against SNCC months ago. "If believing in freedom for all people is 'un-American' then we are un-American too. If believing the people in Vietnam should decide what happens in their country is un-American, we too are un-American. And if believing that black people have something in this country to fight for is un-American, color us un-American too." Subtlety was never the Atlanta Project's strong suit.[11]

The project's success working with Vine City tenants against slumlords had even prompted Martin Luther King Jr. to issue a rare criticism of Atlanta elites. The Southern Christian Leadership Conference also made its home in Atlanta, perhaps the safest city in the South—a safety secured through an unspoken alliance between a tight-knit Black political establishment and city officials. Yet the project's consistent protests prompted King to tour Vine City and declare it "appalling." King said, "I had no idea people were living in Atlanta in such conditions. This is a shame on the community."[12]

Like many SNCC organizers, Gwen and Mike viewed King as a flashy public speaker, a man who parachuted in for the media and helicoptered out afterward, perhaps with a stop in jail in between. Privately, they called him "de lawd." Their loyalties lay with the local communities in which they lived and worked. Still, they were grateful to have his support and hoped to translate his recognition into action by the city. King's presence, together with the ongoing protests from tenants, brought city elites to the table.

One of the people at the table was Martin Luther King Sr. "Daddy King," as everyone called him, was not as gracious to SNCC as his radical son. Daddy King was a Baptist minister who, in his younger years, had led protests on behalf of Black schoolteachers and tenants. But his social gospel teachings joined with his own gospel of prosperity, and by 1966 he was a moderating powerbroker in Atlanta's Black establishment. He was on the board of trustees of Morehouse College and Citizens Trust Bank, a Black bank founded in 1921. And he was a property owner. When Mike mocked Daddy King's moderate and esteemed counsel at a meeting, King fumed and menaced Mike with his cane.

Though he flinched at King's cane, Mike relished these confrontations with Atlanta's small but entrenched Black political establishment. The project hoped to launch a third party as a more authentic voice for Black working-class communities. When Mike, Bill, and Dwight went to register a new political party, Secretary of State Benjamin Forston cursed them and told them to leave his office. *We're not leaving*, the trio informed the irate politician. Forston called JD Hood, a Black state representative, to coax them to leave.

Soon Forston called the state troopers in a rage. *I've got four niggers in here*, Forston fumed. *They've got to get out!* When Hood protested *Not me* as the state troopers approached, Mike broke the news: *He meant you too, motherfucker!*

The obsequious deference that Atlanta's burgeoning Black establishment showed to white power convinced Gwen, Mike, and their comrades that white supremacy was prominent among their would-be allies as well as among their open antagonists. That realization added fuel to the already raging fire of despair and opportunity in Vine City. Project staff began to view white activists in the neighborhood and in the SNCC national office with suspicion. In Vine City, the project clashed with Hector Black, a white Harvard University graduate and Quaker who had moved to Atlanta in 1965. Black ran a Quaker-based tutoring program and helped establish the Vine City Council to fight for the rights of the neighborhood's exploited tenants. Black had been arrested in the standoff with Joe Shaffer, the slumlord and frequent target of Atlanta Project pickets. Project staff increasingly saw Black as competition in their organizing. Driving the sound truck through Vine City, Bill Ware took to the loudspeaker to brand Black a "white Jesus" who had nothing to offer them. Similar critiques could be found in the pages of the *Nitty Gritty*.[13]

The *Nitty Gritty* itself remained an ongoing source of tension within SNCC that only heightened the project's suspicion of white activists. After failing to block the paper's name, SNCC's research department hoped to preserve the organization's respectability on the back end. Two members of the Atlanta Project discovered Minnis, Mendy Samstein, and three other white SNCC staff planning the first issue of the paper in isolation from the rest of the project. Gwen and Mike were furious: they had clearly stated that the paper would be written, edited, and produced by Black members in consultation with the Vine City residents they were organizing alongside. Gwen did not reach for a chair this time. But she felt certain that they would have to do something to preserve the integrity of the project they wanted.

POLITICS IS AN aphrodisiac, Mike thought as he sat down next to Gwen, and the Atlanta Project was all politics. After another long day with tenants and workers in Vine City, they settled into the couches at the freedom house to talk with their comrades. These rap sessions confirmed their young romance as well as their excitement for the project overall. With booze, music, and insatiable curiosity as their companions, members of the Atlanta Project would stay up in the night talking about the city, the movement, the world. Dead tired but alive with possibility, they began to record their conversations. They felt on the cusp of a new understanding, a new strategy, a breakthrough that they didn't want fatigue or alcohol to erase. As they processed their years of struggle in the context of their new campaign, Atlanta Project members kept coming back to how Black people thought of themselves. Whether in rural Mississippi or across college campuses, and now in the inner city, so much of their work had been about developing people's self-confidence. Gwen and Mike had seen how white supremacy had so terrorized Black communities in Laurel and Helena, in Memphis and Philadelphia and Atlanta, too. The bitter conditions, they felt, encouraged poor Black people to believe in their own inferiority and the superiority of whites. It was an attitude Gwen had seen in the smug assurances of white liberals in New York as well, as they told Jim Forman what SNCC should do from the comfort of their posh Manhattan offices.

Through their conversations, Gwen, Mike, and the rest of the project came to believe that Black people needed to see other Black people in positions of power and authority to bolster their collective self-esteem. And to eradicate racism, they would need to target it where it lived and breathed: in white communities and white-controlled institutions. In his time on the front lines, Mike felt that at best he had stanched the bleeding—but he wanted to stop the killer. *When someone gets shot, someone chases the killer and someone heals the wounded*, he rationalized. *If everyone is just healing the wounded, then the people are going to go on shooting.* Black pride and white anti-racism: on these two points, all of the Atlanta Project, including Samstein, its one white member, agreed.[14]

With other women in the project, Gwen transcribed the group's recorded conversations. Some of the men involved then turned the transcript into essay format. None signed their name to it. The Atlanta Project was listed as the author, in honor of the document's collective origins. They called the essay "the Black Consciousness Paper," and they imagined it as the first in a series of strategic documents about urban, electoral, and anti-war organizing. The statement was capacious and uneven, covering everything from jazz to apartheid. At its core was a call for self-determination. "We reject the American Dream as defined by white people and must work to construct an American reality defined by Afro-Americans." In prose that echoed the sweeping critiques of European colonialism raised by the likes of Aimé Césaire, Frantz Fanon, and South Africa's Pan-African Congress, the paper described Black people as "victims of a domestic colonialism" who "could never be" part of "western civilization" on par with whites. Instead, the statement challenged their comrades to interrogate Black people's "relationship to America and the World."[15]

In an occasionally frustrated tone, these seasoned organizers reflected on the intractability of racism. Many of the core legal objectives of the Southern freedom movement had been won. Yet its political, economic, and social objectives remained unmet. The violence, poverty, and disparities of racism still conditioned Black life, while the United States moved deeper into making war abroad. How could the movement move forward? The Black Consciousness Paper said that it was not enough to build power in Black communities, as SNCC had always done. It called for white people to develop an anti-racist constituency in white communities. "There is no doubt in our minds that some whites are just as disgusted with this system as we are," they wrote. "But it is meaningless to talk about coalition if there is no one to align ourselves with, because of the lack of organization in the white communities." Recalling the slave owner who beat the protagonist of *Uncle Tom's Cabin* to death, the statement suggested that centering the movement only in Black communities meant the continuation of white racism. "We have dealt stringently with the problem of 'Uncle Tom,' but we have not yet gotten around to Simon Legree. . . . Everyone knows Uncle Tom, but who knows Simon Legree?"[16]

The Black Consciousness Paper went on to criticize whiteness as a barrier to Black self-advancement: "Whites can only subvert our true search and struggle for self-determination, self-identification, and liberation in this country." Whites had for too long determined the roles Black people could play; the Atlanta Project called to reverse that, saying SNCC "should be Black staffed, Black controlled and Black financed" so that "a Black organization (devoid of cultism) be projected to our people so that it can be demonstrated that such organizations are viable." Black leadership was needed to shatter racist myths of the impossibility of Black leadership. And the struggles over the project newspaper remained a touchstone for the material differences of race. "So that white people coming into the Movement cannot relate to the 'Nitty Gritty,' cannot relate to the experience that brought such a word into being, cannot relate to chitterlings, hog's head cheese, pig feet, ham hocks, and cannot relate to slavery, because these things are not a part of their experience."[17]

As Gwen and Mike discussed it, they reinforced each other's belief in what SNCC was and could be. They wanted their white comrades to develop their own constituency in the communities they called home, much as they would do with Black communities. Gwen sent the statement out widely. She solicited the opinion of her old Spelman College (and Freedom Summer) mentor, Staughton Lynd, as well as Laurel Project alumnus Jimmy Garrett, who was then trying to develop a Black Student Union at San Francisco State University. Garrett saw the paper as a model for how to build Black Power at predominantly white institutions.[18]

The seven-page paper was both unfinished and sclerotic, at once too rigid and too abstract. It bore all the insight and awkwardness of extemporaneous dialogue translated to paper. Bill Ware would later liken it to a jazz improvisation. Still, Gwen and Mike hoped it would anchor a larger political and strategic document.

THE TASK OF presenting the paper to SNCC fell to Bill Ware, Donald Stone, and Askia Toure, a member of the Revolutionary Action Movement who had taken up residence with the Atlanta Project and helped convert the transcribed conversations into essay form. The simmering standoff between the Atlanta Project and the national office, together with the stridency of the statement itself, soured many people to its message. The national office was filled with dedicated SNCC staff who were removed from the daily rhythms of local organizing. They provided funds, public relations, and other administrative support for local projects. Gwen and Mike felt that Vine City residents would be as uncomfortable in the SNCC office as office staff would be in Vine City. The organization rejected the paper forcefully. Yet many in SNCC shared Gwen and Mike's belief in this protean concept of Black Power.[19]

Embedded within the paper was a critique of the national office as having become too staid, too removed from the daily concerns of Black communities. SNCC was no longer the student-based organization led by campus committees it had once been. What it could or should be instead, however, was not yet clear. The same month that the organization rejected a plan for "Black consciousness," several SNCC members conducted a sit-in at the South African consulate in New York City to protest apartheid. A transnational Black consciousness was growing within SNCC. So was the idea that the organization needed a change in leadership.

In May 1966, SNCC staff gathered in Kingston Springs, Tennessee, to elect the organization's national leadership, which had been reliably stable. Jim Forman had been the executive secretary since 1961 and John Lewis the chairman since 1963. Cleve Sellers, the newest addition to the leadership team, had been program secretary for two years.

While Sellers was reelected to his post, Forman resigned his role. He was replaced by Ruby Doris Robinson, SNCC's twenty-three-year-old administrative secretary who had been a leader in the Atlanta student movement and an inspiration to Gwen. When Lewis narrowly won reelection to be the titular head of this ultra-democratic organization in a two a.m. vote taken after a full day of deliberations, several staff revolted.

Lewis's bravery was uncontested. He had been arrested forty times in different protests, beaten so many times that Mike maintained that Lewis had the toughest skull in the movement. Yet Lewis had become removed from SNCC's daily operations. SNCC had to recognize that, as members expressed, "nationalism helps organize in the black community" and that Lewis's pastoral approach was not "what the times required." Many in SNCC felt that the organization needed a chairman who reflected the growth in Black consciousness. With a second ballot, Stokely Carmichael, the SNCC project director for a creative attempt at winning Black electoral power in Lowndes County, Alabama, became the new chairman.[20]

In a way, the Atlanta Project had won. Throughout the meeting, SNCC staff stressed that "Black consciousness" was what the organization needed to advance its work to the next level. SNCC members no longer used the word *Negro* and saw themselves as part of a larger Third World that stretched from Black America to Asia, Africa, and Latin America. Many staff agreed with the Atlanta Project in substance even if they disagreed with its tenor. And Carmichael's work in Alabama was enacting the kind of Black political power and social solidarity that undergirded Gwen and Mike's work in Atlanta. The parallels seemed obvious to several observers, too, even if they arrived from racist media. National white media misunderstood the context, scorned Carmichael's election as a win for Black nationalism and militancy. And within SNCC, Carmichael's leadership aligned with Atlanta Project complaints that the national office had become too isolated from the grassroots.[21]

HOPING TO SMOOTH tensions between the national SNCC office and the Atlanta Project, Jim Forman had invited Gwen and Mike to the meeting in Kingston Springs. But they declined the offer. It would be days before they heard what had happened there. It wasn't just that they were smarting from the organizational drama. They sought expressions of global Black Power.

As national staff arrived in Tennessee, Gwen and Mike were some two hundred miles away in New Orleans. Bob Moses had invited them to a conference there. One of SNCC's moral and strategic anchors, Moses too had found the civil rights movement troubled by white paternalism and American nationalism—dynamics that allowed the United States to project a false image of democracy globally while supporting racist regimes in Africa. He joined Janet Jemmott, Dona Richards, and Tina Fernandez in planning the African–Afro-American Cultural Conference. The conference brought representatives of different African liberation movements to join a group of Black American scholars, including Sterling Stuckey and *Freedomways* editor John Henrik Clarke, to discuss the theme of Black consciousness from a global perspective. Representatives of the Zimbabwe African National Union and the Zimbabwe African People's Union, two organizations leading the fight against the brutal white settler government of Rhodesia, also spoke.

It was at the conference that Gwen and Mike first learned about Sharpeville, the South African township where police murdered sixty-nine and wounded almost two hundred people during a protest against restrictive pass laws imposed by the apartheid regime in 1960. This was also the first conference they had been to that excluded whites from participating. The pressures in SNCC would pass, they thought, more confident than ever that the Atlanta Project was part of a global effort at Black freedom.[22]

STOKELY CARMICHAEL'S ELECTION to SNCC leadership vaulted him to the national limelight. A month after he became SNCC's chairman, the charismatic and photogenic Carmichael was marching arm in arm with Martin Luther King in Mississippi to carry on what had been James Meredith's solo march against racism. Meredith, an Air Force veteran and the first Black student admitted to the University of Mississippi, was on the second day of the 220-mile, three-week "March Against Fear" through the Mississippi Delta when a white supremacist attempted to murder him. While Meredith recovered from a gunshot wound, a broad coalition of civil rights organizations banded together to continue his march. Carmichael was arrested in Greenwood after an argument with local police. Following his release from jail, and two weeks shy of his twenty-fifth birthday, Carmichael alighted a platform and addressed his fellow marchers with a messianic fury. "This is the twenty-seventh time I have been arrested—and I ain't going to jail no more," he exhorted to cheers.

He continued, sounding a lot like members of the Atlanta Project: "The only way we gonna stop them white men from whuppin' us is to take over. We been saying freedom for six years and we ain't got nothin'. What we gonna start saying now is Black Power!" And then, encouraged by Mike's old campus traveling buddy Willie Ricks, who had been testing the phrase with crowds beforehand, he led the crowd in a chant. "What do you want? Black Power! What do you want? Black Power!"[23]

Journalists looked to Carmichael as the chief architect of Black Power. They did not understand its meaning and judged it using the violent barometer of white power. National media quickly inveighed against the term. The *Los Angeles Times* summarized elite media opinion in castigating Black Power as proof that "extremism has not been limited to mobs of white yahoos" and a "great harm" to "advancing racial progress." In a repeat of the response SNCC faced after its anti-war statement months earlier, several prominent Black liberals chastised the organization. At the NAACP national convention, the association's director, Roy Wilkins, called Black Power "a reverse Mississippi, a reverse Hitler, a reverse Ku Klux Klan" and pledged that the NAACP "will have none of this." Martin Luther King feared the phrase "connotes black supremacy and an antiwhite feeling that does not or should not prevail."[24]

In early August, the *New York Times* published an excerpt of the Atlanta Project's Black Consciousness Paper alongside a profile of Carmichael. Reflecting a long-standing indifference to the internal dynamics of Black radical organizations, the newspaper omitted mention of the Atlanta Project. Instead, the Black Consciousness excerpt was said to be "the basis for the organization's 'black power' philosophy." That preface and its placement alongside the profile of Carmichael wrongly suggested that SNCC had endorsed the statement—and that Carmichael was its architect. Although Carmichael, who would soon coauthor a book titled *Black Power: The Politics of Liberation*, increasingly agreed with the outlook contained in the paper, he had joined with the other national SNCC staff in rejecting it months earlier.[25]

The *New York Times* excerpt appeared on Mike's twenty-first birthday. It was hardly the present he wanted. Mike was relieved to hear the news of Carmichael's election and speech. He and Gwen saw their work in the Atlanta Project as an experiment in urban self-determination for Black people, abbreviated as Black Power, much as Stokely's work in Lowndes County had been. If Carmichael, the charismatic and well-liked new head of SNCC, now endorsed what the Atlanta Project had been saying, maybe tensions within the organization would finally ease. Instead, they accelerated. SNCC faced increased funding troubles for its outspoken radicalism, which exacerbated the interpersonal conflicts between the Atlanta Project and the SNCC national office. But Mike found that he and Bill Ware were among the targets of outrage from SNCC's national leadership.

Specious rumors followed: Bill Ware was a CIA agent, Mike a provocateur sent from either the Nation of Islam or the Revolutionary Action Movement. As proof, the rumors pointed to Ware's time in both the military and the Peace Corps prior to joining SNCC, and to Mike's personal connections to the two Northern-based Black nationalist groups whose ideas were becoming increasingly popular among SNCC rank and file. Mike understood the gossip about him, but he shook his head that some people would disregard Ware's dedication with such sloppy allegations.

Nevertheless, work carried on. The Atlanta Project continued to stress that the fate of Black Americans was tied in with that of the Third World majority. This soon led them to double down on the issue that had first inadvertently launched the project: SNCC's Vietnam statement and opposition to US imperialism.

As the summer heat settled on Atlanta that August, Mike turned twenty-one and Gwen turned twenty-two. There was little time to celebrate, though, for Mike had received a notice to report to the Army induction center for evaluation on August 18. He had been dodging these notices for eight months. Whenever he received a letter instructing him to appear for a physical, he'd dash off a lengthy response to the Selective Service Board. *Dear motherfuckers*, one letter began, before launching into a twelve-page broadside about slavery, lynching, and the many ways Black history was at odds with US militarism. Somewhere around page seven, after lecturing the military on Frederick Douglass and SNCC, he would switch his address from Philadelphia to Atlanta, Atlanta to Philadelphia. When the Selective Service application asked his "native country" and "date and port of entry," Mike listed "Africa, 1619." Under "status," he wrote "slave." He checked the box indicating he was not a citizen and, where the form asked if he planned to become one, Mike checked "no."[26]

If the length and content of the letter didn't scare them off, he at least bought himself some time by changing his address. The military would now have to reschedule his induction site to a new city.

These antics kept his induction in abeyance for months. But he could not get away with it anymore. He was being drafted—or he was going to prison. For years, Mike had organized his life around two things: not going into the military and not going to prison for it. He had a plan that he hoped would accomplish both goals. He would present himself to the draft board in such a way as to make *them* reject *him*. Or they would shut down the induction center.

CHAPTER NINE

SELLING WOLF TICKETS

STARTING ON TUESDAY, AUGUST 16, THE ATLANTA PROJECT began a week of demonstrations outside the Twelfth Army Corps and Induction Center on 699 Ponce de Leon. Inductions began at six forty-five, so Mike and the rest of the project staff were outside the center at six thirty that morning carrying signs that read THE VIETCONG NEVER CALLED ME "NIGGER" and asking WHO IS THE ENEMY? over a photo of a white crowd ogling the mutilated body of a Black man they had lynched. A small crowd of white men gathered around shouting to "send all Niggers to Vietnam" or "kill the Black son of a bitches." From the second and third floors, Army personnel spat and threw lit cigarettes at the demonstrators below until they left around ten thirty.[1]

At six thirty the next morning, Mike and Gwen were back with about ten other people, carrying the same signs and trying to enlist recruits for the "freedom fight" instead of the war machine. By seven a.m., Army personnel were once again harassing them and flinging lit cigarettes from the floors above. One of the lit cigarettes landed on a picketer, singeing her hair. Mike and another man marched inside, demanding that they close the windows. Yet three minutes later,

Gwen was hit by a mysterious liquid poured from the second floor by a man in military uniform. Once again, Mike led a small group inside the induction center to complain. *We are not going to take much more of this*, he told the officer in charge as Gwen showed the man what one of his subordinates had done. When the harassment continued, Mike sat down inside the induction center and demanded the full force of the military be brought to bear on soldiers violating citizens. The Army brass said that he would close the windows once Mike and company left the lobby. Instead, other SNCC staff joined Mike in sitting in.

About thirty soldiers surrounded the activists and began dragging two of the men out the door. When they tried to drag one of the woman demonstrators, other men began yelling, *Take your hands off that Black woman or there will be trouble!* Instead, the soldiers grabbed the chairs that two of the women were sitting in and dumped them out the door and onto the sidewalk. When they got to Mike, he went limp. Two soldiers grabbed him and started swinging him, preparing to toss him full force on the street. Instead, he reached back and grabbed the testicles of one of the soldiers. Hard. Mike fell to the ground amid the yelp and saw himself out. The Army agreed to close the windows on the top floors, and the Atlanta Project agreed to end its sit-in and go back to marching outside.

THURSDAY, AUGUST 18: Mike's induction day. They arrived at six thirty a.m., a crowd of about thirty. By six forty-five, the heat of an Atlanta summer day began to set in as Mike approached the door, determined to be turned away. With a friend at his side, he knocked on the door. Bearded and wearing a T-shirt and sneakers, the twenty-one-year-old did not look like someone reporting for induction. And he had no intention of being drafted.

What do you want? sneered one of the soldiers standing guard, annoyed to see that Mike had returned. The door was closed and under heavy guard as a result of the Atlanta Project's ongoing protests.

I have business here, Mike began. *Please get out of my way.*

No, you don't, the soldier averred. *Get back.*

It was all going according to plan. Mike schemed that if he got the soldiers to refuse him entrance, he would be neither drafted nor held at fault. The soldiers denied Mike access to the building despite his insistence that he had business to attend to on the second floor. Rebuffed, Mike rejoined the picket. A few minutes before his scheduled appointment at seven a.m., Mike once again tried to gain entry to the induction center. He even asked to speak to the head of the induction center. Request denied.

He repeated the same sly ritual every ten minutes. After the fifth time, Atlanta police intervened and began to pull him away from the door. *Take your hands off me*, he protested. *I have business in there!* The police disagreed and pulled harder. *Let me go*, Mike pleaded to no effect. *Stop interfering!* The harder the police pulled, the harder Mike and others grabbed onto the door of the induction center. When the door broke, it shattered the police restraint. Officers began dragging people away, choking and beating them into submission.

The sun had set on we-shall-overcome for these SNCC staffers. Weaponless but furious, some of them fought back against the police while others shouted *Racism runs this country*, condemned the *denial of constitutional rights by white racist police*, and pleaded with potential inductees not to *die in Vietnam to support racism at home.* An officer threw Mike into the paddy wagon and headed back to the brawl. So did Mike, who jumped out of the vehicle and back into the fracas only to be arrested again.

It was nine a.m.

As police moved in, Gwen moved out. The Atlanta Project had agreed beforehand that someone should make sure to avoid arrest in order to coordinate media response, alert other movement activists to what happened, and keep the protest going in the days to come. Gwen, the project codirector and an experienced organizer, was the designated survivor.

MIKE WAS ONE of ten men and two women arrested outside the induction center. He felt especially bad for the two women, who were not Atlanta Project regulars. Now they faced the wrath of an irate Atlanta legal system. Everyone was charged with disturbance and most were also charged with resisting arrest and failure to obey an officer. One of the group was also charged with "insurrection." It carried a possible death sentence.

The trial, such as it was, happened the next day. Captain Redding, the local police officer assigned to monitor the Atlanta Project, played the role of prosecutor. Judge T. C. Little found the defendants guilty of all charges, remanding the case of insurrection to a higher court to decide. Addressing SNCC lawyer Howard Moore with a colloquial disregard, Little declared, "But you see, Colonel, I'm not giving them stiff sentences based on their color but because I have a son in Vietnam who is fighting to defend the principles of freedom and democracy." Then he sentenced the group to serve between 90 and 120 days.[2]

BACK AT THE project office, Gwen got to work writing a press release, informing their comrades, and drafting new leaflets. She also organized the next day's picket outside the induction center. Over the weekend, she held vigil in Vine City. The mood alternated between festive and morose. During the day, Bill Ware denounced the Black police officers surrounding them as "white men in Black skins" while Gwen and others passed out flyers. They denounced the war in Vietnam and the arrests, hoping to raise money to support their imprisoned comrades. In the evening, they brought out a barbeque grill, connected the sound system to the record player, and partied in the streets.[3]

The following week, Gwen was back in front of the induction center at six thirty a.m. Now the group was almost entirely women. Police mocked them and two Black officers followed the group as they left. Once they left downtown, the women confronted the police.

You are a disgrace to Black women, Gwen challenged. *How can you stand there while white cops make fun of Black women who are protesting the killing of our Black brothers in a racist war?*

Gwen brought her fury—at the war, the arrests, the intractability of it all—to the next day's demonstration. Feeling that their outrage was too easily absorbed by the back-and-forth shouting they had done with soldiers all week, Gwen shifted tack. Instead, at six forty-five a.m. Gwen led a group of five women to the induction center dressed head to toe in black. Silently, they carried signs reading WE MOURN THE DRAFTING OF BLACK MEN and WE MOURN THE 400 YEARS OF LYNCHING AND CASTRATION OF THE BLACK MEN IN THIS COUNTRY and WE WONDER WHY THE WHITE MAN FEELS THE NECESSITY TO CASTRATE AND LYNCH BLACK MEN? They held vigil outside the induction center and then moved their somber procession to downtown, where Black women would see them on their way to work.

Some of the women recognized the SNCC activists, sources of regular literature on war and racism. *Where you been?* one of them demanded of Gwen. *You made me late! I been here waiting on you!* The woman grabbed the flyer, lamenting, *Now I got to say to my white lady why I'm late.*[4]

MIKE AND THE other eleven SNCC activists were sent to Honor Farm, a three-hundred-acre prison farm in southeast Atlanta where prisoners raised pigs, did agricultural labor, or split rocks. The SNCC group was isolated: the men separate from the women and the whole group kept as far away from other prisoners as the staff could manage.

Still, Mike tapped into a reservoir of bravado and unpredictability in order to aggravate their jailers. It was not long before the SNCC activists went on strike. The guards threw them in the hole, a set of cinderblock cells with a light on twenty-four hours a day and a bread-and-water diet. Every third day they would be given beans. The dismal scene was meant to compel obedience. Instead, the prisoners went on a hunger strike. Not long into the fast, a guard threatened to beat up Dwight for knocking some water onto his foot. Hearing this, Mike figured he could at least draw some heat away from his friend. *You punk motherfucker!* he yelled at the guard. *Come get me! You so bad, kick my ass first, motherfucker, if you're so bad.* Mike insulted the guard's whole bloodline while he waited for the inevitable beating.

But it didn't come. Much to his surprise, Mike's tirade had scared the guard, any guard, from returning to the unit that night. And when they were let out of solitary after a few days, that guard refused to look Mike in the eye. Instead, he would speak to Donald Stone, the oldest in the group of SNCC prisoners, to relay the message. *Stone, explain to Simmons that this is the rule and we aren't trying to pick on anybody.* Knowing he had them spooked, Mike played for his audience. *Stone, man, you don't speak for me, motherfucker.* And then, to the guard: *Who are you talking to?*[5]

Even without the hunger strike, Mike was mercurial in dealing with his captors. In the hole, the guards conducted count—checking no one had escaped—every two hours. A guard named Smith worked the graveyard shift and would kick the doors to wake them up each time. As soon as Mike fell asleep after the last interruption, Smith would be back with another *bam, bam, bam.*

Mike had an idea. *Look, when Smith comes by tonight,* he told his sleep-deprived comrades after a few days, *tell him to kick the door.* That puzzled them; they wanted the kicking to stop. But Mike held firm. *We've got to tell him before he kicks.*

When Smith returned that evening, Mike welcomed his routine. *Kick the door, you motherfucker! Kick the door!* Smith happily obliged and left. When he returned a couple hours later, Mike raised the stakes. *Kick the door, you stupid motherfucker! Kick that goddamn door!* And when he did, Mike chastised: *Is that the best you can do?* All the SNCC workers chimed in, mocking the guard. When he returned again, Smith's puzzlement gave way to stubborn refusal. *I ain't going to kick that door if I don't want to!* he told them. *Y'all can't make me kick the door!* And he never did again, no matter how much they demanded.

WITH MIKE IN prison, Gwen kept the Atlanta Project humming with demonstrations, flyers, meetings. A new practice helped steady her focus. For weeks, she had noticed that two Atlanta Project members, Askia and Aisha Toure, participated in the group's political discussions, but not its socializing. The couple had come to Atlanta from New York City, where they were members of the Revolutionary Action Movement. Yet they always seemed to disappear when the SNCC staff would bust out the cheap wine, crank the music, and dance. *What's wrong with y'all,* Gwen would tease them about their vegetarianism and sobriety. But she also wanted to know.

One morning, she asked them more seriously where they went when the rest of the project unwound. *We meditate,* they told her. She asked them to teach her. They showed her the power of stillness and shared with her *The Autobiography of a Yogi,* the 1946 book by Indian mystic Paramahansa Yogananda. Reading about Yogananda's search for a guru and personal transformation into spiritual leader moved her. She began to meditate, began to match the power of her outward struggle for justice with the focus of an inner search for clarity.

MIKE TAUNTED HIS jailers. He thought he had a good sense of how far he could push—and that was pretty far. One day the group was splitting rocks when Mike initiated a call of *Black Power!* A guard bade them to quiet. *What are you gonna do,* Mike challenged, *put us in jail?* The guard repeated his orders. *Kiss my ass,* Mike replied. Seeing the guard pull out his gun, Mike grabbed the pickax he had been using on the rocks and walked closer to the armed guard. *You motherfucker!* Mike yelled, advancing. *What are you gonna do, shoot us?* The guard seemed to be considering it. *Man, you got six bullets,* Mike told him. *There's ten of us. Four of us are gonna kill you.* Getting close to the guard, Mike commanded, *Put that fucking gun away.* And he did.

It was hard to know who thought Mike was crazier, his captors or his comrades. They all breathed a sigh of relief after these episodes,

Mike included. Later Mike would acknowledge that he'd had no plan, that if the guard had fired even one shot in the air he would have soiled himself. But for now, he'd lived to fight another day.

SUNDAYS WERE VISITING days at the prison. Gwen would visit every week, keeping Mike and her comrades up to date on the Atlanta Project work. In addition to her steady vigil at the induction center and flyering at Five Points, she was also mailing the project's Black Consciousness Paper and other anti-war literature to SNCC's mailing list. The statement reached Black activists far and wide. In Harlem, Black Women Enraged organized a demonstration in solidarity with the Atlanta Project. The solidarity came from other SNCC leaders, too, who would also visit. As tense as things had become between the project and the national office, the clarity of purpose still bonded them—especially in the face of repression.[6]

It was in jail that Mike learned about the four-day uprising in Atlanta's Summerhill neighborhood after police shot Harold Prather three times in the back and side. The rebellion had once again pierced Atlanta's myth of racial innocence. Yet city elites blamed SNCC. "It is now the Nonstudent Violent Committee," police chief Herbert Jenkins said, promising to "deal with it accordingly." Mayor Ivan Allen, who ordered police to "tear the place up" to quell the uprising, vituperated SNCC in the lingua franca of Southern reaction. "Outsiders, not Atlanta Negroes, were responsible for the riot," he said, pointing special blame at Stokely Carmichael. For many elites, the riot confirmed their worst fears of "Black Power," and they directed their rage at the organization most identified with the concept.

Julian Bond resigned from SNCC the day the uprising began. He had won his reelection but was still being denied his seat. Now he faced a third primary as he was focused on taking his case against the Georgia state legislature to the Supreme Court. He distanced himself from SNCC to focus on the legal battle ahead.[7]

FOR MIKE, THE battles were in the streets. After sixty days in the stockade and some savvy maneuvers from SNCC-aligned attorneys, all twelve SNCC workers were released. The next day, Mike returned to the induction center to once again fulfill his responsibility. And once again, the soldiers refused to let him in. *Could it be*, he marveled, *I have outsmarted the US military?* He was free of the draft and of jail.

But he wasn't done with the war machine, not while the United States continued to escalate its assault on Vietnam. Mike was released during the fall semester of 1966, a time many in the still-developing anti-war movement considered the "Year of the Draft." The number of people being called for induction was four times greater than it had been in 1964, yet college students and the children of the elite were spared from consideration.[8]

Hoping to use his experience to develop a larger strategy against the war, Mike coauthored with Atlanta Project member Larry Fox a proposal for a National Anti-Draft Program. Prior to their incarceration, the pair had pitched SNCC on a "National Black Anti-Draft Movement." Now they forged ahead with a bold plan that anticipated where the cutting edge of the anti-war movement would, in two years' time, find itself: draft resistance. They saw it as a matter of principle. "The Draft Program that we envision is not concerned with peace. There can be no peace until our Brothers of color are free from the oppression of the WEST, i.e., [in] Vietnam, Angola, Rhodesia, South Africa, etc. WE MUST DO THIS FOR SURVIVAL." Throughout the fall, Mike and Larry traveled to half a dozen cities in the Midwest and Northeast meeting with Black activists. Some, like Afro-Americans Against the War in Vietnam (Boston), Black Women Enraged (New York), and Inner City Organizing Committee (Detroit), had developed campaigns against the draft. They also met with Detroit's popular Black nationalist minister Albert Cleage, attorney Conrad Lynn, and boxer-turned-draft-resister Muhammad Ali. In a speech, Mike told the Eastern Black Anti-Draft conference, "The problem is not a moral one, but one of white power, which is amoral—the Peace Movement has not assaulted white power."[9]

Gwen accompanied Mike to Philadelphia amid his anti-draft organizing—her first time there. Together, they attended a meeting of the Revolutionary Action Movement, the secretive but influential group that had been central to Mike's initial foray into politics. RAM's emphasis on Black nationalism and armed self-defense appealed to a growing number of SNCC workers. RAM founder Max Stanford had developed close ties with a panoply of Black radicals, from veterans of the Communist Party and the Universal Negro Improvement Association to young militants who didn't jibe with pacifism and patriotism. Mike kept up with RAM through its publication, *The Liberator*, and appreciated Stanford's counsel. Stanford seemed excited by the ideas coming out of the Atlanta Project, and Gwen was eager to connect with other Black nationalists.[10]

When they arrived at Stanford's house, the interior painted all in black, more than a dozen people were there chatting. After some pleasantries, the women were told to leave the room so the men could discuss politics. Gwen was stunned. She was perhaps the most experienced organizer in the room and could hold her own in any debate about high theory. She tried to catch Mike's eye, to protest the women's dismissal. But everyone, including Mike, complied with the order. Over tea with the other women, Gwen railed against the divide. Many of the women politely agreed with her. But none dared challenge their boyfriends or husbands. Confronted with a Black Power effort that sidelined women, Gwen fumed.

GWEN AND MIKE saw Black Power as an expression of self-determination. That meant organizing Black communities to wield political and economic control, they hoped, toward some kind of nonracist socialism, with self-assured confidence of who they were. Others defined the term differently, more fearfully. Though the term was not exactly new, its sudden popularity beguiled practitioners as well as its detractors. Much of the discord concerned two things: the specter of violence and the role of white people. Centuries of white racism had justified itself as a bulwark against the presumed violence of Black Power, and now observers trilled at the thought that the projection might turn real. The threat of physically toppling white supremacy was a cornerstone of Black Power. RAM, like the NOI, championed self-defense against white racism. A new organization out of California, the Black Panther Party for Self-Defense, accelerated that position with the open display of arms as they monitored police stops to prevent brutality.

Beyond the Panthers, 1966 marked the third straight year of ghettos and barrios erupting into fiery rebellion every summer. American cities burned with the pent-up frustration of Black urban communities. The five-day rebellion in the Watts section of Los Angeles in 1965 presaged a recursive summer of riots—in 1966, it was Cleveland and Omaha that saw the biggest disturbances, anticipating the massive uprisings in Newark and Detroit the following year. Some in the movement cheered these insurrections, especially after racist violence and elite intransigence forced Martin Luther King to end his failed attempt to desegregate Chicago housing that summer.[11]

Gwen and Mike did not imagine going toe to toe in a military battle with the US government. When some of her comrades parroted the incendiary slogan from the Watts rebellion, *Burn, baby, burn*, Gwen demurred. *Don't be selling wolf tickets*, she chided. Armed struggle was a check that Black communities couldn't cash. Mike was surprised to one day find a Chicago-based Black nationalist setting up an automatic rifle in the living room of the Atlanta Project freedom house. *My brother*, Mike said, anxiously coaxing the visitor out the door, *it's a bit premature. We ain't got to that level yet.*

The question of white people proved trickier, however. SNCC had always been a Black-led, white-funded organization. Gwen, Mike, and the rest of the Atlanta Project pushed for white people to organize against racism in white communities. Whites who shared those anti-racist goals needed to develop a constituency among white people. Some SNCC-affiliated white activists tried to do just that through the Southern Student Organizing Committee, an initiative some in SNCC lovingly called "the white folks project." Like many in SNCC, Gwen and Mike wanted to both affirm SNCC as a Black organization and encourage white allies in organizing their communities against racism. Stokely, now the prominent spokesman of Black Power, said as much in his coauthored manifesto on the topic.[12]

This long percolating debate came to a head at a SNCC staff meeting in December 1966. Almost sixty SNCC staffers gathered in Kerhonkson, New York, at the Catskills estate of entertainer Peg Leg Bates. The Atlanta Project's influence dominated the meeting: SNCC decided to create "freedom organizations" that would function as "all-inclusive political parties" to combine an insurgent approach to electoral politics with "service and fight[ing] for day-to-day needs" in areas such as employment, education, welfare, and housing. The organization voted to establish a national Black anti-draft program along the lines that Mike had proposed. And it included culture as one of six divisions of a newly established program department, building on the Afrocentric cultural work Bill Ware and others had promoted within Atlanta.[13]

Bill also made a speech in support of a motion to rest SNCC's decision-making power exclusively with its Black members. Such a move, he said, would demonstrate Black Power in action and free white members to organize other white people against racism. He suggested that white people who understood their task would voluntarily leave the organization. But, he concluded: "Those who don't understand that ought to be expelled. They serve no useful purpose and they don't understand what we are saying."[14]

Any sense of victory Gwen and Mike may have felt at the project's resonance with SNCC was replaced with the queasiness that accompanied hours of grueling debate. It was after one a.m. when the group voted on this controversial motion. Nineteen members supported it and eighteen opposed it. Gwen and Mike were among the twenty-four people present who abstained from voting. Everyone in the Atlanta Project abstained, as did all of the white SNCC members present, and for similar reasons: from different vantage points both groups worried that their vote would seem to taint the process. The mood was as determined as it was dour. Even those who supported the new structure, as Gwen and Mike did, felt the heavy uncertainty of their decision. Once more unto the breach.[15]

NATIONAL MEDIA TITILLATED by the Black Power concept had made Stokely Carmichael a household name. He traveled the country giving speeches—while lawmakers sought to arrest him for inciting local protests. After he spoke at Vanderbilt University, members of the Tennessee House of Representatives called for deporting Carmichael, even though he was a citizen of the United States. The constant pressure wore at people and seemed to distract from the organization's effort to retool its model of on-the-ground organizing to meet the demands of the moment. Some in SNCC began calling him "Stokely Starmichael." They charged that he was doing as chairman what John Lewis had done as chairman and what Stokely had been elected to reverse: prioritizing fundraising and speechmaking over organizational development. Stokely saw it differently. "I've come to the conclusion that there is nothing I can do inside of SNCC," he told a convening of the organization's newly established Central Committee in January 1967. "I can best serve the organization during the rest of the term [as chair] by selling wolf tickets and that's what I'm doing."[16]

Yet the ire caused by the organization's woes remained most heavily concentrated on the differences between the Atlanta Project and the national office leadership. Even James Forman, the inveterate organizational peacemaker and SNCC's patrician guide, lost his patience at something inflammatory Mike had said in a talk to some students. Forman showed up at the project house later that night, throwing pebbles at the window and challenging Mike to a fight. Mike ignored him until he left. The worst was yet to come.

IT WAS ABOUT a car. With SNCC, it was always about a car. In January, James Forman sent Mike to Detroit to pick up a Plymouth Valiant that a SNCC worker there had arranged to donate, with the help of Nathan Conyers, whose brother John was first elected to Congress in 1965. It was a nice car, nicer than most of the vehicles SNCC had at its disposal. Mike headed to Detroit, eager not only to get the car but also to connect with the city's audacious radicals. For the better part of a decade, the Motor City had become one of the most significant sites breathing life into the Black Power experiment in America. It was in Detroit where Malcolm X first delivered his famous "Message to the Grassroots" speech in 1963, and the city was still teeming with radical fervor. With increasing militancy, Black workers had been challenging the racism and exploitation of both the auto industry and its unions. Their efforts would soon spark a confederation of "Revolutionary Union Movements" in auto plants throughout the city.

In Detroit, Mike met General Baker, one of the driving forces of this effort, who had also been a member of RAM as well as of a local Black nationalist endeavor called Uhuru. Ever the prodigious firebrand, Baker had been agitating for local union movements to oppose the war in Vietnam as an expression of US imperialism. Mike liked him immensely.[17]

Back in Atlanta, Mike continued to drive the car, as did other members of the Atlanta Project. The Valiant joined a Dodge Dart that SNCC had given Dwight Williams. Like everything else in the Atlanta Project, the cars became communal property. Yet the national office maintained that both cars belonged not to the project but to SNCC. As the relationship between the project and the national office soured beyond repair, the cars became the focus of a petulant tug of war.

In a letter derisively addressed "Dear Black Power boys," Mike protested having to report "from us masses to you elite." But he dutifully obliged with a record of his efforts to build "a Black resistance to the draft not relating to [the] peace movement" that drew predominantly white people. He had been rallying anti-war troops in Atlanta and Philadelphia, Cleveland and Detroit as part of an emerging Black draft resistance network. SNCC leaders then sent a series of letters to Mike and Dwight requesting they turn the cars over to the organization. Mike ignored them; Dwight declined more politely. Cleve Sellers and the SNCC Central Committee dug in their heels as well.[18]

While Mike held on to the car, Gwen held on to a $3,000 donation to the campaign to reelect Julian Bond. Since that was the project's original mission, and since Gwen's fundraising prowess had helped secure the donation, she felt the funds belonged to the Atlanta Project. SNCC's national office requested the money to use for other projects, including the one in Lowndes County. Gwen held out, citing not just principle but the hope that money would entice the organization's leadership to take the project more seriously. Instead, SNCC's national leadership resented the project, describing Gwen, Mike, and the rest of the project as rogue operatives.

When Mike refused to abide by Sellers's demand to return the car, Sellers and Stokely Carmichael went to the Atlanta Police Department to report the Valiant missing and presumed stolen. Sellers used more direct means too. Following a SNCC meeting, Mike discovered that the Valiant wouldn't start. Sellers, who had left the meeting early, flashed him the car's distributor cap, which he had removed.[19]

On February 3, Sellers suspended the Atlanta Project. On Valentine's Day, Ware responded, less to the suspension than to Sellers's use of police, with an unloving letter. "Beware of going to the man to deal with supposedly internal conflicts," he warned obliquely. "It can work both ways. We have tapes and other information that could fall into black peoples [sic] hands across the country. There are several magazines lined up to publish our writings." Stokely Carmichael sent a one-sentence response the same day: "Dear Mr. Ware: You have just been fired from the Student Nonviolent Coordinating Committee." Following a meeting of the organization's Central Committee the next month, Gwen and Mike were fired too.[20]

GWEN AND MIKE remained committed to the promise of the Atlanta Project: its internationalism, its dedication to Black Power and Black people. They would simply have to find other outlets. And those alternatives seemed to be emerging. In March, Mike was in Washington, DC, to help students organize a protest at Howard University against General Hershey. Students disrupted the general's talk with signs blaring AMERICA IS THE BLACK MAN'S BATTLEGROUND and threw eggs and tomatoes.[21]

Days after Gwen and Mike were fired, Martin Luther King finally spoke out against the war in Vietnam. In a powerful speech at Riverside Memorial Church, King condemned the US government as "the greatest purveyor of violence in the world today." Three weeks later, champion boxer Muhammad Ali sacrificed his lucrative boxing career by refusing induction into the military. The quick-witted Ali had for months claimed his objection to the draft and the war more broadly by saying he had "no quarrel with the Vietnamese." When his induction day came, Ali released a prepared statement saying, "I strongly object to the fact that so many newspapers have given the American public and the world the impression that I have only two alternatives in taking this stand—either I go to jail or go to the Army. There is another alternative, and that alternative is justice."[22]

Citing faith and principle, Ali's dignified refusal resonated with Gwen and Mike. Of course, they recognized something of Mike's own struggle against the military in Ali's stance. But it was more than that. For Gwen and Mike embarked on a new phase of their lives the same way Cassius Clay had done in 1961: by joining the Nation of Islam. This perch, they hoped, would allow them to advance the Black Power movement beyond SNCC.

CHAPTER TEN

GETTING OUR XS

No longer in SNCC, Gwen and Mike remained devoted to Black Power. The next two years would stretch their faith, deepen their commitment to both one another and the struggle for freedom, and bring them into contact with a dizzying number of organizations across an ever-widening geography.

Their journey began with Muhammad Mosque 15, the Nation of Islam temple located in Atlanta's Sweet Auburn neighborhood. The temple had been founded in the 1950s by Jeremiah Shabazz, a Philadelphia native who joined the NOI alongside Mike's brother Nate. Jeremiah had been a regular at the Simmonses' house when Mike was growing up. Despite their affinity for Malcolm X, who was expelled from the NOI and later assassinated, Gwen and Mike began attending NOI's Sunday services while they were still in the Atlanta Project. NOI gospel aligned with Atlanta Project priorities. Gwen and Mike heard the minister give a stirring speech condemning mainstream Christianity, the war in Vietnam, and American racism. The sermons made sense to them. The bitter feud with SNCC over Black consciousness, the brutal beatings and imprisonment, high-speed car chases and attempted assassinations they'd both experienced left a mark on them. Recent years led them to nod approvingly when the Nation of Islam preached that white people were uniquely, genetically evil, the dangerous creation of a mad scientist.[1]

THE NOI's APPROACH blended Eastern mysticism, Western patri- archy, and a deep opposition to US racism and empire. The Nation maintained an active recruitment strategy that placed high emphasis on young militants like Gwen and Mike who, for their part, saw in the NOI a robust infrastructure based in Black life. A Black God promising deliverance from white racism was welcome news. Gwen had become convinced that whites were too full of hatred to allow in- tegration, and Mike had even begun to wonder whether white people should be quarantined for the good of the planet.[2]

Muhammad Speaks, the NOI newspaper that Michael's brother John managed, boasted of Black accomplishments in equal measure to its condemnations of white supremacy. The paper reported fre- quently on the civil rights movement and racist violence, the war in Vietnam and the fights to decolonize Africa. Both in person and in print, the Nation of Islam preached Black uplift and self- determination. And it seemed to be practicing it as well: in addition to the mosque and a robust slate of publications, the Nation owned restaurants and property, seeing in them the capital through which to build a sovereign Black nation.

Beyond the eschatology, the NOI appeared to have much of what the Atlanta Project desired: Black-run institutions, with the dream of an independent Black territory. The people they met in the Nation came from every walk of life, with plenty of well-to-do profession- als seated in worship alongside the down-on-their-luck crowd more commonly associated with NOI members. The NOI's focus was on Black people taking care of themselves. The Nation preached that Black men were bold and fierce fighters, duty-bound to protect Black women, their queens. Gwen, who by twenty-one had already helmed a community-organizing project deep in Klan country, was not used to being put on a pedestal and deemed in need of protection. Nor was she used to women having to sit separately from men. She found it both awkward and reassuring. The sermons recalled her grandmother's admonition of the dangers Black women faced at the hands of whites.

The NOI frowned on cohabitation among unmarried couples, however, and so, before Gwen and Mike could join the Nation of Islam, they had to get married. On May 12, 1967, Gwen and Mike wed. It was a small affair, consisting mostly of signing the required papers in front a reverend they knew through the Atlanta Project. They were in love, but marriage was a means to an end. And once married, they could officially get their Xs as members of the Nation.

Joining the Nation of Islam required permission from its enigmatic leader, the Honorable Elijah Muhammad. Gwen and Mike each wrote him a letter requesting membership, affirming their "intention to return to the holy original Nation" and requesting an "Original name." Gwen became Gwendolyn 2X, in recognition that she was the second Gwendolyn in the Atlanta congregation. Mike became Michael 10X.[3]

Married and members of the Nation, Gwen and Mike still needed jobs. Meager as it was, SNCC had been their source of income. Since their firings, Mike had even gone to the blood bank a few times for some cash. They needed something more permanent.

Gwen was excited when Doris Dozier approached her with a job. At twelve, Dozier had been head of the Montgomery NAACP Youth Council when the bus boycott began. Now she was the Southern field representative for the National Council of Negro Women (NCNW), a service organization established in 1935 by legendary educator Mary McLeod Bethune. Throughout its three-decade history, the NCNW had blended middle-class uplift with responding to the needs of Black communities, anchored in the vanguard role of Black women. The NCNW was an early supporter of Black labor leader A. Philip Randolph's March on Washington Movement in the 1940s, organized hundreds of buses to ferry people to the March on Washington in 1963—and, following the exclusion of women from the speakers' roster at the historic demonstration it helped create, proclaimed that Black women's fight for justice could not be subordinated to a male-dominant civil rights movement.[4]

The NCNW's emphasis on women's empowerment allowed its moderate mission to house radical action. It had amassed a membership of more than three million people, connected through a skeleton staff. After decades of being primarily volunteer driven, the NCNW secured a two-year, $300,000 grant from the Ford Foundation to direct a new project, Project WomanPower, which sought to develop Black women leaders. With thirty locations nationwide, Project WomanPower was an experiment in developing Black Power at the grassroots. It combined the bourgeois aspirations of the NCNW's mission with the people-powered localism Gwen had implemented in SNCC. Using targeted microloans, Project WomanPower brought together middle-class reformers with Black nationalist militants. The theme of economic empowerment united socialist stalwarts with capitalist entrepreneurs.[5]

One of several former SNCC women on staff, Gwen was hired as the Midwest field representative for Project WomanPower. She would be responsible for projects in Illinois, Michigan, Missouri, and especially, Ohio. She and Mike chose Chicago as their new home. They lived with Gwen's aunt Jessie, whose tour of the Windy City a decade earlier had first showed Gwen a world beyond the South. A new name, a new faith, and a new job, Gwendolyn 2X began her next adventure.

GWEN WAS NERVOUS about leaving the South. She wasn't familiar with the conventions of Black communities in the North, and before moving there had spent only days in the Midwest. As a regional field director, Gwen had to figure out what work was already happening in a given area and identify local women leaders. It was similar to the work she had done when she was unexpectedly made project director in Laurel in 1964—except, instead of one town, she now was responsible for seven. Her terrain included major cities such as Chicago, Detroit, and St. Louis, midlevel cities Cleveland and Columbus, and smaller Ohio towns like Lorain and Elyria. On the road constantly, armed for the first time with a corporate credit card, she hoped that lessons honed in Atlanta and Mississippi would translate to Chicago and Ohio. She relied on social networks to meet some of the known leaders in a given town and, through them, identify women interested in developing their leadership and organizing skills.[6]

The geography was new, but the mission familiar. Project Woman Power aimed to train mostly working-class Black women around the country to be community organizers in two years' time, expanding the mission and focus of NCNW in the process. Gwen's SNCC education served her well in recognizing indigenous community leadership. In every city she traveled to, she stayed with local families rather than in hotels. She needed to build trust, to see how people lived, if she was going to assist them in advocating for themselves.

Project WomanPower set out to identify community leaders and deepen their organizing skill sets. Gwen was part of a cohort of young staff politicizing the NCNW's long track record of community service and uplift. The NCNW provided recognition of women's community enrichment efforts, which the former SNCC members now on staff placed within a broader context. Gwen was particularly attuned to the shame many women expressed about their family structure. Two years earlier, the Department of Labor had published a report by sociologist Daniel Patrick Moynihan that described Black families as embedded in a "tangle of pathology" that originated in its "matriarchal structure." Blaming Black women as too-powerful barriers to Black collective progress pervaded schools, welfare systems, and the media. Many of the women Gwen worked with confided that their work outside the home and their power within it prevented Black men from being given their due. As in Mississippi, Gwen had to develop the confidence of the women she worked with to shed decades of devaluation.[7]

GWEN'S CONSTANT TRAVEL posed an unexpected complication for her faith. Through the Muslim Girls Training and General Civilization Class, the Nation of Islam had a formal structure for women's leadership. Yet it was unaccustomed to women occupying such powerful roles external to its structure. Women traveling without their husbands needed to have a letter from the minister of their local temple to present to the minister at the temple where they would worship while on the road. But Gwen was on the road a lot, which raised suspicion. Even with her authorized letter, she was not greeted kindly. Local ministers and women parishioners interrogated her: *Why are you traveling alone? Where is your husband?* Her answers, acknowledgment of her life beyond the Nation, never satisfied.

It was not just her travel. Gwen selectively followed NOI's strict regimen of women's health, dress, and diet. She ate only one meal a day, as Elijah Muhammad proscribed in his "How to Eat to Live" column in *Muhammad Speaks*. She submitted to being weighed at her local mosque and tried to keep her weight under the required limit of 120 pounds. But she never dressed in uniform. Gwen wore colorful African garb, including for her head scarf. She refused to even purchase the virginal white gown she was expected to wear. While the NOI spoke of "an Asiatic race," Gwen was still loyal to a Black one. The Sister Captains of the Muslim Girls Training, the auxiliary group that enforced the NOI's gendered expectations and served as the only source of organized power for NOI women, regarded Gwen severely. In every town she visited, her travel letter failed to address another question: *Where is your uniform?*[28]

Gwen's travel did bring her closer to Islam if not the Nation. In Detroit, she visited with original members of the Nation of Islam who were now part of her extended family. Before marrying John Ali—Mike's brother and the only non–blood relative in Elijah Muhammad's inner circle—Minnie Coleman had been raised in the Nation. Her parents had joined the mercurial faith even before Elijah Muhammad did. They remained in it still. Yet their practice differed. They had traditional Qurans in addition to the translation that Elijah

Muhammad had approved, and they observed salat, the ritual prayer of traditional Islam that involves both standing and kneeling. The Nation's prayer ritual did not incorporate the bodily postures. Watching them read from the holy book, seeing them bow in reverence, Gwen was riveted.

GWEN'S TRAVEL ALSO posed a challenge for Mike. He was bored. The NOI was no more part of his social world than it was for Gwen. His family connection to NOI leadership meant that he never sold a copy of *Muhammad Speaks*. Mike skipped over what was a rite of passage for most men who joined the Nation. Though Chicago boasted a thriving political movement, he couldn't get a job and was too restless to appreciate that he had a free place to stay in a thriving Black metropolis. By summer of 1967, he decamped for New York City, where a SNCC associate had arranged for him to get a job working with youth through a War on Poverty–funded organization called the United Block Association. He stayed with an aunt before getting an apartment for him and Gwen, a fifth-floor walk-up on Eighty-First Street between Columbus and Amsterdam. Gwen now added another city to her roster.[9]

Their time in New York also brought the couple in close contact with the most prominent member of the Nation of Islam outside Chicago: Louis Walcott. Known within NOI as Louis X, he had joined the Nation in the 1950s as a calypso musician. In *The Hate That Hate Produced*, a 1959 documentary that first brought the Nation of Islam to a national audience, his voice can be heard issuing a stirring indictment to a large gathering of Muslims. "I charge the white man with being the greatest liar on earth," he intoned, before rattling off a list of charges for drunkenness, gambling, assault. The clip was from a one-act play he had written, *The Trial*, based on NOI eschatology. A mentee of Malcolm X, Louis X had, like John Ali, sided with Elijah Muhammad in 1964 and risen through the ranks following Malcolm's expulsion and murder.[10]

By 1967, Louis X had been given the surname Farrakhan and had been assigned Malcolm's duties as head of the Nation in New York. He welcomed Gwen and Mike to the city, seeing in them the Nation's future. All three shared a hope that the NOI could be a vehicle for promoting Black Power, a way to translate the uprisings against white racism into a sustained program. Mike was particularly star-struck, having heard recordings of Farrakhan's play *The Orgena: A Negro Spelt Backwards* and song "A White Man's Heaven Is a Black Man's Hell" in his house growing up.

Gwen and Mike were the seasoned organizers Farrakhan needed to expand inroads into the civil rights movement. Like the leader of the NOI temple in Atlanta when Gwen and Mike first joined the Nation, Farrakhan seemed to share their vision that the NOI could be a righteous political vehicle. He was an affable teacher, driven and charismatic. His lectures at the Harlem temple spoke not just to the Muslim faith but also to its political vision of self-help and Black capitalism. Greeting them after Sunday services, Farrakhan assured them that he shared their vision of what the Nation could be. *We need people like you to bring a new light to the Nation*, he told them. Farrakhan made sure they knew that he had dismissed the complaints from midwestern NOI women about Gwen's frequent travel and lack of uniform.[11]

MIKE LASTED ONLY three months in New York before Dwight persuaded him to return to Temple University. He moved back to Philadelphia in late fall, shortly before the winter semester. He took a job with a social service agency that placed him at the Paschall Betterment League. Headed by an ambitious and efficient administrator named Wilson Goode that everyone called Willie, the league was part of a network of neighborhood-based projects advocating for housing security. It was enmeshed in the city's rising Black political establishment, including an ambitious lawyer named Hardy Williams who, liked Goode, would soon become an elected official.

Mike's work there was more prosaic. He served as Goode's surrogate at meetings and, on November 17, 1967, at a demonstration organized by Black high school students. A lot had happened in the two years Mike had been gone from Philadelphia. Seven months of daily picketing in 1965 had targeted the walled fortress of Girard College, a segregated school in North Philadelphia. Alongside those efforts, a group of Freedom Library partisans launched the Black People's Unity Movement, which, by 1967, spearheaded a vibrant student movement demanding "Black history curricula, recognition of Black student unions, and repeal of school policies that banned African clothing, hairstyles, and names." Their demands were eclectic, righteous. Among others, the students wanted to change Ben Franklin High School to Malcolm X High School.[12]

When Mike arrived at the Board of Education building on Twenty-First Street and Benjamin Franklin Parkway, he found more than three thousand students from twelve area high schools calling for Black Power and community control. Frank Rizzo, the police commissioner who had long terrorized Philadelphia Black activists, was there. Mike heard Rizzo instruct his officers to *get their black asses*, and then the cops were everywhere, clubbing with rage. It was indiscriminate: students, reporters, school board employees—everyone fell under the thrashing batons. When someone near him was clubbed to the ground, Mike helped her up, and they made their escape.[13]

Coming amid a spirited student campaign, the police assault jump-started a series of emergency meetings on how to respond. Mike attended as many as he could, not just as Goode's representative. He wanted to know what students were doing, for in January 1968, he would be one again.

WHILE MIKE LOOKED to students as a basis for Black Power, Gwen continued to organize mothers and daughters in the Midwest. She moved to Philadelphia but continued to travel frequently in 1968. As the NCNW opened itself to the Black Power initiative, it came to

define Black women as the leading, most advanced current of transformation—the vanguard. To ensure that these community leaders
were ready for the awesome challenges ahead, NCNW organized
two Vanguard trainings. Both of them were weeklong intensive
educational sessions involving three women from each of the participating locations around the country. The participants ranged in
age from seventeen to seventy-one and were mostly based in cities.
The majority of Vanguard women were married, had children, and
worked jobs outside the home, from domestic work and teaching to
nursing, machine operation, and clerical labor.[14]

At the first Vanguard training in June 1967, several of the women
expected the workshops to prescribe what they needed to do afterward. They were discomfited when Gwen and other NCNW staff
said they would need to draw upon their own emergent strengths in
responding to the needs of their community. To help them fight their
own battles, the Vanguard sessions were dedicated largely to workshops on Black history, economics, and education—a Black Power
agenda. The second Vanguard training, held in Nyack, New York, in
March 1968, even opened with a chant of "Black Power!"

The training was more than slogans. Pan-African scholars John
Henrik Clarke, Keith Beard, and James Campbell lectured on Black
history, both in Africa and its diaspora, and the power of Black women.
Fannie Lou Hamer, the NCNW field organizer in Mississippi, spoke
about NCNW's efforts in the context of the bitter struggles against
white supremacy. Organizers from the Afro-American Association
in California spoke about the causes behind the country's urban rebellions and the President's Commission on Civil Disorders. Though
Vanguard women were a mix of young firebrands and respectable
moderates, they shared a focus on collective care for young and old.
That the majority of Vanguard participants were parents struggling
with underfunded and segregated school systems placed a high emphasis on education. John Churchville was one of several speakers to
highlight the development of community-led preschools. A central
pillar of the conference was devoted to cooperative economics, and

women left the conference planning to organize cooperative childcare centers and food and clothing distribution, as well as to share first aid and self-defense skills with others in their community.[15]

On her way back from Nyack, Gwen stopped in Cleveland to pick up members of the Republic of New Libya, a Black nationalist group she had befriended there. The group was led by Fred Ahmed Evans, a tall bearded man who considered himself a mystic. Evans was the proprietor of the Afro-Culture Shop and Bookstore on Cleveland's east side. Like followers of the Nation of Islam, Evans believed in numerology, the belief that numbers—from the distance between the sun and earth to the number of letters in your name—held power in one's life. He also believed in astrology, seeing in birthdays and times divine insight. Evans claimed that the stars told of an impending war between Black and white. As they became friendly, Gwen accepted his offer to read her astrological chart. She found him eccentric and enigmatic. He was well connected throughout the region, and he invited her to the Black Government convention in Detroit. Gwen agreed to drive him and whoever else from Cleveland's nationalist community would fit in her car.[16]

The Detroit convention followed Black Power gatherings in Berkeley, Newark, and Philadelphia. But unlike its predecessors, this one aimed to launch a new organization and a new constitutional order. Brothers Milton and Richard Henry, prominent Black nationalists, organized the conference under the umbrella of their organization, the Malcolm X Society. (An attorney, Milton had joined the legal team to free Mike and others from the Atlanta Stockade in 1966.) The brothers had garnered support from a broad cross section of the Black liberation movement, including Betty Shabazz (widow of Malcolm X), Mauluna Karenga of the US organization, BARTS cofounder Amiri Baraka, and Lawrence Guyot of SNCC and MFDP. The convention pledged to inaugurate a new claim for reparations and Black sovereignty in the former slave strongholds of Alabama, Georgia, Louisiana, Mississippi, and South Carolina. Robert Williams, the former NAACP activist run out of the country for his armed self-defense efforts, was to be the nominal president of this new country, the Republic of New Africa.

Looking forward to the conference, Gwen's stomach dropped when she saw Evans and two compatriots approach her NCNW-rented car with a small arsenal. *Oh, no, no, no!* Gwen protested. *What are you doing? You can't put these guns in my car!* Evans told her, *We don't travel anywhere without our heat.* Cleveland police had recently evicted Evans from his store, the storm Evans predicted growing ever closer.

Begrudgingly, Gwen relented. But her anxiety increased when she noticed the car obviously following them, the well-dressed white men inside—who Gwen presumed were from the FBI—taking pictures of them any time they stopped. *I am not dying here with y'all*, Gwen cursed her companions. *If there's going to be a shootout, I'm getting out!*

Almost two hundred miles separate Cleveland from Detroit, and Gwen was relieved when they made it to the Shrine of the Black Madonna unharmed. The church that hosted the gathering was pastored by the outspoken nationalist Rev. Albert Cleage. She was glad to participate in the conference, to cocreate its grand ambition about building an independent Black republic within the United States. The position echoed that of the Nation of Islam, but it was more outwardly revolutionary in its demands. The gathering affirmed that the Middle Passage had created a new identity, that of the New African, who now demanded independence from the United States. After three days of spirited discussion, the time had come to sign a New African declaration of independence from the United States. March 31, 1968, the start of a new Black republic in the Western Hemisphere. The first to sign was Audley "Queen Mother" Moore, a Louisiana native born in 1898 and a veteran of both Marcus Garvey's Universal Negro Improvement Association and the Communist Party of the United States. Moore rejoiced at the opportunity: "Hallelujah, Hallelujah, I've lived to see the day."[17]

Gwen was proud to join the signatories, to imagine transforming the states that had almost killed her into a Black national homeland. She was just as glad to have survived the journey without any bloodshed. Heading east that night, she paid no attention to Lyndon Johnson's address from the Oval Office. "The Communists may renew their attack any day," Johnson said of the Tet Offensive that had surprised US forces in Vietnam and demonstrated the indominable perseverance of the National Liberation Front. At the end of his message, the president declared that he would not stand for reelection that fall. One way or another, there would be a new republic.[18]

FOUR DAYS LATER, April 4, 1968,Gwen was in New York City for an all-day NCNW meeting. The NCNW had put her up at the Tudor Hotel. But when she arrived at the posh midtown hotel, everyone in the lobby stared at her. Panicked, sullen. The clerk at the front desk offered her condolences. *Why?* Gwen asked. *What happened?*

Martin Luther King Jr. had been assassinated. He had been in Memphis, Gwen's hometown, supporting a strike by sanitation workers when a gunman killed him as he stepped onto the balcony of the Lorraine Motel.

Gwen didn't know what to do. She turned on the television in her room and saw reports of rioting. She knew she had to be outside, where unadorned grief fueled inchoate protest. She put on jeans and stepped into the streets. Unbeknownst to her, fires burned around the country, a rageful inferno reaching within blocks of the White House. John Lindsay, the liberal Republican mayor of New York City, greeted crowds in Harlem in an attempt to quell a more riotous outburst. That was also the objective of five thousand cops and firefighters dispatched to Harlem and Black sections of Brooklyn. Gwen walked the streets with the crowd, outraged and despondent. For the first time in her life, she threw rocks at police and storefront windows. She stayed in the streets, surrounded by people, as long as she could. Then she went back to her hotel room and cried until the tears ran dry.[19]

MIKE WAS IN Philadelphia when he heard the news about King's murder. Like Gwen, he instinctively headed to the streets, to be with the people, numb with uncertainty. The night was uneventful, at least for him. He processed his sadness at King's murder in relation to his newfound project: the Black Student League.

Temple was a newly public institution when Mike renewed his studies there in the winter of 1968. The university did not represent the local public, however. Located in the majority Black neighborhood of North Philadelphia, its student population was mostly white. The small number of Black students on campus easily found each other, and the Black Student League was the most political of the few Black organizations on campus. The league published *Maji Maji*, a "Black Power newsletter" named after a 1905 uprising in East Africa against German colonialism. Mike joined right away.

When King was killed, the league was already embroiled in a campus battle: protesting a fraternity's blackface minstrel show. Beyond the offense of the performance itself, league members used the opportunity to campaign to make the university responsive to Black students and the surrounding Black community. By the end of the month, more than one hundred white students held a sit-in outside the university president's office in support of five demands generated partly by the Black Student League. The demands called for Black students to comprise at least a quarter of the next freshman class, university curriculum to incorporate Black authors and issues, students and the surrounding Black community to have "a say in university expansion" into North Philadelphia, and students to have a say in campus governance. The protests at Temple did not generate the international headlines that students at Columbia University did when they went on strike that month against their university's planned expansion into Harlem. But the issues involved were similar.

Unlike Columbia, however, some of Temple's projected growth was underwritten by the Model Cities program of the War on Poverty, a federally funded attempt at "urban renewal."[20]

Seizing the potential, the Black Student League established the Steering Committee for Black Students to serve as an umbrella organization for any Black student group interested in bettering the university. Its member organizations included fraternities, sororities, and civic groups, such as Conscience, the tutoring organization Mike cofounded after the Selma protests in 1965. How far he had come in those three years. The Black Student League, with its mix of Black nationalism, Marxism, and Pan-Africanism, was exactly his desired milieu. It was what he and Gwen had hoped the Nation of Islam would be, and in fact several members of the league were also members of the NOI. Gwen joined Mike in visiting the Philadelphia temple. But neither of them joined the temple.[21]

The Steering Committee proved a nimble way to challenge Temple's racism. A month after the protests against the white fraternity, the Steering Committee was calling out racism in Temple's dorms, where Black women were subject to harassment and abuse from white administrators and jocks—issues that the Steering Committee saw as intimately connected to the university's imperious role in North Philadelphia. In a letter to the administration that spring, the Steering Committee charged that Temple, "this oasis in the black ghetto, must now accept the responsibility of listening, accepting, making qualitative changes and redressing valid grievances felt by black students and the black community." And so, the letter closed, the university "should have the opportunity to prove that it can become a humane and responsive part of the black community."[22]

Mike was ecstatic. He had recently read the four-volume collected works of Mao Tse-tung, and the Steering Committee exemplified to him what the Chinese communist leader had theorized as the united front. Any organization that believed in its broad mission of building an anti-racist university could claim membership, and the mission encompassed both campus and community. Its tent was broad, its demands unifying. *If Mao and Chiang Kai-shek could get along, we should be able to get along with the Greeks*, Mike told himself. The Black Student League continued to function as a radical element within the broad coalition, helping to lead meetings but careful not to project its ideology onto the committee as a whole. While the Black Student League had *Maji Maji*, the Steering Committee for Black Students published the *Black Torch*. (The editorial staff of both publications overlapped significantly.)

The league began to operate in two directions simultaneously: the Steering Committee mobilized Black students on campus, while the league began to initiate partnerships with other Black Power campus groups throughout the region. Mike traveled to the University of Pennsylvania, Swarthmore College, and the University of Connecticut in an attempt to develop a mid-Atlantic Black Power coalition. The Black Student League was adamant that Black Power politics needed to engage with the university's relationship to the surrounding geographic community and to Black people's concerns off campus. The league held and joined frequent meetings at Philadelphia's Church of the Advocate and at local community centers to support the organizing happening off campus as well. Gwen joined Mike and other members of the league in the Sankoré Society, a Black nationalist study group named after a traditional African place of learning. They read W. E. B. Du Bois's *Black Reconstruction*, a magisterial reconsideration of the period following the Civil War. Among other things, Du Bois cast Black workers as the midwives of universal goods like the modern public school, under assault from a racist system of private ownership.[23]

Inspired as he was by the work he was doing, Mike felt dejected at what seemed to him to be a rising tide of nihilism in some corners of the Black Power movement. The deaths of Malcolm and King hastened an already prominent view that the United States was too racist to accommodate social change. Oakland police killed seventeen-year-old Bobby Hutton in a shootout with the Black Panthers there on April 6, 1968, inaugurating a series of bleak attacks on the group as it spread beyond California. Police commissioner Frank Rizzo used King's death as an opportunity to institute a state of emergency that banned gatherings of more than twelve people. Even after it was rescinded, police pressure remained high and failed to stop a mob of white racists from threatening Black youth at a South Philadelphia high school that fall. America was at a potentially fatal precipice, and the millenarian worldview of some Black nationalists seemed more vocal, more bleak after King's murder. That summer, Ahmed Evans, the Black nationalist mystic that Gwen had befriended through her work with NCNW, was involved in a bloody shootout with Cleveland police that killed seven, injured fifteen, and sent him to prison for life. Even in *Maji Maji*, the first editorial after King's death forewarned that "we black people are moving inevitably towards a final confrontation from which we will indeed emerge free at last, either victors or dead heroes."[24]

Mike hoped that Black artists could help reverse course. He wrote in *Maji Maji* about what he saw as two branches of nihilism: one he labeled "the Black People, you ain't shit theme" that emphasized "only the ugliness, the brutality of Black Society with no alternative to this way of life being given." The other was "the Guerilla-like Black Revolutionary" who was a "sub-human machinistic [*sic*] guerilla whose only goal in life is to take the heads of 100 white men, 50 white women, 10 white children and to carry the heads of thousands of Black Uncle Toms on Spikes through blood-drenched liberated streets." The arts could be the North Star guiding Black people toward the future, which he understood as a nation. Artists, he wrote, should create works "that will turn the negro into a Black man. . . . That's really what the people of the future are going to be looking for: How to get out of this that we're in. We need to begin to show, to get into the whole Black History thing, to begin writing epics again, to begin to show our visions of the future."[25]

BY THE FALL of 1968, Gwen had left NCNW. Beyond the exhaustion of constant travel, she had a bigger reason to slow down: she was pregnant. The morning sickness was so intense that she lost weight while growing a baby. Subsisting on ginger ale and soda crackers, she rested in Philadelphia as she and Mike planned to bring a child into the whirlwind.

When she could, she joined protests organized by the Steering Committee for Black Students. The opposition to Temple's expansion into North Philadelphia now included a plan for recruiting Black students and staff. The Steering Committee also demanded an Afro-Asian Institute, in recognition of what *Maji Maji* described as "nonwhite Internationalism" and a "turn to the East (Afro-Asian world) for correct answers."[26]

There were no Asian students at Temple as far as Mike or anyone in the Steering Committee knew. The 1965 immigration reform act that eliminated the prohibition on Asian migration was still too recent to have much impacted the campus demographic. A smattering of Puerto Rican students, some of them with deep roots in North Philadelphia and all of whom Mike considered at least politically Black, joined the Black Student League in its demands. Their demands of Temple included an "open-door" policy for Black and Puerto Rican people, who they hoped would make up at least one-quarter of Temple's student body.[27]

Mike shared notes on his organizing experience with Jimmy Garrett, whom Gwen had worked with in Mississippi in 1964. Gwen had invited Garrett to a Midwestern Regional Training Conference for Project WomanPower in Ohio the previous summer to help organize a Black Student Association. Garrett was now at San Francisco State University where, that November, students launched a five-month strike. They called themselves the Third World Liberation Front, and their demands mirrored those of the students at Temple. San Francisco had a more multiethnic population than Philadelphia, however, where the demand for an Afro-Asian Institute expressly recalled the 1954 Asian-African conference in Bandung, Indonesia. The Black students saw Afro-Asia as the geopolitical axis at the forefront of the world's struggles to be more human by throwing off the yoke of colonialism, whether in apartheid South Africa or US-occupied Vietnam.[28]

The Steering Committee pressured Temple to commit to hiring Black and nonwhite faculty and admitting Black and nonwhite students. The administration initially responded by falsely inflating the number of Black students enrolled. In continued protests, the Steering Committee mobilized the Black staff on campus, as well as the students. And then they won. In the summer of 1969, the university created a Special Recruitment and Admissions Program to increase the number of Black students on campus, appointed a Black professor as director, and allocated a budget of $22,000 to the effort. Temple would soon agree to launch an Afro-Asian Institute as well, with a teaching staff that truly was Afro-Asian.[29]

But by the time it opened, Mike was in prison.

FOR YEARS, MIKE had organized his life around how to avoid going into either the military or prison. He was optimistic that his cat-and-mouse scheme with the Selective Service System, moving often and then getting soldiers to refuse him admission to the induction center, might persuade the court that he had followed the letter if not the spirit of the law.

Mike had felt good about his chances heading into trial for draft evasion in 1967. But when he saw a uniformed soldier, arm in a sling, head toward the witness stand, he knew his fortunes had changed. The man, who had declared his occupation as "professional soldier" upon taking the stand, had been flown back from Vietnam in order to testify. He had been inducted into the military the same day Mike was arrested for blocking the induction center. *Oh man*, he told himself. *We are going to jail.* He was convicted on September 19, 1967.[30]

His attorney, SNCC lawyer Howard Moore, had succeeded in delaying sentencing for two years. In the summer of 1969, however,

Moore told Mike that the Supreme Court had refused to hear their appeal. A judge had given him one more chance to enlist, which he once again refused. Twelve credits shy of graduation, he would now have to turn himself in to serve a three-and-a-half-year sentence for draft resistance and damaging the induction center.

Gwen thought they could delay it even longer. *We can leave the country*, she suggested. Already a network of draft resisters had taken up refuge in Canada. There were even more exciting vistas overseas. By 1968, Eldridge Cleaver had established an international branch of the Black Panther Party in Algeria, where he fled to avoid returning to prison after a shootout with police. Gwen and Mike had met Cleaver shortly after Mike's conviction, when he was in Atlanta for the funeral of SNCC organizer Ruby Doris Robinson, who died of a rare cancer. They found Cleaver brash and macho and wanted nothing to do with him.

There were other international outposts, however, ones that might have been more appealing. Black revolutionary Robert Williams, the nominal head of the Republic of New Africa, had already circumnavigated the Third World, from Cuba to China. And SNCC comrades had traveled to Tanzania, Ghana, Senegal. Suppressed in the United States, Black revolutionaries were finding or making home elsewhere. If it was her, Gwen thought, she might leave rather than go to prison.

Mike considered it. But he remembered his visit with two RAM members laying low in Toronto to escape federal charges. They seemed miserable, isolated. He didn't know anything about Canada, much less the farther-flung sites where US radicals had sought refuge. Besides, his mother was sick, running out the clock on the five-year prognosis doctors had given her after a cancer diagnosis. Going might mean never coming back. He couldn't abandon his mother. It was only three and a half years. He had done two months in the Atlanta Stockade, had spent various other stints in jail. *I'm gonna do the time*, he said.

On April 22, 1969, after more than twenty hours of labor, Gwen pushed a healthy baby girl into the world. After mapping her astrological chart, they named her Aishah Shahidah Simmons. Aisha was the name of the Prophet Muhammad's third and youngest wife, who had led an army against the Fourth Caliphate in the seventh century. It was a far cry from the diminutive role offered Gwen in RAM and the Nation of Islam. Shahidah was the name of a close family friend, a fellow organizer who had taken a Muslim name upon joining the NOI. Their ranks bigger by one, Gwen and Mike were elated.

Seventy-eight days later, on September 4, 1969, Mike turned himself in to authorities in Philadelphia to begin his prison term.

CHAPTER ELEVEN

PRISON AND OTHER METAPHYSICS

THREE WEEKS AFTER MIKE TURNED HIMSELF IN TO THE PHILA-delphia Detention Center, officers shackled his legs and wrists to his waist and loaded him in a transport van. Next to him was an old classmate from elementary school. The man had robbed a bank and then escaped from jail. During his time on the run, Mike had given him a ride to see his wife. He hadn't heard that he had been recaptured. Now they were headed toward the red-brick walls of Lewisburg federal penitentiary together.

Once in Admission and Orientation at Lewisburg, Mike was officially a federal prisoner. He was assigned the number 36305. He spent only a couple weeks there before being deposited at what would be his new home: the federal prison camp at Allenwood. The prison sat on grounds of a once thriving town in central Pennsylvania that had been turned into a munitions depot during World War II. The prison opened in 1952, some decommissioned munitions bunkers still on the grounds. New highway construction joined the almost two hundred miles separating the prison from Philadelphia.

Camp was the lowest security option within the federal prison system. It held people convicted of white-collar crimes, midlevel mobsters, those finishing a long prison sentence, and, by the time Mike arrived in fall of 1969, conscientious objectors. Prisoners slept in bunkbeds in fifty-person dormitories rather than in private cells. During the day, they wore Army-style khakis and worked in the prison's furniture factory, rock quarry, or cattle farm. The chain-link fence surrounding the prison was not tall enough to stop a determined climber.

Allenwood fielded four softball teams, microcosms of the prison's social world. The teams were determined by race and politics: Black, white, Latino, and conscientious objector. The COs, as people knew them, were a motley crew of radical Quakers and Catholics, Jehovah's Witnesses, members of the Nation of Islam. While all of them had a religious objection to serving in the military, the Quaker and Catholic COs had come out of the anti-war movement. Mike joined the Black softball team, which also included some of the NOI members. At the same time, he was keen to befriend the activist COs, the war resisters who shared his movement orientation. Incarcerated at a time when Black people were becoming the majority of prisoners nationwide, Mike's organizing in federal prison would demonstrate the tactical creativity and multiracial solidarity of Black Power behind bars. As an organizer, Mike saw his job as building what social life he could across the four major groups inside. They would make a lot of good trouble together.[1]

WHEN MIKE WENT to prison, Gwen and Aishah moved into a house owned by one of Mike's old Heritage House friends. Gwen had a new baby and no employment. They lived rent-free in the rehabbed first-floor West Philadelphia apartment. The support eased her time considerably. But food and utilities costs still loomed, and so Gwen applied for government assistance. At the time, Black women in the burgeoning National Welfare Rights Organization (NWRO) were fighting drastic cuts to welfare programs. The cuts began at the state level but were being federalized under newly elected president Richard Nixon, who wanted to both limit cash payments and attach them to a work requirement. The welfare rights movement had a different idea. Insisting that "every man, woman, and child has the right to live," the NWRO demanded that the government provide Americans a guaranteed income. Welfare payment could be a protean example of the social benefit every American deserved. Gwen supported the demand. She also had a personal reason to apply for welfare. *Uncle Sam, you have locked up my husband and the father of my child*, she thought while filling out the application, *so you are gonna pay me!*[2]

Though she succeeded in receiving welfare benefits, Gwen was not spared its indignities. There were the condescending looks from some in the grocery checkout aisle as she paid with food stamps. The real insult was her welfare case worker, who often functioned more like a police officer. He was particularly interested in whether Gwen had any male relationships, as that would be reason to end her payments. In between searching under her bed and inside her closet, he saw her overflowing bookshelves as evidence of a man's presence. *Whose books are these?* he scoffed. *They're in my house*, she said coldly. *Whose books do you think they are?*

Gwen visited Mike as often as she could. Sometimes, especially those cold winter months when she didn't want to brave the snowy mountains in her blue Volkswagen alone, she drove with friends or with Mike's family. Increasingly, she came to know the family networks of other radical conscientious objectors. One of the other CO wives had moved near the prison, since locals could visit daily, and offered her a place to stay. Gwen would also catch rides with the parents or wives of other COs. Powelton Village, the Philadelphia neighborhood where Gwen and Mike lived before his incarceration, was home to many anti-war activists—some of whom visited or wrote their comrades who were now incarcerated with Mike. Gwen knew several of them, and she also began volunteering with the American Friends Service Committee (AFSC), the Quaker peace and justice organization headquartered in downtown Philadelphia. Gwen had first been introduced to Quakerism at Spelman. At the time, she had found the Quakers strange: a religion that had no singing, no preaching or pastor, and a lot of silent meditation was unlike her understanding of religion. Now she was grateful for their progressive and contemplative ethos. The AFSC offered various support to Quaker COs, including regular visits from a Quaker minister as well as correspondence. Gwen availed herself of the more informal support mechanism the Quaker association provided. She often caught a ride to prison with the well-to-do parents of a Quaker CO who were prominent supporters of the AFSC.[3]

MIKE KEPT HIS letters positive so as not to worry his mother. "I'm doing fine and looking slim (smile)," he wrote her. It was also true: he was doing fine and looking slim.

Mike had taken a martial arts class at Temple in anticipation of being incarcerated. He was a vegetarian, a legacy of seeing pigs slaughtered at the Atlanta Stockade in 1966 that had hardened in his Muslim period. Embracing the slow-run exercise that had recently become popular in America, Mike jogged four miles regularly. He fasted one week out of the month, cleansing and testing his body. He spent the weekends playing chess as much as possible. Reading Gandhi and Nehru (the first prime minister of India and a proponent of Third World solidarity), practicing yoga and meditation, his mind wandered to India as a site of both spiritual enlightenment and anti-colonial politics.[4]

Initially, Mike hoped to busy himself through his prison term. The prison was a small town: it had both a farm and a factory that built furniture for federal government offices. Mike was excited to learn welding, until the assignment came to weld iron bars. *Fuck you, I'm in jail*, was his resignation. Maybe he could lathe? But he didn't want to make furniture for the people who, directly or indirectly, put him away. *I ain't making shit for you motherfuckers of any value.* His attitude once again cost him the job. He wound up doing jobs around the facility, cleaning bathrooms and staffing the library.

When he had unstructured time, Mike would listen to Pharoah Sanders and John Coltrane and think of home. He also developed a social life with other prisoners. He met Carmine DeSapio, the disgraced Tammany Hall leader convicted of bribing the New York water commissioner. Bobby Baker, Lyndon Johnson's former fixer, who was at Allenwood for larceny, fraud, and tax evasion, gave Mike a tip on a hot stock. Mostly, though, Mike divided his time between the Black population, most of whom were not COs, and the other activists, who tended to be white COs. (Mike found most of the other Black conscientious objectors, Muslims or Jehovah's Witnesses, disinclined to politics.) Mike was already crossing the line by spending time with white people—even if just the white people whose politics made them a nuisance to other white people. As prison systems nationwide confronted strikes and rebellions, Mike dared to see how far he could push against the capricious rules of prison life.

The prison order was maintained not just by guards and fencing but also by its racial hierarchy. "The Italians"—as those connected to the mafia were called—were the leading enforcers of the prison's racial divisions. According to the jeremiad circulating Allenwood, *You've got to look out for your own, and the Italians know how to do that.* Theirs was a predatory knowledge. When a Black prisoner everyone called Gucci was caught leaving Allenwood for a tryst at a nearby hotel, he was sent to solitary confinement at Lewisburg. Unofficial prison rules held that Black prisoners would recoup his property. Instead, the mafia claimed it. Irate, Mike went to Blinky Palermo, a Philadelphia mobster incarcerated for fixing boxing fights. *I don't mean to be disrespectful or anything*, Mike said, *but you've got to give us Gucci's stuff back.* Mike saw that Palermo looked disgusted. But he didn't say no. *You all know how this works*, Mike continued. *You all probably set the goddamn rule! That belongs to us. I'm not trying to be no tough guy.* Bravado and sincerity got the job done. Gucci's stuff was returned, and Mike's stock rose exponentially.[5]

Mike also partnered with white COs on another act to circumvent the mafia's hold on prison life. The Italians controlled the prison's informal economy of booze and drugs. Some prisoners labored long hours to make moonshine. The impressive coordination it took to make contraband alcohol was a large part of its allure. The mafia had quality liquor, plus drugs. Bob Eaton, a Quaker draft resister who had sailed medical supplies to Hanoi in 1967 to aid Vietnam against US aggression, had concocted a plan to break another blockade: the COs would sell alcohol inside, using the proceeds to support indigent prisoners who were being released. Mike liked the plan right away. *I'm sure glad you're a Quaker*, he told Eaton, *because you'd be a dangerous white dude.*

The plan itself was dangerous. Most contraband entered prison with staff, but that wasn't an option for the COs. They would use their family support. Most of the COs worked on the farm and so were familiar with the prison's landscape. They drew a map of the area, noting where to deposit the goods. Gwen packed a box of turkey, sweets, and a case of liquor. She loaded the box, and Aishah, in the car. The wife of another CO buckled in her two kids next to Aishah. Together they drove to Allenwood, hoping their kids wouldn't make a noise. They buried the illicit groceries and left without incident. Later, COs would load the box onto a farm truck and drive it back to the dormitories. Mike opened the package, excited for his first good meal in prison.

The mafia's extortion of other prisoners was made more egregious considering how little money prisoners had. Prison jobs paid between 17 and 42 cents an hour. Earning no more than $35 a month and having to buy food and supplies from the prison commissary, prisoners had little money to send home to their loved ones. Enforced desperation plus restricted liberty was a combustible frustration that exploded in prisons around the country. Prisoners in California had staged a series of labor and hunger strikes in 1968 and 1969, and 1970 saw a series of fatal encounters between guards and prisoners. There were prison uprisings in Carson City, Nevada, the New York City jail system, and Holmesburg, Pennsylvania, that summer. In New York, a group calling itself the Inmate Liberation Front took five guards hostage. Prisoners at New York's Attica and Leavenworth in Kansas went on strike for better pay.[6]

Two weeks after the Leavenworth strike began, signs appeared at Allenwood: NO WORK—SUPPORT LEAVENWORTH. More than half of the prison refused to go to work that day. More than three hundred people, over half the prison, joined the strike. Participants came from all of the prison's main social factions—except for the Italians, Jehovah's Witnesses, and Muslims, all of whom avoided organized politics.

Everyone at Allenwood was on their way home soon enough, which was normally enough incentive to quell any disturbance. The threat of extended prison time sent most people back to work. Mike was one of fifty-two people, mostly COs, to hold the line as long as they could, until prison officials isolated them from the rest of the prison. Still, the Bureau of Prisons had agreed to a 10 percent raise.[7]

When it was all over, someone approached Mike. Another Black prisoner, who called himself Prince and claimed to be African royalty, had helped break the strike. *He has to be punished*, the man told Mike. Mike was shocked—not opposed, though. That night, he hit the lights in the dorm while the other man whacked Prince on the behind with a two-by-four.

WHILE MIKE HELPED mete out retaliation behind bars, Gwen rushed sixteen-month-old Aishah to the hospital. She wouldn't stop crying, especially when she tried to stand. X-rays revealed that Aishah had a broken leg and a severe case of rickets. Her leg bones were bowed and porous. Gwen's family had already given her grief for being vegetarian throughout pregnancy and now during parenthood. She knew they would blame her for this. She already blamed herself.

The doctors at the children's hospital wanted to put Aishah on an experimental drug to cure the rickets. Gwen was dubious. With medical personnel threatening to call Child Protective Services, Gwen scooped up Aishah and left the hospital. Soon after, she broke down crying at a health food store. *My daughter can't walk and the hospital wants to experiment on her and I don't know what to do,* she sobbed when another customer asked after her. *Have you heard of homeopathy?* the other woman inquired. Gwen had not. The countercultural and natural foods movements of the era had begun to resuscitate the alternative medical practice that dates back to the 1700s and uses plants and minerals to stimulate the body's healing powers. With a bit of research, she located a homeopathic doctor in Philadelphia.

Walking into the office, she was nervous. It was in a white neighborhood, and the other clients were all white too. No one was friendly. *Mother, what is the problem with this child?* asked the doctor, an octogenarian with a thick German accent. She explained, including the hospital's prescribed course of action. *Mother, we can take care of this very easily.* That spooked Gwen—the hospital had given a severe diagnosis. But he affirmed her instincts. He quickly popped some white tablets in Aishah's mouth and turned to a stunned Gwen. *Mother, this child's appetite is going to increase rapidly.* Delirious but hopeful, she left his office. Within days, Aishah's appetite doubled and she began to heal rapidly. Besides getting Aishah's cast removed, Gwen wouldn't return to Western medicine. The homeopathy doctor became Aishah's pediatrician.

As she breathed a sigh of relief at Aishah's recovery, Gwen got an unexpected phone call from her former landlords. The couple, a Black man and a Chinese woman, were headed to Tanzania to work with the Peace Corps. They invited Gwen to move into the three-story Victorian home adjoining Gwen and Mike's old apartment. *What am I going to do with a whole twelve-room house and a baby?* Gwen asked. *Well, can't you get someone else to join you?* they offered. It was a novel idea. Gwen set out making her own freedom house.

Located at 3700 Spring Garden Street, the house soon became an all-Black commune. Cooking and cleaning were collectivized, everyone had a shift—even if some of the men needed to learn how. Everyone in the house was involved in some kind of political or cultural project, which brought them into contact with similar efforts elsewhere in the city. Gwen came to think of their house as a sister to a similar commune in the Germantown neighborhood, the Kazana Family. Gwen visited the Kazana house for an annual Kwanzaa celebration, an Afrocentric holiday founded by Ron Karenga in 1966. Based in Los Angeles, Karenga was the head of the US organization. While Karenga's group had fallen out of favor in some activist circles after some of its members killed two members of the Los Angeles Black Panther Party, Kwanzaa's popularity endured. The weeklong holiday honors a different principle each night, including Umoja (unity), Nia (purpose), and Imani (faith). Gwen attended Karenga's talk at the Kazana house. She liked the emphasis on African culture and Black solidarity, but she rebuffed efforts to entice her to join the Kazana group. She didn't want to get too close to an organization that endorsed polygamy and sidelined women's leadership.

Gwen loved the principles of Kwanzaa, however. Combining that ethos with a focus on natural foods, she and her housemates soon turned their house into a small-scale food co-op. People would place orders for bulk grains, legumes, and other dry goods. People would pick up their food at designated times from the covered porch in the backyard of the house. They dubbed the effort Ujamaa, a Swahili word meaning cooperative economics (and one of the seven principles of Kwanzaa). Ujamaa would soon grow too large for the house to handle and moved to the basement of the Church of the Advocate. Gwen also supported a local Black independent school that the Kazana Family ran. And the house itself, its big bay windows flushing light onto Gwen's many plants, functioned as its own little school for Aishah. She played hide-and-seek with aunties Ameenah and Mumina, her laughter breathing life into the old house.[8]

MEANWHILE, MIKE'S WORLD seemed to be getting smaller. Allenwood did not allow prisoners to make phone calls. Mike wrote letters and received visits, but the men around him were his primary social life. As he earned a reputation among prisoners for his bravery, Mike sought to be heard for his morality. *Don't take my TV*, he would advise people of their pre-prison antics. *Go to the TV store and take all the TVs.* As was true of the larger movement brewing among Black prisoners at the time, his was a message of solidarity, not legality. The pimps tried to maintain detachment, claiming they never harmed their own sisters. *But it's somebody's sister*, Mike replied.

In his first winter in prison, Mike tried to follow the moral vision of the arts that he identified in *Maji Maji* by writing a play about Black history. Black students around the country had transformed an early-twentieth-century idea of "Negro History Week" into something called Black History Month. It didn't yet have official buy-in, but students used it as an organizing opportunity. Mike hoped the play could educate fellow prisoners about the Black radical tradition. He never fancied himself a writer. But the prison was full of outcast autodidacts who learned to play guitar, write poetry, file lawsuits, or carve wood. Why couldn't he try his hand at being a playwright?

His play incorporated passages from notable figures like Frederick Douglass and W. E. B. Du Bois. He corralled other Black prisoners to perform it. A seasoned organizer, Mike felt confident at his directorial abilities. He neglected the artistic temperament: the men were late to rehearsal, if they showed up at all, and Mike fumed. *If you're going to be late, don't even bother me*, Mike threatened. But everyone kept at it, and they were able to perform it in front of the prison population.

When the next February drew near, Gucci asked Mike about doing another play. *No, man, it was too much trouble*, Mike said. *I don't feel like it.* Then Gucci was transferred out of Allenwood in retaliation for his off-campus departure, and others asked Mike to do something in his honor. He agreed, so long as the men took a more active role in its creation.

The result was *Mirror on Lennox Avenue*, a satirical look at the factors that sent people to prison. Ventriloquized through the characters and weaving in contemporary R&B music, the men reflected on the predatory crimes of poverty. As with Gwen's experience bringing the Freedom Southern Theater to Laurel in 1964, *Mirror on Lennox Avenue* was the first time many people, including the participants, had seen a play. Their appreciation for the performance redounded. The play drew from the well of prisoner talent: prisoners had written, performed, and designed the entire play. Mike marveled that the set, a silhouette of downtown Manhattan, was fit for Broadway.

If not Broadway, it was at least ready for Bucknell, the small liberal arts college located twenty minutes away. A Bucknell professor teaching a class on human rights and social movements had brought his class to Allenwood for the play. Afterward, he arranged for it to be performed at the university. That meant a night out of prison. Mike was elated. He set to work immediately: he doubled the speaking parts and stage directions so that more prisoners could enjoy a few hours reprieve from the institution. Several of the white COs now found themselves in *Lennox Avenue*, while people whose latent talents had never been recognized now set foot on a college campus as invited guests.[9]

Not long after *Mirror on Lennox Avenue* made its debut, another performance at Allenwood showed that cultural expression fostered a unity that prison officials would not tolerate. Some of Mike's comrades from the Steering Committee for Black Students at Temple University had formed a cultural group called Seeds of Blackness. In the two years of his incarceration, Mike remained an absent presence in SCBS, often invoked in conversations about strategy and focus. Now the group was coming to him.

Or at least they would try. Days before the planned performance, hundreds of prisoners marched to the visiting room to protest a disciplinary write-up two prisoners had received for not being in their beds at nighttime count. Then, the morning of the show, prison officials snatched up George Mische. Mische was one of the Catonsville Nine, a group of Catholic leftists who had destroyed almost four hundred draft files in Maryland in 1968, a major escalation of draft resistance. Mische waged a more minor rebellion at Allenwood, stealing fifteen hard-boiled eggs from the mess hall and then protesting a guard search of his property. When authorities placed Mische in a truck to transfer him out of the facility, a group of COs staged an impromptu sit-in to block them. Officials ultimately relented.[10]

Afterward, prison staff demanded that Mike cancel the Seeds of Blackness performance. He refused. *Well, if they come, we're not going to let them in*, the sergeant said. *So you've got to go down to the gate and tell them*. Mike refused again. *If you don't want them to come in, then you tell them*, he said. *But I'm not doing that*.

Magically, Seeds of Blackness was allowed in that night. About thirty SCBS members, together with some honorary members like Gwen, came. They brought with them large djembe drums and ornate costumes. (Allenwood wouldn't let them wear the metal ankle chains they usually performed in.) Mike greeted Gwen, his old SCBS comrades, and new recruits with equal enthusiasm. Before the incarcerated people had to take their seats separate from visitors, Mike thanked everyone for coming. The performance, titled *The Ritual*, began. It was an Afrocentric mixture of poetry, drumming, and dance. Performers reenacted slave revolts, chanted Claude McKay's legendary 1919 paean to resistance "If We Must Die," and celebrated Africa as the birthplace of civilization and its future. Mike delighted at seeing that even racist white prisoners there just for a night off were entranced. Cheering.

The Ritual always ended the same way: Seeds of Blackness performers danced out into the audience and brought people onstage to dance. Several prisoners tried their hands at the djembe drum. It was a jubilant affair, an orchestrated chaos the joy of which lingered into the evening.

The next morning, Mike and eighteen others—mostly conscientious objectors but also apolitical people Mike played chess with— were called into the visiting room. Guards in full riot gear, batons at the ready, loaded them onto a prison bus and sent them to what prisoners called The Wall: United States Penitentiary, Lewisburg.[11]

ONLY TWELVE MILES away from Allenwood, Lewisburg was a different world. It was a medium–maximum security prison, harsh and severe. It had cells, not dorms. At first, the prison held them seven or eight people to a cell. After they went on hunger strike, the prison transferred all of them to solitary confinement. The thick steel doors and isolation from the rest of the population undercut their ability to organize. Segregation was divided into five levels. Mike and his friends were in the most severe level: alone in a cell, sparse meals brought to them twice a day.

Mike joined a one-day work stoppage of prisoners while antiwar activists picketed outside the gates of Allenwood to protest the transfers. The well-connected parents of one CO persuaded Edward Brooke, a liberal Massachusetts Republican and the first Black politician popularly elected to the US Senate, to call Lewisburg. Soon, the prison began transferring people to other federal prisons around the country: Minnesota, Florida, Kansas, and as far away as California. Mike stayed—at Lewisburg, and in solitary. The only way out of solitary was to convince the prison's Adjustment Committee that you deserved it. At Mike's hearing, Allenwood's assistant camp administrator Ralph Jones sank his chances. *He's a troublemaker,* Jones advised Lewisburg staff. *He's always writing to his congressman and challenging the rules.* Even worse, Jones admonished, *He can talk his way out of anything. Don't listen to him.* They didn't. When guards caught Mike talking to another prisoner through the small windows of their cells, they marched the pair to the prison's boiler room and forced them to strip. The guards insulted them and threatened to beat them but ultimately sent them back to their cells unmolested.[12]

Gwen got reports on Mike from Fay Honey Knopp, a well-respected activist who visited as part of a Quaker prison fellowship. She also visited as soon as she could. It was their first visit in weeks, shrouded in a mutual but understated concern at his isolation. When he walked into the visiting room, Mike's chest tightened. He had been separated from most human contact, and the sight of Gwen overwhelmed him. His body tensed at the sight of her, the reminder of her, of life beyond the small cage in which he had been spending every day. If he gave in to his body's urge to cry, he might never stop. He barricaded his emotions behind shallow breath and pat assurances.

After Gwen left, officials moved Mike to the prison hospital. He had been on a water-only fast for three weeks, and they were starting to panic. Mike continued to refuse food in the hospital until Robert Thompson came in. Thompson was an Air Force veteran convicted in 1965 of sharing military information with the Soviet Union. *Is there anyone here named Simmons?* the husky thirty-five-year-old asked in the prison hospital. When Mike responded, Thompson shared the bad news. *I heard they're about to send you to Springfield*, he said, refer-ring to the federal prison hospital in Missouri. *They're going to declare you insane. And when they declare you insane, your time stops until you become sane again.* Mike had already seen other prisoners declared insane be made catatonic on Thorazine. Self-preservation kicked in. *Fuck the fast*, he thought.[13]

LEAVING THE PRISON, Gwen saw three people she knew who had been part of the retaliatory transfer from Allenwood. They were chained together and being placed on a prison bus to be transferred again. One of them was Prince, who had befriended Mike despite his role in breaking an earlier strike at Allenwood. *Tell my daughter where they're taking me*, he shouted to her. *They won't let me call her.*[14]

Gwen called Prince's daughter. She also reached out to people in Lewisburg on her own behalf. Of the more than six thousand people who lived in Lewisburg in 1971, fewer than one hundred were Black. Since Bucknell University was the other place Black people could be found in Lewisburg, Gwen sent a letter to Seventh Street House, the unofficial hub for Black students on campus, to see if they would house her during prison visits.[15]

Her first night at Seventh Street, Gwen stayed up until five a.m. talking with one of the Bucknell students who had been part of the class that saw *Mirror on Lennox Avenue* at Allenwood. The woman shared Gwen's spiritual hunger and recommended that Gwen visit a psychic in New York City. Gwen persuaded her roommate Agnes, a member of the Black Student League and close with Mike, to accompany her to the West Side apartment building where the psychic had her chapel.

Gwen didn't know what to expect as she and Agnes took the elevator to the fourth floor. When they arrived, a man in a small booth handed each of them a piece of paper and instructed them to write down their questions and place them in a wooden box. Gwen wrote down: *Is Michael going to be safe? Will Aishah be ok?* And: *Are you my teacher?*

Gwen and Agnes sat in a pew in the back row. Slowly, the chapel filled up. And then the psychic, a small woman of about fifty with a thick accent Gwen placed as Italian, appeared and took her seat in a raised bench above the pews, like a judge. Gwen and Agnes grew indignant as one by one the psychic called on everyone else to sit with her until only Gwen and Agnes remained. *I saved you all for last*, she said at their grimaced looks. And then she began to answer their questions. To Agnes, perpetually struggling with money, Reverend Calli assured her, *You are going to become a very rich woman, and you're going to have an incredible life.* Agnes and Gwen almost laughed at the idea. Her reassurances continued as she turned her attention to Gwen. *Your husband did nothing wrong*, she said. *He has no business being in that prison. He's innocent, but he will be taken care of.* Gwen exhaled. *Your daughter will be healed. You will heal her.* Gwen's skepticism mixed with hope. Finally, the psychic told Gwen that her teacher was on his way. *He's coming very soon for you. He is so beautiful, and he may be the only one of his kind left in the world.*

Driving back to Philadelphia, Gwen and Agnes did not know what to think. They could not know that Agnes would soon become a millionaire CEO and Gwen would indeed find her teacher. An act of generosity at Lewisburg federal penitentiary would help lead her to him.[16]

PRISON REFRACTED MIKE's love of rebellion through an appreciation for what encouraged people to act in service of others. That
was a central theme of his voracious reading inside, whether *Zen
in the Art of Archery* or *Soledad Brother*, an epistolary book by a California prisoner named George Jackson. At eighteen, Jackson had
been sentenced to serve between one year and life in prison after a
$70 gas station robbery. In January 1970, Jackson was one of three
Black prisoners charged with murdering a Soledad guard in retaliation for a guard's murder of three Black prisoners. In tracing Jackson's own evolution as a political thinker, largely in the confines of
solitary confinement, *Soledad Brother* summarizes the explosion of
Black radicalism in prison. "There are still some blacks here who
consider themselves criminals—but not many," Jackson writes. "This
camp brings out the very best in brothers or destroys them entirely."[17] In the final letter, Jackson pays tribute to his seventeen-year-old
brother, who attempted to free another three Black prisoners from a
California courtroom on August 7, 1970. Police killed most of the
group, including Jonathan Jackson, as they attempted to flee.

Soledad Brother* exploded in Mike's mind. Much as the record of
Malcolm X offered Gwen succor from the desolation of Mississippi,
Soledad Brother rescued Mike from incarceration. He couldn't believe
that Jackson could tarnish the prison system so boldly and still live
within it. Jackson often signed his letters "from Dachau with love,"
likening the racism of the American penal system to the Nazi concentration camp, whose name Mike had not heard until then. Jackson lacked Mike's movement experience but had arrived at a similar
conclusion of its potential for togetherness. "If there is any basis for a
belief in the universality of man," Jackson declares, "then we will find
it in this struggle against the enemy of all mankind."[18]

Less than a month into Mike's time at Lewisburg, San Quentin
guards shot and killed Jackson during a bloody uprising on August
21, 1971, in which five others were also killed. Three weeks later,
more than a thousand people incarcerated at Attica prison in New
York seized the prison's D-yard. They had taken several guards as

hostages and proceeded to issue a series of demands for better wages, religious freedom, the right to organize, access to education and healthy food, and an end to censorship. "We are men," L. D. Barkley told the assembled media. "We are not beasts and we do not intend to be beaten or driven as such. The entire prison populace, that means each and every one of us here, has set forth to change forever the ruthless brutalization and disregard for the lives of the prisoners here and throughout the United States."[19]

Mike's excitement at the uprising gave way to panic as New York officials refused to consider several of the prisoners' demands. Governor Rockefeller wouldn't even visit the prison. Mike broached the subject with his captors. *They're gonna kill those guards*, he told them. *You watch. They don't give a fuck about you. You're doing time too.*

On September 13, four days after the rebellion began, Mike's premonition came to pass. Rockefeller ordered state troopers to retake the prison. They gassed the D-yard and opened fire, killing twenty-nine prisoners and ten guard-hostages. Mike saw the sunken faces of his captors, who wouldn't admit that he was right.

We gotta do something here, several prisoners pleaded with Mike after the slaughter at Attica, in deference to his political experience. But he didn't have it in him. *They got this one, blood*, he replied. *Ain't shit we can do about that.*

Mike hadn't given up all hope, however. With eight other COs, he joined a lawsuit against the federal Bureau of Prisons. Weeks after the Attica massacre, Mike was in court for a hearing. Brought by a team of COs, the lawsuit alleged that the men were denied an opportunity to challenge or appeal the prison's decision and punished more harshly as a result of their political motivations. On the witness stand, the warden likened himself to Captain Bligh, saying he had to prevent a mutiny. But Mike enjoyed reconnecting with his troupe of troublemakers, and even the admission of the "mutiny" seemed like a fitting testament to the collective power they had built inside. Both the trial judge, a Nixon appointee, and the Third Circuit Appellate Court upheld that depiction of events.[20]

LIKE GWEN ON the streets, spirituality helped Mike process his surroundings. Though he maintained a respectful relationship with the Muslims in prison, he kept his distance from the Nation of Islam. Before he went to prison, Mike and Gwen both were concerned to hear that some people connected to the Philadelphia NOI were selling drugs, committing robberies, even assassinating rivals. The couple even hoped they might reform the local branch—until Jeremiah told Mike to back off. Not everyone in their group stood down, however, as Mike discovered when Gwen reported that their friend had been beaten with an iron pipe for criticizing the local NOI minister.

He continued to return to matters of the spirit. An older Black man being released after more than two decades passed on his books to Mike. Among them were the collected works of Indian musician Hazrat Inayat Khan. In the early twentieth century, Khan had traveled England and the United States lecturing on mysticism and harmony. Mike found the books soothing, and Khan's origins cemented Mike's fascination with India. Khan wrote of a divine universalism present in music, saying that music "contains the fountain of all knowledge within itself."[21]

Mike knew that Khan's approach would speak even more to Gwen. On her next visit, Mike arranged for a friend working in the prison kitchen to include the book on her lunch tray. Gwen had lined Aishah's diaper bag with plastic and she placed the book under this protective cover. When she opened the book back in Philadelphia, she did not simply read it. Gwen felt as if Khan materialized next to her, reading his books to her directly. The words came alive, began to fill a deep longing she had within her. In Khan's mystical teaching, she found the divine present within her—if only she could access it. "In all things there is God," Khan wrote, "but the object is the instrument, and the person is life itself." God was not found in the edicts of Baptist priests and Muslim ministers, nor in the teachings of the stars. God resides within. "Self is the wall between you and justice," he wrote.[22]

Alive with possibility, Gwen couldn't wait to go back to prison—to continue sneaking out each volume of Khan's collected works.

GWEN CONTINUED TO seek out a teacher to guide her but found Santeria and Yoruba rituals did not speak to her. She had been taking yoga in the Germantown neighborhood of Philadelphia with Virginia Demby, the only Black woman yoga teacher Gwen knew. At the end of class, Demby welcomed Mohamed Maroof to greet the class. Originally from Ceylon, Maroof was a graduate student studying anthropology at the University of Pennsylvania. He wanted to bring a guru from Ceylon to the United States. *His message can help solve the racial issues in this country*, Maroof offered. He needed people to sponsor the visa. Maroof passed around a picture of and pamphlets by the guru, Bawa Muhaiyaddeen. Gwen liked what she read and felt connected to the slender man of peace whose soulful eyes met hers through the picture. She agreed to cosponsor Bawa's visa.[23]

Two months later, not long after testimony in Mike's lawsuit wrapped up, Gwen eagerly joined the four-car caravan to the airport. Bearing flowers and enthusiasm, a dozen adults and four children awaited Bawa at the airport. Bawa was a slender man with a white beard and, to Gwen's eyes, radiating light. The first person he approached was Aishah, sitting in her stroller, head back in wonderment. He gently kissed each of her cheeks. Gwen's knees turned wobbly as he greeted her. She saw not his face but a luminous power surround her as she tried not to faint.

The group drove back to Maroof's house on Forty-Sixth and Pine in West Philadelphia. Bawa began a discourse, talking to the assembled group for the next several hours in Tamil, as Maroof or Bawa's travel companions translated. Of Gwen, he said, *I've been watching you for many years, and I have seen you go up to that prison. I see you in a little car driving up that mountain. Sometimes it's quite dangerous for you—snow and ice on the roads. Your husband has no reason to be in prison. He hasn't done anything, and I'm working to get him out.*

It was the first thing he said to her. She was transfixed. She would be with him almost every day over the next eight months. Daily he would speak with whatever crowd had assembled—first at Maroof's house and then in a house that disciples rented across the street to serve as his temple. So connected was he with the energy around him, his advisors said, that he did not need food. Besides drink tea and smoke cigarettes, Gwen only saw him eat garlic or the occasional mango slice. Everyone called him *guru* or simply Bawa.

And he in turn gave them names too. One day, he looked at Gwen and spoke. His translator relayed the words. *God puts half the beauty of the constellations in Zoharah and her son. That's your name. Zohar* means "splendor." It appears in Hebrew, Persian, and Arabic, always connected to light or stars. Like the light she saw when Bawa arrived, like the stars she gazed at as a twelve-year-old girl wondering why the world had such suffering. She shed "Gwendolyn" and her decades of searching for the divine. She was now Zoharah. Her teacher had arrived.

IN THE LAST weeks of his incarceration, Mike finally made it out of the maximum security unit to the dairy farm at Lewisburg. From midnight to seven a.m., he worked cleaning out the prison's coal heater. The actual labor didn't take that long, however, and he relished the time alone to read and think. To plot what was next.

And then it came. On February 11, 1972, Mike waited eagerly. Impatiently. After two and a half years in federal prison, he was going home. Prison rules held that returning citizens were entitled to twenty-five dollars and a jacket. The jacket type depended on the weather. Though it was still winter, authorities offered him only a thin trench coat. He demanded the heavier jacket that he had seen others wear. *I want the peacoat*, Mike insisted. *I'm not leaving until I get my peacoat.*

When Gwen arrived at the prison with Aishah, Mike's brother Reginald, and several friends, Mike was wearing a peacoat. He had won his final fight against the prison system. He was free.

Rhoda Bell Temple Douglass, Zoharah's grandmother, circa 1930s. CREDIT: *courtesy of Aishah Shahidah Simmons family collection.*

Mike and his mom, Rebecca White Simmons, at the beach in Atlantic City, circa 1956. CREDIT: *courtesy of Aishah Shahidah Simmons family collection.*

Gwen, the project director, measures a window while SNCC volunteer Ulysses Everett prepares the ceiling at the first Laurel COFO office during Mississippi Freedom Summer. CREDIT: *photograph by Marian Davidson, courtesy of Zoharah Simmons.*

When police attacked a voting rights demonstration in Selma, Mike co-organized a protest of Temple University students, March 1965. CREDIT: *Special Collections Research Center, Temple University Libraries, Philadelphia, PA.*

After mass arrests during a protest against the Mississippi legislature, demonstrators sing freedom songs while incarcerated at the Mississippi State Fairgrounds, June 1965. CREDIT: *Getty Images/ Bettmann.*

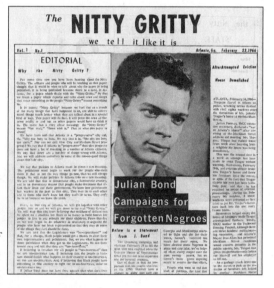

The inaugural issue of *Nitty Gritty,* the Atlanta Project newspaper, spotlights the fight for Julian Bond's congressional seat and protests against evictions in Vine City. CREDIT: *courtesy of the New York Public Library.*

Mike and Gwen in June 1968, a few months after they relocated to Philadelphia. CREDIT: *courtesy of Aishah Shahidah Simmons family collection.*

Gwen and Aishah picnic on East River Drive in Philadelphia, circa 1970. CREDIT: *courtesy of Aishah Shahidah Simmons family collection.*

Mike and Aishah celebrate his release from prison, February 11, 1972. CREDIT: *photograph by Dwight Williams, courtesy of Aishah Shahidah Simmons family collection.*

With Zoharah behind him, a seated Bawa addresses his community of supporters at their newly acquired headquarters, circa 1973. CREDIT: *photograph by Carl Marcus, courtesy of Bawa Muhaiyaddeen Fellowship of Philadelphia.*

Michael during his visit to India, April 1974. On the far left is T. S. Sundaram, the Quaker activist who coordinated the trip, and Bessie Williamson, one of the other Third World Coalition members on the trip. CREDIT: *courtesy of Michael Simmons.*

Michael, third from left, with the rest of the planning committee for the National Minority Marxist-Leninist Conference in Detroit, June 1979. Tyree Scott is on the far right. CREDIT: *University of Washington Libraries, Special Collections, SOC4904.*

Michael cuddles his newborn son, Tyree Cinque Simmons, spring 1979. CREDIT: *photograph by Dina Portnoy, courtesy of Dina Portnoy.*

A poster advertising the founding convention of the National Black Independent Political Party in Philadelphia, November 1980. CREDIT: *courtesy of Sylvia Wright.*

Zoharah reunites with Mrs. Spinks at her Laurel home during the thirtieth anniversary of Mississippi Freedom Summer, 1994. CREDIT: *photograph by Aishah Shahidah Simmons, courtesy of Aishah Shahidah Simmons family collection.*

Zoharah in Beijing with other members of the American Friends Service Committee delegation, plus two women from Japan, at the United Nations Fourth World Conference on Women, 1995. CREDIT: *courtesy of Claire Jung Jun Yoo.*

Michael delivers a press conference in Budapest following the Roma–African American exchange, December 1995. He is sitting between former SNCC organizer Fay Bellamy and Roma activist—and future member of the Hungarian Parliament—Aladár Horváth. CREDIT: *courtesy of Michael Simmons.*

Zoharah received her PhD from Temple University in 2002—forty years after she began as a freshman at Spelman College. She is joined by her mother, Juanita Cranford. CREDIT: *courtesy of Zoharah Simmons.*

Michael celebrates his birthday in 2016 with his children, Aishah, a filmmaker, and Tyree, better known as DJ Drama. CREDIT: *courtesy of Aishah Shahidah Simmons family collection.*

Michael, Aishah, and Zoharah Simmons at the #FromNO2Love conference, Philadelphia, October 2019. CREDIT: *photograph by Becca Haydu, courtesy of Aishah Shahidah Simmons family collection.*

PART III

THE KEY OF LIFE

CHAPTER TWELVE

FRIENDS AND COMRADES

MIKE WAS WELCOMED BACK TO PHILADELPHIA WITH A BIG party. Amid the reverie, friends encouraged him to ease into civilian life. But he was eager to make up for lost time. *I'm about my father's business*, he had once teased his mother, echoing what a young Jesus told Mary—only now in service of explaining his commitment to the freedom struggle. With prison in his rearview mirror, that intensity magnified. Thanks to Dwight's credit card, he had an all-new wardrobe. He wanted to work and to travel. The revolution lay ahead.

Within a month of his release, he got a job as deputy director of Safe Streets Philadelphia. Funded in part by a federal grant authorized by the War on Crime, Safe Streets attempted to ease tensions between rival gangs throughout North and West Philadelphia. Mike's former boss Wilson Goode helped get him an interview. At $12,000 a year, Mike was making more money than he ever thought possible.

He was also bored out of his mind. He had to wear a tie and sit in an office. Four months into his tenure there, Mike was invited to become the organizational director after the board fired the former police officer occupying that role. The promotion would nearly double his salary. He declined.[1]

Instead, in October 1972, he took a job with the American Friends Service Committee (AFSC), the Quaker peace and justice organization. Any child of Philadelphia is at least provisionally acquainted with Quakers. William Penn, who established the commonwealth of Pennsylvania with Philadelphia as its beacon, was a Quaker. Originating in seventeenth-century England as the Religious Society of Friends, the Quaker faith espoused a pacifist and nonhierarchical Christianity. Instead of a minister to guide them, Friends believed that everyone had a bit of God—a light—in them. (Detractors said that Friends "quaked" at the word of God, and the name stuck.) The AFSC began in 1917 as an alternative service for Quakers opposed to World War I, and by the 1970s it comprised an activist expression of Quakerism. Many of the bravest activists Mike was incarcerated with at Allenwood were Quakers, often from the Philadelphia area, as were some of their staunchest supporters.[2]

Mike was excited to learn that his neighbor Rosemary Cubas was working at the AFSC with an auspicious new entity called the Third World Coalition (TWC). Borrowing the term that had provided a conceptual unity for the national liberation struggles across the decolonizing world in Africa, Asia, and Latin America, the Third World Coalition aimed to provide the infrastructure for coalitional work among Black and other people of color supported by the AFSC— and to shift the AFSC in the process. Though the AFSC had a long history of work in nonwhite communities, the staff remained mostly white. That began to change as a number of people like Rosemary, who cut their teeth in the civil rights, anti-war, and feminist movements of recent years and now looked for ways to make social justice their career as well as their calling, joined the staff. The AFSC offered these young militants an organization rooted in consensus decision-making and a philosophical commitment to nonviolence. It was also an office job at a historically white organization whose sense of justice—and funding— originated in the pacific and at times paternal doctrine of Quakerism.

The TWC formed in 1971 with the hope that it would provide the vehicle through which the AFSC hired more people of color and would act as an anti-racist compass for AFSC programs. It became a standing body of the AFSC a year later. The Third World Coalition harmonized the insights of the Atlanta Project's Black Consciousness Paper with the principles of national liberation struggles in Africa and Asia. "The principle of self-determination is a right of Third World peoples to have complete control over decisions which affect their lives," an early memo declared. "As regards programs operating within Third World communities it is essential . . . that Third World people involved have total decision and policy making powers." Their goal, TWC staff later admitted, was to be a "formalized pain in the ass" to the AFSC.[3]

The AFSC seemed as good a place as any for Mike to ply his revolutionary trade. Mike applied for an opening in the Community Relations Division, the branch of the AFSC that supported domestic initiatives. The head of the program was Barbara Moffett, who in 1963 had persuaded the AFSC to print ten thousand copies of Martin Luther King's until-then obscure "Letter from Birmingham Jail," which offered a poignant critique of white moderates and championed the use of direct action. Almost a decade later, Moffett was trying to challenge the moderates within AFSC. Notwithstanding its strong human rights stand, the organization preferred to hire Quakers to leadership positions. This practice kept the organization mostly white. Moffett, a white woman who was not a Quaker, tried to expand the organization in an effort to make it more responsive to the communities it aimed to serve.

The job opening was for the national representative for housing and employment—*two issues I know absolutely nothing about*, Mike thought as he applied. He was eager to learn. The job involved supporting social movement campaigns around the country, linked through the AFSC's ten regional offices. First he had to make it through the interview. Mike had one-on-one meetings with more than two dozen Quakers over three days. Each meeting surfaced similar questions. *Are you committed to nonviolence? What about if someone is attacking your mother?*

Mike was repulsed at the needling questions. He wondered if white applicants had their nonviolent pedigree questioned with similar intensity. But his excitement for a job doing social change won out. He got hired, at $8,500—almost a third less than what he had been making at Safe Streets. He traded in the tie that had been part of the stifling attire of Safe Streets Inc., but kept a bit of professionalism as he introduced himself as Michael.

Two AND A half years in prison well acquainted Michael with living communally. Now he got to live collectively. His body eased into the comfort that comes from the removal of arbitrary authority. It tensed again when he realized he would have to cook for a full house. (Zoharah helped at first.) Besides Zoharah and his Black Student League comrade Agnes—who had now taken the name Ameenah, courtesy of Bawa—Michael had little prior relationship with the other people living in the house. Even Aishah greeted him as a part stranger. *This is Mommy's room*, she confronted him soon after his return. *What are you doing here?*

It was a question he was increasingly asking himself. Zoharah was spending most of her days listening to Bawa's discourses in West Philadelphia. At times, Michael accompanied her. Bawa even named him Hamza: lion, brave. But Michael stuck with the name his parents had given him. He was turned off by the intensity of the devotion surrounding Bawa. As a kid, Mike hated the few hours his parents forced him to spend at church each week. But at least he could wait out the clock. Sessions with Bawa lasted as long as the spirit moved him. It grated on Michael's patience.

He was also increasingly frustrated at those who had come to learn from Bawa. Zoharah first told Michael about Bawa when he was still in prison. Mauroof, the Dembys, and Zoharah were effective recruiters: The people going to hear Bawa were largely Black.

Zoharah brought several people from the Black Student League and from Ujaama Co-Op. Yet by the time Michael got out of prison, the community around Bawa was largely white. And as he saw some of these devotees worship at the feet of this holy man, imbuing him with supernatural authority, he lost any fleeting interest he once had.

Meanwhile, Zoharah's commitment to Bawa deepened. She proposed to Michael that they embrace celibacy as an opportunity to enhance their spiritual pursuits. Michael already felt that Zoharah had abandoned him for Bawa. Now he was being asked to sacrifice another facet of their relationship to embark on a journey that was not his own.

This is your thing, he told her. *You've been searching, in one way or another, since I've known you. I'm not driven to this like you are.* The fellowship was hers, he knew that. And it was not his, she now saw.

Bawa held their hands in his, consecrating a new phase in their relationship. *You are soulmates,* he declared. And then, to Michael, *Have patience with her as she heals from this heartbreak.*

Within a few months, Michael moved to an apartment—a few blocks from the house where Bawa held his meetings, as it turned out, though he did not return there. No lawyers, no paperwork accompanied the separation. As he left the commune, Michael and Zoharah hugged and wished each other well.

When Michael's mother heard the news, she affirmed Bawa's determination. *You married your sister,* she said of her beloved daughter-in-law. Their bond was indeed permanent, joined by parenthood and principle. In the decades to come, each one would stay on freedom by bringing Black Power politics to ever-widening geographies. They shared, broadly, an outlook on the world's problems and an abiding commitment to transformation. They would compare notes often. Yet theirs would be parallel journeys.

MICHAEL'S EXPERTISE LAY not in the specifics of housing policy or employment law but in knowing which way the wind was blowing. In the early 1970s, he felt the gale of an insurgent labor movement.

While he was doing much the same in prison, workers in the early 1970s staged a series of uproarious strikes. In 1970 alone, there were more than 5,000 strikes involving more than 3 million workers—one-sixth of the nation's union members. Yet the strikes, which targeted both private industry and the public sector, were often organized independently of traditional unions. Most dramatically, 150,000 postal workers walked off the job in an illegal strike in 1970. There were 1,400 strikes in 1972, a quarter of them wildcats. Autoworkers, steel workers, coal miners, construction workers, and others were revolting. Black workers were particularly in the lead against racist trade unions that upheld a segregated labor market and, with it, private white wealth.[4]

Michael was particularly inspired by what was happening in Seattle. The city was in the midst of a deep recession when he first visited in October 1972, shortly after starting at the AFSC. His host was a man named Tyree Scott. Gregarious and focused, Tyree was a Marine veteran from Texas who never finished high school. He was also an electrician, which should have been a boon in Seattle at the time, given the federal grants the city had received under the Model Cities program. Yet both contractors and local unions blocked Black workers in the building trades from being apprenticed, hired, or given the same hours. At the time, all but 29 of the 14,821 members of the Seattle building trades were white. The racist local economy worsened when Boeing, the largest employer in the region, laid off more than 60,000 people in three years, leading to massive unemployment and exodus from the city. As Michael was preparing to enter prison in the late summer of 1969, Tyree was organizing dramatic protests that disabled construction vehicles at the University of Washington and leading more than a hundred people onto the tarmac at Sea-Tac Airport to protest Black workers' exclusion from the construction trades.[5]

Tyree worked with the Seattle AFSC office to outline a campaign to break Jim Crow unionism. Already, Tyree's efforts had prompted a Department of Justice lawsuit against five Seattle trade unions that, in June 1970, led to an ambitious court ruling to open employment opportunities for Black workers. A month later, he was head of a new effort, supported by the local AFSC, to mobilize Black worker power through an organization called the United Construction Workers Association (UCWA). Unions dragged their feet on court-ordered integration. Even in the Central District, the historic Black neighborhood created out of decades of redlining, construction crews were all white. Tyree led a series of shutdowns to block segregated construction sites— much like the one Mike attended in high school, his first protest. As the UCWA grew, it drew in Chinese and Filipino American workers too. With the mantra *What would the workers do?* Tyree's unshakable faith in the brilliance of ordinary workers proved inspiring.[6]

Some in the AFSC were anxious to see how these two intemperate men, a conscientious objector just out of prison and a Marine leading his troops into battle, both possessed by great urgency, would get along. Michael arrived late on a Thursday. The next night, Tyree took him to Beacon Hill School so that they could join a sit-in being carried out by Chicana/o activists in demand of a community center. They spent the night there, surrounded by other Black workers from UCWA and Asian American radicals joined in solidarity with the Chicana/o organizers. Despite the overwhelming whiteness of Seattle, the movement there seemed a physical manifestation of the Third World Coalition precept. *This is a liberated zone*, Michael marveled of multiracial Seattle. And Tyree was his new best friend.[7]

IN THE DECADE since John Kennedy had first used the phrase "affirmative action" to identify the principle of nondiscriminatory hiring, the concept was subject to the whims of judges and political appointees. At the Department of Labor, Washington state Black Republican Arthur Fletcher implemented a plan that established minimum goals for hiring Black workers on federal construction projects. Yet Fletcher's boss, Richard Nixon, courted the support of reactionary white construction workers who attacked the anti-war movement.

Tyree and the UCWA saw in affirmative action a vehicle for working-class power. They would use the law as a fulcrum to unite Black workers and remake the building trades. Their way in was through Title VII of the 1964 Civil Rights Act, which outlawed employment discrimination on the basis of "race, color, religion, sex or national origin." While the public recognition of the Civil Rights Act focused on education and public accommodations, Title VII covered workers. It had already given birth to the UCWA after a judge ruled that Seattle labor unions had violated its provisions. In the summer of 1973, a $75,000 grant from the Equal Employment Opportunity Commission (EEOC) provided the UCWA a chance to bring its method south. Created through the 1964 Civil Rights Act, the EEOC expanded its mission as a result of the 1972 Civil Rights Act. Along with the money, the EEOC gave UCWA population breakdowns of several counties in the South. Tyree and UCWA member Todd Hawkins selected seven cities that ringed Arkansas, Louisiana, Oklahoma, and Texas. Their plan was to use Title VII not only as a legal avenue against segregated employment practices but also as a political method to bring Black workers together.[8]

Michael was a quick study on the intricacies of Title VII. New for him was organizing people as workers. In SNCC his focus had been the community, working mostly with high school youth and their parents to contest social and educational marginalization. At Temple he organized other students; in prison, other prisoners. Now the workplace was the terrain—and with it, the economy. With Todd and Tyree, he hoped to use affirmative action to build the power of Black workers.

Michael's official job duties included administrative support for the project, particularly in the form of helping secure grants to support its efforts. Todd and Tyree traveled widely throughout the South. Michael joined them in the field as much as he could, meeting with attorneys and churches in a series of midsized Southern cities with Jim Crow economies. As the one with the office job and almost four years of college, Michael often got the most respect from some of the professionals they met in places like Tulsa and Shreveport. As the office worker and youngest of the group, Michael had to ride in the back of the tiny sports car that the trio drove across the South.[9]

Michael was thrilled to join sixty workers from across the region at a planning meeting in Dallas in July 1973 for what became the Southwest Workers Federation. By December, three hundred people—the vast majority of them workers from project locations—attended what Michael thought of as a constitutional convention of Black labor militancy. "Our ancestors were used by the man as free labor," Michael said in his opening remarks. Now, he advised, Black workers were in control. "We should not just push for better jobs, we need to build a base, for instance, an economic base, from which we can care for and about one another, help our brothers and sisters. No one *gave* us the EEOC or Title VII—*we* got them. Government is working for *you*, it is *your* servant. *You* deserve applause, not some government heavy."[10]

The federation hoped to harness affirmative action laws as a tool to empower Black workers. The strategy called for use of the courts, but it was not primarily a legal effort. Rather, the law was an organizing tool. *The UCWA is merely a catalytic agent*, Tyree told Michael. Its job was to *demystify the law*. Antidiscrimination lawsuits might provide temporary relief, but the federation viewed them as successful only to the extent that workers could better fight their own battles. Above all, Tyree hoped that the workers set the agenda. Even some movement lawyers were loath to give up their power. But in the Southwest Workers Federation, they took a back seat to the workers. *Poor people should be able to treat their lawyers like rich people treat their lawyers— they tell them what to do*, Tyree liked to say. The law was a tactic, to be utilized by workers as it served them. The federation would train the lawyers, both on how to file Title VII discrimination claims and on how such claims advanced the Black working class. And indeed, the federation filed more EEOC complaints than the understaffed agency could handle. Even local attorneys found it hard to keep up. Each new claim demonstrated a renewed self-possession among Black workers at American Airlines and Reynolds Aluminum, at Olin Kraft and the St. Francis Hospital, and other sites across the region.[11]

When Michael had first gone to Arkansas in 1965, the duplicity of the local FBI convinced him that the movement could not pin its hopes on turning the hearts of those in charge. Returning to Arkansas, and neighboring areas, in 1973 reinforced his belief that the struggle was about transformation and that oppressed people needed to lead the charge. In a note to federation staff, Michael reminded them that the fight was not about jobs. "Finally, we should remember that there was a time when Black people were guaranteed employment, food and shelter and it was called slavery," he wrote. "We must not settle for wage-slavery but should fight for power over our lives."[12]

MICHAEL RELISHED ALL the travel required by his new job. Besides his time in the South, he traveled to other AFSC projects. There were times when he flew between Denver and Philadelphia twice in a seven-day period. He went to Seattle so much that he was sure some thought he lived there. If it weren't for his daughter and his mother—both of whom he saw as much as he could, often together—Michael would have moved to Seattle.

Travel brought him into contact with the broader possibilities of the Third World. Michael had come into the TWC believing African Americans to be the prototypical victims of racism and thus uniquely positioned to end it. The smattering of Puerto Ricans around the Black Student League or Asian Americans in SNCC were partisans of the Black struggle. He thought the Hispanic people he saw in popular culture—Desi Arnaz, Ricardo Montalbán—were white people with accents. Indeed, he was surprised to find that someone he and Zoharah knew as a white woman in SNCC, Elizabeth Sutherland from the New York Friends of SNCC office, was now Elizabeth "Betita" Martinez, a leading voice of the rising Chicana/o movement. She had hidden her Mexican ancestry to find work in the publishing industry.[13]

Beyond the refuge from the otherwise white world of the AFSC, the TWC offered a space of constant challenge. What did it mean to be Third World people and what was the basis of unity—both within the United States and between the United States and the rest of the Third World? Rosemary Cubas, the Third World Coalition staffer who lived near Michael and Zoharah's Spring Garden Street commune, suggested that racism was an insufficient basis for Third World unity. "For there are forces that put us in the position of oppressed and exploited minorities which also affect the continents we come from which go beyond race and which we must learn to recognize and fight in USA society, in these continents where it saps the vitality for development, as well as 'in ourselves' as products of this exploiting and dehumanizing society," Cubas wrote in a memo to TWC members. She outlined three such "forces": economics ("bread and butter, how we get it, who owns the means to produce it, and what happens when one person or country wants more?"), social relationships ("why and how we work together"), and political organization ("what structures do we create that will assure our participation in vital decisions affecting our lives"). Cubas maintained that racism was "a thread that runs throughout these forces but it is not the cause." And their resolution required a more cohesive restructuring of the economy in particular.[14]

Rosemary's economic emphasis reinforced what Michael learned from Tyree's approach. Tyree teased that Michael, decked in daishikis, was missing the Third World's promise. *Don't bring that Black nationalist shit out here*, Tyree mocked, referring to multiethnic Seattle as much as the South.

Increasingly, Michael brought a spirit of global solidarity with him. Having gone to prison out of the belief that the US Black freedom struggle was linked to anti-colonial movements around the world, Michael came primed for the TWC's framework. The existence of the TWC enabled interdivisional connections between the AFSC's domestic work, where all of the people of color were employed, and its white-staffed international campaigns. Soon after joining the staff,

Michael joined a South Africa Working Group to explore the possibilities of conducting education on apartheid, blocking US support for racist regimes there, and organizing for an "African nuclear-free zone." The TWC also developed campaign work in support of Puerto Ricans in the United States, another rising social movement of the early 1970s. After the US-backed military coup in Chile overthrew the democratically elected socialist president Salvador Allende, Michael worked with the Tulsa affiliate of the Southwest Workers Federation to hold a picket outside the federal building.[15]

Travel provided Michael the clearest indication that difference was the basis of Third World unity. Site visits to AFSC projects revealed that exploitations of land, labor, and body were not unique to African Americans. Michael accompanied AFSC staff from Brownsville, Texas, on a day trip to Mexico. Returning stateside, Michael breezed through without incident, only to watch the Border Patrol give his Chicano coworkers the third degree. Another trip sent him to a different kind of border town: Rapid City, South Dakota, the border between white settlers and Oglala Sioux. It was the closest city to the Pine Ridge Reservation, site of the infamous 1870 Wounded Knee massacre—and of a low-intensity warfare then unfolding between traditionalist Indians and the local, federal, and tribal governments. When Michael saw that local bars let him in but refused service to Native Americans, it was the first time he felt that people were being treated worse than Black people. And when he saw members of the American Indian Movement grab guns and hit the lights rather than accede to a threatened police search of the community center where they were meeting, he thought he might die with them too.[16]

THROUGHOUT HIS INCARCERATION, Mike's wildest hope was to go to India. Both Martin Luther King and Bayard Rustin had traveled to India, and coteries of radical pacifists in the United States had honored the Indian anti-colonial struggle in creating community centers they called ashrams. The country seemed to combine his fleeting spiritual interests with his pronounced political passions. *I have no idea*, he would say of his travel plans, *but I'm convinced that circumstances will take me there one day.*[17]

That circumstance arose in 1974. T. S. Sundaram, a member of the AFSC's International Affairs Program, shared with TWC members that they needed to engage with the geographical as well as the political dimensions of the Third World. Thanks to the British history of both Quakerism and colonialism, the Quakers already had a presence in India. The TWC agreed to send three people on a six-week delegation to the subcontinent. TWC decided the only fair way to select participants would be drawing names from a hat. Mike knew with all his heart that he would be on that trip. Sure enough, his name came out of the hat.

On March 1, 1974, Mike joined with Frank Sifuentes and Bessie Williamson for a three-day orientation at a Quaker retreat center outside Philadelphia to prepare for the trip. The trio would receive a crash course in Indian politics and culture, drawing on the resources of Quakers in the area. Bessie was a Black woman who worked in the financial department of the Philadelphia office, Frank a Chicano activist from Los Angeles. That same day, seven former aides to president Richard Nixon were indicted for conspiracy and, for many, obstruction of justice, related to an attempted cover-up of a 1972 break-in to the Democratic National Committee at the Watergate Hotel. Nixon himself was named as an unindicted coconspirator in the crime. It was the latest in a series of events that would set the stage for impeachment hearings and Nixon's resignation. But for now, Michael was more focused on India, a place that had felled not just a ruler but an empire.

In planning for the trip, Mike wanted to do it all. He wanted to visit a prison and talk with former political prisoners, to meet Hindus and Muslims, to visit cities and countryside, to meet young and old, right and left, artists and politicians. He barely slept across three flights and twenty-four hours, he was so excited. They arrived in Delhi along with the warm weather. The city burst with amber orange, forest green, and more people than Michael had ever seen. More than 3.5 million people lived in Delhi at the time, and their movements throughout the city produced a thick congestion.[18]

Their hosts in Delhi were well-to-do Quakers who lived in a posh house and had an ambivalent relationship to India. Mike fumed when one of them told him that starvation in the Sahel was *God's punishment for kicking the British out*. Nevertheless, they along with Sundaram had arranged an exciting catalog of dignitaries for the group to meet. The speakers included economists, social workers, industrialists, labor leaders, journalists, and prominent Quakers. In prison Mike had read biographies of Gandhi and Nehru and was eager to discuss revolutionary nonviolence and the transition from colony to sovereignty. But solidarity was not the watchword of the new nation in the way he had hoped. India had just finished a brutal war with Pakistan in 1971, and saber-rattling nationalism still lingered across religious divides. While the Quakers celebrated Gandhi as a beacon of nonviolent action, many of the Indians Michael was introduced to treated him as a symbol of Hindu national greatness. While there were fourteen languages spoken in India, religion seemed a growing chasm—along with the foundational difference of caste.

Mike made conversation with everyone he could, the Sikh cab drivers, the lower caste Hindus pulling the rickshaws, people on the streets he walked when not in meetings. The trip was conceived as a ten-thousand-mile "seminar on wheels" that spanned the subcontinent from Kashmir to Madras, and they traveled by many different kinds of wheels: horse-drawn tonga, taxi, bus, scooter, rickshaw, as well as trains, planes, even—when they got to Kashmir—a houseboat. The group met with Sheikh Abdullah, a Muslim politician and leader of Kashmir, who supported self-rule for the northern India territory. Michael liked him immensely. He also liked hashish, which he smoked for the first time aboard the houseboat.

The travel was exhilarating, the poverty relentless. Michael was uncomfortable being part of the weight that someone would pull with their bodies in the wooden rickshaws. He hated when the train stopped. Impoverished mothers would hold their babies, many of them visibly sick or disabled, up to the windows, begging for money. Michael did not want to look but could not look away.

The intensity of the poverty aligned with other troublesome observations. Among the people they met was a Christian missionary who promoted sterilization as a response to overpopulation. Even if she was an outlier, other problems could not be so easily dismissed. Michael was disturbed to see that women were not on the street after dark and rarely alone; people often assumed that Bessie was married to either Mike or Frank. His exposure to the caste system shocked him. It seemed to correspond, unevenly, to a color schema he felt he knew well from the United States. There were dark-skinned Brahmins, it's true, but no light-skinned Shudras or Dalits. Personal ads in the newspaper specified the desired caste and even color of their prospective dates. Yet many of the people they spoke with in the prearranged meetings justified the caste system. When Michael called the caste system racist, he was criticized for *bringing American reality to India. There was no animosity between castes*, people told him. *It is god's design.*[19]

MIDWAY THROUGH THE trip, Mike separated from the group and flew to Sri Lanka. Located off the southeastern tip of India, the island had gained partial independence from Britain in 1948, not long after India. Mike's mission there was personal: Bawa Muhaiyaddeen, Zoharah's guru, was back in his native country, which had recently shed its British name of Ceylon for Sri Lanka. Mike wanted to see Bawa in his own land. Maybe it would help him reconcile his separation from Zoharah—or send him back to her. He knew that she wanted to get back together, but he didn't know if he could coexist with her spiritual commitments. Bawa lived in the house of some well-to-do supporters in Jaffna where he spoke at length to devotees, much as in the United States. Michael's visit coincided with a delegation from the United States. All of the fifteen visitors were white except for

Zoharah's friend, who, like her, had stuck around through the demo-graphic shift. Bawa had given her the name Jeharah.

The delegation stayed at the house with Bawa, mostly sleeping on the floor and eating the communal meals provided by the hosts. Michael remained impressed with Bawa's unassuming simplicity and sincerity. He had no possessions, no fixed address, he slept little and ate less. He lived only through the generosity he asked others to share in the world. Yet that generosity seemed to flow in one direction. The seekers ignored the dark-skinned domestic worker who maintained the house. None thanked her for cleaning up after them, invited her to learn with Bawa, or otherwise acknowledged her presence. They just pretended she wasn't there. Mike thought about his own mother, who had worked as a domestic worker six days a week before he was born. He seethed at the disregard among the devoted, people so loyal to Bawa they slept at his feet but in their waking moments would not acknowledge a Black woman who cared for them. *Devotion to Bawa is an act of absolution for these people,* Michael thought about these white spiritual seekers.

He flew back to Calcutta newly resolved that the spiritual path would not be enough to change the material realm, knowing too that although he and Zoharah were forever bound together by their com-mitment to the movement and their daughter, that bond would never again be romantic.

Finally, the group was at Delhi's Palam Airport to begin their journey home. *I might never come back here again*, Michael thought. *I can't leave right now.* He bid adieu to his companions and went back into the Delhi night. He spent the next week revisiting some of the same locations and exploring new ones, now acting as his own tour guide. He hoped to go to Pakistan, but the tensions between the two countries prohibited the journey. He remained in India, soaking in all he could.

He returned to Philadelphia at the end of April 1974. "One of the main things I learned was how much I had to learn," Michael said in an AFSC statement about the trip. "For example, it wasn't clear what holds the people of India together. Was it religion? Skin color? Historic experience?" The AFSC circulated the press release on May 23, 1974. Five days earlier, in the desert of Rajasthan, India had exploded Smiling Buddha—its first nuclear bomb. And Michael was abandoning the metaphysical for a budding romance with Marxism.[20]

His new love blossomed quickly. Not long after his return from India, he joined the Philadelphia Worker Organizing Committee (PWOC), a communist group that formed out of the radical edge of the city's anti-war movement. PWOC combined union campaigns in the city's dwindling factories with international solidarity. Michael saw it as a local echo of what he and Tyree tried to build through the Southwest Workers Federation. International events as much as local ones steadied his faith in Marxism. In February 1976, he traveled to Cuba with twenty-five other US radicals, mostly Black, to meet with representatives of the Popular Movement for the Liberation of Angola (MPLA in Portuguese). The MPLA was battling both incursions from the racist apartheid regime in South Africa and US- and China-backed Angolan militias stoking civil war to destabilize the country.

He embraced communism alongside Tyree, who had gone on a twenty-eight-person delegation to China in 1975 and returned enthusiastic about its possibilities. By 1976, the two of them had become cochairs of the Third World Coalition at AFSC and, beyond that, leading members of an attempt to build a new communist movement in the United States. His days, and his nights and weekends, were filled with meetings of the most urgent task he could imagine: building mass movements to overthrow racism and capitalism.[21]

CHAPTER THIRTEEN

WATCHING OVER

LIKE MICHAEL, ZOHARAH FELT AWAKENED TO NEW POSSIBILITIES. At twenty-eight, she had spent almost two decades trying to reconcile her belief in the larger mysteries of existence with her frustration at what organized religion—whether Baptist or Islamic—failed to explain about human suffering. Her experiments with Yoruba, Rosicrucian, Zoroastrian, and astrological practices all left her seeking more.

In Bawa, this gentle prophet with piercing eyes and a warm smile, she began to find the fulfillment she had long sought. Slowly the insights she gleaned from him began to coalesce into a deeper truth: *We are spiritual beings living a human existence.* The spirit demanded nurturance that exceeded what religion could offer. Bawa preached a syncretic faith, drawing from elements of Christianity and Islam, together with Hinduism and Zoroastrianism, to come up with something his own. He hesitated to put a name to his teachings. Eventually, some in the community dubbed it Sufism—the mystical branch of Islam.

Zoharah shook with excitement at his insistence that "if a true human being is there, God is also there." The fog of uncertainty that first clouded her mind as a child growing up in segregated Memphis and asking why had begun to break. *Human beings can become God!* She was overcome with the revelation. Bawa was the teacher she had been waiting for, the one who could help her understand why she was put on this earth. She spent as much time with him as she could, pursuing answers to her biggest questions.[1]

Zoharah didn't grasp how much stress her time with Bawa caused at home. There was no programming to occupy the few children whose parents came to hear Bawa, and Aishah struggled to observe the reverential silence needed to allow Bawa's message about consciousness to reach the assembled seekers. Zoharah did not pay much heed to the fact that Michael, fresh out of prison, wasn't coming either. Bawa noticed. *Go be with your husband*, he encouraged her. But when someone announced that *Guru Bawa is speaking*, Zoharah was at her teacher's side.[2]

MICHAEL AND ZOHARAH's separation initiated a larger turnover. Zoharah recruited two other single moms from the Bawa Muhaiyaddeen Fellowship, as the community now called itself, to move into her house. She also rejoined the workforce. She got a job at the RW Brown Boys and Girls Club in North Philadelphia as a "drug prevention officer." The position was funded by a federal grant, part of an escalating concern over both heroin and marijuana that had, in 1971, become targets of a national war on drugs. While encouraging the government to adopt "a period of 'benign neglect'" when it came to addressing inequality, Republican orthodoxy stressed a punitive approach to disorder. Republicans rallied behind boosting arrests and incarceration. Politicians from President Richard Nixon to New York governor Nelson Rockefeller led this get-tough push around drugs that echoed support for punitive policing. The leading avatar of this position at the local level was Philadelphia's new mayor, Frank Rizzo. The former police commissioner, who called himself "the toughest cop in America," had a long track record of terrorizing Philadelphia's Black community. He campaigned exclusively in white neighborhoods and was elected under the vaguely menacing slogan "Rizzo means business." Nixon's most prominent Democratic supporter, Rizzo took office two months after the War on Drugs launched.[3]

But drugs were not just a right-wing concern. Black activists had spoken with increasing alarm about drugs, particularly heroin. In New York, the Black Panther Party described heroin as a plague and "the scourge of the Black colonies of Babylon," and a BPP offshoot, the Black Liberation Army, targeted drug dealers along with police as sources of oppression. Zoharah's former SNCC comrade H. Rap Brown was arrested in October 1971 for an alleged robbery of a drug den on the Upper West Side. Other community activists took aim at the heroin trade by pressing for greater law enforcement.[4]

Zoharah saw drugs like heroin as a scourge that sapped political potential. Her work at the Boys and Girls Club involved both children and parents in the neighborhood around the community center, a few blocks from Temple University. Her SNCC training informed her work, especially with kids. She felt certain that a prideful embrace of Black history would empower kids to make positive decisions. She set about trying to build her own Freedom School, teaching children Black history. She prompted them to create plays, poems, and talent shows—performances that would bring even the most suspicious parents to the community center, where Zoharah also delivered "parent-effectiveness trainings" from scripted programs provided through the federal grant that funded her job. When funds and timing allowed, she took the kids on field trips to the local zoo or the art museum, foreign lands in the city they called home. She even hosted sleepovers for some of the girls at her house.

The job required a new layer of coordination for her personally. She and Michael were sharing a car, a green Volkswagen, which they used to get Aishah to and from her school in Germantown and to her most loyal babysitters, Michael's mother and stepfather, who still lived in the North Philly house he grew up in.

Now living in a two-bedroom apartment with Aishah, Zoharah filled her days with work and parenting. Sorrow came at night. With Aishah asleep, Zoharah sobbed uncontrollably, tears of sorrow that her marriage could not be healed. Bawa, who was back in Sri Lanka, came to comfort her in the form of a cool air that blanketed her as she tried to sleep. She awoke to his comforting presence. Then, she would repeat one of the Zikrs, an Islamic meditational prayer, that Bawa had taught her and begin the day anew.

MUCH AS ZOHARAH enjoyed doing good, she was excited when Barbara Moffett, Michael's boss at the AFSC with whom Zoharah had worked as a volunteer during his incarceration, and her former SNCC comrade Ed Nakawatase encouraged her to apply for a job with a new AFSC project investigating government surveillance.

The AFSC had been a target of government spying, both directly and as a result of its coalitional work. Revelations of government malfeasance dominated the news since March 1971, when an unknown group of pacifists broke into a regional FBI office in Media, Pennsylvania. The files they stole revealed a massive, years-long FBI campaign "to expose, disrupt, misdirect, discredit, or otherwise neutralize the activities of Black nationalists" and other left-wing groups. The FBI called its macabre effort a counterintelligence program, or COINTELPRO. Under its auspices, the FBI had spied on dissidents, broken into their offices, sent poison-pen letters to sabotage coalitions, planted false stories in the press, infiltrated organizations, and coordinated police attacks. The FBI even sent an anonymous letter to Martin Luther King encouraging him to commit suicide.

The pilfered files circulated alongside publication of the so-called Pentagon Papers, which showed that US presidents and military had lied about the war in Vietnam. The attempted cover-up of the 1972 burglary of the Democratic National Convention headquarters at the Watergate Hotel only added fuel to the fire once it became clearer that the White House was behind it. After Richard Nixon resigned in

August 1974, Congress turned its attention to the larger edifice that enabled his crimes. Idaho senator Frank Church chaired the leading congressional effort to document abuses by government agencies and implement reforms. Starting in January 1975, the Church Committee interviewed eight hundred witnesses before releasing its voluminous report fifteen months later.[5]

The AFSC was among the initial recipients of files taken from the raid in Media. The organization joined a lawsuit against the FBI after the bureau broke into the apartment of an AFSC staffer in a misplaced effort to find the burglars. The AFSC Project on Government Surveillance and Citizens Rights would continue this research on the impact of state repression.[6]

The AFSC did not pay well, and the job was only guaranteed for six months. But Zoharah liked the volunteer work she did with the AFSC, and the chance to do something more overtly political was enticing. The grueling two days of one-on-one interviews with AFSC leaders from different branches of the organization, all of whom were white people testing her commitment to "Quaker principles" of non-violence and consensus, tied her stomach in knots. But, in February 1976, she took the job.

A RETURN TO organizing as her avocation, the AFSC was Zoharah's first time working in a majority-white environment. The AFSC building is made of deep-red bricks whose color matches their location on Cherry Street, blocks from Philadelphia City Hall. Though most AFSC programs involving domestic issues, particularly those involving people of color, were housed in the Community Relations Division, Zoharah's job was curiously located in the Information Services Division—its public relations department. And indeed, communication would play a big part in her job. The only other staff devoted to the project would be her supervisor, an exacting woman named Thelma Segal.

While COINTELPRO, the pet project of megalomaniacal FBI director J. Edgar Hoover, was the most sustained operation, every branch of government seemed to be involved in spying on dissidents. Using the Freedom of Information Act, which was amended in 1975 to make it easier for citizens to request files from the government, the AFSC had learned that the CIA, Air Force, Navy, IRS, and Secret Service had also spied on them. So had local police departments. The AFSC issued a bold response. "Believing in the Quaker ideal of an open society in which all are free to promote peace, equality and justice without fear, the American Friends Service Committee unhesitatingly adds its voice to those which say that the CIA and the Internal Security Division of the FBI must be abolished." The statement, which was spearheaded by Ann Davidon—whose husband, a physics professor at Haverford College, had, unbeknownst to anyone at the time, masterminded the raid on the Media FBI office—connected the problems of federal agencies to local police. "We recognize that, sometimes in league with federal agencies and sometimes independently, state and local police forces are engaged in some of these practices," the report continued. "They, too, must be stopped."[7]

Stopping them was part of Zoharah's job. She would be encouraging members and affiliates of the ten AFSC regional offices to apply for records of their surveillance under the Freedom of Information Act, to develop public educational materials about and legal remedies to political repression. She soon learned that the police spying efforts revealed through COINTELPRO had deep roots in decades of American anti-communism. She worked closely with former labor lawyer turned civil liberties researcher Frank Donner, an intense man with slicked-back hair and a slight Brooklyn accent, who directed the ACLU's Project on Political Surveillance. Donner, who spoke in Philadelphia that summer, had been subpoenaed by the House Un-American Activities Committee (HUAC) for representing accused communists. Donner stressed the long history of "Red Squads." These anti-communist surveillance units of metropolitan police departments targeted all manner of political activists—each city with its own FBI. Though formally disbanded by 1976, many cities had reconstituted their Red Squads under other names. In Chicago, it was the Gang Intelligence Unit, while the Mississippi Sovereignty Commission kept tabs on the civil rights movement and served as the umbrella coalition for the police, the Klan, and the Chamber of Commerce. Zoharah knew the Sovereignty Commission well. But she didn't know how similar forms of surveillance, infiltration, and repression had been used as a bludgeon against social change elsewhere.[8]

Zoharah focused her research on local police departments. Her goal was to create a handbook for activists to use in contesting government surveillance and develop local campaigns against police abuse. She spent her first months on the job sorting through records AFSC affiliates had garnered from different police agencies. With media attention focused on federal wrongdoing, Zoharah wrote to AFSC contacts, "very little has been mentioned concerning the role of local police in the intelligence network." As a result, conversations about surveillance focused far away or on famous people. But policing was not so limited. "We hope our education and action program will help citizens realize that what is happening nationally and abroad is, at another level, also happening in their own back yards and that it can affect the most unsuspecting citizens."[9]

Her experience in Philadelphia illustrated the malignancy of police surveillance. As police commissioner, Frank Rizzo and the head of the Philadelphia Police Department's Civil Disobedience Unit bragged on national television of having files on eighteen thousand Philadelphians and six hundred political organizations. He directed his cops to bust SNCC in 1966 and RAM in 1967, led the assault on student activists and anti–police brutality protestors in 1967, and forced Black Panther activists to strip to their underwear before taking their pictures in handcuffs after a predawn raid in 1970. As mayor, Rizzo was caught spying on city councilors with a team of thirty-four police officers in 1973, was accused by a state commission of blocking investigation of police brutality in 1974, and won reelection in 1975 after promising to "make Attila the Hun look like a faggot."[10]

Zoharah was a main organizer of the Coalition Against Police Abuse (CAPA), which documented police brutality and tried to stop the Philadelphia police from getting the federal grants that, Zoharah knew, had funded local police expansion nationally. She knew as well the random terror of police aggression. One morning, police stormed her two-bedroom apartment unannounced while Aishah was eating pancakes. *Get out of the way,* they barked on their way in, claiming to be looking for an unknown fugitive. The police made Zoharah show them every closet, bed, nook, and cranny of the apartment before they left.[11]

Even when they were not barging into her bedroom, police were a constant presence in her neighborhood. Blocks away from her apartment, police had trained their sights on an idiosyncratic group called MOVE. Founded by a Korean War veteran and handyman with a third-grade education who took the name John Africa, MOVE was a sui generis religion that emphasized the natural order. Its members took the surname Africa, ate raw foods, exercised diligently, and pursued confrontation. They fought with neighbors and disrupted public events. The city took out an injunction against MOVE protests in 1974. MOVE people were bound and gagged in court. By 1976, MOVE members had been arrested four hundred times in protests against the city school board, the zoo, and even an annual meeting of veterinarians. MOVE people lived and ate collectively in a large dilapidated Victorian twin at 309 North Thirty-Third Street, just blocks from where Zoharah and Aishah now lived. An early morning celebration to welcome home a group of MOVE people freed from jail on March 28, 1976, turned into a brawl with police in which one-month-old infant Life Africa was crushed to death. MOVE rejected police authority so fully that they buried the body on their own. Police insisted that the baby never existed.[12]

Zoharah rallied neighbors in West Philadelphia to attend meetings at the Church of the Advocate, the cavernous Episcopal house of worship in North Philadelphia that had long allied with the city's Black movements for justice. CAPA had tallied complaints against the police from a cross section of the city. Yet MOVE's confrontational élan derailed meetings. MOVE members addressed the church with a boisterous *fuck the police*. Cursing was their philosophy. *The system is profane*, MOVE members declared, *you have to talk about it with profanity*.

Zoharah worried that such language would alienate people. But she had no love for the police. Leading into the summer of 1976, Rizzo had requested the federal government send fifteen thousand National Guard troops to quell what he baselessly described as a planned insurrection during the city's bicentennial celebrations.[13]

She joined the thirty thousand people who peacefully protested in Philadelphia for a "Bicentennial without Colonies" on July 4. Three days later, she embarked on a month-long research trip for the AFSC that would bring her to eleven cities in six states, deep into the land of the unfree.

SHE BEGAN IN Cleveland, where FBI agents had followed her years earlier. The New Libya movement had faded with Ahmed Evans's incarceration, however, and she spent most of her time with local anti-war activists and civil liberties attorneys. From there, she headed to Chicago. With four different lawsuits active against local, state, and federal law enforcement, Chicago activists were leading the fight against government surveillance. One of the lawsuits involved the killing of Black Panther leader Fred Hampton. Zoharah toured the apartment where the police had murdered the twenty-one-year-old in his bed seven years previously, the bullet holes still evident in the walls. Flint Taylor, an attorney for the People's Law Office, told her about the FBI informant who supplied Chicago police with a map of Hampton's apartment and likely drugged him so he wouldn't wake up when police stormed in at four a.m.[14]

Zoharah recoiled in horror. Hampton's murder was gruesome, and the FBI had orchestrated it. She thought back to Freedom

Summer, when she had welcomed the FBI's regular safety checks. Like a teacher taking attendance, the agent would check off the names of all the project staff on his clipboard. At twenty-one, Gwen viewed this ritual as a benevolent bulwark against the Klan-friendly local police. It felt necessary at the time. Now standing in Hampton's bullet-riddled apartment, Zoharah felt naive.

The more she traveled, the more overwhelmed she felt at the scale of police surveillance. Of 125 people to attend an anti-war demonstration in Fort Carson, Colorado, 59 were government agents. Of 200 arrests for jaywalking in Denver, 185 of them took place in front of a gay bar. Denver police arrested the wives and girlfriends of men killed by police and had a special focus on the Crusade for Justice, a radical Chicano organization that worked in tandem with the American Indian Movement. Police used provocateurs and planted drugs and weapons at the Crusade office to justify arrests of its members, she learned.[15]

Infuriated at these revelations, Zoharah was eager to speak with as many people as she could. From the Denver AFSC office, she confirmed her appointment with the local National Lawyers Guild. *Can I come with you?* a man asked her as she hung up the phone. He was unfamiliar, but then again, this was her first time in Denver. She agreed. As she drove, she questioned the line between paranoia and reasonable concern. She couldn't be too careful. Once they arrived at the office, he persisted. *Well, who are you meeting with next?* he asked. *Boy, I'd like to go in and hear that too.* Concerned, Zoharah declined his invitation.[16]

People she spoke with illuminated how government spying prevented trust among activists. She saw this firsthand in Seattle, Michael's adopted second home. Concerns over informants ran rampant there, especially after police killed a Vietnam veteran who was solicited by an informant to plant a bomb. When a new rash of bombings occurred in 1975, some feared it was a secret police operation. Already the Seattle police chief admitted to destroying surveillance files of

730 activists in the city in 1974 rather than submit them to public scrutiny. Zoharah enjoyed meeting the AFSC and UCWA organizers she knew of from Michael. She was shocked, though, to find a prosaic disunity. Even though the ACLU and National Lawyers Guild officers were in the same building, some of those involved had not met each other until Zoharah's visit brought them together. *Wait a minute, you all can talk after I leave*, she interjected as the lawyers hit it off too much. *Let me try to understand what you're doing here already first.*[17]

In Los Angeles Zoharah met with Frank Wilkinson, the cherubic former Los Angeles Housing Authority manager who oversaw the city's first integrated housing development before being fired for refusing to answer whether he had been a member of the Communist Party. Wilkinson headed the National Committee Against Repressive Legislation (NCARL), which, along with the ACLU, had been a central coalition partner in Zoharah's work. Wilkinson had spent much of 1961 in prison, along with civil rights activist Carl Braden, for refusing to answer questions from House Un-American Activities Commission (HUAC) on the grounds that it violated the First Amendment. Now he was her tutor on the history of Red Squads. Zoharah didn't know where to sit, Wilkinson's house was so overflowing with records of the surveillance state.

Everyone Zoharah talked to seemed terrified of the police. Respectable professionals told her that *the police blackmail everybody with their files*. Even Tom Bradley, the city's first Black mayor and a former cop, was said to be compromised in this way. She met with Rev. Edgar Edwards, whose Immanuel United Church of Christ was only blocks away from the Compton house where Los Angeles police incinerated six alleged members of the guerrilla group Symbionese Liberation Army on live television in 1974. The house caught fire after five hundred officers fired twelve hundred rounds of ammunition and countless tear gas cannisters. Police blocked the firefighters from dousing the blaze and blocked the militants from exiting. When Edwards criticized the killings in a press conference, he received visits from six different police agencies—local, state, and federal. She learned that the LAPD kept records of children as young as seven, mostly Black or Brown, who police deemed "likely to get into trouble with the law." And she learned of the Law Enforcement Intelligence Unit. It was, she would tell the AFSC, a private "fraternity" of police chiefs and heads of Red Squads nationwide run by the California governor's brother-in-law and funded by public money without any oversight or regulation.[18]

Zoharah found the information dizzying. She was glad that the AFSC had allowed her to stay at a hotel instead of with local Quakers—she needed space to decompress. But when she got back to her hotel room after another long day of interviews, she found that her room had been ransacked. Someone had rifled through her notes and taken the tapes of her interviews. Panicked, she called the Philadelphia AFSC office, who found her a local Quaker family to stay with.[19]

When she reported her findings to an AFSC staff meeting in September, Zoharah was unequivocal. "I returned convinced that the most important, yet toughest-to-get-at segment of the intelligence network is the local and state police red squad."[20]

ZOHARAH COULDN'T BEAR the thought of having to rewrite another memo. Her supervisor seemed to take a red pen to every document she wrote and second-guessed her suggestions for the project. Zoharah was an accomplished organizer with years of experience directing projects. Yet Thelma's constant doubts left Zoharah feeling disempowered. One of the only Black people in any kind of leadership position at the AFSC, especially outside of the Community Relations Division where Third World Coalition staff worked, Zoharah felt under surveillance herself. For the first time in her years of activism, she doubted her credibility and worried that people disliked her. *How can I be in a leadership position?* she fretted. *I didn't even finish college.*

She had never worried about her place or pedigree before. But so many people around her seemed highly educated. And contrary to her almost two decades of experience in social movements, nearly everyone she worked with was white. (Zoharah would not find out until later that Thelma, her demanding supervisor, did not have a college degree either.) Now she questioned her ideas, her writing, her qualifications, and that constant pain in her stomach.

For months, she had battled an agonizing indigestion that had only grown more severe. It became unbearable. When she finally went to a doctor, she found out that she had an ulcer. *I made it through Mississippi okay, but developed an ulcer at AFSC,* she chuckled. *Of course, I wasn't trying to please the Klan.*

After a few weeks off, she returned to work in September with renewed appreciation for what both her grandmother and her years fighting for Black Power had taught her: white dominance created myths of Black inferiority that even Black people might believe. The AFSC would not be the Black-staffed and -financed project Zoharah and her comrades tried to make of SNCC. Still, it was not just in rural Mississippi or urban slums where Black people needed to see each other exercising authority and fighting for change. She had to find validation outside the formal AFSC leadership and find her voice within it.

She sought refuge in the Third World Coalition. Zoharah would eat lunch with TWC comrades, including Michael when their schedules aligned, and seek counsel from coalition staff. She also presented her work at TWC staff meetings. The coalition worked to break the silos that the AFSC's structure created between discrete projects. Zoharah enlisted the coalition in her efforts to broaden the work of the surveillance project. She asked the TWC, whose members were well experienced with police harassment, to appoint a representative to the project task force—each AFSC project reported to a unique advisory board—so that the coalition and its priorities could shape the project.[21]

Zoharah was also the AFSC representative to a nascent coalition against government surveillance. Originally called the National Campaign Against Lying and Spying, the effort launched in February 1977 as the Campaign Against Government Spying. More than sixty organizations endorsed the campaign, a broad cross section of progressive and radical organizations that had been targeted by various law enforcement agencies. Zoharah found herself in the familiar role of bringing together liberal and faith-based organizations with big budgets and reputable reputations with the unruly urgency of the grassroots—Black, Chicano, and Puerto Rican nationalists, international solidarity activists, environmentalists, and others. Even the Church of Scientology was on board.

The anchor organizations of the Campaign Against Government Spying—the ACLU, the AFSC, NCARL, and the Center for National Security Studies—were mostly white, however, and at the campaign's founding convention Zoharah insisted on the priority of "Third World and victim participation in the Campaign." She signed up to be a member of a five-person "special committee" that would propose making the campaign responsive to the communities it claimed to serve. Her other committee members came from NCARL, the National Conference of Black Lawyers, the National Organization for Women, the National Jesuit Social Apostolate, and the Puerto Rican Solidarity Committee. After a three-month process, they recommended that the campaign reserve seven (of twenty-five) seats on the executive committee for "representatives of minority/victim organizations," with that determination to be made by the special committee. They also recommended that the campaign provide scholarships and other support to regional branches to attend national meetings and empower local groups through "regional conclaves" that would serve as hubs for strategy and action.[22]

The campaign met often in DC, where several of the participating members had national offices. But to Zoharah, the action was in the local branches. She was particularly inspired by the work in

Minnesota, where she spent a freezing winter week observing the efforts of Native American activists and their allies investigating the FBI. Surrounded by snow banks taller than she was, Zoharah's teeth chattered. Her hosts took her to buy long johns and sturdy boots. She didn't know it could be so cold. Inside, as people from the Rosebud Reservation revealed FBI efforts to break their movement, Zoharah warmed by the fire of public testimony.[23]

CHAPTER FOURTEEN

ALL OF US

MICHAEL AND ZOHARAH BOTH KNEW THAT WORKING AT A majority-white institution would come with its share of frustrations. Yet they still saw in the AFSC an opportunity to pursue Black Power's transformative promise of solidarity, particularly amid the late 1970s thaws in Cold War orthodoxy. They looked both inward and outward. As liberation movements in southern Africa advanced their campaigns to end white rule, Michael and Zoharah labored to democratize the AFSC as an anti-racist institution through an affirmative action program. These were twinned projects, stitching the conditions of organizing to its desired ends.

Despite being a social justice organization, the AFSC siloed its staff. Early in his time there, Michael bitterly called the Community Relations Division—the section of the organization dedicated to issues such as housing and employment—the "nigger program division." It was there where all of the people of color at AFSC, other than custodial and secretarial staff, worked. As the Third World Coalition took up campaigns in support of Puerto Rican independence and an end to apartheid, some in the AFSC told Michael that the organization's international efforts drew upon white staff and audiences because *Black people don't care about peace* and *Africans don't like Black people.* Michael thought that the AFSC too often assumed the limits of others' concerns.[1]

Michael rejected the narrow casting of what concerned Third World people—both those on staff and in the communities AFSC claimed to serve. Much of his political life had been spent identifying the intimate proximity of far-off events. The same system that threatened his life in Arkansas and Atlanta made the war in Vietnam that sent him to prison in Pennsylvania. To transform the world meant changing the AFSC. The global fight against apartheid allowed him to do both.

Michael had paid close attention to events in southern Africa since his days in SNCC. As co-coordinator of the Third World Coalition, he had come to see it as the "Vietnam of the 70s," the urgent site of colonial violence that could bond an international solidarity movement. He screened anti-apartheid documentaries with the Southwest Workers Federation, read anything he could on African liberation movements, and grilled former SNCC comrades who had attended the 1974 Pan-African Congress in Dar-es-Salaam. Much like the Atlanta Project's Black Consciousness Paper, Michael saw the Black Consciousness Movement in South Africa as a harbinger of a new phase of struggle. In 1976 the Black Consciousness Movement helped catalyze an uprising in the Soweto township. The stakes were high: prominent Black consciousness activist Steve Biko was arrested and beaten to death by police on September 12, 1977. He was thirty, not two years younger than Michael. The severity of repression in the aftermath of Soweto renewed both popular protest and armed resistance to the apartheid regime, and Michael was eager to support the reinvigorated liberation movements.[2]

He took on apartheid as director of the AFSC's new Southern Africa Program. The AFSC board made an organizational commitment in 1974 to oppose "the status quo in southern Africa" and "support African efforts towards self-determination." That framing, endorsed by the Third World Coalition, recognized the need for a truly international approach: backed by the United States, apartheid South Africa was fighting to uphold racist domination across the region. The South African government banned anti-apartheid organizations and hounded activists who had fled into neighboring countries that had provided them cover. Michael's program reflected the work he and others had been doing to demolish the siloing of issues and staff within the organization. Although other progressive groups lobbied against the South African regime specifically, the AFSC pursued a broader offensive.

Hiring Bill Sutherland, based in Tanzania, secured the organization's regional orientation. Sutherland was a Black American pacifist who was imprisoned as a conscientious objector during World War II and had cofounded the New York Congress of Racial Equality, which launched the first Freedom Rides against segregation in 1947. Inspired by African liberation movements, Sutherland moved to Ghana, then called the Gold Coast, in 1953, and worked in the ministry of finance after the country secured its independence in 1957 before he relocated to Tanzania in 1963.[3]

Michael worked to align all of the AFSC behind the strategic agenda highlighted by movements within southern Africa. Under Michael's leadership, the Southern Africa Program transformed the AFSC's international solidarity work—and became a lightning rod for those upset by the deviation from a pacific Quakerism.[4]

The Third World Coalition cosponsored Sutherland's speaking tours in the United States. Michael made sure Bill had the opportunity to address members of the Southwest Workers Federation. In Little Rock, Tulsa, and Shreveport, Bill spoke about the corporate exploitation linking Black workers on both sides of the Atlantic. Michael saw Bill's tour as a rejoinder to Quaker parochialism. "As we see the effects of the United States policy in Vietnam on all of the American people we in AFSC should realize that the issue of peace should not be confined to a small segment of the American public," Michael wrote of Bill's trip. "World events affect all of us."[5]

EVEN FOR A progressive organization, the idea that *all of us* would have a stake in change redefined the organization's constituency and moral compass. That shift came into focus when the TWC proposed to formalize an affirmative action plan in 1976. Also that year, the Nationwide Women's Program (NWP), established two years earlier and composed predominantly of white women staffers involved in the feminist movement, initiated a Racism Sexism Task Group to investigate what kept the AFSC from living up to its mission. And secretaries in the AFSC's southeast office, overwhelmingly women, tried to unionize.[6]

Through his work with the Southwest Workers Federation, Michael had seen the power of affirmative action to transform a workplace. Affirmative action could both open doors that had been previously closed by race and gender and empower disenfranchised workers to fight for themselves and others. The parallel efforts by TWC and NWP united in a campaign to make AFSC an affirmative action employer that would attend to different but linked forms of domination. In effect, women and people of color were asking the organization to adjust both who was in the room and how they were treated when they got there. That combination would, of necessity, shift the organization's approach in other domains.

In joining the AFSC's affirmative action committee, Michael urged the organization to focus more on impact than intent. "I maintain that if we begin to strip through what's said and look at what's done," Mike said, "that the essence of the Service Committee does not depart too much from many institutions in this society that we attack." While some framed the issue as cultural differences between Quaker and non-Quaker, Michael noted that this concern applied only to Third World people: Most AFSC staff and several executive leadership bodies were white, but not Quaker. The organization's print shop was all white, its maintenance staff all Black. And prior to his role with the Southern Africa Program, the only Black staff in either the Peace Education or International divisions were secretaries with no influence on program. Noting that "this may be the only time that I'll ever suggest this," he offered the federal government, which outlawed discrimination in hiring or promotion, as a model for Quakers.[7]

Prominent Quakers' fear of nonwhite violence was especially galling in light of recent history: the civil rights movements of Black and Chicano people had reinvigorated nonviolence. "We get the test, not you; we get the test, those of us that were out there, those of us who put our lives on the line, we're the ones who are asked if we're violent," Michael inveighed with obvious frustration during an AFSC retreat on racism in the organization. Why, he asked those assembled, which included the organization's top leadership, are applicants of color asked to "'state your position on pacifism,' but you never have to state your position on racism?"[8]

Anchored in the Third World Coalition, the affirmative action planning committee responded to these concerns in an ambitious plan that concerned AFSC policies for hiring, promotion, and program development. Rejecting quotas as an operating logic, the plan recommended the AFSC work to have its staff at a minimum be 20 percent Third World and 40 percent women within five years. The plan also highlighted the need to include gay and bisexual people in affirmative action plans, although it did not specify an ideal percentage. In 1978, the AFSC became an affirmative action employer.[9]

Also that year, Michael became a father for the second time. What spare time he had was devoted to the Philadelphia Worker Organizing Committee, the communist organization he joined after his return from India. There he began dating another member, a white Jewish woman named Dina Portnoy. They welcomed their son into the world on April 22, 1978—Aishah's ninth birthday. They named him Tyree Cinque, after two great revolutionaries: Tyree Scott and *Amistad* slave rebel leader Cinque. Michael was present at Tyree's birth, delighted to welcome a child without a prison term on the horizon.

As MICHAEL WORKED to transform the AFSC's structure, Zoharah was surprised to be invited to apply for a job in the AFSC's Financial

Services Division. She assumed that the job was reserved for *weighty Quakers*, as prominent people of the faith were called, with a preference for *birthright Quakers*, those raised in the faith. In practice if not design, that meant a preference for white men. The AFSC had five fundraisers in its national office, together with one fundraiser in each of its ten regional offices. All of them were white, most of them men. The fundraisers in the national office were all white men. The job paid well, though, and unlike the Government Surveillance Project, whose budget relied on grants and renewal from AFSC leadership, its future seemed stable. The salary boost would keep Aishah in the private Quaker school she had been attending near the AFSC. Zoharah liked that Aishah could walk over after school and turn the Friends Center into her playground, visiting both her parents and a slew of grown-up friends.

Zoharah steeled herself for another grueling several days of interviews. This time the process included a psychiatric evaluation—she presumed the doctor was a Quaker who volunteered his services to the AFSC—to test her mental fitness for the job. She must have passed, for the job was soon hers.

The Finance Division was next door to the Information Services Division, but the work differed tremendously. Much of the AFSC's budget came from its eighty thousand individual donors. Anyone who gave a substantial amount, over $500 at the time, had a dedicated fundraiser assigned. Fundraisers would visit large donors at their request to discuss what the Service Committee was doing. Zoharah spent her early days on the job studying the three-by-five index cards that the fundraisers kept on the larger donors, getting to know their interest areas and donation histories. She introduced herself to them on the phone. And then she began the house visits.

You know, you are the first Black person I have ever entertained, a member of the DuPont family gushed to Zoharah over tea at their Delaware estate. She became well practiced at seeming unfazed at being greeted by maids and butlers. She answered bemused *How did you get this job?* questions with a patience determined not to trigger her ulcer. And she remained calm even when the Quaker donors did not. *Don't you remember?* Zoharah smiled gently through the closed door to a wealthy white woman startled to find a Black woman on her property. *We spoke on the phone.* Eventually, the door opened for Zoharah to share news of the peace and justice activism the woman had funded.

To keep the funders updated, Zoharah had to have her finger on the pulse of the AFSC's many projects. She met often with AFSC program heads in Philadelphia and from regional offices to understand the grassroots projects Quakers were involved in—and what they could do with greater funding. In time, she would bring funders to the field. She wanted the organizing to drive the funding, not the other way around.[10]

KNOWING THAT MANY Quakers saw him as apostate, Michael loved his work more than his job. His approach to southern Africa was twofold: following the request of the movements in the region, he wanted to end US government and corporate support for apartheid. And, following the model of the Third World Coalition, he wanted "to connect the struggle against racism in southern Africa with the struggle against racism in the United States," an effort he saw as both strategic and practical. As Michael put it in a memo to his colleagues, "only Africans will liberate their respective countries from oppression. It is our role, indeed our duty, to support those struggling for freedom."[11]

As the apartheid regime became more menacing—killing or imprisoning demonstrators, banning political organizations and publications, conducting military raids in neighboring countries—some of the liberation movements turned to violent tactics. It wasn't a new conflict for the AFSC: the pacifist organization's opposition to the US war in Vietnam raised similar concerns with regard to the National Liberation Front, and some Quakers shared Michael's belief that movements on the ground set the terms of their own freedom struggles. As Jim Bristol, a weighty Quaker with whom Michael traveled to Cuba in 1976, put it, "It is up to the Latin Americans and the Africans to decide how they will wage their struggle for freedom. We cannot decide for them. Certainly we dare not judge the morality of their choices."[12]

Echoing Bristol, Michael took the position that the status quo in southern Africa—and many other parts of the world—was itself a form of violence. If pacifism was about eradicating violence, Michael thought, the AFSC had a moral obligation to support those who refused the violent structure itself. The AFSC could no more cling to pacifism than it could mandate that people under the yoke of apartheid respond according to the dictates of Western Quakerism. Against the charge that the Southern Africa Program *wasn't Quakerly*, Michael worked to clarify the nature of violence itself. Though Quakers had supported or even participated in some righteous insurgencies as far back as the English Revolution, *Quaker values* remained a bludgeon against the insurgents within the AFSC, especially nonwhite staff.[13]

Michael hoped to translate the respect Bristol and Sutherland enjoyed among Quakers to make solidarity more than pacifism the driving principle. In 1977, he helped organize a Quaker delegation to southern Africa to "provide opportunities for creative exchanges" transnationally in ways that would help the AFSC determine how to balance its "concern to support movements for self-determination and a concern to seek nonviolent solutions to conflicts." Unlike most AFSC trips, this one consisted primarily of Third World staff.[14]

Michael wasn't on the tour, which visited five "frontline" countries in southern Africa, but considered it a great success. He was quick to fold reflections from the tour into the developing calls to boycott and divest from South Africa. But he had to contend with white South African Quakers, in tandem with conservative members of the AFSC, who called the tour and its subsequent proposals biased. They demanded a second visit, one that would stress the Quaker presence in South Africa, dialogue, and a negotiated resolution to apartheid. Among their complaints, they griped that white Quakers were not consulted in the plans of the Southern Africa group, that AFSC delegations should consist only of Quakers (effectively shutting out TWC members), and that divestment was a form of violence that would hurt the South African economy—especially for Black people.[15]

Michael said the proposal was as absurd as "anything George Wallace has written." Channeling the outrage of AFSC staff members, Michael alleged that the Afrikaner proposal rejected nonviolence far more than anything the Southern Africa Program did. After all, "Economic boycotts have long been a major weapon in the arsenal of nonviolent struggle" and the "struggle in South Africa has already sustained over twenty five years of nonviolent activity. . . . Yet nonviolence and violence is always the issue when we discuss South Africa. Why?"[16]

When Michael found out that the Quaker UN representative sent a snide criticism of a press conference by a Black Consciousness Movement organizer Michael had brought to the United States, he was furious at what he saw as white arrogance. "Except for some particular aspects of this situation," he wrote back, "I do not see your approach as distinct from many within the AFSC family." The "total disregard" of Third World Staff was an old problem. "It is usually passed off based on 'Quaker purity,' but I suggest that this is a smoke screen for implicit and explicit racism," Michael said. He longed for the day that white people within AFSC would challenge these attitudes. But he knew that the organization lacked the infrastructure to do it. "As we embark on an affirmative action plan we should realize that it is more than adding non-white faces," Michael explained. "If you or others do not feel that I am competent to represent AFSC on Southern Africa then say that! Until then I only ask the respect that I have seen given to white staff for the past five years."[17]

Six months later, a group of weighty Quakers drafted a proposal to AFSC leadership to muzzle Michael. Their plan called for subjecting the Southern Africa Program to a thorough review by

Quakers in order to bring it in line with dominant Quakerism. And they called for suspending its budget. One of its authors, a decorated economist named Kenneth Boulding, had earlier flown from Colorado to Philadelphia to hold a one-man vigil outside the AFSC to mourn its departure "from the light of the Gospel and of science." Michael, one of the heretics prompting Boulding's exorcism, found the display entertaining.[18]

Well accustomed to being the target of Quaker piety, Michael responded that Quakerism was not a moral prophylactic. *You mean to tell me it's a coincidence that Richard Nixon and Herbert Hoover were both Quakers*, he would goad his critics of the two Quakers who had served as US president, one a corrupt war criminal, the other whose policies helped launch the Great Depression. *And how do you explain Quaker slave owners?* At other times, he would offer an olive branch in the form of a Bible passage. His opponents were nonplussed. *Even the devil can quote scripture*, an antagonist said of Michael after yet another heated exchange. Michael, who considered himself a *born-again heathen*, had to laugh.

WHILE MICHAEL WEATHERED the storm of conflicts within the AFSC, Zoharah found herself facing a police state. She watched the police erect a blockade of reinforced eight-foot wooden slats around her neighborhood. Even though she lived just outside the perimeter, she was terrified at living adjacent to an occupied zone.[19]

She had seen police brutality worsen under Mayor Frank Rizzo. When ten police officers broke their nightsticks in beating a Black man who ran a stop sign, Rizzo bemoaned, "It's very easy to break some of these nightsticks nowadays." He refused to remove six detectives from duty even after they were convicted of torturing confessions. The *Philadelphia Inquirer* concluded that "many homicide detectives, in beating or coercing suspects and later denying it under oath, have come to accept breaking the law as part of their job."[20]

Rizzo and the police concentrated their attention on the disruptive MOVE organization. The blockade followed almost a year of round-the-clock surveillance of MOVE. The official rationale for the blockade was to arrest eleven members of the organization who had displayed (nonfunctional) guns on the porch in a rally of their Powelton Village home. Rizzo and the police commissioner described their efforts as a "starvation blockade" that shut off water to the house and denied food coming in. The police sealed off a four-block area around the MOVE house. As in South African Bantustans, residents of the area had to show passes to get in and out.[21]

Zoharah continued to participate in community meetings against police brutality. She had recently joined a local anti-apartheid group as well. Both apartheid and police violence seemed evident in the eight-foot fence enclosing her neighborhood. From the bus, she saw snipers and sandbags ring the roofs. MOVE's unkempt style—children naked and unschooled, the property rife with stray dogs and rats—had alienated many neighbors. So did the police response. Concerned about the children in the house as well as the suppression of the larger neighborhood, Zoharah joined neighborhood and citywide efforts to end the blockade. Two weeks into the standoff, she locked arms with a thousand others to surround city hall in an interfaith protest. She supported the AFSC in offering MOVE land in the country, where the organization could establish a commune. Yet neither the police nor MOVE backed down. Heading past the blockade to yet another community meeting at the Church of the Advocate, Zoharah was angry and afraid.

MICHAEL DIDN'T WANT to be bothered with MOVE. He had first encountered MOVE in the early 1970s disrupting anti-war events and Quaker meetings. He assumed MOVE was a right-wing group. When the blockade went up, he was focused on southern Africa. But the blockade was oppressive, and the widespread Black opposition to the police occupation deserved support on principle alone. He helped gather food to donate. Some members of PWOC who lived in the Powelton neighborhood under siege broke through police lines to deliver food.[22]

His attention remained on toppling the political cover and economic support that US institutions provided apartheid South Africa. The apartheid regime fired bullets from US guns, rationed food using US computers, paid salaries through US banks, drove vehicles powered by US oil companies, and escaped consequences for its actions by US government veto at the United Nations. Michael increasingly focused his energies on divesting from South Africa. Anti-apartheid campaigners targeted Mobil Oil, Citibank, and Chase Manhattan, the bank that SNCC protested in its 1965 demonstration against apartheid. Michael wanted to expand divestment. He knew it would ruffle feathers. Targeting the pocketbook always does.

Michael's approach, and that of the South Africans themselves, contravened the preferred approach of prominent Black leaders. Leon Sullivan, the scion of Philadelphia's Black political establishment and director of the board of General Motors, proposed a set of six principles to end segregation in South Africa without disrupting GM's business there. Andrew Young, the former confidant of Martin Luther King turned UN ambassador under Jimmy Carter, eschewed international sanctions against South Africa. Instead, Young proposed a "negotiated settlement" to apartheid. Both men claimed that divestment and sanctions would worsen conditions for those it was designed to assist, Black South Africans.[23]

Michael had grown up with Sullivan as a model of Black success; he even heard him preach a sermon once. But he knew that the terrain opened up by Jim Crow's decline required sharp opposition to capitalism as a barrier to the emancipatory Black politics he wanted to build. In a 1975 article, Tyree Scott described Black politicians as the new "Buffalo soldiers," well-educated members of a rising Black middle class who, like their nineteenth-century Indian-hunting forebears, cosigned the exploitation of the world's racialized working class.[24]

Against the Buffalo Soldiers, Michael organized an immersive freedom project in the summer of 1978. From June to August, Michael led the AFSC's "Southern Africa Summer" program that trained forty high school and college students from around the country in the politics of apartheid and the strategies of resistance. The project trained the mostly Black participants to organize where they already lived. It operated in eleven cities nationwide and was organized on the theme of "U.S.–Apartheid: Break the Links." Through Michael's efforts, the AFSC provided documentaries, flyers, and other educational materials for the cohort to use in organizing in their own communities. The AFSC also pitched Bill Sutherland's speaking schedule to cities where Southern Africa Summer projects were located.[25]

Michael felt in his element coordinating Southern Africa Summer. It was a boot camp in divestment organizing, political education, and global solidarity. The project pledged its support to "the peoples of Southern Africa in their struggle for self-determination." He knew that approach would not disabuse hesitant Quakers of the notion that he was a fifth column within the AFSC, sabotaging its nonviolent mission. In protest of Michael's approach, the Quaker meetinghouse in Chicago refused to let members of the summer project eat lunch there, despite it being an AFSC initiative.[26]

Michael's challenge to the AFSC exceeded the cafeteria. He had followed the money of apartheid enough to know that even the AFSC's portfolio was implicated. When this came up during an orientation session for the project, several volunteers revolted. The debate lasted until one a.m., volunteers threatening to leave or scale back their operations. The AFSC became a target of its own initiative. The group issued a statement demanding that the organization's board "divest itself of stock in corporations with business operations in South Africa, and withdraw funds from banks which refuse to state they will not continue to make loans in South Africa." At stake was "the moral and political foundation for our work."

The protest prompted the AFSC, in Quaker fashion, to dialogue with fifteen companies about their business ethics. Michael resented flying to Battle Creek for a pro forma meeting with Kellogg executives about apartheid. He was more nervous to meet with Leon Sullivan. It was a means to an end. By the end of the summer, the AFSC publicly announced that it had sold forty-five thousand shares of stock, worth $1.3 million, of US companies operating in South Africa. "We don't think anyone should be making profit from apartheid," AFSC executive secretary Lou Schneider averred. Michael had rebuffed opponents of divestment for months. It was a nonviolent tactic. It was a moral necessity. It was what Black South Africans had asked of the international community. And now Michael, the alleged apostasy of Quaker pacifism, had helped a cohort of new organizers push the AFSC to enact its nonviolent ideals in defense of human rights.[27]

No such divestment campaign targeted the Philadelphia police. Although the police lifted the neighborhood blockade in May, it resumed in August when MOVE refused to vacate. On August 8, as police surrounded the house, Zoharah joined many of her neighbors by the police line, hoping their presence would prevent a police assault. But then the police pumped water into the basement to flood MOVE out. Then she heard the fusillade of gunfire. Soon, one police officer lay dead. Nine MOVE members had been arrested, one of them badly beaten, half-naked and with his arms outstretched.

Crestfallen, Zoharah walked the three blocks home. The police bulldozed what had been MOVE's house and, as neighbors protested, rampaged the neighborhood with truncheons.[28]

Her horror turned to rage a month later when she learned that Frank Rizzo, who had given a farewell speech lamenting the need for "white rights," announced his intention to amend the city charter to allow him an unprecedented third term as mayor. Rizzo's campaign platform was an odious blend of opposition to affirmative action, busing, and public housing and support for the death penalty. He encouraged supporters to "vote white." Zoharah, Michael, and almost everyone they knew joined one of the citywide coalitions to defeat Rizzo's power grab. An independent forum, the Black Political Convention, marshaled candidates to respond to community demands rather than subsume them under party control. Sure enough, Black voters heard the message. The charter amendment was soundly defeated, thanks to a unified Black vote. In other races on the ballot, however, Black voters were a heterogeneous group: supporting Democrats and Republicans, Black and white politicians. Zoharah and Michael delighted at the news. Not only had they defeated Rizzo, but Black voters had proved themselves independent of loyalties to either political party. That realization would embolden Zoharah and Michael in different attempts at developing oppositional political parties.[29]

LIKE MICHAEL, ZOHARAH was a Third World Coalition partisan. After four Black women resigned or were fired from the AFSC in as many months, Zoharah helped plan a TWC retreat to address racism and sexism in the organization. "We are hopeful, in fact, we feel that the majority of the non-Third World people in the Service Committee recognize our unique contribution and are appreciative of it," she opened. "We are also clear," she continued "that there is within the Service Committee as without, in the greater society, a growing trend of conservatism which is frightened of change in power relationships and seeks to wipe out, for a number of reasons, gains that have been made here in the United States and within the AFSC to eradicate racism and sexism." Part of that conservatism within the AFSC included voices suggesting that affirmative action obviated the need for the Third World Coalition. To Zoharah the reverse was true: "We live in one very small world, and what effects [sic] any group in any part of it affects us all." That understanding could anchor bridges between the AFSC's traditional white base and Third World communities. It could serve as the basis for coalition, for unity across differences. That was her hope.[30]

Michael participated in the TWC retreat, always glad to be with TWC members from around the country. But he had hit his breaking point with the Service Committee. Conservative Quaker opposition to southern African liberation movements wore him down. And there were more promising opportunities. He had played a leading role in the Philadelphia Worker Organizing Committee's efforts to consolidate a network of communist groups into a national organization. Weeks after the TWC gathering, Michael was in Detroit for the National Minority Marxist-Leninist Conference. More than forty people from around the country attended the gathering he and Tyree co-organized to bring more Third World workers into the mostly white groupings that made up what partisans called the New Communist Movement in the United States. Liberation movements across southern Africa continued to press on, and left-wing guerrillas were poised to take power in Nicaragua. He would throw his lot in with the communist movement. He resigned his post at the AFSC that summer, vowing never to return.[31]

DESPITE HER CONCERNS, Zoharah still hoped that the AFSC could be a vehicle for global solidarity. She got to put that hope to the test when she was invited to join an AFSC delegation to Southeast Asia to bear witness to the catastrophic aftermath of the US war in the region. The United States dropped more than two million tons of bombs on Cambodia alone, more than the Allies dropped in all of World War II. The war killed approximately three million people across Vietnam, Cambodia, and Laos. The war's end brought a new phase of horror, particularly between a newly unified Vietnam and a post–civil war Cambodia. Led by Pol Pot, Cambodia enacted a genocidal campaign to depopulate the cities, eradicate any Vietnamese or Buddhist influence, and impose a rural agrarian society. After years of conflict, Vietnam captured Phnom Penh in January 1979. China attacked Vietnam in retaliation, exacerbating grief across the region.[32]

The AFSC, which had a long history of peace work in the region, rushed into the crisis. The organization assembled a delegation of five people—two board members and three staff, including Zoharah—to go to Southeast Asia. They arrived in Laos on September 6 and spent two days meeting with government officials and visiting AFSC projects there. In Vietnam, Zoharah marveled at how thirty years of war was built into the geography. She squeezed her way through the tunnels where Vietnamese fighters hid during French, US, and most recently Chinese attacks. She visited a makeshift museum with jars of deformed fetuses born prematurely due to Agent Orange poisoning and toured "schools"—reeducation centers—dedicated to making juvenile delinquents and former prostitutes into productive workers.

At an orphanage, Zoharah observed a little girl of obviously mixed parentage; Zoharah assumed her father had been a Black American GI. The girl took her hand and began to talk quickly to her. *Come quick*, Zoharah called for a translator, *and tell me what this child is saying to me.* But the girl quieted when the interpreter arrived. When they were alone again, the girl pulled and pointed and talked to Zoharah at length, her tiny hand gripped tightly around Zoharah's as they toured the facility. *Does she want me to take her home with me?* Zoharah wondered. The girl shooed away other children when they tried to talk to Zoharah. *She wants to go with you*, one of the nuns who ran the orphanage told Zoharah. *There's no place for her here.* When it came time to go, the girl followed Zoharah to the door with earnest attachment. Zoharah quivered. Had she failed this girl?

ZOHARAH VIEWED THE challenges of Vietnam as the challenges of the Third World overall, including within the oppressed communities of the United States. She was impressed with how much the translators seemed to know about Black struggle in the United States and hoped to prove herself similarly educated about their history. But the delegation had a difficult decision to make: Did they still want to go to Cambodia? *It will be dangerous*, the Vietnamese officials said, *and we can't guarantee your safety.* They couldn't even guarantee a way out. Few Westerners had been allowed into the country since Pol Pot assumed power in 1975, and fighting between his forces and Vietnam continued. The five went into a silent Quaker meditation to decide. Zoharah, the only delegate with a young child at home, was hesitant. If anyone balked, she was ready to decline. But when they returned, she found herself agreeing with her Friends. They would go to Cambodia.[33]

Zoharah thought the Phnom Penh airport, large and made of glass, resembled a winged bird. The beauty soon turned eerie as she realized theirs was the only flight. There were no land personnel on the ground, no other passengers as they exited into the eerie stillness of a haunted land emptied of human life. Two Khmer women in their early twenties served as the group's translators. As the pair explained how they had abandoned miniskirts and jeans for traditional garb as a sign of cultural reclamation, Zoharah thought back to when she first donned kente cloth.

The group drove the wide avenues past empty buildings overgrown with grass and weeds but no people. Zoharah felt transported to *On the Beach*, the postapocalyptic movie where nuclear fallout wiped out all but a small group of survivors. Through incarceration, execution, and forced removal, the once sprawling city had been shrunk from more than two million people down to ten thousand. Intellectuals, doctors, people who wore glasses had all been killed. Starvation was rampant, electricity spotty.

As in Vietnam, their meetings began with the offer of tea. Only, in Cambodia, their hosts had to scour for cups, spoons, tea itself. Zoharah choked up at their apologies. *Please*, she thought, *we don't need tea. Please, let us help you.* Once again they toured an orphanage, some of the children there bald and with bellies distended from malnutrition. They toured a prison that had once been a high school, now a museum to Pol Pot's atrocities. In blood-splattered rooms, Zoharah saw chains, tools of torture, a mountain of clothing left by thousands of executed Cambodians. Pictures of the slain adorned the halls, with their ages and occupations: architects, doctors, lawyers next to children ages fifteen, twelve, ten. Outside she saw the human remains stacked in mass graves.

Zoharah was numb. Cambodia unleashed in her a frightful realization: Europe and its descendants had no monopoly on genocide. Nightmares consumed her until she abandoned the idea of sleep.

ALTHOUGH POL POT had been deposed, fighting between Vietnam and the Khmer Rouge continued. Zoharah's Vietnamese hosts were afraid that Khmer Rouge fighters would shoot down any airplanes. Instead, their Vietnamese hosts arranged for someone to drive from Vietnam to get them. The van arrived armed with petrol containers, water jugs, and rifles. *This will be the worst ride of your life*, the driver told them. Zoharah didn't doubt it. Throughout the eight-hour journey, she prayed for the strength of the vehicle's axles as the van rumbled onto riverbanks to avoid the craters that bombs had left in the war-torn country. Thinking about the Black Vietnamese girl at the orphanage and hoping to see her own daughter once again, Zoharah heard gunfire in the distance.

CHAPTER FIFTEEN

THERE MUST BE SOMETHING WE CAN DO

Sensitive to the AFSC's limitations, both Zoharah and Michael looked for opportunities to scale out their organizing. Revolution remained on the horizon around the world, whether in the form of overthrowing racist regimes or learning to govern newly independent countries. The defeat of Frank Rizzo's attempt at a third term as mayor showed the power of mobilized Black communities to contest America's rightward turn. Each in their own way, Michael and Zoharah committed to organizations tenacious beyond their small numbers. Yet while they carried the torch of Black Power into a new era of uncertainty, a violation they thought unimaginable burned their family.

As Michael had done in India, Zoharah stayed in the Asian Pacific after the delegation ended. In Japan and Hawaii, Zoharah partnered with AFSC connections to hold press conferences about what the delegation saw in Cambodia, which had been the focus of global condemnation. She continued to travel and lecture about the trip in the United States. She appeared on *Good Morning America* and lectured to peace groups around the country. With its purported embrace of Marxism, the Khmer Rouge was often cast in Western media as a Cold War morality tale vindicating capitalism. The willful sacrifice of millions seemed the work of a singularly possessed madman's bankrupt delusions. But Zoharah saw the Cambodian atrocities as a more human drama. She spoke not of ideology but of people, the impact on those with no loyalties to the great powers. "You see, they had this *whole plan*," Zoharah told the *New Yorker* of Pol Pot's designs. "But it didn't work."[1]

The traumas of the US war in Vietnam echoed in Zoharah and Michael's own family. Michael's brother Reginald, who had served two tours of duty in Vietnam, was in the hospital. Again. In his decade as a civilian, Reginald had traded in his Marine greens for the SEPTA blues of a Philadelphia bus driver. Zoharah learned to bite her tongue around him years earlier, when he told her, *I'm not Black, I'm a Marine.* Yet he was a loving man. He never criticized Michael's anti-war stance, had visited him in prison, and went with Zoharah to pick him up when he was released. His own journey since leaving the military had been fraught. He had married, lost a child to crib death, and had a growth under his arm removed. The growth had returned, however, and he had been diagnosed with a rare form of cancer.

The family decamped to the VA Hospital, Michael's mother most especially. A diagnosis of multiple myeloma had driven Rebecca from the workforce fifteen years earlier. By 1979, she had long outlived the doctor's initial prognosis. But she had been given so much radiation that her bones were too brittle for her to spend time in the sun. She refused to accept defeat. Rebecca prided herself on a clean home and a protected family. She was determined to care for her firstborn child. Rebecca and Michael visited Reginald every morning. Rebecca stayed in the hospital until staff kicked her out each day. Worried that it was too much for her, Michael offered that they could alternate days at Reginald's bedside. *If you don't want to go, fine,* she told him, *but I am.* And that was that. Michael went every few days, Rebecca daily. She became an unofficial nurse in that VA, fulfilling her childhood dream in the context of her personal night-mare. She made her daily rounds, looking after not only her son but other patients.

Early in Reginald's hospitalization, the doctors told Michael and Rebecca that it was terminal. When someone Michael knew from college coincidentally became Reginald's doctor, he told them that the news was even worse. *If you say something, I'm going to deny it*, the doctor informed Michael and Rebecca, *but, man, he got this from Vietnam. This is Agent Orange*, he said of the chemical weapon the US military used to defoliate Vietnam. The orange-colored herbicide contained the toxic chemical dioxin. More than four million US troops and un-told numbers of Vietnamese were thought exposed to Agent Orange. Its presumed linkage to cancer, diabetes, and birth defects among vet-erans and their families had prompted a class-action lawsuit against the chemical manufacturers. The lawsuit was filed months before Reginald's hospitalization. Michael's family did not even know about it. They did not tell Reginald that Agent Orange—the US military—was likely the cause of his suffering. He wouldn't have cared anyway.

They didn't discuss that he was dying. When they brought him to Rebecca and Willie's house for Thanksgiving, it took nurses forty-five minutes to calm his pain enough to get him down the stairs. Watch-ing his excruciating decline, Zoharah recalled the gruesome display of spontaneously aborted fetuses and deformed infants that she saw in jars at a Hanoi museum, casualties of the same poison now eating away at her former brother-in-law. Her heart sank for Michael and Rebecca, for Reginald's wife and surviving children.

Reginald Simmons died on March 7, 1980. At his funeral, a team of soldiers fired the customary three-volley salute given to fallen vet-erans. Both his daughter and granddaughter would also die premature deaths from cancer.[2]

EVEN AMID SUCH tragedy, Zoharah and Michael both traveled fre-quently: Zoharah fundraising for AFSC and speaking about what she witnessed in Vietnam and Cambodia, and Michael consolidating a national effort among communist organizations aligned with the PWOC. With Rebecca attending to Reginald, and then her own grief, care of Aishah often fell to Willie. Zoharah's relationship with Michael's stepfather was more cordial than close, but Michael knew him to be a good man: devoted to Rebecca and her chronic illness, a hard-working employee of the gas company who relished his role as provider for the family. Michael had even tutored Willie in math as he studied for the test that made him a supervisor. During Reginald's illness, Aishah was with Willie often at the house where Michael spent his teenage years.

Zoharah was standing at the kitchen sink of her own house when Aishah broke the news. *Pop-Pop came into my room at night*, Aishah said, before revealing that Michael's stepfather had molested her. Aishah had her own room at Rebecca and Willie's house, so often was she there. Willie had fondled her while she, terrified, pretended to sleep. The violation, she reported, was preceded by several incidents where he had kissed her inappropriately.

Zoharah didn't believe it. *That must have been a bad dream*, she insisted. Willie had carried Aishah from the hospital bed to the car when she was first born while Michael pushed Zoharah in the wheelchair. *Are you sure it wasn't a dream?* she asked. *You could have dreams that are so real that you think they're real.* Rebecca ran a tight house; she would never allow that. *That can't be true.* Aishah stayed with Willie and Rebecca often—Zoharah needed them. She couldn't believe it. *Maybe it was bad energy, it was Satan.* Something, anything, not this.

Disoriented, Aishah insisted on what happened, which soon gave way to tears, rage and sorrow in every drop. Zoharah did not know what to do. The possibility of its truth devastated her. Both she and Michael relied on Rebecca and Willie's childcare to support their public political lives. She couldn't process this violation in light of her extensive commitments. She felt an urge to deny Aishah's testimony. Yet she also knew from experience the betrayal of being dismissed, powerless and unheard, after recounting sexual abuse at the hands of a trusted figure. She resolved to talk with Michael about what to do.[3]

ONE OF THE few PWOC members not working in a factory, Michael made $150 a week as a full-time revolutionary. It was a throwback to his subsistence wages as a SNCC worker, only he was fifteen years older and had two kids to support. His work for PWOC was multifaceted. He planned gatherings, sold newspapers, and ran study groups. About one-quarter of PWOC's membership was Black, and much of Michael's work concerned the organization's Black Liberation Commission. The commission anchored a local anti-apartheid coalition; protested cuts to infrastructure, factory closures, and police brutality; and participated in teacher and transit worker strikes. As in several major US cities, Philadelphia's population grew older, Blacker, and poorer throughout the 1970s as the city lost 150,000 manufacturing jobs and experienced greater white flight.[4]

Since 1978, Michael had been active in PWOC's attempt to lay the groundwork for a new national communist party. They called their effort the Organizing Committee for an Ideological Center (OCIC). The OCIC adopted the PWOC approach of Marxist politics and shop-floor organizing in a handful of deindustrializing cities. PWOC leader Clay Newlin served as the OCIC's chair. The group aimed to develop a shared theoretical framework—an "ideological center"— around which to unite disparate Marxist groupings that could then organize the multiracial working class into a new political party.

That was the idea anyway. In practice, the effort included a lot of polemical battles with other communists. China and the Soviet Union were at odds, and many US communists lined up behind one—and against the other. Although Michael had been partial to China in the 1960s, he now joined the PWOC in supporting the Soviet Union. This owed in part to the USSR's aid to liberation movements, particularly in southern Africa. Yet in for a penny, in for a pound: When the Soviet Union invaded Afghanistan in December 1979, Michael saw it as a necessary move to protect women's rights and the possibility of a secular democracy against a theocratic threat.[5]

Michael criticized communists as sharply as he once had Quakers—including within his own organization. At an OCIC gathering in Chicago, Michael objected when one of the local hosts described the conference location as *a bad and dangerous neighborhood* that visitors should *walk through quickly and never alone*. Michael tried to address the matter. "The question that I raised, though, is what is a safe neighborhood in Chicago? What are the criteria for a safe neighborhood in Chicago, and safe for who?" One of the locals interrupted, assuring him that he had misunderstood their intent. "Why is it I can't speak?" he asked, the distance between Quakers and communists suddenly feeling very small.

As discussion continued, Tyree raised another problem. One of the flyers that Chicago activists had prepared to orient the out-of-towners said of the city's bus drivers *despite appearances, CTA drivers can be quite friendly and helpful if treated politely.*

Michael was appalled to see people he assumed to be comrades dismiss primarily Black working-class people, both on the bus and around the South Chicago Y where the gathering occurred, with such contempt. How could the OCIC build anything with such attitudes? Michael saw it as a problem within the organization itself. "And I'm not trying to be cute with words," he said as the discussion wrapped up, "but I just want for people to be clear that had this [incident] never occurred, it [racism] still will happen." Communists would have to confront racism. The conference concluded with a resolution that read, in part, "we recognize that we have not taken our criticism and rectification deep enough. The process has only begun."[6]

MICHAEL AND ZOHARAH only ever fought about parenting. But parenthood offered a lot of fodder. Michael's libertine lifestyle, with family, music, and alcohol, contrasted with Zoharah's ascetic spiritualism. Schooling was a constant source of conflict. Zoharah wanted to keep Aishah in Quaker school. But when Aishah, repeating something she heard at school, made a vaguely disparaging reference to *those people*, Michael knew she couldn't stay there. *We are 'those people,'* he told her. After years of the posh Friends School, Michael won his campaign to switch her to public school in fifth grade.

Then Zoharah confronted him with something he thought unimaginable—Willie's abuse of Aishah.

Mike, we've got to do something, Zoharah pleaded. *She's telling the truth.*

His initial impulse had been the same as hers—disbelief. He thought Zoharah was looking for reasons to criticize him. They argued about it. But Zoharah pressed on. Those tears, such pain. It happened. *We've got to do something.*

Michael switched to crisis management. *We can't tell my mom*, Michael said, numb. *It will kill her.* Zoharah agreed. Everything about their extensive commitments and fragile schedules relied on Rebecca and Willie to care for Aishah when one or both of them was out of town. If not Aishah, they vowed to protect Rebecca—and themselves.

With fear and uncertainty, they agreed to a plan: Michael would confront Willie, and Aishah would never be alone with him again. But it was chimerical. Their hectic travel commitments in fighting for liberation around the world came at a terrible price for their safety at home. Each one hoped that denial would make the horror of this violation disappear. And so they never enacted the plan: Feeling confident that Michael would do it, Zoharah never confronted Willie. But neither did Michael, and they did not speak about it again for decades. And Aishah continued to go to Rebecca and Willie's house, both with others and alone. While their public lives stayed on freedom, a horrible silence consumed their family.[7]

It was an uncharacteristically dry summer when Zoharah stepped off the airplane in New Orleans on August 21, 1980. She had flown with two friends, part of a nineteen-person delegation from Philadelphia, one of the largest delegations, to participate in the fourth National Black Political Convention. Recently released from prison, Republic of New Afrika cofounder Imari Obadele was among the Philadelphia group, as was PA state representative David Richardson, whose frustration with the Democratic Party led him to refuse to support Jimmy Carter's reelection bid. Zoharah cochaired the group with a member of the Kazana Family whom she had worked with a decade earlier.

The gathering was boldly titled "Developing a Progressive Black Agenda from the Grassroots for the 1980s." In support of that agenda, the Philadelphia delegation was there to urge the convention to adopt a "vote-no campaign" for the 1980 presidential election in protest that "none of the candidates are willing to make the substantial commitments required to improve the life quality of the masses of Black people in the U.S." The group also opposed registration for the draft, which Carter had recently reinstituted, and supported the Provisional Government of the Republic of New Afrika. Despite promising a "human rights" administration and appointing several Black cabinet members, President Carter largely followed Republican and business interests. His pick for the Federal Reserve, Paul Volcker, instituted a steep hike to interest rates that exacerbated an unemployment crisis that fell particularly hard on Black workers in the United States and a debt crisis in the broader Third World. Carter's softer approach to the Cold War still sided the United States with abusive dictators against leftist movements.[8]

The first National Black Political Assembly (NBPA) had been a raucous 1972 gathering in Gary, Indiana, where the town's first Black mayor, Richard Hatcher, joined Congressman Charles Diggs and Black nationalist Amiri Baraka to preside over an unwieldy gathering of radicals, liberals, and progressives. Eight thousand people attended the first convention and endorsed a "Gary Declaration" that committed participants to an "independent" Black politics. Subsequent, though smaller, national gatherings in Little Rock (1974) and Cincinnati (1976) reaffirmed that agenda.

Michael had been part of developing a similar infrastructure in the Philadelphia Black Political Convention. After helping mobilize Black voters to defeat Rizzo, the Philadelphia convention movement pivoted to a standing forum to address issues such as schools, policing, affirmative action, and other needs of the city's Black masses. Michael was thrilled to see a forum outside the Democratic machine and where would-be candidates had to prove their mettle in regard to concrete community demands. Though the convention's preferred candidate failed to win the mayoralty after Rizzo, the group's efforts helped ensure that Wilson Goode, Michael's old boss from the Paschall Betterment League and a gadfly at the convention process, served as chief of staff of the new administration. Writing in PWOC's *The Organizer*, Michael praised the convention effort as "a great step forward and . . . the cutting edge for progress in the city of Philadelphia."[9]

Zoharah hadn't participated in the local conventions but approached the National Assembly with an urgency that blanketed despair. On May 17, 1980, an all-white jury in Miami acquitted four officers in beating a Black motorist to death and tampering with related evidence. The acquittal sparked an uprising, during which eighteen people were killed and almost a thousand arrested as the National Guard patrolled the streets. Twelve days later, a white supremacist shot and wounded Urban League president Vernon Jordan in Indiana. The day the NBPA gathering began, news came that another Black child—the thirteenth in as many months—had been killed in Atlanta. Zoharah had followed the story since it first made national news in November 1979, when the child of former Atlanta Project members Camille and John Bell was killed. As the killings continued, Camille Bell became a leading voice in the Committee to Stop Children's Murders. The killer(s) of eleven Black women in Boston in 1979 had still not been found while the Klansmen and American Nazi Party members who killed five communist activists in Greensboro, North Carolina, were soon to be acquitted of all charges.

And in his first speech since becoming the Republican nominee for president, Ronald Reagan went to the town where three Mississippi Freedom Summer volunteers were murdered in 1964 and pledged his support of "state's rights."[10]

Surveying this bleak landscape, Zoharah sought rejuvenation. She was glad to be among two thousand delegates at the New Orleans convention, hoping that the assembly could offer a poignant response to recrudescent white supremacy. She didn't know what it might be. No one seemed to. As Jimmy Carter's genteel austerity prepared to square off against Ronald Reagan's open revanchism, NBPA attendees shared a despondent rejection of the status quo. But what to do instead?

At the Friday night plenary, Zoharah nearly leapt out of her seat when NBPA leader Barbara Sizemore, the former superintendent of Washington, DC, schools, declared, "The revolution is now." The first Black woman to head a metropolitan public school system, Sizemore urged NBPA to reorganize itself as a political party. The next day, Ben Chavis read a formal proposal on party building to the crowd, finishing with a call to arms: "It is not only Nation time, it is independent Black political party time!" Queen Mother Moore, the eighty-two-year-old Black nationalist Zoharah had met at the Republic of New Afrika conference twelve years earlier, urged the group to forge ahead. Zoharah joined the crowd in applause and chanting, "We're fired up, can't take no more." Rather than just vote-no, the convention had come around to an affirmative position: build a new party.[11]

The closing day of the conference was devoted to launching the party. The NBPA agreed to host a founding convention in Philadelphia, site of the first Convention of Colored People of the US (1830), and home to a formidable cadre of activists committed to independent Black politics. Zoharah volunteered to be the chief coordinator for the local planning committee.

THE NEXT THREE months were a blur of daily meetings and constant logistics. With $800 to its name, the organizing committee established a meeting space for the late November gathering and food and housing for the five hundred expected attendees. Zoharah led the small team of volunteers in availing themselves of whatever networks they could through Pennsylvania state representative Dave Richardson, the Black Political Convention, and the Philadelphia Alliance of Black Social Workers. With Zoharah's phone number on the bottom, flyers distributed around the city and nationwide announced the goal as "a popular, mass based, Community-building, Nation-building Party."[12]

More than fifteen hundred people from twenty-six states and the District of Columbia gathered in Philadelphia for the National Founding Convention for a Black Independent Political Party on November 21, 1980. The gathering fell two weeks after Ronald Reagan's landslide victory over Jimmy Carter and three days after six Klansmen and neo-Nazis were acquitted of killing five communists in North Carolina a year earlier. The fury at events propelled the conference forward. Overwhelmed at the number of attendees, Zoharah and the local organizing committee scrambled to find food and housing for a gathering three times the expected size. Despite her anxiety at the task, Zoharah viewed it as a good problem. Most of those who attended were under forty, worked professional careers, had never attended a similar gathering, and considered themselves Black nationalists or Pan-Africanists. *These people have come from everywhere*, she marveled.[13]

The conference took place at Ben Franklin High School in North Philadelphia and moved quickly to establish itself as the National Black Independent Political Party (NBIPP), with Zoharah as its treasurer. NBIPP cochair Ron Daniels introduced Zoharah to the crowd as *Sister Sojourner*. She outlined the group's context. "We know that our conditions have worsened in the last two decades, regardless of the things that are quoted of how many of us are now in the middle class," she said. The reasons were many: "Black men are languishing in the jails," "sisters are having to go it alone," "neighborhoods are deteriorating. Not only the buildings, but the quality of our lives."

Children are "miseducated, undereducated and suffering from mental and cultural genocide" and "senior citizens live alone, on pitiful incomes." She declared a mission of self-determination. "We are going to pay for this out of our own pockets, because we are going to be independent and answerable to our Black selves," she told the cheering attendees. Seeing how SNCC's funding had collapsed as the organization took on more controversial stances, Zoharah was adamant that NBIPP be funded by its members. She saw the NAACP as a model. NBIPP members were expected to pay two dollars a month.[14]

NBIPP modeled itself on the idea of a liberation party like the African National Congress or, for that matter, the Mississippi Freedom Democratic Party: a mass-movement organization of local chapters, giving form to popular demands so that they may shape electoral outcomes. Its plan was to develop the capacity to challenge the existing party system before running its own candidates. Zoharah's friend Sylvia typed up the NBIPP charter at night at her job, to be sent out to two hundred delegates for approval. The charter laid out the minutiae of party structure alongside an ambitious platform of Black self-determination. The platform covered everything from jobs, education, and health care to energy policy, international relations, and incarceration. Learning from the recent past of male-dominated organizations, NBIPP instituted a strict policy of gender parity: every committee had to have at least one woman as cochair. There were two exceptions: the Women's Caucus had no men on it, and Zoharah served as the sole treasurer, with no male counterpart.[15]

She couldn't wait for what came next.

MICHAEL WAS FLYING to Seattle yet again. While his visits there were once about coordinating worker organizing, now it was to criticize his comrades. Michael was a commanding figure in the Struggle Against Racism, the formal response sparked by incidents at the OCIC's Chicago conference. All local groups within the OCIC participated in this internal campaign to purge the communist movement of white racism. It soon became the group's dominant concern. As with the rest of the OCIC, Philadelphia was the campaign's epicenter. Alongside Clay Newlin, who was the chairman of both OCIC and PWOC, Michael led group meetings to address racism.[16]

Their technique involved a process common among communist groups: criticism/self-criticism. In theory, the process allowed people to challenge themselves and each other in the interests of personal and collective growth. Everyone was subject to criticism. After women in PWOC criticized him for relying on his mom's uncompensated labor, Michael stopped having her iron his clothes. Michael and Clay often led the sessions, both in Philadelphia and with OCIC groups nationwide, which often excused them from the harshest critique.

Michael's faith in the purity of their purpose soured as he saw the process devolve into show trials and self-flagellation. *Michael, when you're around, you just bring out my racism*, a communist in Boston reported. Others overcompensated. People confusingly divulged deep hatred for Black people, a claim at striking odds with their public activism against racism. Lacking the capacity to deal with the nuance of sharing power in an unequal society, people resorted to cartoonish confessions. At one point, even Clay came to Michael privately to disclose three acts of racism in his past—one of which was failing to challenge Michael's sexism. Down the pecking order, members were subjected to criticisms of "white chauvinism" and berated to do better. Some made sincere change, but with great discomfort. The confessional nature of the proceedings mistakenly isolated racism to discrete individual acts to purge rather than social relations to transform.

It was falling apart—even in the middle of its collapse, Michael recognized that much. But recognition could not stanch the bleeding of membership, for both PWOC and OCIC. Those who didn't resign were expelled for failing the OCIC's campaign. "The campaign has developed into a destructive ritual, permeated with moralism and a crusade-like atmosphere," a group of OCIC members from around the country wrote in October 1980.[17]

For all the creative talent the new communist movement attracted, it used few tools. Those who stayed, including Michael, swung the hammer of polemics into the nail of organizational decline. Where *The Organizer* had for years featured reports of shop-floor organizing and the crisis of Philadelphia's deindustrialization—factory layoffs, cuts to public transportation and the city schools, police brutality—its pages now thudded with denunciations. The organization had shed so many members it couldn't put out the paper in a timely fashion. "These resignations are one aspect of the split in our movement over the campaign against white and petit bourgeois chauvinism," the paper offered by way of apology in an unsigned editorial for having skipped an issue before further polemicizing the split.

Instead, criticism became its own reward. The OCIC rebranded the Struggle Against Racism as a Campaign Against White Chauvinism, and rebranded again to include opposition to "petit bourgeois chauvinism." The expanded scope was meant to include the ways cadre dismissed the potential of working class. The campaign surfaced critiques of sexism as well. Finally they added "accommodation to racism," that is, the role that Black and other people of color played in tolerating or internalizing racism. In *The Organizer*, Michael explained the move. The campaign clarified for him how racism diminished his own impact, leading him to distrust his own ideas or insights around white leftists at times. It was the same struggle Zoharah had when she began at the AFSC—an extension, even, of what they both observed in Vine City and elsewhere. Black people needed to reckon with the toll racism took on their own psyches. He hoped that other Third World Marxists would benefit similarly. This expanded effort put nonwhite members on the hot seat.[18]

From the outset, it took an intimate turn. Most of the Third World people in the group were partnered with white people, and, sex being an obsession of Western racism, the campaign took its inexorable turn to examining interracial relationships. Like any member in an interracial relationship, Michael and Dina were subject to demanding questions, from themselves as well as others, about their attraction and whether they treated each other differently from how they would treat romantic partners of the same racial background. And like other members', Michael and Dina's relationship couldn't withstand the genuine insight and withering self-doubt generated by the campaign. No one ordered them to break up, but it was nearly impossible to stay together, and stay in the organization, after such an intense process.[19]

Dina moved out of their Germantown house. Things between them were tense as they negotiated coparenting. Michael had baby Tyree nine days at a time compared to her four days. It was a custody arrangement shaped by the Struggle Against Racism, which affirmed that biracial children should spend more time with the nonwhite parent in order to foster a stronger sense of racial identity.

The critique of accommodation to racism impacted Michael's other intimate relationship, too—his friendship with Tyree. In an earlier criticism session, Tyree had gotten so disoriented that he accused himself of plagiarism for writing poems inspired by Langston Hughes. One of the most prominent bona fide proletarians in the group, Tyree had a lot of influence in the OCIC. Yet the criticism process wore at him, and Michael thought he'd lost a sense of himself. Now with Michael and Clay in Seattle, Tyree was nowhere to be found. Other local activists were similarly MIA. *Are we going to have this meeting or what?* Michael asked. His Seattle comrades were evasive, making excuse after excuse until it was clear that no one was coming. The meeting wasn't going to happen. Michael returned to Philadelphia, defeated.

ZOHARAH CRISSCROSSED THE country to build the National Black Independent Political Party. When not in her living room, meetings brought her to Pittsburgh or Baltimore, Indianapolis or Chicago, Memphis or Rocky Mount, North Carolina. Between NBIPP and her AFSC responsibilities, she was on the road constantly. Zoharah left Aishah with Michael or his parents during these trips, straining their already quarrelsome relationship.

The biggest Black nationalist effort of the early Reagan years, NBIPP quickly attracted a large reputation—even beyond the United States. In March 1981, four months after its founding, Zoharah and Ron Daniels represented NBIPP on an official visit to Grenada. The Caribbean island off the coast of Venezuela was celebrating the second anniversary of its socialist revolution. Zoharah saw her spot on the dais next to dignitaries from Cuba and Nicaragua (which also experienced a socialist revolution in 1979) as a sign of NBIPP's potential. Beyond the planned festivities, she enjoyed staying up late swapping movement stories with women and girls she met there. The ruling New Jewel Movement planned sweeping educational reforms—its name stood for Joint Endeavor for Welfare, Education, and Liberation—and Zoharah hoped that her Freedom School history could be of some use. An African revolution in the Western Hemisphere! Zoharah was elated. Dreaming of a six-month sabbatical from AFSC to work in Grenada, she promised the Grenadians she met that she would return soon.[20]

In the meantime, the exigencies of NBIPP weighed on her. Despite or perhaps because of its procedural sophistication—committee structure, decision-making process, chapter certification procedure, points of unity—NBIPP still had too few devotees. As Michael had done with the OCIC, Zoharah participated in study groups and member meetings, locally and nationally. And as with Michael, Zoharah's party-building effort failed to launch. NBIPP was besieged with division on its purpose and strategy. Groups like the Socialist Workers Party and the African People's Party sought to force NBIPP to endorse their separate organizational planks. Meetings ran late into the night as people jockeyed for position, attempting to get the organization to refuse to run candidates or to begin running candidates immediately, to support or denounce the Soviet Union, to scrap or adopt its charter. NBIPP became bogged down in proceduralism, what critics would later describe as "wage war by resolution." The group spent precious time debating ethereal positions without having much ability to implement them. She grew frustrated battling with partisans who seemed uninterested in NBIPP itself.[21]

As NBIPP became a bruising debate club, attendance dwindled—both at national meetings and within local chapters. The organization's budget bore the bad news. Two months after the founding convention, Zoharah had proposed the organization needed a budget of $75,000 to enact its plans. Six months later, Zoharah reported no incoming funds from state or local chapters. NBIPP's existing monies depleted in supporting its meetings and brochures, Zoharah had no time to rouse a volunteer fundraising committee. "The reason [for the committee's inactivity] being an overcommitment of my time and a physical inability to handle all the responsibilities I have attempted to shoulder," she wrote in exhaustion. "I self-criticize myself for not haveing [sic] more insite [sic]."[22]

MICHAEL FOUGHT THE sadness enough to go to the meeting. Local journalist Mumia Abu-Jamal, who had covered some of Michael's organizing over the years, had been shot and arrested following a late-night altercation in which a police officer was killed. The ad hoc defense campaign included people Michael knew through the Black Political Convention and AFSC, including the lawyer who sued the Bureau of Prisons after he and others were transferred from Allenwood. But the campaign divided early on. Michael's old boss, Wilson Goode, was now city manager, and he had privately assured people that he would take care of it. *How's he gonna take care of it?* Michael wondered. *He can't take care of shit. He's not the mayor!* Some of Abu-Jamal's journalist colleagues feared his political stances, particularly his closeness with MOVE, and left the coalition. Some of those who stayed had Michael's leftist associations in mind when they derisively demanded, *We only want people in all-Black organizations to be part of this.* Not long after Mumia was sentenced to death, Michael left the group.[23]

His social life dwindled along with PWOC's membership. His connection to Tyree, already frosty, froze completely after Tyree flew from Seattle to Philadelphia to testify in an acrimonious custody battle involving divorcing PWOC members. Michael saw Tyree's testimony, choosing sides among former comrades, as a betrayal. When Tyree gave a speech suggesting possible common cause with Allan Bakke, the white man whose anti–affirmative action lawsuit against the University of California was beloved by the Right, Michael was furious. They ceased talking altogether.

With PWOC extinguished, Michael began driving a taxi to make ends meet. The cars were run-down, the medallion that cab drivers needed was expensive. *We really need a union*, he thought. But he was too unsure of himself to try. The closest he got to politicizing his job was his willingness, unlike many other drivers, to take customers deep into North or West Philadelphia. His son was a bouncy preschooler now. Michael would drop him off at his parents' house, drive all day, and pick Tyree up on the way home. When Tyree was asleep or with Dina, Michael watched whatever sports was on TV. Occasionally he drank too much. He didn't do much else. He couldn't. He was too depressed.

ZOHARAH'S DESCENT FOLLOWED Michael's. Her mom had moved in with her, convalescing from shingles and difficulties with her husband. An NBIPP comrade Zoharah was dating also moved in. He was only supposed to be there a short time, but it was already clear he had no plans of moving out by the time he stole her credit card. When her mom and Aishah were not around, she called for other NBIPP members to help her throw him out.

Beyond the unpleasantness of the situation, Zoharah felt weak and afraid. Her pants were too big, her shirts too bulky. She was eating but losing weight. She grew concerned enough to visit a doctor, someone on the fringes of NBIPP. When the tests began, Zoharah was relieved when they ruled out cancer. But the diagnosis still offered cause for concern. *What are adrenal glands?* she wondered when the doctors reported that hers had failed. Triangular groupings of cells located on top of the kidneys, adrenal glands regulate the body's response to stress. The years had taken a toll. *Whatever you're doing, you've got to stop*, the doctor told her. Zoharah's two weeks in the hospital served as her resignation letter from NBIPP. The organization had little steam left in it anyhow. She abandoned her planned sabbatical in Grenada when Reagan sent US troops to invade the island in October 1983.

Michael was depressed. Zoharah was on leave from AFSC and organizing. Their bodies wore the declining fortunes of Marxism and Black nationalism, lodestars of their faith. What's worse, the Right was winning: with little Democratic opposition (and increasing support), Republicans eviscerated the already threadbare social safety net, while anti-colonial movements and leftist governments worldwide were beset with civil war, punitive debt, and autocratic rule. It would take all of Michael and Zoharah's strength to renew their freedom fight. And it would be many more years before they confronted their failures to protect their daughter.

CHAPTER SIXTEEN

THE WORLD AND ITS PEOPLE

FROM THE MID-1980S TO THE DAWN OF THE TWENTY-FIRST century, few would be able to identify anything approximating a Black Power movement. Many of the standard-bearer organizations—SNCC, RAM, the Black Panthers—had long folded by the time Ronald Reagan was reelected in 1984, when the idea of Black Power was most readily associated with the attempt to elect Black people to higher office. Jesse Jackson's presidential campaign brought a social movement ethos to the Democratic primary under the banner of the "Rainbow Coalition." The name itself was taken from an earlier multiracial effort by the Chicago Black Panther Party. Though Jackson's campaign lost, local electoral campaigns that trafficked in diluted notions of Black Power helped elect mayors and other local officials.[1]

Philadelphia was a telling example. Wilson Goode—Michael's former boss—beat Frank Rizzo to become mayor in 1984. The city's first African American mayor, Goode also oversaw the police devastation of a Black neighborhood in West Philadelphia. MOVE had returned to the city, once again drawing complaints from the neighbors. In response, officers dropped a three-and-a-half-pound bomb from a helicopter on the house where MOVE people lived. Zoharah saw thick plumes of black smoke fill the air as she listened to the conflagration on the radio. *Lord have mercy, they're going to kill them all*, she thought. The police and fire commissioners decided to let the fire burn. The inferno killed six adults and five children, all part of MOVE, and incinerated the whole block—sixty-one houses.

The MOVE bombing was an extreme example of the new national orthodoxy that treated Black people as disposable. Reagan's regressive policies slashed social spending and drove Black unemployment to records not seen since the Great Depression—in June 1985, it was 15 percent for African Americans, and 40 percent for Black teenagers, compared to 6 and 19 percent, respectively, for the country overall. Incarceration rates skyrocketed, particularly for poor Black men. Reagan's saber-rattling patriotism also funded proxy wars against leftist movements in Central America and supported apartheid South Africa and Israeli expansionism. With different inflections, the United States would continue to be bellicose abroad and callous at home into the new millennium.[2]

Within this grim landscape, the politics of Black Power still offered a vital framework that connected Black Americans to the wider world. Michael's work with Southern Africa Freedom Summer, for instance, helped seed what was, by the mid-1980s, thriving campaigns on college campuses to divest US support from apartheid South Africa. Coming out of their own mental and physical health challenges, Michael and Zoharah remained stayed on freedom by applying Black Power's emphasis on self-determination and internationalism to a changing world. As the Cold War ended, with conservativism reigning in the United States and capitalism triumphant globally, Black Power provided part of the foundation for renewed social movement. Black Power's influence in the late twentieth century required more than plying hard-fought lessons from the past. Michael and Zoharah adapted their methods to meet the moment. Not yet able to process Willie's violation of Aishah, Michael and Zoharah nonetheless recognized that the treatment of women and girls was a bellwether for social conditions. Their organizing, always anti-racist and internationalist, became increasingly devoted to feminism.

WHILE WORKING AT Crisis Intervention Network, an anti-violence organization that employed former gang members to deescalate potentially violent situations and to protect Black and Puerto Rican youth from racist attacks, Michael also reentered the Quaker fold. Prompted by Ronald Reagan's bombastic foreign policy, he began doing anti-draft organizing with Quaker groups in Philadelphia and New Jersey, conducting workshops on militarism and how to become a conscientious objector. And in 1986, he was invited to join a two-week delegation to the Soviet Union. The group included distinguished academics from MIT, the Bulletin of Atomic Scientists, and the American Enterprise Institute. Michael was the only nonacademic member—the only one without a college degree, in fact—and the only Black person.

He said yes immediately. Still a Marxist, Michael was thrilled to visit the land Lenin once ruled, the place that had inspired Paul Robeson, Langston Hughes, and so many others in the Black world. Combined with Soviet aid to Third World liberation movements, the historic support of Black radicals for the Soviet Union led Michael to think he was headed to a place that not only built socialism but transcended racism.

The AFSC partnered with the US-USSR Friendship Association to coordinate these delegations, which alternated annual trips between the two countries. The format for trips to the Soviet Union was well established by the time the six-person delegation landed there in mid-April 1986. The group would spend most of their time in Moscow, together with a trip to one of the Soviet Republics—theirs would be to Lithuania—meeting with various government representatives, academics, and others.

Michael was eager to discuss imperialism and the future of socialism. Mikhail Gorbachev had come to power in the Soviet Union a year earlier, promising widespread reform to revive the Soviet future, while US jets had just bombed Tripoli and Benghazi in retaliation for the bombing of a West Berlin nightclub that killed a US soldier and wounded more than two hundred people. Michael found his hosts taciturn with such political questions. Formal presentations did not broach these topics. On the train to Lithuania, he overheard his companions speaking with Soviet representatives about nuclear weapons and Reagan's proposed plan to build military capacity in space. Yet the people seated next to Michael would only discuss Duke Ellington. *Listen, man, I don't mean to be rude*, Michael said at last, *but I didn't come here to talk about that. I love jazz, I promise to send you some records when I get back. But*, he said, gesturing at the other delegates, *I want to talk about what they're talking about.* They offered some perfunctory remarks as Michael stewed.

If not in conversation, Michael tried to steer the delegation toward sites that might reveal something of Soviet politics. The Soviets stalled on his request to visit a synagogue, however, and refused to discuss antisemitism. He was disappointed to find that the Patrice Lumumba Institute, the university named after the slain Congolese leader and held out as a beacon of Soviet support for Third World struggles, was not in the heart of Moscow as he had thought but tucked in its suburbs. When party apparatchiks distanced themselves from African liberation struggles or offered support for Ethiopia's military occupation of Eritrea, Michael questioned his romantic attachment to the Soviet Union.

Man, he realized, *these motherfuckers are racist.* They weren't more racist than Americans, certainly—just racist.

The night the group left Moscow, an explosion at the nuclear power plant in Chernobyl released a radioactive cloud ten times more deadly than the blast at Hiroshima. Coming just seven years after the Three Mile Island catastrophe in Pennsylvania, Michael wondered if anyone else in the world had been within five hundred miles of the two largest nuclear meltdowns in history. While the group returned to the United States, Michael booked a Eurail Pass and traveled the region by train. In the Netherlands, which had a dynamic anti-apartheid movement, he reconnected with an old AFSC comrade he knew from their work on southern Africa. Spain was his first time at a nude beach. On his last night in Europe, he met a Black US soldier who became his tour guide around Frankfurt, Germany. He stayed up all night, a flaneur in a foreign land.[3]

Not six months later, in the fall of 1986, he was back at the AFSC—working as director of a new East-West Program. Fifteen years of Third World Coalition agitation for the organization to hire people of color for programs that were not deemed overtly "racial" had softened management to Michael's return. He did, after all, know a lot about the Soviet Union.

The job was divided between the Peace Education Division, focused domestically, and International Affairs, which meant travel and the chance to work on the ground abroad as well as within the United States. That arrangement would solve some of the problems of his earlier position in the Southern Africa Program. It was only a one-year job. But he knew that Zoharah, who would soon be fundraising in support of his program, was eleven years in to what began as a six-month position.

For the perfect job, he was willing to answer the same questions from 1972 about his writing ability and his commitment to nonviolence, happy to *yessir* his way through admonitions to respect Quaker principles this time around.[4]

Michael found the AFSC more formal than when he had left it. The looser, experimental atmosphere that had marked his time there in the 1970s had given way to a more conventional nonprofit. Since he'd left in 1979, the organization had instituted a sign-in at the front desk. Yet when he noticed that Black people, even regular visitors, always had to sign in, while white people, even complete strangers, did not, he instructed Aishah and Tyree to skip the sign-in. *Mine ain't doing nothing yours don't do*, he thought.[5]

Still, Michael enjoyed setting up the East-West Desk. The job allowed him to subscribe to dozens of publications across the ideological spectrum in order to track developments in and with the Soviet Union. His first task was to hire an assistant director who could help him read the foreign language press. Some of his friends in the Third World Coalition objected when he hired John Feffer, a white man and recent graduate of Haverford College. But Michael took to John right away: he spoke fluent Russian and didn't seem to care whether he got the job. It was a perfect fit of what Michael needed and what he wanted.

From a windowless room in the basement of the Friends Center, surrounded by piles of publications, Michael chain-smoked while he and John tried to determine the extent of the Soviet Union's transformation. The job was well suited to Michael's lifelong love of newspapers. As Soviet elites opened up the country to public scrutiny, the foreign language press was particularly helpful. They were keen to see whether Gorbachev was another apparatchik or sincere in his professed commitments to democracy, human rights, and nuclear disarmament. Whereas some saw Gorbachev's call to abolish nuclear weapons as smoke and mirrors, Michael was optimistic. Calling it an opening, Michael encouraged peace activists "to take a visionary step without always knowing what the next step is."[6]

Michael got to see how the Soviets imagined that next step when he returned there in November 1987, two weeks before Reagan and Gorbachev met at the White House. He met with Soviet officials and academics, together with two former AFSC staff members who had been part of the 1979 delegation to Cambodia with Zoharah and had since relocated to Moscow. Michael's conversations entailed not only human rights within the Soviet Union but also the government's relationship to Europe, the United States, and the Third World. His already dashed hopes of Soviet internationalism faded further in the face of isolationist sentiment. Eight years of seemingly pointless war in Afghanistan, together with poverty and deprivation throughout the Soviet Union, had created a nationalistic sentiment while Gorbachev's governing coalition was badly fractured. Days before Michael arrived, conservatives on the Politburo removed Boris Yeltsin as head of the Moscow Communist Party after Yeltsin criticized Soviet leadership and the slow pace of reform.

Other than reacting to Reagan's plans to militarize space, Michael's Soviet hosts seemed aloof to global politics. Though they offered ongoing support for Angola, Cuba, and the African National Congress, they also expressed that *the ANC needed to develop more patience* in its fight against apartheid. They backed away from expressing support for Nicaragua, where the socialist government faced blistering attack from the United States, or for the Palestine Liberation Organization, despite Israel's "iron fist" policy that saw a dramatic increase of arrests without charges and the closure of Palestinian newspapers—issues that would, within weeks of Michael's departure, lead to a general strike in Gaza. Although Jesse Jackson had recently launched his second insurgent run for president, Michael found Soviet interest in US politics stopped at Gus Newport, the radical mayor of Berkeley, California.

Michael returned stateside in December doubtful that the Soviet Union had a future. "Within the next twelve months," he wrote in a January 1988 summary of his trip, "we may be able to determine if the current direction the two countries are now in is a hiatus or whether we are witnessing the slow, tedious death of the post war era." Thirteen months later, Soviet troops withdrew from Czechoslovakia, and the Polish workers movement began negotiations with the government that would soon lead to independent elections and a non-communist government. The Cold War was dying; a new geopolitics was being born.[7]

ZOHARAH WAS GLAD to see Michael back at the AFSC. Yet life inside the organization had deteriorated amid budget cuts and an administrative bloat that viewed with hostility the activist spirit people such as Zoharah and Michael represented. Although the Third

World Coalition and Nationwide Women's Program advocated for a dignified and principled workplace, they lacked collective bargaining power. Zoharah joined the growing effort to organize a staff union. She participated in furtive meetings in the TWC office and, as the initiative grew, at the American Federation of State, County, and Municipal Employees (AFSCME) building nearby. Earlier attempts to organize an independent AFSC union had faltered, so the group sought support from the municipal workers union. The executive leadership opposed the effort, saying unionization *goes against Quaker principles* by "involving built-in adversarial relations with outside parties." Zoharah had heard it all before. *Well*, she thought, *racism goes against Quaker principles too. But you're still doing that.* Zoharah didn't see the AFSC belief in consensus on display when the AFSC board hired lawyers to oppose the unionization effort or suggested disbanding the Third World Coalition, a base of union support.

Like her grandfather before her, Zoharah was all in on the union. She was part of the organizing committee. And when the AFSC staff union was certified by a vote of 63 to 41 in the spring of 1988, Zoharah was on the first bargaining team.[8]

Yet management had dragged its feet on contract negotiations and used the leeway it provided to summarily fire longtime staff member Bahiya Roberts. Toward the end of the workday on Valentine's Day 1989, two managers walked to Bahiya's desk and told her to pack her things immediately. She was escorted off premises. As bad as the firing itself, management declared that Bahiya had to repay twenty-five dollars from a recent per diem expense.

Word of the humiliating disregard for a longtime staff member—and the most senior person of color in the personnel department—spread quickly through the Friends Center. The Third World Coalition fumed at the pettiness of it all. *So much for Quaker values*, Zoharah said bitterly. Livid, Michael had an idea. *We're gonna pay them back*, he said. Once he had collected the money Bahiya allegedly owed, Michael snuck into the manager's office and spread twenty-five hundred pennies across her desk.[9]

THROUGHOUT 1989, MICHAEL's premonition on the collapse of the Soviet empire came true in a staccato burst. Soviet troops left Czechoslovakia in February and Hungary in April. The Solidarity union movement forced the Polish government to the negotiating table in February, initiating a process that would, by August, create the country's first non-communist government since 1948. Masses of Germans dismantled the Berlin Wall in November, hastening the decline of East Germany and the Soviet bloc. Throughout Eastern and central Europe, communist regimes collapsed. And with the exception of Romania, where a mob murdered dictator Nicolae Ceaușescu and his wife, Elena, on Christmas Day, it was a largely nonviolent revolution. The ripple effects would soon dissolve the Soviet Union itself.[10]

The Cold War was ending, but what followed was undetermined. Michael hoped to devote his energies to the struggles of women and workers in making the new Eastern Europe. Worker movements had been at the forefront of the push for democracy in Poland and Czechoslovakia, and Hungary led the region with a strong feminist movement. Ostensibly a workers' state, the Soviet Union had formal structures for women's leadership in government and support in childcare throughout the Eastern Bloc. Michael hoped that the recognition of workers and women's leadership would provide a third way between the Stalinist repression Eastern Europe had overthrown and the capitalist exploitation he worried lay in wait. He arranged for John Feffer to visit Europe and interview people on the ground to develop a possible project, and he began organizing "East-South" dialogues to bring social movements from the global periphery into conversation.

Michael's rejection of Cold War orthodoxy led him to recalibrate his job from the "East-West Desk," which emphasized US-Soviet exchange, to what would ultimately become the AFSC's Central European Affairs program. When history finally overtook the Soviet Union at the end of 1991, Michael was already developing a forward-thinking human rights outpost responsive to the fluctuating situation on the ground in a pivotal region. He opened an office in Budapest, the only AFSC office in Europe.

Michael divided his time between Philadelphia, Budapest, and the rest of the world. He saw Eastern Europe as a window into a possible future beyond orthodoxies of capitalism and communism. The world's axis was shifting, in ways yet undetermined. His East-South seminars promoted trilateral exchange focused on the Third World. In Harare, Zimbabwe, he met with leaders of the African National Congress, the Pan-African Congress, and the new social movements in South African townships. The gathering in Mexico City brought together Eastern European economists with those from El Salvador, Honduras, Nicaragua, and elsewhere in Central America. The final meeting, held in Greece, planned connections across Western Europe, Eastern Europe, and the Caucasus states.

His focus remained in central and Eastern Europe, where old dangers threatened the hope sparked by communism's collapse. Absent the state guarantees of formal equality and dedicated minority political representation, racism and sexism now flourished. Women were being laid off, harassed, and denied childcare supports. Right-wing movements and conservative politicians targeted nonwhite Europeans, particularly the diasporic Roma communities, who were segregated and despised throughout the region, and migrants. Limited as it was, the state support for equal rights that communism offered had disappeared. Market-sanctioned discrimination joined frequent street harassment of women, the loss of gender parity in government, and occasional racist attacks by skinheads.

One of the first public events that Michael and Judit Hatfaludi, the Hungarian feminist he hired to staff the AFSC central Europe office, organized in the post–Cold War Eastern Europe was "Women in the Workplace." The seminar brought about fifteen feminist organizers from the region to Budapest in the summer of 1994. The featured speaker was Marty Langelan, the former president of the Washington DC Rape Crisis Center and author of *Back Off!*, a guidebook for women on confronting sexual harassment.

Participants received a copy of the book to use it developing local campaigns.[11]

Ilona Zambo, founder of the Gypsy Mothers Association, spoke at the conference about the growing racist discrimination Roma women faced. Michael recognized the Roma plight, defined as it was by ghettoization in both housing and employment, police violence, and the popular acceptance of racist stereotypes. He had heard Roma organizations speak of the Black American civil rights struggle as a model they could emulate. To them, that meant Martin Luther King—a prominent and eloquent spokesman. Michael knew it should mean widespread community mobilization.

In December 1995, Michael brought groups of Roma activists into dialogue with African Americans to discuss civil rights organizing. The group of twenty gathered for four days in the Budapest suburb of Szentendre. "We all come here as students and teachers," Michael said in opening the conference. "Over the last few years, there have been a lot of Westerners who have come to this region solely as teachers. The spirit of this meeting is that we are here to learn from each other. While the African American community has many organizing experiences, we too are in search of a movement. . . . We are here to learn about each other, collectively and as individuals."

The group shared stories to identify points of unity, forged in difference as much as in commonality. The end of communism eviscerated the Roma workforce, much as deindustrialization and mass incarceration had done for Black youth in the United States. Questions of assimilation and stereotypes, the unique pressures women of both groups faced, and whether to work within or from outside mainstream politics loomed large. "We know everything about each other and we know nothing about each other," one of the Roma participants offered. "We know everything because the relevant issues are the same. . . . But our civic movement is a new one. Yours is an old one."[12]

After a day of heady discussion, the group celebrated with a raucous party in a working-class Roma neighborhood. The alcohol flowed freely—a bit too freely, Michael thought, as he hid in the bathroom at one point to avoid a woman's advances. He took it in stride, having been to his fair share of exuberant gatherings. The next day, the Roma at the meeting apologized. *It's no big deal*, Michael reassured them. Still, they insisted on bringing the group to meet middle-class Roma. *We are not all like that*, someone said of the previous night. Michael saw it differently. *We are everything*, he told them. *It's not this or that. It's this and that.* When Roma pined for their equivalent of Martin Luther King, Michael tried to tell them *you are Martin Luther King!* There was no leader to save them—they needed a movement. *The process of liberation is as important as being liberated*, he told them.[13]

As with the Women in the Workplace seminar, Michael and Judit left the Roma–African American exchange with big plans to support campaigns throughout the region. But their hopes were dashed by the brutal violence cannibalizing Yugoslavia.

ONCE UPON A time, Michael had seen Yugoslavia as an example of multiethnic cohabitation. But that changed as nationalist militias orchestrated ethnic massacres beginning in the early 1990s.

He flew to Eastern Europe an average of every other month, staying about two weeks each time. As violence spread, Michael spent more time in Yugoslavia. Some of Michael's friends worried about his frequent dashing into a war zone, especially one characterized by ethnic massacres. Though cautious, Michael was not scared. *They're not shooting at me*, he rationalized. The warring parties invoked centuries' old grievances of faith and language—none of them involving Africa or its descendants. *I might accidentally get shot—but that could happen anywhere*, he reasoned. Besides, he thought, and as many Eastern Europeans would come to see of him, Jim Crow had taught him the urgency, empathy, and adaptability needed to survive a war.

Though he felt as safe as one could feel in such a situation, his experience in refugee camps proved that racism structured even crisis relief. Within two months of setting up a refugee camp in Macedonia, people there had access to hot water and international phone calls. Michael learned that these small comforts were rare. *Damn, these folks get warm water, and we couldn't even get clean water in Africa,* a professional aid worker who had spent time in Rwanda and the Congo said to him. Michael found the economy of international aid startling. As humanitarian relief workers flooded war-torn Sarajevo, the city became suddenly metropolitan. Mexican and Indian restaurants—plus inflation—catered to the sudden flood of NGOs. As the war pivoted to Kosovo, the relief industry followed. Wherever he was, Michael hoped to build projects that could endure. He also wanted to spend money on programs, not creature comforts. He even took a taxi from Bulgaria to Kosovo, spending a fraction of the money a flight would have cost, to have more money for relief efforts.

His only luxury expense was Shalimar, the fanciest Indian restaurant in Budapest, where he held lengthy planning meetings. The meetings spilled over from the restaurant to the AFSC office and back again. The office was buzzing with activity, doubling as an overflow space to the AFSC-sponsored refugee center in the city. People slept on the desk of the conference room or on the floor of the makeshift guest room they had fashioned at the office. *The office is like a freedom house,* Michael beamed. He ran interference between his AFSC superiors and the meager staff on the ground in Eastern Europe. He knew that there was no way the organization could truly grasp dire circumstances from afar. When the new head of the AFSC's International Division demanded more precise reports to align the organization's work with its funders, Michael said enough to keep the spigot, small as it was, running.

In 1987, NINE months after Bawa died and twenty-five years after she matriculated at Spelman, Zoharah returned to college to complete her bachelor's degree. Antioch College, where Staughton Lynd and Coretta Scott King had encouraged her to attend in 1964, had a Philadelphia campus designed for working adults. Zoharah took night classes while working full-time and maintaining her busy travel schedule. She loved being a student again. A former Freedom Rider turned Temple University professor, John Raines, encouraged her to pursue graduate study. (Unbeknownst to her or anyone at the time, Raines had also been among the group who broke into the suburban Pennsylvania FBI office in 1971 and stole the files that revealed COINTELPRO, ultimately paving the way for Zoharah's first job with the AFSC.)

As the Cold War ended and the AFSC union succeeded, Zoharah graduated from Antioch. She began a PhD program in religion at Temple University in 1990, with an emphasis on women and Islam. If Islam was to be her faith, she needed to know there was a place for the feminist politics she had increasingly adopted as her own. Her concern over the treatment of women and girls was global, which meant it was also local. As Michael had found in Yugoslavia, where rape became a weapon of war, Zoharah was beset with how emboldened right-wing movements, both in the United States and internationally, consolidated their power on the backs of women. After years of reluctance, Zoharah began to describe herself as a feminist, or sometimes a womanist, using the neologism of Black feminist theology proffered by Rev. Dr. Katie Geneva Cannon, with whom Zoharah studied.

Zoharah felt called into action when George H. W. Bush nominated Clarence Thomas, the Black arch-conservative jurist, to replace retiring justice and civil rights icon Thurgood Marshall on the Supreme Court. Thomas described opposition to his appointment as a form of racism. "I will not provide the rope for my own lynching," Thomas said in refusing to address allegations that he had sexually harassed Anita Hill when he was her supervisor. Following Thomas's inflammatory statement, Hill testified to a visibly hostile Senate.

Watching Hill's testimony in October 1991, Zoharah was ready to fight back. She identified with Hill, who described being hospitalized with stress-induced stomach pain around the same time as Zoharah had suffered adrenal gland failure. She was quick to join an ad hoc effort, led in part by her former NBIPP comrade Elsa Barkley-Brown, to challenge Thomas's nomination and voice support for Hill. On November 17, 1991, three weeks after Thomas was sworn in to the court, Zoharah and Aishah were two of sixteen hundred Black women to sign a statement under the name African American Women in Defense of Ourselves. The document appeared as a full-page ad in the *New York Times* and five other publications. "We pledge to continue to speak out in defense of one another, in defense of the African American community and against those who are hostile to social justice no matter what color they are," the statement thundered. "No one will speak for us but ourselves."[14]

Zoharah continued to emphasize feminist responses to the increasing conservatism of both Democrats and Republicans. She joined the AFSC's Justice for All campaign launch in July 1995. The effort was aimed at countering the new Republican congressional majority's plan to slash social welfare spending, expand mass incarceration, and shield corporations from litigation. "The right wing has targeted our very fragile safety net and put it on a 'hit list,'" Zoharah said. Of Republican Speaker of the House Newt Gingrich's signature document, Zoharah said, "The so-called Contract with America is a real misnomer . . . it's more a contract *on* America." The conservative assault, as she saw it, aimed to disempower those it disenfranchised. "Let us set the record straight that we are not powerless, voiceless, apathetic, or hopeless. Let us join with others and break out of single-issue ghettos and set the record straight. We will redefine what America is with our community-based movement for justice!"[15]

Six weeks later, Zoharah joined with others to redefine not just an American but also a global sense of justice as head of an AFSC delegation to Beijing for the United Nations Fourth World Conference on Women. Zoharah, now a leading member of the AFSC's Nationwide Women's Program, headed the fourteen-person AFSC delegation. The group included women from both the United States and Mexico. The passage of the North Atlantic Free Trade Agreement (NAFTA) a year earlier had exacerbated low-wage and dangerous working conditions for women in Mexican maquiladoras (sweatshops). The AFSC's binational delegation was a deliberate attempt to highlight a women- and worker-centered form of globalization. Aishah, who was now working in the Communications Division at the AFSC and was shop steward of the staff union, wrote the press release.[16]

Zoharah's group took a bus from the Beijing airport to Huairou, a suburb about fifty kilometers north of the city, for a weeklong summit of NGOs preceding the formal gathering of the UN. Though a recognized part of the conference, the NGO forum did not have much infrastructure behind it. Zoharah's delegation slept in scattered accommodations, the workshops were in too-small rooms in far-flung parts of the city, and most of the food offered to participants had pork in it. Zoharah cleared a convenience store of its potato chips and Snickers supply as her subsistence. And the weather was unforgiving. "We have had an incredible amount of rain," Zoharah wrote in a letter to AFSC director Kara Newell, "turning the NGO Forum Site into a sea of mud, puddles, grit and grime. This was added to workshop sites incredibly far apart, collapsing tents, confusion on top of confusion re: workshop sites, bus stops, bus schedules, and the almost impenetrable language barrier."

And yet, it was a great success. Zoharah delighted being in the throngs of more than thirty thousand women, "many of whom are grassroots from all over the world in every color, hue and shape to be found in the human family," she wrote, "who have come to add their voices and to lend their talent to the effort to improve the lot of women across the globe." Despite her sense of worldliness prior to the conference, Zoharah was moved to tears at what she learned from the gathering. "One wonders about the obvious hatred and misogyny which is unbounded by geography, race, religion or culture," she wrote. "But what has buoyed me up is the women of the world's determination to expose the violence and to end it in their lifetime."

Zoharah collected literature from women's groups around the world. She joined in protests against Structural Adjustment Programs, the punitive austerity pushed on Third World countries by the

World Bank and International Monetary Fund that exacerbated what had been dubbed the feminization of poverty. Her main focus was the Muslim world. She thrilled hearing women from Iran, Saudi Arabia, Jordan, Morocco, Egypt, Mali, Syria, Pakistan, and elsewhere describe their organizing. Presentations offered feminist interpretations of the Quran that rebutted the patriarchal interpretations of marriage and gender roles hardening under something Zoharah learned was called Shari'ah law. When she saw a group of Iranian exiles chase away Iranian men sent by the government to chaperone the country's official delegates to the conference, she felt inspired that the effusive solidarity among Muslim feminists could better the lives of women and girls around the world.[17]

After the NGO forum ended, the AFSC delegation headed to a hotel and hot vegetarian meals in Beijing. Zoharah and another member of the group had been granted "observer credentials" for the governmental conference. This allowed them the chance to shape the "Platform for Action," the official conference document of recommendations. In meeting after meeting, Zoharah channeled the fighting spirit of the women who inspired her to press the US delegation to adopt more progressive positions.[18]

She returned to Philadelphia committed to using the platform to guide ongoing feminist organizing, particularly among Muslim women in the United States. While the Nation of Islam leader Louis Farrakhan defended boxer Mike Tyson from rape allegations and organized a "Million Man March" to celebrate Black patriarchal authority, Zoharah's former SNCC colleague H. Rap Brown—now an imam named Jamil al-Amin—headed a congregation where women wore niqabs, full body and face coverings, and were expected to be subservient to men. Zoharah's meeting with al-Amin went nowhere. When she organized a report-back session on the conference aimed at Black women, she learned that a local imam had disparaged the session and discouraged his congregants from attending.

Six months after returning from Beijing, Zoharah received a Fulbright Fellowship, a prestigious grant that funds American researchers working overseas. She chose Jordan, where English was widely spoken, for her dissertation research. She took a yearlong unpaid sabbatical from AFSC, a benefit offered to longtime employees, and in June 1996, she boarded a plane to Amman.

This would be her third time in the region in as many years. In 1994, she had joined a delegation with the US Interreligious Committee for Peace in the Middle East to Israel, Palestine, Jordan, Egypt, and Syria. The group visited soon after Israeli and Palestinian officials signed the Oslo Accords, establishing the Palestinian Authority and a limited form of self-government in the occupied territories of the West Bank and Gaza Strip. At the Tel Aviv airport, Israeli customs officers seeing her Arabic name accused her of being Palestinian and threatened to deny her entry. The cautious optimism she felt in meeting with Jewish and Palestinian officials in Israel and the West Bank was dashed by her time in Gaza, where wire-encased checkpoints staffed by hostile soldiers controlled Palestinian movement. Inside Gaza, her heart broke listening to a psychologist describe his trauma center for Palestinian children.

The next year she made *umrah*, the Islamic pilgrimage to Mecca, with eighty members of the Bawa Muhaiyaddeen Fellowship. Sufism was banned in Saudi Arabia, and patriarchal control was widespread. In one of her outings, a store owner threatened Zoharah for walking without a male chaperone. Yet these trips also nurtured her soul. In the Old City of Jerusalem, she felt herself return to a place she had never been as she worshipped at the holy sites of the three Abrahamic religions. Prayers, both learned and adopted, poured out of her as she worshipped at the Church of the Holy Sepulchre, the Dome of the Rock, and the Wailing Wall. And circling the Kaaba, the giant black cube in Mecca outside Islam's holiest site, Zoharah felt what Malcolm X had described of his own experience in Mecca thirty years earlier: *It is the world and the world's heart united here*, she beamed.[19]

Now with the Fulbright Fellowship, Zoharah would have a full year to study Arab and Muslim feminist organizations. Like many countries, Jordan was undergoing dramatic social change that pitted the moderate royal family against progressive (both secular and religious) challengers and an even larger Islamist opposition that sought to stem the disruptions of globalization through enhanced patriarchal authority. The Muslim Brotherhood controlled one-third of the seats in Parliament. The debate, such as it was, concerned everything from women's literacy to their holding elected office. Her time there coincided with a pivotal national election in 1997 that had mobilized women's groups. Toujan al-Faisal became the first woman elected to Jordan's Parliament in 1993, but not long after Islamists took her to court to forcibly divorce her from her husband as an "apostate." Zoharah followed al-Faisal's reelection effort in 1997, along with the campaigns of sixteen other women who ran for Parliament that year. As she listened to one candidate describe the physical threats she had endured for her run and saw the hope evident among campaign volunteers working to change a historically inaccessible electoral system, Zoharah recalled her time trying to elect Black people to office in Mississippi and Georgia.[20]

In part because of that experience, Zoharah was not surprised when all the women lost their campaigns. Her focus was elsewhere: the efforts to transform the social status of women in Jordan. She worked part-time as a researcher at the Princess Basma Resource Center. The eponymous women's organization was led by the king's sister, whom Zoharah had heard speak in Beijing. She also observed educational sessions, both in Amman and in several rural towns. Even through a translator, Zoharah recognized the organizers' attempt to use their meetings as "consciousness raising" sessions, where women could recognize their concerns as collectively suffered and structurally based. Conditions made that difficult. In one small village, a group of men crashed the workshop and refused to leave.[21]

Challenging as conditions in Jordan were, Zoharah took heart from the rich ferment of women's activism. She made friends quickly, forging a cosmopolitan community among Palestinian, Syrian, and other expatriates as well as many Jordanians. As she learned the country and its language, deepening her ties to its social and political

life, Zoharah considered staying in Jordan. With the support of another fellowship, she had already extended her time there another six
months. Friends assured her that her skill set could yield a job at the
UN Development Programme, headquartered there. But she wanted
to finish her long-winding educational journey.

She returned to Philadelphia to find that the AFSC had eliminated her position. Suddenly, at fifty-four, she found herself out of
work. She moved in with a friend, resumed her below-minimum-wage
teaching assistantship at Temple, and took out student loans. Soon,
she became a secretary in Temple's Women's Studies Department.

Thanks to the union contract, she was able to receive three months
of severance pay from AFSC. But the organization offered her a rate
only at the part-time salary she had been working prior to her travel
abroad. She felt discarded. "Given that I worked for over 20 years,
with only four, possibly five of those years as a part-time employee,
I think that the least the organization could do would be to give me
severance pay which reflects what I earned," Zoharah wrote in a letter
to AFSC's executive director. "I am truly flabbergasted at what I feel
is the insensitivity, the callousness, and disregard exhibited in this decision." Zoharah likened the AFSC's treatment of Black women staff
to having "served time in Muncie (a women's prison in Pennsylvania)
on a drug possession charge or the like." She was wounded by the
organization's disregard. "My time back home has been very difficult
as I have tried to piece together employment, health insurance and
beat back fears, anxieties and worry about how I would survive each
month."[22]

With just one chapter of her dissertation written, Zoharah applied for full-time teaching positions. She interviewed at Earlham
College, a Quaker school in Indiana, and the University of Florida.
UF offered her the chance to teach classes on both Islam and the
civil rights movement, and she preferred Florida's heat to Indiana's
snow. In December 1999, her car stuffed with clothes, books, and
files, Zoharah returned South to live once again.[23]

While she quickly worked her way into progressive activism in North Central Florida, Zoharah remained focused on the Middle East. Between teaching and finishing her dissertation, Zoharah cofounded the US Campaign to End the Israeli Occupation. She joined scholar Edward Said, researcher Phyllis Bennis, and three faith-based peace activists on the campaign Steering Committee. The group then recruited a broad coalition of human rights organizations working to cut US military aid to Israel. The strategy shared much in common with the global anti-apartheid movement Michael had been part of.[24]

Through the campaign, Zoharah was invited to join an international Quaker delegation to Israel, Palestine, Syria, Jordan, and Lebanon in June 2002. The group of fourteen came mostly from the United States—including someone she traveled with to Vietnam and Cambodia twenty-three years earlier—but also from Canada, England, South Africa, and Palestine. Seeing the itinerary, Zoharah was pleased that the group would visit many of the same people she had met with on her first trip there, eight years before. But the trip was hardly a reunion.

Oh my god, it's so much worse, she thought almost immediately upon arriving in Israel. Any sense of optimism garnered in 1994 had been evacuated by a hardening of the occupation and its discontents. Heavily armed soldiers were everywhere. The second intifada began after right-wing politician Ariel Sharon, who had allowed a massacre of Palestinian refugees in Lebanon as defense minister, staged a heavily armed visit to the Temple Mount in September 2000. A veiled threat, Sharon's visit sparked militant protests and recriminations that soon included Palestinian suicide bombings and Israeli military incursions into West Bank and Gaza. The context was as grim as it was asymmetrical: by the time Zoharah's delegation visited in June 2002, Palestinian combatants had killed 470 Israelis (including 58 minors) while the Israeli army and settlers had killed 1,399 Palestinians (including 234 minors).[25]

Waiting at the same checkpoint into Gaza that she had passed through in 1994, Zoharah no longer saw groups of Palestinians on the other side trying to gain entrance into Israel, for Gaza had been sealed off entirely. The people she spoke with in Gaza told her that Israeli helicopters flew overhead all night, shining bright lights into their homes. When they visited the Gaza Community Mental Health Center, the same psychologist she had met eight years earlier showed her the Palestinian children's drawings. Zoharah saw small stick figures with arms raised standing in front of thick-lined helicopters. Elsewhere, she heard how Israel rationed water and cut the caloric intake for Palestinians in Gaza. She despaired at the pressures of life in an open-air prison.

It wasn't just Gaza. Palestinians in the West Bank covered their roofs in chicken wire to catch the debris that Israeli settlers tossed down on their houses. In Hebron, a small band of armed settlers had forcibly closed Palestinian businesses and terrorized people off the streets. Elsewhere, Zoharah's group photographed a housing demolition until the Israeli soldiers turned the bulldozers at them and Zoharah ran, terrified they would run her over. The Church of the Nativity, said to be the birthplace of Jesus, still bore bullet holes from a recent assault by the Israeli army. The group waited all day trying to get in to Ramallah, the West Bank city with a historic Quaker presence. But it was in vain: the Israeli army had placed Palestinian leader Yasser Arafat under house arrest there and refused to let anyone enter.

The situation in Israel proper was little better. In Jerusalem, Zoharah marched in a somber feminist demonstration against the occupation. The group, Women in Black, used the same approach Zoharah had used after Michael and others were arrested at the induction center demonstration in August 1966: funeral attire and a silent march. The only Black woman in the group, Zoharah felt the palpable acrimony in the Hebrew phrases hurled at her by Israeli onlookers. *What are they calling me?* she asked the other women. *You don't want to know* was all they told her.[26]

Zoharah was despondent at her trip. *We're not doing enough*, she thought. As the group drafted a book-length report on the trip, Zoharah engaged a couple of AFSC staff who worried that the statement was too harsh on Israel. Zoharah was adamant that the text describe the situation as they saw it: an asymmetrical battle rooted in a US-funded occupation. "Because we believe that there is that of God in everyone, we call on Quakers and others to work energetically and nonviolently for a solution based on the equal worth and dignity of each person, and on the power of love, forgiveness, moral imagination, and generosity of spirit to find a way to resolve even those conflicts that may appear intractable," the group wrote. The AFSC published the book under the title *When the Rain Returns* and sent copies to Congress, the United Nations, and peace groups. Zoharah delivered that message in several lectures. And still, she thought: *We're not doing enough.*[27]

SOMETIME IN THE early 1990s, Michael became the AFSC's Director of European Programs. Quakers who never batted an eye at having white people lead programs in Africa or Asia asked Michael how he became the face of the AFSC in Europe. They also suggested interfaith dialogue as a solution to the genocidal nationalistic enmity devouring Yugoslavia. Michael balked, at the source as much as the suggestion. *You don't have one relationship in the United States that is not with white people*, he fumed. *But you're going to go over there and teach them to talk to each other?*

He knew otherwise: He was not a leader of people but a conduit for them to lead themselves. People would recognize each other through collective action for their community, not through discussions facilitated by people foreign to their context. With Michael's support, AFSC staff in Sarajevo began simply: with a garden. In helping Bosnian, Serb, and Croat neighbors grow their own food, Michael saw his vision blossom. That first garden ultimately seeded fourteen different locations across the region, involving three thousand people.[28]

Michael continued to travel the world, attending any conference that would put him in conversation with rumblings of change. He went to the Socialist Scholars Conference in New York and the Journalists of Color Conference in Atlanta. He brought Tyree with him to Atlanta, and the pair attended the Black Arts Festival happening there at the same time—paving the way for Tyree's blossoming DJ talent that would ultimately see him become a prominent hip-hop artist. Aishah, too, was becoming an artist: around this time she made a short film, *In My Father's House*, about coming out as a lesbian. She dedicated the film to Michael, "my father and comrade in the struggle to end all forms of oppression."

In 1997 he traveled to Tahiti for Abolition 2000, an international coalition pursuing the eradication of nuclear weapons by the new millennium. The conference took place fifteen months after massive protests against French nuclear testing on the small colonized Pacific island. As Michael had asserted so many times before, the Moorea gathering affirmed "that indigenous and colonized peoples must be central" in the process of eradicating nuclear weapons and that the "inalienable right to self-determination, sovereignty and independence is crucial in allowing all peoples of the world to join in the common struggles to rid the planet forever of nuclear weapons."[29]

He and Zoharah both attended the founding conference of the Black Radical Congress (BRC), held in Chicago the Juneteenth weekend of 1998. Organized by a coalition involving many prominent academics, the BRC attempted to update Black Power radicalism for the coming new millennium. Leaders from both the National Black Independent Political Party and the African American Women in Defense of Ourselves effort played key roles in the BRC. The conference allowed Michael to reunite with Tyree Scott, as well as someone he first met at Lewisburg prison. Zoharah, still adjusting to being back in the United States, but not one to miss a gathering of such importance, welcomed reconnecting with her NBIPP comrades.

But as US funding sources for AFSC's Europe program dried up in the new millennium, Michael needed to find new ways of sustaining his work. Michael's boss suggested he move to Europe for a two-year term as the Quaker International Affairs Representative there. He arrived in Budapest on March 31, 2003. The US-led war in Iraq had begun two weeks earlier, and much of Eastern Europe, including Hungary, joined the "coalition of the willing" in supporting the US and UK invasion. But the fevered push for war that dominated American politics had recessed in Budapest. Being there, he immediately felt liberated—from US politics, from the AFSC, from an unhappy second marriage.

He busied himself with Roma organizing, drawing on the support of Budapest's extensive expat community. One of those expatriates was a woman who confided in Michael that her ex-boyfriend had stalked and harassed her. Michael sent the man a threatening letter. When his AFSC superiors summoned him back to Philadelphia immediately, he knew that he had pushed the envelope on Quaker principles too far. His supervisors told him to leave Hungary immediately. They also demanded he apologize to the man, who had threatened to sue for libel. Michael refused. *Fuck that*, he said. *The only way I'll apologize is if the woman tells me she lied.* As his mother had taught him, never back down when you think you're right.

Still in AFSC's employment, he returned to Budapest about two months later and picked up on a proposal to organize a conference on sex trafficking. New to the issue, Michael relied on his contacts across the region. He traveled around Hungary, Serbia, Albania, and beyond to arrange the seminar. The more he accomplished, the more the AFSC pulled back. Funds dried up, staff support disappeared. He received an urgent telex prohibiting him from screening Aishah's documentary-in-progress about sexual violence in Black communities. Still, he pulled off the conference in June 2004, a success beyond his hopes, with Black American and multiethnic European women in conversation across multiple languages.[30]

He returned to the United States in mid-June to meet with AFSC executives about his programs. The organization's new leadership had become more controlled, less radical. Management had thinned staff ranks, and most of those laid off seemed to be troublemakers of Michael's generation and temperament. Still, he hoped the success of the conference would persuade them to launch a coordinated campaign against sex trafficking. June became July and then August as he sat in the AFSC office without any response from AFSC leadership. Finally, on August 31, his supervisor called him in. *Michael, we are closing your program at the end of the month*, they told him. *We no longer have need for your services.* He was laid off, effective immediately.[31]

Michael wasn't shocked—two months of silence had prepared him for the worst. But when the AFSC bosses told him to relocate back to Philadelphia, he decided then and there: he was moving to Budapest. Though spite drove his choice, it made perfect sense. It's a big world, people everywhere working to better it.

MANY MOONS

MICHAEL SPENT THE FIRST MONTHS OF THE PANDEMIC IN AT-
lanta, living with his son, Tyree, now a Grammy-winning artist
known as DJ Drama. Michael still thrived on politics, still enjoyed,
as he put it, *being a pain in somebody's ass*. But the world had tested
his faith in recent years. His adopted home of Hungary was enter-
ing its second decade of autocratic rule. The Roma movement, with
a lot of NGO dollars but bereft of grassroots organizing, had little
to show for itself. Not for lack of trying: Michael had spent years
encouraging community mobilization. He joined a Roma youth activist in protesting racist stereotypes at Comic-Con in New York
City in 2016, and he and Linda, his partner of almost two decades,
spent months in southeastern Spain to support Roma organizing.
Introduced as a minister who had worked with Martin Luther King,
Michael met with local authorities to prevent them from harassing a
Roma church there. Still, the combination of authoritarian governments and ineffectual nonprofits had nearly broken Michael's steady
consumption of the news, so depressing were the headlines.[1]

When I called him in the summer of 2020, he sounded positively
giddy. *I knew it*, he effused about the nationwide uprising against

police violence. *People can only accommodate their oppression so long.* He asked me what was happening in Seattle, where, two miles from my house, the intense protests outside the police precinct had turned into a prolonged occupation. All over the country, people yet unknown to history were making history.

Six months later, the summer fires had cooled. Now began the work of making sense of it all, the more tedious push and pull of social change. In the winter of 2021, I invited Michael—still one semester shy of his college degree—and Zoharah, professor emerita, to speak virtually to my African American Studies class about their work in the civil rights movement. Students quickly brought the conversations to the present. One of them, a Lebanese immigrant, raised a pressing question. This student is the father of someone I had taught two years earlier. His son was one of my sharpest students, and the father, gregarious and determined, was about to complete his own undergraduate degree. "My son graduated last year," he began, "and he believes that the whole system cannot be repaired. I just want to ask your opinion: Do you think we can fix it, or the whole thing, it's just impossible?"

That age-old question—reform or revolution. Michael, however, resisted the divide.

"A flip way of answering it," he began, "would be to say, what's the option? Really. I don't mean to be insulting when I say that, don't misunderstand me. I feel that way too sometimes." But, he said, whether the system can be repaired or not elided the reality that the only way out is through. "I always tell people, wherever you're at, there's a contradiction—some people are being oppressed. You don't have to go and find something to do. Wherever you're located, whatever profession you're in, it's there. You just have to look for it. Your starting point should always be wherever you're living at any particular point."

Zoharah agreed. She had spent the last decade as a member of the National Council of Elders, a self-conscious attempt from twentieth-century organizers to encourage contemporary social justice movements. For her, that included mentoring members of the Dream

Defenders, a Florida organization that began after the murder of seventeen-year-old Trayvon Martin, and joining the local Unitarian Church. "Black Lives Matter is a continuation of the long freedom struggle that African Americans—and others—have been engaged in," she said. The movement's foundational outrage, police violence, is an old problem, she said, with examples going back at least as far as the nineteenth century. But a spark needs more than flint and stone to make a fire: it needs oxygen and tinder. "This movement has grown beyond focusing on police violence. I am very, very excited at how they've expanded. . . . It's a continuation of the long freedom struggle that really began in the enslavement period."

After an hour, the students enthusiastically waved Michael and Zoharah farewell, little hands in little boxes filling the screen, as we begrudgingly turned our attention to discussing course readings. But their message, of possibility and inspiration, of endurance and initiative, is one that has defined my conversations with Zoharah and Michael over many years. And not just conversation. As they would be the first to admit, actions speak louder than words, and I have observed some of their practice here as well.

One of the last trips I went on before the pandemic upended the world was to Philadelphia in the fall of 2019 for an international conference that Aishah organized. "FromNO2Love: Black Feminist Centered Forum on Disrupting Sexual Violence" was both a celebration and an intervention. It marked twenty-five years since Aishah began work on her multi-award-winning documentary, *NO! The Rape Documentary*, which is the first feature-length film about intraracial sexual violence against Black women and girls. Aishah spent twelve years on the film, which debuted in 2006 and has been screened around the world—everywhere from Florida to Hungary, and many points beyond and in between. Zoharah and Michael both feature prominently in the film, and they both spoke at the anniversary screening of the film, which opened the conference.

After a day of panels on Black feminist anti-violence activism and the crises of sexual violence, the conference ended with an event celebrating the release of *Love WITH Accountability: Digging Up the Roots of Child Sexual Abuse*. The book, which Aishah edited, features writings by forty diasporic Black survivors and advocates working to confront sexual violence outside of, as Aishah writes, "the criminal injustice system" that offers neither protection nor accountability. The book, which went on to win a Lambda Literary Award, provides a chorus of strategies to both confront and prevent the scourge of child sexual abuse. While the topic remains taboo for many families who experience it, Aishah's persistent activism on the issue made it possible for Michael and Zoharah to confront their failures to intervene at the time—and to speak publicly about it.

Zoharah's essay opens the volume. Recognizing that most people are, like she once was, afraid to address such violations, she wrote of her own attempts at accounting for the harm she and Michael caused by not protecting Aishah as a child or not confronting Willie before his death in 2010. She also offers four action steps for families confronting child sexual abuse: "First and foremost, Believe the child! Check it out. Confront the perpetrator. Second: Remove her/him/them from the site of the molestation and do not make the child continue to go there and act as if everything is normal. Third: Report the crime to family members and possibly to authorities—unless he or she makes amends, especially within the family unit. Fourth: Get professional help for your child, other family members, and yourself." Zoharah joined Aishah on stage for a tearful and moving presentation at the 2019 book party, a scene of their shared work to stay on freedom. They also partnered on a June 2021 webinar on Black family trauma for the #MeToo movement.[2]

Accountability, like the freedom fight itself, is a process. It is not a box to be ticked but a relationship to be tended. It continues, forever unfinished. Aishah, Michael, and Zoharah—so bound together in purpose and affect—have cultivated it in their own way. Amid the pandemic-inspired turn to Zoom in the spring of 2020, Aishah tells me that she had a breakthrough conversation with her parents. It was not the first time in the years I've been writing this book that I've heard such reports, either of breakthroughs or of new barriers. They have been vulnerable, disagreeable, and generous with each other. I know these conversations will continue, including in Aishah's forthcoming memoir.

Nonetheless, a positive breakthrough in either interpersonal or social relationships, the product of so much difficult and often unseen work, is something to celebrate. It is one of the many small rumbles needed to create tectonic shifts. When the earth will shake is unknown. But in asking what it is we owe each other and how we extend our capacities for change, the Black struggle for freedom continues to remake the world.

Acknowledgments

In the before-times, I benefited greatly as a Scholar in Residence at the Schomburg Center for Research in Black Culture, unquestionably one of my favorite public institutions. My deep appreciation to Brent Hayes Edwards for directing the fellowship with such wisdom. Riley Snorton encouraged me to apply for, and to accept, the fellowship when I thought parenting responsibilities would make it impossible. Additional fellowships from the UW Harry Bridges Center for Labor Studies and the UW Simpson Center for the Humanities allowed me to finish the manuscript. I thank Kathy Woodward, Andrew Hedden, and Kim England for their support via these marvelous centers, and the research fellows I worked alongside at the Schomburg and the Simpson Center.

Thanks to all the librarians and archivists who fielded my questions, especially those at the Schomburg (Cheryl Barado, Shola Lynch, and Maira Liriano), and to Don Davis, who supported my research in the American Friends Service Committee archives.

When travel was more possible, Jeff, Emma, Milo, and Eira Frank; Kathy Boudin (RIP); Craig and Ruthie Gilmore; Rebecca Hill and Warner Belanger; Matthew Lyons, Claire McGuire, and Evelyn

Lyons-McGuire; and Irit Reinheimer housed me on research trips. B. Loewe and Neidi Dominguez offered a celebratory refuge toward the end. I'm grateful to all for the warm beds and enduring friendships. When every minute to write was a gift, Claire McGuire and Jenna McDavid provided precious childcare from afar. Emma Wendel did so in person. The Hanson-Stansbury and Martin-Berliner families provided much-needed local lifelines.

Thank you to everyone who sat down for an interview—in person, over the phone, or on the computer. Louise Newman introduced me not only to Zoharah Simmons but also to the idea of being a historian, thereby changing my life in two interrelated ways. When I was a kid, my parents told me that writing wasn't a viable career, and I told them not to move our family to Florida. I'm glad that we were both wrong, and I appreciate the enthusiasm they've shown for my work.

Lots of love to the many friends who provided good cheer over the years. For help with various aspects related to this project, thanks to John Carl Baker, Orisanmi Burton, Alex Colston, Andy Cornell, Nathan Connolly, Susie Day, Chris Dixon, Bradley Duncan, Garrett Felber, Max Felker-Kantor, Laura Foner, David Goldberg, Trevor Griffey, Matthew Guariglia, Rebecca Hill, Wesley Hogan, Catherine Jacquet, Walter Johnson, Mariame Kaba, Robin DG Kelley, Julilly Kohler-Hausmann, Timothy Lombardo, Toussaint Losier, B. Loewe, Josh MacPhee, Rowan McNamara, Laura McTighe, Lauren Mottle, Tej Nagaraja, Megan Kate Nelson, Dennis O'Neil, Judy Polumbaum, Chandan Reddy, Charlotte Rosen, Michael Staudenmaier, David Stein, Carl Suddler, Heather Ann Thompson, Rebecca Tuuri, Laura Whitehorn, and Rhonda Williams.

Comments from Mika Ahuvia, José Alaniz, Denise Andrade, Abena Asare, Keisha Blain, Sarah Brucia Breitenfeld, Katia Chaterjie, Stephanie Clare, Michelle Commander, Ashley Farmer, Garrett Felber, Susan Gillman, Wesley Hogan, Michael Honey, Jasmine Johnson, Brian Jones, Kelly Josephs, Hajin Jun, Louisa Mackenzie, Charles McKinney, Leigh Mercer, Xin Peng, Erin Pineda, Guillermo

Rebollo-Gil, David Stein, Richard Watts, and Christopher Willoughby improved different parts of the manuscript.

Deep gratitude to LaTaSha Levy, Josh Myers, Jasson Perez, and Barbara Ransby for their careful read of a penultimate draft. Special thanks to Kay Whitlock, for serving as the book's rabbi and jester; and to Linda Carranza, for general enthusiasm and a last-minute fact check.

Margaret Odette and Jay Driskell provided research assistance, Penny Miller the transcriptions. Conversations with Katy O'Donnell and Brandon Proia shaped my thinking on the project early on. Katy also introduced me to Lisa Adams of the Garamond Literary Agency, whose discernment and encouragement steadied me lo these many years. I am overjoyed to have found a home at Basic Books, where first Claire Potter and then Kyle Gipson championed the project with care and insight. Thanks to everyone at Basic for their support.

Zoharah, Michael, and Aishah welcomed me into their family, and Dana and Julian created one with me. Zoharah, Michael, and Aishah placed their trust in me to do something I often came to believe was impossible, or maybe just foolish. I hope to have done right by their faith in me. Dana anchored our collective with loving creativity and offered abundance when the pandemic made time both infinite and scarce. Julian could only babble when this project began but was old enough to lament that I am "not famous at all" when I neared its completion. To Julian, forever with a song on his heart and skip in his step, the magical being from Planet Invisible who named the dog Jedi and whose endless jokes provided so many distractions— to Julian, I owe the world. May he know a better version of it than the one we now call home.

Archival Collections and Interviews

Aishah Shahidah Simmons personal papers, Washington, DC
American Friends Service Committee, Philadelphia
- Community Relations Division (CRD)
- General Administration (Genl Admin)
- Government Surveillance and Citizen Rights (Gov Surv/Cit Rts)
- International Division (ID)
- Nationwide Women's Program (NWP)
- Peace Education Division (PED)
- Third World Coalition (TWC)

Butch Cottman personal papers, Philadelphia
Columbia University, Rare Book & Manuscript Library, New York
- Malcolm X Project Papers
- Manning Marable Papers

Bradley Duncan personal papers, Philadelphia
Emory University, Atlanta
- Howard Moore Papers
- Veterans of Hope Project Interviews

Encyclopedia of Anti-Revisionism Online
- New Communist Movement

Federal Bureau of Investigation, Washington, DC
- Jeremiah Pugh Shabazz File
- Student Nonviolent Coordinating Committee

National Archives for Black Women's History, Washington, DC
- National Council of Negro Women

ProQuest History Vault, Black Freedom Struggle in the 20th Century, Organizational Records and Personal Papers, Part 2
- Student Nonviolent Coordinating Committee Papers

Schomburg Center for Research in Black Culture, New York
- August Meier Papers
- Betty Garman Robinson Papers
- Ella Baker Papers
- Larry Neal Papers
- Malcolm X Papers
- National Black Independent Political Party microfilm
- Northern Student Movement Papers
- Roberta Yancy Civil Rights Collection
- Ruth Schein Papers

SNCC Legacy Project, Critical Oral Histories Conference Interviews, 2016–2018, Duke University, Durham, North Carolina

Tamiment Collection, NYU
- Communist and Socialist Serials
- David Sullivan US Maoism Collection
- Labor Movement Serials
- National Lawyer Guild Papers

University of Southern Mississippi, Hattiesburg
- Center for Oral History and Cultural Heritage
- Lawrence Spears Collection

University of Washington, Seattle
- Labor Archives—Tyree Scott Papers

Wisconsin Historical Society, Madison
- Mendy Samstein Papers
- Social Action Vertical File
- Staughton and Alice Lynd Papers

INTERVIEWS CONDUCTED BY THE AUTHOR UNLESS OTHERWISE NOTED
Paul Beach, July 16, 2020
Kathy Bergen, November 16, 2021

John Braxton, July 8, 2020

Linda Carranza, February 13, 2019

Pat Clark, March 27, 2019

Butch Cottman, April 11, 2019

Ron Daniels, April 18, 2019

Ulysses Everett, interview by KZSU Project South, (n.d.), 1965

John Feffer, August 24, 2020

Vicente Fernandez, August 19, 2020

Tom Ficklin, February 12, 2021

Laura Foner, May 20, 2020

Keith Forsyth, August 7, 2021

Michael Fox, July 24, 2020

James Garrett, July 7, 2020

Domingo Gonzalez, October 17, 2021

Beverly Guy-Sheftall, June 15, 2020

Judit Hatfaludi, August 24, 2021

Todd Hawkins, interview by Trevor Griffey, September 11, 2006

Gerald Horne, July 23, 2020,

Gloria House, September 8, 2020

Darryl Jordan, May 9, 2019

Rafiq Kalam id-Din, August 5, 2020, August 10, 2020

Rachael Kamel, March 4, 2020

Robin D. G. Kelley, October 15, 2021

Ken Lawrence, March 9, 2019, email

Clarence Lusane, September 24, 2021

Staughton Lynd, March 23, 2019

Elizabeth (Betita) Martinez, interview by Loretta Ross, March 3, 2006, Voices of Feminism Oral History Collection, Sophia Smith Collection, Smith College, Northampton, MA

Thad Mathis, April 10, 2019

Adrian McCray, July 15, 2020

Rosemari Mealy, October 14, 2021

Ed Nakawatase, March 24, 2019

Al Pertilla, February 28, 2019

Dina Portnoy, June 2, 2019

David Rudovsky, April 12, 2019

Fannie Rushing, September 14, 2020

Aishah Simmons, May 12, 2021, September 15, 2021

Michael Simmons
- 2012: April 12
- 2019: February 10, February 11, February 12, July 10
- 2020: January 3, January 10, January 17, January 24, January 29, January 31, February 14
- 2021: January 29, February 12, February 17, March 24, March 25, March 31, April 1, April 9, April 16, September 2, September 17
- 2022: February 8
- Interviewed by Zsuzsa Beres, May 3, May 7, May 21, and May 30, 2016
- Interviewed by John Feffer, September 13, 2012
- Interviewed by Trevor Griffey, September 16, 2007
- Interviewed by Klancy Miller, December 2, 1991
- Interviewed by Veterans of Hope, May 18, 2001

Tyree Simmons, October 6, 2021

Zoharah Simmons
- 2017: May 24, July 3
- 2018: February 23, February 24, November 9
- 2019: January 11, January 21, March 8, March 27, December 7, December 8
- 2020: January 10, January 17, January 24, January 31, June 25, October 2, October 16
- 2021: January 29, February 17, May 21, May 28, June 11, June 18, July 16, August 20, August 27, October 22, October 29, November 5, November 12, November 19
- 2022: February 4, February 8
- Interviewed by Juliette Barbette, December 20, 2018
- Interviewed by Justin Dunnavant, October 25, 2021
- Interviewed by Catherine Jacquet, November 25, 2017
- Interviewed by Joseph Mosnier, September 14, 2011
- Interviewed by Catherine Murphy, January 21, 2019
- (Gwen Robinson), interviewed by Ted Polumbaum, Summer 1964
- Interviewed by Robyn Spencer, August 18, 2018
- Interviewed by Rebecca Tuuri, May 24, 2017
- Interviewed by Veterans of Hope, June 24 and June 25, 1998, June 21, 2005

Eberta Spinks, interview by Kim Adams, spring 1995, Mississippi Oral History Program, University of Southern Mississippi, Hattiesburg

David Sogge, July 20, 2021
Lawrence Spears, June 26, 2020
Geri Walker, August 11, 2020
Reginald Walker, August 4, 2020
Gaye Walton-Price, February 12, 2021
Ron Whitehorne, April 10, 2019
Michael Woo, July 14, 2020
Sylvia Wright, March 25, 2019

Notes

INTRODUCTION: A LOVE SUPREME

1. I am glossing a vast literature on civil rights and Black Power. Among the most influential, see Joshua Bloom and Waldo E. Martin Jr., *Black Against Empire: The History and Politics of the Black Panther Party* (Berkeley: University of California Press, 2012); Taylor Branch, *Parting the Waters: America in the King Years 1954–63* (New York: Simon & Schuster, 1988); John Dittmer, *Local People: The Struggle for Civil Rights in Mississippi* (Champaign: University of Illinois Press, 1995); Wesley Hogan, *Many Minds, One Heart: SNCC's Dream for a New America* (Chapel Hill: University of North Carolina Press, 2007); Manning Marable, *Malcolm X: A Life of Reinvention* (New York: Vintage, 2011); Charles Payne, *I've Got the Light of Freedom: The Organizing Tradition and the Mississippi Freedom Struggle* (Berkeley: University of California Press, 1995); Barbara Ransby, *Ella Baker and the Black Freedom Movement: A Radical Democratic Vision* (Chapel Hill: University of North Carolina Press, 2005); Thomas J. Sugrue, *Sweet Land of Liberty: The Forgotten Struggle for Civil Rights in the North* (New York: Random House, 2008); Jeanne Theoharis, *The Rebellious Life of Mrs. Rosa Parks* (Boston: Beacon Press, 2013). Other scholars have told the history of Black radicalism that anticipated the 1960s upsurge. See, for instance, Keisha N. Blain, *Set the World on Fire: Black Nationalist Women and the Global Struggle for Freedom* (Philadelphia: University of Pennsylvania Press, 2018); Glenda Elizabeth Gilmore, *Defying Dixie: The Radical Roots of Civil Rights, 1919–1950*

(New York: Norton 2008); Erik S. McDuffie, *Sojourning for Freedom: Black Women, American Communism, and the Making of Black Left Feminism* (Durham, NC: Duke University Press, 2011).

2. Robin D. G. Kelley, *Freedom Dreams: The Black Radical Imagination* (Boston: Beacon Press, 2002), 9.

3. The connection between love and justice runs deep in the Black radical tradition. For one recent example linking the pairing to material culture, see Tiya Miles, *All That She Carried: The Journey of Ashley's Sack, a Black Family's Keepsake* (New York: Random House, 2021).

4. "Ella Baker Address to a Mass Meeting in Hattiesburg," January 21, 1964, box 1, folder 6: Writings, Ella Baker Papers, Schomburg Center for Research in Black Culture, New York.

5. Chris DeVito, ed., *Coltrane on Coltrane: The John Coltrane Interviews* (Chicago: Chicago Review Press, 2010), 119–120; Daniel Fischlin, Ajay Heble, and George Lipsitz, *The Fierce Urgency of Now: Improvisation, Rights, and the Ethics of Cocreation* (Durham, NC: Duke University Press, 2013).

6. Saidiya Hartman, *Wayward Lives, Beautiful Experiments: Intimate Histories of Social Upheaval* (New York: Norton, 2019), 348.

7. Vincent Harding, *There Is a River: The Black Struggle for Freedom in America* (New York: Vintage, 1981), xxi.

8. Imani Perry, *May We Forever Stand: The Black National Anthem* (Chapel Hill: University of North Carolina Press, 2018).

9. Ashley D. Farmer, *Remaking Black Power: How Black Women Transformed an Era* (Chapel Hill: University of North Carolina Press, 2017); Angela Davis, Gina Dent, Erica Meiners, and Beth Richie, *ABOLITION. FEMINISM. NOW* (Chicago: Haymarket Books, 2021); Aishah Shahidah Simmons, *Love WITH Accountability: Digging Up the Roots of Child Sexual Abuse* (Chico, CA: AK Press, 2019).

1. A MEMPHIS EDUCATION

1. Laurie B. Green, *Battling the Plantation Mentality: Memphis and the Black Freedom Struggle* (Chapel Hill: University of North Carolina Press, 2007), 15–45; Michael K. Honey, *Going Down Jericho Road: The Memphis Strike, Martin Luther King's Last Campaign* (New York: Norton, 2007), 7–22; Brian D. Page, "'In the Hands of the Lord': Migrants and Community Politics in the Late Nineteenth Century," in *An Unseen Light: Black Struggles for Freedom in Memphis*, ed. Aram Goudsouzian and Charles W. McKinney Jr. (Louisville: University Press of Kentucky, 2018), 15–18; Mia Bay, *To Tell the Truth Freely: The Life of Ida B. Wells* (New York: Hill & Wang, 2009), 83–85;

Darius Young, "'The Saving of Black America's Body and White America's Soul': The Lynching of Ell Persons and the Rise of Black Activism in Memphis," in Goudsouzian and McKinney, *An Unseen Light*, 39–60. Lincoln, quoted in Honey, *Going Down Jericho Road*, 7.

2. Zoharah Simmons, "From Little Memphis Girl to Mississippi Amazon," in *Hands on the Freedom Plow: Personal Accounts by Women in SNCC*, ed. Faith S. Holsaert, Martha Prescod, Norman Noonan, Judy Richardson, Betty Garman Robinson, Jean Smith Young, and Dorothy M. Zellner (Champaign: University of Illinois Press, 2010), 19; Zoharah Simmons, interview with Rebecca Tuuri, May 24, 2017.

3. Theda Skocpol and Jennifer Lynn Oser, "Organization Despite Adversity: The Origins and Development of African American Fraternal Associations," *Social Science History* 28, no. 3 (2004): 397–401; Eloise Bibb Thompson, "Liberty and Protection Object of Secret Order," *Chicago Defender*, September 5, 1914, 1.

4. Skocpol and Oser, "Organization Despite Adversity," 398, 401. More generally, see Hortense Powdermaker, *After Freedom: A Cultural Study of the Deep South* (New York: Viking, 1939).

5. David T. Beito, *From Mutual Aid to the Welfare State: Fraternal Societies and Social Services, 1890–1967* (Chapel Hill: University of North Carolina Press, 2000), 53–55, 181–194; Katrina Rochelle Sims, "'Take the Mountain': The International Order of Twelve Knights and Daughters of Tabor and the Black Health Care Initiative in the Mississippi Delta, 1938–1983" (PhD diss., University of Mississippi, 2016).

6. Zoharah Simmons, interview with author, February 23, 2018, and June 25, 2020; David Robertson, *W. C. Handy: The Life and Times of the Man Who Made the Blues* (Tuscaloosa: University of Alabama Press, 2011).

7. Mrs. Addie Jones, Mr. E. A. Teague, and Mrs. Willa McWilliams, "The History of Manassas," n.d., http://historic-memphis.com/memphis-historic/blackeducation/historyofManassas.pdf.

8. Zoharah Simmons, interview with author, February 23, 2018, and December 7, 2019; Beverly Guy-Sheftall, interview with author, June 15, 2020.

9. Timothy Tyson, *The Blood of Emmett Till* (New York: Simon & Schuster, 2017).

10. Zoharah Simmons, interview with author, February 23, 2018; and Simmons, "From Little Memphis Girl to Mississippi Amazon," 11–13.

11. Zoharah Simmons, interview with Rebecca Tuuri, May 24, 2017; Zoharah Simmons, interview with author, February 23, 2018.

12. Green, *Battling the Plantation Mentality*, 216–250; Steven A. Knowlton, "'Since I Was a Citizen, I Had the Right to Attend the Library': The Key Role

of the Public Library in the Civil Rights Movement in Memphis," in Goudsouzian and McKinney, *An Unseen Light*, 203–227.

13. Hogan, *Many Minds, One Heart*, 13–42; Raymond Arsenault, *The Freedom Riders: 1961 and the Struggle for Racial Justice* (New York: Oxford University Press, 2006), 86–106, 179–209.

14. Simmons, "From Little Memphis Girl to Mississippi Amazon," 9–31; Zoharah Simmons, interview with Veterans of Hope, June 24, 1998, tape A-1 and tape A-2, box 14, Emory University, Atlanta; Zoharah Simmons, interview with author, February 24, 2018.

15. Zoharah Simmons, interview with author, February 23, 2018; Beverly Guy-Sheftall, interview with author, June 15, 2020.

2. WORLDMAKING IN PHILADELPHIA

1. Rebecca White Simmons Chapman obituary, personal collection, Aishah Shahidah Simmons; Michael Simmons, interview with author, February 10, 2019.

2. Daina Ramey Berry and Kali Nicole Gross, *A Black Woman's History of the United States* (Boston: Beacon Press, 2020), 68–69; Manisha Sinha, *The Slave's Cause: A History of Abolition* (New Haven, CT: Yale University Press, 2016), 73–74, 137–138; Eric Foner, *Gateway to Freedom: The Hidden History of the Underground Railroad* (New York: Norton, 2015), 11–12, 50–52; P. Gabrielle Forman, Jim Casey, and Sarah Lynn Patterson, eds., *The Colored Conventions Movement: Black Organizing in the Nineteenth Century* (Chapel Hill: University of North Carolina Press, 2021).

3. Michael Simmons, interview with author, February 10, 2019; Matthew J. Countryman, *Up South: Civil Rights and Black Power in Philadelphia* (Philadelphia: University of Pennsylvania Press, 2006); Paul M. Washington, *Other Sheep I Have Known* (Philadelphia: Temple University Press, 1994), 26. My use of *worldmaking* in the chapter title comes from Washington's framing, but it shares much in common with Adom Getachew's depiction of national liberation movements in *Worldmaking After Empire: The Rise and Fall of Self-Determination* (Princeton, NJ: Princeton University Press, 2019).

4. James Wolfinger, *Riding the Rails: Capital and Labor in the Philadelphia Transit Industry* (Ithaca, NY: Cornell University Press, 2016), 137–159.

5. Michael Simmons birth certificate, personal collection, Aishah Shahidah Simmons; Michael Simmons, interview with author, February 10, 2019.

6. Michael Simmons, interview with author, February 14, 2020; Rebecca White Simmons Chapman obituary, personal collection, Aishah Shahidah

Simmons; Michael Simmons, interview with Vincent Harding, May 18, 2001, tape A-1, series 1, box 14, Veterans of Hope Project, Emory University.

7. Michael Simmons, interview with Vincent Harding, May 18, 2001, tape A-2, series 1, box 14, Veterans of Hope Project, Emory University; Michael Simmons, interview with author, February 10, 2019.

8. Michael Simmons, interview with author, February 10, 2019; Russell Rickford, "John Ali, Biographical Sketch," box 39, folder: Bios of Key Figures, Malcolm X Project Papers, Columbia University, New York.

9. Judith Weisenfeld, *New World A-Coming: Black Religion and Racial Identity During the Great Migration* (New York: NYU Press, 2016).

10. Les Payne and Tamara Payne, *The Dead Are Arising: The Life of Malcolm X* (New York: Liveright, 2020), 235–284, passim; FBI, "Background of Cult of Islam," January 31, 1956, 6–33, box 13, folder: Report of Political Activities, Malcolm X Project, Columbia University; Karl Evanzz, "The FBI and the Nation of Islam," in *The FBI and Religion: Faith and National Security Before and After 9/11*, ed. Sylvester A. Johnson and Steven Weitzman (Berkeley: University of California Press, 2017), 148–167; Michael Simmons, interview with author, February 10, 2019.

11. Michael Simmons, "Progress Report, Philadelphia Public Elementary School," June 1956 and June 1957, private collection, Aishah Shahidah Simmons.

12. Timothy Lombardo, *Blue-Collar Conservatism: Frank Rizzo's Philadelphia and Populist Politics* (Philadelphia: University of Pennsylvania Press, 2018), 39; Countryman, *Up South*, 51–57.

13. Donald Freeman, "Orientation to a Black Mass Movement, Part 2," 3–4, Malcolm X Collection, reel 15, box 15, folder 19: Revolutionary Action Movement, Schomburg Center for Research in Black Culture.

14. Tony Martin, *Race First: The Ideological and Organizationl Struggles of the Universal Negro Improvement Association* (Dover, MA: Majority Press, 1991); Blain, *Set the World on Fire*.

15. Michael Simmons, interview with author, February 10, 2019; Michael Simmons, interview with Veterans of Hope, May 18, 2001, tape A-2; Timothy B. Tyson, *Radio-Free Dixie: Robert F. Williams and the Roots of Black Power* (Chapel Hill: University of North Carolina Press, 1999).

16. Melanye P. White-Dixon, "Marion Cuyjet: Visionary of Dance Education in Black Philadelphia" (PhD diss., Temple University, Philadelphia, 1987), 84–86; Jeffrey S. McMillan, "A Musical Education: Lee Morgan and the Philadelphia Jazz Scene of the 1950s," *Current Musicology* 71–73 (Spring 2001–Spring 2002): 2158–178.

17. Michael Simmons, interview with author, February 11, 2019; Reginald Walker, interview with author, August 4, 2020; Geri Walker, interview with author, August 11, 2020; Michael Simmons, interview with Veterans of Hope, May 18, 2001, tape A-3, series 1, box 14, Veterans of Hope Project Interviews, Emory University.

18. "Malcolm X Draws 800 in Camden," *Baltimore Afro-American*, July 20, 1963, 14; Sandeep S. Atwal, *Malcolm X: Collected Speeches, Debates, and Interviews (1960–1965)* (self-published, 2020), 331.

19. Michael Simmons, interview with author, February 10, 2019; Countryman, *Up South*, 139–140.

20. Charles R. Weiner, letter to Michael Simmons, August 1, 1963, personal collection, Aishah Shahidah Simmons.

3. SNEAKING TO SNCC

1. Frances D. Graham and Susan L. Poulson, "Spelman College: A Place All Their Own," in *Challenged by Coeducation: Women's Colleges Since the 1960s*, ed. Leslie Miller-Bernal and Susan L. Poulson (Nashville, TN: Vanderbilt University Press, 2007), 239–240; Zoharah Simmons, interview with author, June 25, 2020.

2. Albert E. Manley, "The Role of the Negro College in Retrospect and Prospect," *Journal of Negro Education* 27, no. 2 (1958): 133; Beverly Guy-Sheftall, interview with author, June 15, 2020; Graham and Poulson, "Spelman College," 238–239; Tomiko Brown-Nagin, *Courage to Dissent: Atlanta and the Long History of the Civil Rights Movement* (New York: Oxford University Press, 2011), 144; Henry Lefever, *Undaunted by the Fight: Spelman College and the Civil Rights Movement* (Macon, GA: Mercer University Press, 2005).

3. Al Pertilla, interview with author, February 28, 2019; Zoharah Simmons, interview with author, June 25, 2020.

4. Tobin Miller Shearer, "Moving Beyond Charisma in Civil Rights Scholarship: Vincent Harding's Sojourn with the Mennonites, 1958–1966," *Mennonite Quarterly Review* 82, no. 2 (2008); Zoharah Simmons, interview with author, June 25, 2020.

5. Al Pertilla, interview with author, February 28, 2019; Staughton Lynd, interview with author, March 23, 2019; Zoharah Simmons, "Mama Told Me Not to Go," in *Time It Was: American Stories from the Sixties*, ed. Karen Manners Smith and Tim Koster (Upper Saddle River, NJ: Pearson, 2008), 99.

6. Baker, quoted in Cleveland Sellers with Robert Terrell, *The River of No Return: The Autobiography of a Black Militant and the Life and Death of SNCC* (Jackson: University Press of Mississippi, 1990), 34. More generally, see Clayborne Carson, *In Struggle: SNCC and the Black Awakening of the 1960s*

(Cambridge, MA: Harvard University Press, 1995); Hogan, *Many Minds, One Heart*; Ransby, *Ella Baker and the Black Freedom Movement*.

7. Ransby, *Ella Baker and the Black Freedom Movement*; Howard Zinn, *SNCC: The New Abolitionists* (Chicago: Haymarket Press, 2013).

8. Pertilla, interview with author, February 28, 2019; Simmons, "From Little Memphis Girl to Mississippi Amazon."

9. Zoharah Simmons, interview with author, June 25, 2020; Ed Na-kawatase, interview with author, March 24, 2019; Zoharah Simmons, interview with Robyn Spencer, August 18, 2018.

10. Zoharah Simmons, interview with Catherine Jacquet, November 25, 2017.

11. Zoharah Simmons, interview with author, January 29, 2021; William P. Jones, *The March on Washington: Jobs, Freedom, and the Forgotten History of Civil Rights* (New York: Norton, 2013), 193–194.

12. Albert Manley to Howard Zinn, June 1, 1963, in Howard Zinn Papers, box 3, folder 23, Tamiment Library and Robert F. Wagner Labor Archives, Tamiment Collection, New York University, https://tamimentlibrary.tumblr.com/post/83244664840/the-archive-speaks-howard-zinn-and-the-spelman.

13. Brown-Nagin, *Courage to Dissent*, 231–251; Kevin Kruse, *White Flight: Atlanta and the Making of Modern Conservatism* (Princeton, NJ: Princeton University Press, 2005); "'Open City' Drive Begins," *Student Voice*, January 14, 1964, 3; Winston A. Grady-Willis, *Challenging U.S. Apartheid: Atlanta and Black Struggles for Human Rights, 1960–1977* (Durham, NC: Duke University Press, 2006), 40.

14. "Protestors Will Spend Christmas in Jail," *Student Voice*, December 23, 1963, 1; "SNCC Meets Klan: Seventy-Three Arrested," *Student Voice*, January 20, 1964, 3; "Jails Fill as Protests Rise," *Student Voice*, January 27, 1964, 1; "Demonstrations Gain Additional Support," *Student Voice*, February 3, 1964, 1, 4.

15. Simmons, "From Little Memphis Girl to Mississippi Amazon," 17–20; and Simmons, "Mama Told Me Not to Go," 102–104.

16. Cynthia Griggs Fleming, *Soon We Will Not Cry: The Liberation of Ruby Doris Smith Robinson* (Lanham, MD: Rowman & Littlefield, 1998), 174–175; Zoharah Simmons, interview with author, June 25, 2020.

17. Simmons, "From Little Memphis Girl to Mississippi Amazon," 20–22; Zoharah Simmons, interview with author, June 25, 2020.

18. Fleming, *Soon We Will Not Cry*; Zoharah Simmons, interview with author, June 25, 2020; Zoharah Simmons, interview with Catherine Murphy, January 21, 2019.

19. "Miss. Summer Project Set," *Student Voice*, March 1964, 3; Carson, *In Struggle*, 96–110; Doug McAdam, *Freedom Summer* (New York: Oxford University Press, 1990); Bruce Watson, *Freedom Summer: The Savage Season That Made Mississippi Burn and Made America a Democracy* (New York: Viking, 2010).

20. Zoharah Simmons, interview with Catherine Murphy, January 21, 2019; Simmons, "From Little Memphis Girl to Mississippi Amazon"; Staughton Lynd, interview with author, March 23, 2019.

21. Lynd, interview with author, March 23, 2019; Zoharah Simmons, interview with author, June 25, 2020; Simmons, "From Little Memphis Girl to Mississippi Amazon."

22. Zoharah Simmons, interview with author, June 25, 2020; Gwen Robinson (Zoharah Simmons), interview with Ted Polumbaum, summer 1964.

23. Zoharah Simmons, interview with author, June 25, 2020; Simmons, "From Little Memphis Girl to Mississippi Amazon."

24. Zoharah Simmons, interview with Jacquet, November 24, 2017; Zoharah Simmons, interview with author, June 25, 2020.

4. MISSISSIPPI AMAZON

1. Bob Moses, "Memo to Accepted Applicants," box 1, folder 2: Ruth Schein Personal Account, Ruth Schein Papers, Schomburg Center for Research in Black Culture.

2. Carson, *In Struggle*, 110.

3. Zoharah Simmons, interviews with author, December 7, 2019, January 24 and January 31, 2020; Jimmy Garrett, interview with author, July 7, 2020.

4. Victoria E. Bynum, *The Free State of Jones: Mississippi's Longest Civil War* (Chapel Hill: University of North Carolina Press, 2001).

5. Untitled document, p. 21, box 1, folder 2: Personal Ruth Schein, Personal Account, Ruth Schein Papers, Schomburg Center for Research in Black Culture. See also Patricia Michelle Boyett, *Right to Revolt: The Crusade for Racial Justice in Mississippi's Central Piney Woods* (Jackson: University Press of Mississippi, 2015).

6. Zoharah Simmons, interview by Joseph Mosnier, September 14, 2011, 10, Civil Rights History Project, Archive of Folk Culture, American Folklife Center, Library of Congress, https://www.loc.gov/item/2015669148; Simmons, "Mama Told Me Not to Go," 113.

7. Zoharah Simmons, interview with author, January 31, 2020; Simmons, "From Little Memphis Girl to Mississippi Amazon"; Eberta Spinks, interview with Kim Adams, spring 1995, Mississippi Oral History Program, Center for Oral History and Cultural Heritage, University of Southern Mis-

sissippi, Hattiesburg, https://researchworks.oclc.org/archivegrid/collection
/data/46317629; Zoharah Simmons, interview with Catherine Murphy, January 21, 2019, 4.

8. Zoharah Simmons, interview with Mosnier, September 14, 2011,
13; Ulysses Everett, interview, tape 0402, KZSU Project South Interviews,
SC0066, Stanford University, Department of Special Collections and University Archives.

9. Gwen Robinson, interview with Ted Polumbaum, summer 1964, 13;
Wide Area Telephone Service, July 10, 1964, 8–9, and Wide Area Telephone
Service, July 11, 1964, 7, both in Student Nonviolent Coordinating Commit-
tee Wide Area Telephone Service Reports, folder 252253-015-0401, ProQuest
History Vault: Black Freedom Struggle in the 20th Century; Ruth Schein,
"Brutality by Citizens," 3, box 1, folder 2: Personal Account, Ruth Schein Pa-
pers, Schomburg Center for Research in Black Culture.

10. Simmons, "From Little Memphis Girl to Mississippi Amazon," 28;
WATS Line Digest, July 21, 1964, 1, in SNCC Papers, Subgroup A, Atlanta Office, Series VII. Communications Department, Internal Communication,
1962–1966, folder: WATS Report, July 1964, ProQuest History Vault.

11. COFO press packet, 7, box 3, folder 7, Betty Garman Robinson Papers,
Schomburg Center for Research in Black Culture; Simmons, "Mama Told Me
Not to Go," 114–115; Simmons, interview with Mosnier, September 14, 2011,
16; Zoharah Simmons, "Critical Oral Histories Conference: The Emergence of
Black Power, 1964–1967," 113, in SNCC Legacy Project, Critical Oral Histories Conference Interviews, 2016–2018, Conference Dossier, July 9–11, 2016,
folder 1, Duke University.

12. Jimmy Garrett, interview with author, July 7, 2020.

13. Gwen Robinson, interview with Ted Polumbaum, summer 1964, 13.

14. Larry Spears, interview with author, June 26, 2020; Zoharah Simmons,
interview with author, January 24, 2020; Zoharah Simmons, interview with Rebecca Tuuri, May 24, 2017; McAdam, *Freedom Summer*.

15. Jimmy Garrett, interview with author, July 7, 2020.

16. Zoharah Simmons, interview with author, January 24, 2010; Simmons,
"From Little Memphis Girl to Mississippi Amazon," 29; Larry Spears, email to
the author, January 6, 2020.

17. Simmons, "Mama Told Me Not to Go," 116–118; Simmons, interview
with Mosnier, September 14, 2011, 20–21.

18. Watson, *Freedom Summer*; Simmons, "Critical Oral Histories Conference," 98–99, 104–115, in SNCC Legacy Project, Duke University.

19. Hogan, *Many Minds, One Heart*, 164; Jimmy Garrett, interview with
author, July 7, 2020; SNCC Executive Committee minutes, June 9, 1964, in

Ella Baker Papers, box 6, folder 3: SNCC Executive Committee Minutes, 1963–65, Schomburg Center for Research in Black Culture. More broadly, see Akinyele Omowale Umoja, *We Will Shoot Back: Armed Resistance in the Mississippi Freedom Movement* (New York: NYU Press, 2013).

20. Zoharah Simmons, interview with author, March 8, 2019; Simmons, "From Little Memphis Girl to Mississippi Amazon," 30; Simmons, "Critical Oral Histories Conference," 93, in SNCC Legacy Project, Duke University.

21. Simmons, "From Little Memphis Girl to Mississippi Amazon," 30; Gwen Robinson, interview with Polumbaum, summer 1964, 12; SNCC Digital Gateway, "Sojourner Motor Fleet," https://snccdigital.org/inside-sncc/sncc -national-office/sojourner-motor-fleet/.

22. Freedom Democratic Party vote results, fall 1964, box 6, folder 5: SNCC Correspondence, Ella Baker Papers, Schomburg Center for Research in Black Culture.

23. Zoharah Simmons, interview with author, March 8, 2019; Larry Spears and Jimmy Garrett, email to the author, February 1, 2020; Larry Spears, interview with author, June 26, 2020; Jimmy Garrett, interview with author, July 7, 2020; Bernard Martin, "Freedom Summer," *Stanford Magazine*, July 1, 1996, https://stanfordmag.org/contents/freedom-summer.

24. Larry Spears, interview with author, June 26, 2020; Simmons, "From Little Memphis Girl to Mississippi Amazon."

25. Gwen Robinson, "Dear Laurelites," September 24, 1964, letter in Staughton and Alice Lynd Papers 1938–2008; Archives Main Stacks, ms. 395, box 4, folder 13, Wisconsin Historical Society, https://content.wisconsin history.org/digital/collection/p15932coll2/id/4184/rec/1.

5. FREEDOM NORTH

1. Taylor Branch, *Pillar of Fire: America in the King Years, 1963–1965* (New York: Touchstone, 1999), 456–476 passim; Chana Kai Lee, *For Freedom's Sake: The Life of Fannie Lou Hamer* (Urbana: University of Illinois Press, 1999), 85–102; George Cable Wright, "Two Rights Groups Begin Sit-In to Support Mississippi Party," *New York Times*, August 25, 1964, 24.

2. Michael Simmons, interview with author, January 29, 2021.

3. Michael Simmons, interview with author, February 14, 2020; Michael Simmons, interview with Zsuzsa Beres, May 3, 2016.

4. NSM Report, "Summer Tutorials—1962," "First Annual Report to Foundations, September 1, 1962–August 31, 1963," Philadelphia Tutoring Project "Progress Report, December 1962–April 1963," all in Northern Student Movement Papers, box 7, folder 11: Philadelphia Tutoring Project

Prospectus and Reports, 1962–64, Schomburg Center for Research in Black Culture; William G. Weart, "Students in Philadelphia Tutor Youths from Minority Groups," *New York Times*, August 5, 1962, 69; Peter Countryman, "The Philadelphia Experiment," *Integrated Education* 1, no. 1 (January 1963): 14–15.

5. John Churchville, "Freedom Library Project—Philadelphia," undated letter, and "Northern Student Movement Freedom Library Report," in Northern Student Movement Papers, box 7, folder 18: Philadelphia Tutoring Project Freedom Library, Schomburg Center for Research in Black Culture; "Philadelphia—NSM Freedom Library," *Freedom North* 1, nos. 4–5, p. 28, in Northern Student Movement Papers, box 3, folder 3: Publications, Schomburg Center for Research in Black Culture; Al Hasbrouck, "Director Explains Freedom Library's Employment Policy," *Temple University News*, December 7, 1969, 1; *Youth Broadcast* newsletter in Northern Student Movement Papers, box 7, folder 16: Philadelphia Tutoring Project Tutorial Administration, 1963–64, Schomburg Center for Research in Black Culture.

6. Karlyn Forner, *Why the Vote Wasn't Enough for Selma* (Durham, NC: Duke University Press, 2017), 150–156.

7. Michael Simmons, interview with author, February 11, 2019; Mark Bricklin and Jim Magee, "12,000 Ring City Hall in Protest Demonstration," *Philadelphia Tribune*, March 16, 1965, 1.

8. Paul Lyons, *The People of This Generation: The Rise and Fall of the New Left in Philadelphia* (Philadelphia: University of Pennsylvania Press, 2003), 91–92; Michael Simmons, interview with author, February 11, 2019.

9. Saul Alinsky, *Reveille for Radicals* (Chicago: University of Chicago Press, 1946), 94; Michael Simmons, interview with author, February 14, 2020; David H. McCuen, "Conscience on Campus," *Temple Alumni Review*, Spring 1965, 1–6.

10. Carson, *In Struggle*, 81, 86; Payne, *I've Got the Light of Freedom*, 163; Hogan, *Many Minds, One Heart*, 88.

11. Countryman, *Up South*, 170–172.

12. Michael Simmons, "Arkansas Roots and Consciousness," in *Arsnick: The Student Nonviolent Coordinating Committee in Arkansas*, ed. Jennifer Jensen Wallach and John A. Kirk (Fayetteville: University of Arkansas Press, 2011), 107–114; Michael Simmons, interview with author, February 10, 2019.

6. FREEDOM IS NOT ENOUGH

1. Drew Pearson, letter to Roy Wilkins, November 9, 1965, in Papers of the NAACP, Part 20: White Resistance and Reprisals, 1956–1965, Group III,

Series A, Administrative File: General Office File—Mississippi Pressures, folder: State Bonds, 1964–1965, ProQuest History Vault; SNCC "Incident Summary, Dec. 10–Dec. 31, [1964]," entries for December 16, December 23, and December 25, in SNCC Papers, Subgroup A, Atlanta Office, Series VII, Communications Department, Internal Communication, 1962–1966, folder: WATS Reports, December 1964–February 1965, ProQuest History Vault.

2. SNCC WATS Report, February 8, 1965, 2–3, in SNCC Papers, Subgroup A, Atlanta Office, Series VII, Communications Department, Internal Communication, 1962–1966, folder: WATS Reports, December 1964–February 1965; WATS Report, January 13, 1965, 2, in SNCC Papers, Subgroup C, Washington Office, 1960–1968, Series I, Administrative Files, folder: WATS List, Revised, November 1965, ProQuest History Vault.

3. SNCC WATS Report, February 8, 1965, 2–3, 5, WATS Report, February 10, 1965, 1, WATS Report, February 16, 1965, 2, all in SNCC Papers, Subgroup A, Atlanta Office, Series VII, Communications Department, Internal Communication, 1962–1966, folder: WATS Reports, December 1964–February 1965, ProQuest History Vault; COFO Office Burned in Laurel, February 16, 1965, Wide Area Telephone Service Report, in box 7, folder 7: SNCC WATS Reports, Ella Baker Papers, Schomburg Center for Research in Black Culture.

4. COFO News, "Incident Summary," n.d. [circa March 11], 3, in SNCC Papers, Subgroup A, Atlanta Office, Series VII, Communications Department, Internal Communication, 1962–1966, folder: WATS Reports, December 1964–February 1965, ProQuest History Vault.

5. "MS. Freedom Labor Union Strikers Evicted from Plantation" [press release], May 31, 1965, and "15 Strikers Walk Off Sen. James O. Eastland's Plantation" [press release], June 5, 1965, in Ella Baker Papers, box 7, folder 6: SNCC News Releases, 1965–1968, Schomburg Center for Research in Black Culture; "To the Freedom Democratic Party," meeting notes, Waveland, Mississippi, April 14–16, 1965, 3, in SNCC Papers, Subgroup A, Atlanta Office, Series XVII, Other Organizations, 1959–1969, folder: Council of Federated Organization, March 10, 1963–1965, ProQuest History Vault.

6. Dittmer, *Local People*, 344.

7. Dittmer, *Local People*, 344–346; Zoharah Simmons, interview with author, March 8, 2019; Paul M. Montgomery, "Rally Tomorrow Set in Mississippi," *New York Times*, June 17, 1965, 21; Paul M. Montgomery, "Voting Rights Bills Pass in Jackson," *New York Times*, June 18, 1965, 27; Paul M. Montgomery, "103 More Pickets Held in Jackson," *New York Times*, June 19, 1965, 14.

8. Zoharah Simmons, interview with author, March 8, 2019; "Notes from Mississippi," *Student Voice*, July 5, 1965, quoted in Jasmin A. Young, "Strapped:

A Historical Analysis of Black Women and Armed Resistance" (PhD diss., Rutgers University, 2018), 168; Unita Blackwell, interview with Mike Garvey, April 21, 1977, 30–32, Center for Oral History and Cultural Heritage, University of Southern Mississippi.

9. Zoharah Simmons, interview with author, March 8, 2019; Blackwell, interview with Mike Garvey, April 21, 1977. Hudson survived and enjoyed a storied career as an activist and local leader; see Constance Curry, *Mississippi Harmony: Memoirs of a Freedom Fighter* (New York: Palgrave, 2002).

10. Gene Roberts, "Rights Prisoners Find Food 'Awful': They Say Police Brutality in Jackson Has Subsided," *New York Times*, June 26, 1965, 13; "Jackson Brutality Charged by Clerics," *New York Times*, June 23, 1965, 19; Zoharah Simmons, interview with author, July 3, 2017.

11. Zoharah Simmons, interview with author, January 10, 2020; WATS Report, July 1, 1965, 1, WATS Report, July 15, 1965, 2, WATS Report, September 2, 1965, 1, all in SNCC Papers, Subgroup C, Washington Office, 1960–1968, Series I, Administrative Files, 1960–1968, folder: WATS List, revised, November 1965, ProQuest History Vault; Boyett, *Right to Revolt*, 131; Ulysses Everett, interview with KZSU Project South, 1965.

12. Jennifer Jensen Wallach and John A. Kirk, eds. *Arsnick: The Student Nonviolent Coordinating Committee in Arkansas* (Fayetteville: University of Arkansas Press, 2011); "On Arkansas in General," n.d. [circa February 1965], in SNCC Papers, Subgroup A, Atlanta Office, Series VIII, Research Department, Southern States, 1960–1967, folder: Arkansas, Administrative, n.d., ProQuest History Vault.

13. Brent Riffel, "In the Storm: William Hansen and the Student Nonviolent Coordinating Committee in Arkansas, 1962–1967," *Arkansas Historical Quarterly* 63, no. 4 (Winter 2004): 404–419; Jennifer Jensen Wallach, "Replicating History in a Bad Way? White Activists and Black Power in SNCC's Arkansas Project," *Arkansas Historical Quarterly* 67, no. 3 (Winter 2008): 268–287; Anne Reeves, "Hansen Resigns SNCC Post; Says Negroes Should Lead but He'll Stay as Advisor," *Arkansas Gazette*, August 26, 1964, 10, reprinted in Jensen Wallach and Kirk, *Arsnick*, 202–204; "SNCC Arkansas Summer Project Begins" [press release], June 27, 1965, in SNCC Papers, Subgroup C, Washington Office, 1960–1968, Series I, Administrative Files, 1960–1968, folder: Press Releases, Oct. 1963–Jan. 5, 1968, ProQuest History Vault.

14. "What to Bring with You" and "Orientation Schedule," reprinted in Jensen Wallach and Kirk, *Arsnick*, 218–219; Simmons, "Arkansas Roots and Consciousness," in Jensen Wallach and Kirk, *Arsnick*, 110; Laura Foner, interview with author, May 20, 2020; Michael Simmons, interview with Veterans of Hope, May 18, 2001, Series 1, Emory University.

15. Megan Ming Francis, *Civil Rights and the Making of the Modern American State* (New York: Cambridge University Press, 2014), 132–143; Nan Elizabeth Woodruff, *American Congo: The African American Freedom Struggle in the Delta* (Cambridge, MA: Harvard University Press, 2003), 75–109.

16. "Helena," *Arkansas Voice*, October 25, 1965, 3; "On Arkansas in General," n.d. [circa February 1965], 4–5, in SNCC Papers, Subgroup A, Atlanta Office, Series VIII, Research Department, Southern States, 1960–1967, folder: Arkansas, Administrative, n.d., ProQuest History Vault.

17. Laura Foner, interview with author, May 20, 2020; Jason Manthorne, "The View from the Cotton: Reconsidering the Southern Tenant Farmers' Union," *Agricultural History* 84, no. 1 (Winter 2010): 20–45; Donald H. Grubbs, *Cry from the Cotton: The Southern Tenant Farmers' Union and the New Deal* (Chapel Hill: University of North Carolina Press, 1971); Woodruff, *American Congo*, 152–227.

18. Simmons, "Arkansas Roots and Consciousness," in Jensen Wallach and Kirk, *Arsnick*, 110–111; Alfred L. Barrow, "West Helena Teens Attempt Pool Integration," *Arkansas Voice*, July 16, 1965, 4.

19. Michael Simmons, interview with author, February 11, 2019; Michael Simmons, "In Search of a Left Agenda: A Personal Journey" (unpublished article in author's possession); Simmons, "Arkansas Roots and Consciousness," in Jensen Wallach and Kirk, *Arsnick*, 111.

20. Simmons, "Arkansas Roots and Consciousness," in Jensen Wallach and Kirk, *Arsnick*, 111–112; Michael Simmons, interview with author, February 12, 2019, and January 17, 2020.

21. Michael Simmons, interview with author, February 11, 2019; Simmons, "Arkansas Roots and Consciousness," in Jensen Wallach and Kirk, *Arsnick*, 112–113.

22. Simmons, "In Search of a Left Agenda."

23. College Campus Travellers [*sic*] memo to staff, "Observation of a College Campus Program," Stuart Ewen Papers, MSS531, box 1, folder 4, Wisconsin Historical Society.

24. Jeanne Breaker, "Campus Travelers Report," and Mike Simmons, "Report on Colleges in Virginia," both in box 2, folder 2: Executive Committee Minutes, 1963–1965, Betty Garman SNCC Files, SCM 08-41, Betty Garman Robinson Papers, Schomburg Center for Research in Black Culture.

7. THE MONSTER WE LIVE IN

1. Fanon Che Wilkins, "The Making of Black Internationalists: SNCC and Africa Before the Launching of Black Power, 1960–1965," *Journal of African*

American History, Fall 2007, 468–490; Zoharah Simmons, interview with author, January 10 and October 16, 2020.

2. Komozi Woodard, *A Nation Within a Nation: Amiri Baraka (LeRoi Jones) and Black Power Politics* (Chapel Hill: University of North Carolina Press, 1999), 64–65; see also Cynthia A. Young, *Soul Power: Culture, Radicalism, and the Making of a U.S. Third World Left* (Durham, NC: Duke University Press, 2006), 18–53; James Smethurst, *The Black Arts Movement: Literary Nationalism in the 1960s and 1970s* (Chapel Hill: University of North Carolina Press, 2005), 147–153.

3. James T. Patterson, *Grand Expectations: The United States, 1945-1974* (New York: Oxford University Press, 1996), 604–628; Fannie Rushing, interview with author, September 14, 2020; Jimmy Garrett, interview with author, July 7, 2020.

4. Pamela Horowitz and Jeanne Theoharis, eds., *Julian Bond's Time to Teach: A History of the Southern Civil Rights Movement* (Boston: Beacon Press, 2021), 294–296; Carson, *In Struggle*, 166–167.

5. "SNCC Position Paper: Women in the Movement," and Casey Hayden and Mary King, "Sex and Caste: A Kind of Memo," both in Alexander Bloom and Wini Breines, eds., *Takin' It to the Streets: A Sixties Reader* (New York: Oxford University Press, 1995), 45–51, quotes from 45, 46, 48.

6. "Tentative Agenda, 3rd Staff Meeting for 1965," 1–3, in SNCC Papers, Subgroup A, Atlanta Office, Series III, Staff Meetings 1960–1968, folder: Minutes, Aug. 1, 1960–Oct. 30, 1968, ProQuest History Vault.

7. "SNCC Staff Meeting Minutes, Nov 24–29, 1965," 19–25, box 2, folder 2: Executive Committee Minutes, 1963–1965, Betty Garman Robinson Papers, Schomburg Center for Research in Black Culture.

8. Gloria House, interview with author, September 8, 2020; Hasan Kwame Jeffries, *Bloody Lowndes: Civil Rights and Black Power in Alabama's Black Belt* (New York: NYU Press, 2009), 81–83; SNCC Digital Gateway, "International Awareness," https://snccdigital.org/our-voices/emergence-black-power/international/.

9. Student Nonviolent Coordinating Committee, "Statement on Vietnam," January 6, 1966, www.crmvet.org/docs/snccviet.htm; James Forman, *Sammy Younge, Jr.: The First Black College Student to Die in the Black Liberation Movement* (New York: Grove Press, 1968).

10. "NAACP Disassociates Itself from Attack on Vietnam Policy," *New York Times*, January 9, 1966, 4; Roy Reed, "Rights Group Widely Criticized for Attacking Vietnam Policy," *New York Times*, January 16, 1966, 60; Carson, *In Struggle*, 188–189; Brown-Nagin, *Courage to Dissent*, 261.

11. Penny M. Von Eschen, *Race Against Empire: Black Americans and Anticolonialism, 1937–1957* (Ithaca, NY: Cornell University Press, 1997); Mary L.

Dudziak, *Cold War Civil Rights: Race and the Image of American Democracy* (Princeton, NJ: Princeton University Press, 2000); Gilmore, *Defying Dixie*; Michael Simmons, interview with author, January 10, 2020.

12. Text of the Voting Rights Act of 1965, https://www.archives.gov /milestone-documents/voting-rights-act.

13. Brown-Nagin, *Courage to Dissent*, 257.

14. On the Bond campaign, see Carson, *In Struggle*, 166–168; Roger M. Williams, *The Bonds: An American Family* (New York: Atheneum, 1972); Michael G. Long, ed., *Race Man: Julian Bond Selected Works, 1960–2015* (San Francisco: City Lights, 2020). On Dahmer murder, see "Editorial," *Nitty Gritty*, February 23, 1966, 1; and Payne, *I've Got the Light of Freedom*, 398. On the connection to Reconstruction, see Atlanta Project, "The Julian Bond Campaign," n.d. (circa spring 1966), 4, in SNCC Papers, Subgroup A, Atlanta Office, Series XV, State Project Files, 1960–1968, folder; Georgia, Atlanta, Organizations , ProQuest History Vault.

8. BLACK CONSCIOUSNESS

1. Brown-Nagin, *Courage to Dissent*, 268, 275.

2. Al Pertilla, interview with author, February 28, 2019; Michael Simmons, interview with author, February 12, 2019; Donald P. Stone, *Fallen Prince: William James Edwards, Black Education, and the Quest for Afro-American Nationality* (Snow Hill, AL: Snow Hill Press, 1990); Jason Perkins, "The Atlanta Vine City Project, SNCC, and Black Power, 1965–1967" (master's thesis, Ohio State University, 2007), 38–39.

3. Kathryn L. Nasstrom, "Women, the Civil Rights Movement, and the Politics of Historical Memory in Atlanta, 1946–1973" (PhD diss., University of North Carolina, 2003), 218; Michael Simmons, interview with author, January 3, 2020; Michael Simmons and Zoharah Simmons, interview with author, January 10, 2020.

4. James R. Ralph Jr., *Northern Protest: Martin Luther King, Jr., Chicago, and the Civil Rights Movement* (Cambridge, MA: Harvard University Press, 1993).

5. Mendy Samstein, "Prospectus for an Atlanta Project," 1966, 2, 3, Archives Main Stacks, SC3093, WIHVS260, Mendy Samstein Papers, Wisconsin Historical Society, Madison, http://content.wisconsinhistory.org /cdm/ref/collection/p15932coll2/id/17696.

6. SNCC News Service, "Purpose of the Atlanta Project," 1966; Atlanta Project, "Some Proposals for a Housing Campaign," in Mendy Samstein Papers, Wisconsin Historical Society; affidavits are quoted in Grady-Willis, *Challenging U.S. Apartheid*, 85.

7. "Slumlords Must Go!" (flyer), in Mendy Samstein Papers, Wisconsin Historical Society; "The Markham Street Affair," n.d. (circa April 1966), 21–22, SNCC Papers, Subgroup A, Atlanta Office, Series XV, State Project Files, 1960–1968, folder: Georgia, Atlanta, Organizations ProQuest History Vault; Nasstrom, "Women, the Civil Rights Movement, and the Politics of Historical Memory," 241–224. Despite his reelection, Georgia state representatives still refused to seat him. With the help of attorney Howard Moore, who represented SNCC, Bond sued the state. In December 1966, the US Supreme Court unanimously agreed with Bond that his First Amendment rights had been violated, and he would ultimately take his position as an elected legislator. See Brown-Nagin, *Courage to Dissent*, 290–295.

8. Ella Baker and Marvel Cooke, "The Bronx Slave Market," *The Crisis*, November 1, 1930.

9. Atlanta Project, "The Necessity for Southern Urban Organizing," 3, 1966, in SNCC Papers, Subgroup A. Atlanta Office, Series XV. State Project Files, 1960–1968, folder: Georgia, Atlanta, Black Paper ProQuest History Vault.

10. Derek Seidman, "The Hidden History of the SNCC Research Department," *Eyes on the Ties*, May 2, 2017, https://news.littlesis.org/2017/05/02/the-hidden-history-of-the-sncc-research-department/; James Forman, *The Making of Black Revolutionaries* (Seattle: University of Washington Press, 1997), 443; Michael Simmons, interview with author, February 12, 2019; Michael Simmons and Zoharah Simmons, interview with author, January 10, 2020; Al Pertilla, interview with author, February 28, 2019.

11. "Editorial," *Nitty Gritty* 1, no. 1 (February 23, 1966): 1.

12. Quoted in SNCC News Service, "Purpose of the Atlanta Project," n.d. (circa March 1966), 5, crmvet.org/docs/660000_sncc_atlproj.pdf.

13. Nasstrom, "Women, the Civil Rights Movement, and the Politics of Historical Memory," 226–227; "Clarification Needed," *Anniston (AL) Star*, July 11, 1966, 4; Carson, *In Struggle*, 239; Michael Simmons, interview with author, January 3, 2020.

14. Zoharah Simmons and Michael Simmons, interview with author, January 10, 2020; the quote from Simmons comes from Grady-Willis, *Challenging U.S. Apartheid*, 88.

15. SNCC Vine City Project, *Black Power* (reprint of "Black Consciousness Paper") (Atlanta, GA: SNCC Vine City Project, n.d.), 5, 4, 7, https://www.crmvet.org/docs/6604_sncc_atlanta_race.pdf.

16. SNCC Vine City Project, reprint of "Black Consciousness Paper," 2.

17. SNCC Vine City Project, reprint of "Black Consciousness Paper," 4, 1.

18. Staughton Lynd, interview with author, March 23, 2019; Jimmy Garrett, interview with author, July 7, 2020; Martha Biondi, *The Black Revolution on Campus* (Berkeley: University of California Press, 2012), 43–78.

19. Carson, *In Struggle*, 199; Simmons, "Critical Oral Histories Conference," 42–52, 130–148, in SNCC Legacy Project, Duke University.

20. The quotes are, respectively, from Ivanhoe Donaldson and Jack Minnis and are quoted in Carson, *In Struggle*, 201, 203. See also Carmichael with Ekwueme Michael Thelwell, *Ready for Revolution: The Life and Struggle of Stokely Carmichael* (New York: Scribner, 2003), 477–482; Sellers, *The River of No Return*, 157–160.

21. Sellers, *The River of No Return*, 156–157; Carson, *In Struggle*, 204.

22. Carson, *In Struggle*, 330; Bob Moses, email to author, January 19, 2020; Michael Simmons and Zoharah Simmons, interview with author, January 10, 2020; David Llorens, "On the Civil Rights Front," *Negro Digest*, June 1966, 70.

23. Carmichael's account is in Stokely Carmichael, *Ready for Revolution*, 505–508.

24. "The Uses of 'Black Power'" (editorial), *Los Angeles Times*, June 24, 1966, A4; M. S. Handler, "Wilkins Says Black Power Leads Only to Black Death," *New York Times*, July 6, 1966, 1; Jack Jones and Ray Rogers, "NAACP Director Condemns Moves for 'Black Power,'" *Los Angeles Times*, July 6, 1966, 3.

25. "Excerpts from Paper on Which the 'Black Power' Philosophy Is Based," *New York Times*, August 5, 1966, 10.

26. Michael Simmons, interview with author, February 11, 2019; Michael Simmons Selective Service System, Transfer for Armed Forces Physical Examination or Induction, August 5, 1966, private collection, Aishah Shahidah Simmons; *Michael Waldo Simmons v. United States of America*, 406 F.2d 456 (March 10, 1969).

9. SELLING WOLF TICKETS

1. The following account is based on SNCC, "Report on Draft Program," circa August 24, 1966, available at www.crmvet.org/docs/6608_sncc_draft -resist.pdf; Michael Simmons, interview with author, February 11, 2019; Michael Simmons and Zoharah Simmons, interview with author, January 10, 2020.

2. "Report of Court Proceedings, August 18, 1966," www.crmvet.org /docs/6608_sncc_draft-court.pdf.

3. SNCC, "Report on Draft Program," 6–7.

4. SNCC, "Report on Draft Program," 8; Zoharah Simmons, "Critical Oral Histories Conference," 130–131, in SNCC Legacy Project, Duke University; Zoharah Simmons, interview with author, July 3, 2017, and January 17, 2020.

5. Michael Simmons, interview with author, February 11, 2019; Michael Simmons, email to Dwight Williams, December 17, 2017.

6. Michael Simmons, interview with author, February 11, 2019; Zoharah Simmons, interview with author, January 17, 2020; Muhammad Ahmad, conversation with author, July 27, 2020; Lauren Mottle, "'We Resist on the Grounds We Aren't Citizens': Black Draft Resistance in the Vietnam War Era," *Journal of Civil and Human Rights* 6, no. 2 (Fall/Winter 2020): 38.

7. Maurice Hobson, *The Legend of Black Mecca: Politics and Class in the Making of Modern Atlanta* (Chapel Hill: University of North Carolina Press, 2017), 44–47; Roy Reed, "SNCC Assailed on Atlanta Riot," *New York Times*, September 8, 1966, 1; Ruby Doris Robinson, "Description of 'Riot' in Atlanta, Georgia, on Sept. 6, 1966," and "Statements Made by 'Important People' About SNCC and the Riot," in SNCC Papers, 1959–1972, Subgroup A, Atlanta Office, Series XV, State Project Files, 1960–1968, Georgia, Atlanta, Black Paper, Aug. 25, 1966, ProQuest History Vault; Peniel E. Joseph, *Waiting 'Til the Midnight Hour: A Narrative History of Black Power in America* (New York: Henry Holt, 2006), 160; Carson, *In Struggle*, 231–232; notes on office staff meeting, July 27, 1966, 1–2, in folder: Miscellaneous, SNCC Papers, 1959–1972, Subgroup A, Atlanta Office, Series III: Staff Meetings, 1960–1968, ProQuest History Vault.

8. Michael S. Foley, *Confronting the War Machine: Draft Resistance During the Vietnam War* (Chapel Hill: University of North Carolina Press, 2003), 52–54.

9. The first quote is from Michael Simmons and Larry Fox, "National Anti-Draft Program" memo to SNCC Staff, November 28, 1966, 2, https://www.crmvet.org/docs/661128_sncc_draft-rpt.pdf; the second quote is from "Excerpts from Michael Simmons' Speech, Minutes of the Eastern Black Anti-Draft Conference, Harlem, New York City," January 21, 1967, box 32, folder: National Coordinating Committee of Black Organizations Against the Draft, Social Action Vertical File, Wisconsin Historical Society. See also "A Black Anti-Draft Program," August 1966, in Subgroup C, Washington Office, 1960–1968, Series II, Subject Files, 1963–1968. folder: Vietnam, June 23, 1965–1968, SNCC Papers, ProQuest History Vault.

10. Michael Simmons and Zoharah Simmons, interview with author, January 24, 2020; Maxwell C. Stanford, "Revolutionary Action Movement (RAM): A Case Study of an Urban Revolutionary Movement in Western Capitalist Society" (master's thesis, Atlanta University, 1986).

11. Muhammad Ahmad, *We Will Return in the Whirlwind: Black Radical Organizations 1960–1975* (Chicago: Charles H. Kerr, 2008); Robert Allen, *Black Awakening in Capitalist America: An Analytic History* (Garden City, NY: Anchor Books, 1970); Bloom and Martin, *Black Against Empire*; Malcolm

McLaughlin, *The Long Hot Summer of 1967: Urban Rebellion in America* (New York: Palgrave, 2014).

12. Gregg L. Michel, *Struggle for a Better South: The Southern Student Organizing Committee, 1964–1969* (New York: Palgrave Macmillan, 2004); Stokely Carmichael and Charles V. Hamilton, *Black Power: The Politics of Liberation* (New York: Random House, 1967).

13. "SNCC Staff Meeting of December '66 and Follow-up," *New York SNCC Newsletter*, February 1967, 1–2, in SNCC Papers, Subgroup A, Atlanta Office, Series III, Staff Meetings, 1960–1968, folder: Minutes, Aug. 1, 1960–Oct. 30, 1968, ProQuest History Vault.

14. Bill Ware, "Some Comments on the Staff Meeting," reprinted in Fay Bellamy, ed., "Special Report to SNCC Staff," March 1967, 3, box 1, folder 11, Roberta Yancy Civil Rights Collection, Schomburg Center for Research in Black Culture.

15. Carson, *In Struggle*, 238–242; Elizabeth Sutherland, "Black, White and Tan," June 1967, 4–5, in SNCC Papers, Subgroup B: New York Office, 1960–1969, Series I, Fundraising, 1960–1968, Administrative Files, 1960–1968, folder: Staff Memos, Apr. 19, 1963–June 1967, ProQuest History Vault; Gloria House, interview with author, September 8, 2020.

16. SNCC January 20, 1967, Central Committee meeting notes, 7–8, folder 4: SNCC Minutes (1961–1967), Ella Baker Papers, Schomburg Center for Research in Black Culture; Joseph, *Waiting 'Til the Midnight Hour*, 179.

17. Michael Simmons, interview with author, January 3, 2020; Dan Georgakas and Marvin Surkin, *Detroit I Do Mind Dying: A Study in Urban Revolution* (Boston: South End Press, 1998); Grace Lee Boggs, *Living for Change* (Minneapolis: University of Minnesota Press, 1998), 75–190, passim; Stephen Ward, *In Love and Struggle: The Revolutionary Lives of James and Grace Lee Boggs* (Chapel Hill: University of North Carolina Press, 2016).

18. In addition to the items cited below, this account draws on the recollections provided in the transcript of the March 4, 1967, SNCC Central Committee meeting in SNCC Papers, Subgroup A, Atlanta Office, Series II, Executive and Central Committee, 1961–1967, folder: Central Committee, 1965–1967—Memoranda, Aug. 23, 1965–Mar. 22, 1967, ProQuest History Vault; Michael Simmons, "Dear Black Power Boys," January 12, 1967, letter, in Subgroup A, Atlanta Office, Series VI, Bookkeeping Department, 1960–1967, Personnel Records, 1962–1967, folder: Biographies, ProQuest History Vault.

19. Sellers, *The River of No Return*, 185–187; Michael Simmons, interview with author, January 3, 2020; Michael Simmons and Zoharah Simmons, interview with author, January 10, 2020.

20. See Cleve Sellers, letter to Bill Ware, February 3, 1967, and Bill Ware, telegram to James Forman, February 14, 1967, both reprinted in Fay Bellamy, ed., "Special Report to SNCC Staff," March 1967, in box 1, folder 11, Roberta Yancy Civil Rights Collection, Schomburg Center for Research in Black Culture.

21. "Angry Howard Students Force Draft Director to Flee," *Philadelphia Tribune*, March 25, 1967, 4.

22. Martin Luther King Jr., "Beyond Vietnam: A Time to Break the Silence" (speech, Riverside Church, New York, April 4, 1967), https://www.americanrhetoric.com/speeches/mlkatimetobreaksilence.htm; Thomas Hauser, *Muhammad Ali: His Life and Times* (New York: Touchstone, 1991), 169–170.

10. GETTING OUR XS

1. Hauser, *Muhammad Ali*, 81–112; Payne and Payne, *Dead Are Arising*; FBI, "Nation of Islam: Cult of the Black Muslims" (monograph, Washington, DC, May 1965), 20, https://en.wikisource.org/wiki/Nation_of_Islam:_Cult_of_the_Black_Muslims; Russell Rickford, "John Ali, Biographical Sketch," box 39, folder: Bios of Key Figures, Malcolm X Project Papers, Columbia University; Michael Simmons and Zoharah Simmons, interview with author, January 10, 2020.

2. "Why Nasser Calls U.S. 'Very Rich' and 'Very Stupid," *Muhammad Speaks*, March 31, 1967, 7; "Freedom and Justice for the American Blackman" (cover), *Muhammad Speaks*, April 7, 1967; "Justice for USA Muslims—or Suffer" (cover), *Muhammad Speaks*, April 14, 1967; "Are Rights, Viet Nam War Compatible? NAACP Cries 'No!' But SCLC Says 'Yes!'" and "Why Should Blacks Be Cannon Fodder in Devil's Unholy Viet War," *Muhammad Speaks*, April 14, 1967, 4, 5; "Justice on Trial" (cover), *Muhammad Speaks*, April 21, 1967; "United with the Muslims!" (cover), *Muhammad Speaks*, April 28, 1967; Rafiq Kalam id-Din, interview with author, August 10, 2020.

3. Zoharah Simmons and Michael Simmons, interviews with author, January 10 and January 17, 2020; Mattias Gardell, *In the Name of Elijah Muhammad: Louis Farrakhan and the Nation of Islam* (Durham, NC: Duke University Press, 1996), 54. Marriage date comes from *Michael Waldo Simmons v. United States of America*, case no. 25,170, Court of Appeals for the Fifth Circuit, No. 25371, transcript, September 19, 1967, 134, box 48, folder 11, Howard Moore Papers, Emory University.

4. Rebecca Tuuri, *Strategic Sisterhood: The National Council of Negro Women in the Black Freedom Struggle* (Chapel Hill: University of North Carolina Press, 2018); Zoharah Simmons, interview with author, January 10, 2020;

Mrs. Dorothy Dozier Crenshaw biography, https://omgdigitalmediasolutions
.com/wp-content/uploads/2016/12/Doris-Dozier-Crenshaw-Bio.pdf.

5. Tuuri, *Strategic Sisterhood*; "Report to NCNW President: Development
of Project WomanPower," December 1966, box 28, folder 583, and National
Council of Negro Women, Inc., "Project Womanpower: Final Report to the
Ford Foundation," August 31, 1968, box 29, folder 586, National Council of
Negro Women Papers, National Archives for Black Women's History, Mary
McLeod Bethune Council House, Washington, DC.

6. Zoharah Simmons, interview with Rebecca Tuuri, May 24, 2017; Zoharah Simmons, interviews with author, November 9, 2018, and January 11, 2019.

7. Zoharah Simmons, interview with Rebecca Tuuri, May 24, 2017; US Department of Labor, "Chapter 4: The Tangle of Pathology," in *The Negro Family: The Case for National Action* (Washington, DC: Office of Policy Planning and Research, 1965), https://www.blackpast.org/african-american-history/moynihan-report-1965/#chapter4.

8. Zoharah Simmons, interviews with author, January 10 and January 17,
2020; Ula Yvette Taylor, *The Promise of Patriarchy: Women and the Nation of
Islam* (Chapel Hill: University of North Carolina Press, 2017), 44–56; Leo
PX McCallum, "You and Your Dental Health," *Muhammad Speaks*, March
10, 1967, 21.

9. Michael Simmons and Zoharah Simmons, interview with author, January 17, 2020; Fannie Rushing, interview with author, September 14, 2020.

10. *The Hate That Hate Produced*, produced by Mike Wallace and Louis Lomax, aired July 13–17, 1959, on WNTA-TV, News Beat; E. U. Essien-Udom,
Black Nationalism (Chicago: University of Chicago Press, 1962), 188; Marable,
Malcolm X, 112–114.

11. Zoharah Simmons and Michael Simmons, interview with author, January 17, 2020, and January 24, 2020; Zoharah Simmons, interview with Veterans of Hope, June 25, 1998, tape A-4, Emory University; Michael Simmons,
interview with Veterans of Hope, May 18, 2001, tape A-4, Emory University.

12. Countryman, *Up South*, 198–199, 223–238.

13. Michael Simmons, interview with author, April 1, 2021; Muhammad
Ahmad, "On the Black Student Movement, 1960–70," *Black Scholar*, May–June
1978, 2–11; Countryman, *Up South*, 223–238; "Racist Rizzo Rides Again," *Maji
Maji* 2, no. 3 (December 1967): 4.

14. National Council of Negro Women, "Project Womanpower: Final Report to the Ford Foundation," August 31, 1968, box 29, folder 586; and "Report
to NCNW President: Development of Project WomanPower," December 1966,
box 28, folder 583, in National Council of Negro Women Records, National
Archives for Black Women's History.

15. National Council of Negro Women, "Project WomanPower: Final Report," 7–40; Tuuri, *Strategic Sisterhood*, 130–132.

16. Zoharah Simmons, interview with author, October 16, 2020; James Robenalt, *Ballots and Bullets: Black Power Politics and Urban Guerrilla Warefare in 1968 Cleveland* (Chicago: Lawrence Hill Books, 2018).

17. Edward Onaci, *Free the Land: The Republic of New Afrika and the Pursuit of a Black Nation-State* (Chapel Hill: University of North Carolina Press, 2020); the Moore quote is page 1.

18. Lyndon Baines Johnson, "Withdrawl Speech," March 31, 1968, https://voicesofdemocracy.umd.edu/lyndon-baines-johnson-withdrawal-speech-31-march-1968/.

19. Zoharah Simmons, interview with Rebecca Tuuri, May 24, 2017; Zoharah Simmons, interview with author, February 23, 2018; Zoharah Simmons, Facebook post, April 5, 2020, https://www.facebook.com/gwendolyn.z.simmons/posts/10220181884831746; Clay Risen, *A Nation on Fire: America in the Wake of the King Assassination* (New York: Wiley, 2009), 60–75.

20. Michael Simmons, interview with author, January 17, 2020; Rafiq Kalam id-Din, interview with author, August 5, 2020; John Brantley Wilder, "Temple Students Demand Apology for 'Blackface' Minstrel Show," *Philadelphia Tribune*, April 2, 1968, 3; Len Lear, "125 Stage Sit-In to Support Demand," *Philadelphia Tribune*, April 27, 1968, 1; Guian A. McKee, *The Problem of Jobs: Liberalism, Race, and Deindustrialization in Philadelphia* (Chicago: University of Chicago Press, 2008), 256–269.

21. Kalam id-Din, interview with author, August 5, 2020; Michael Simmons and Zoharah Simmons, interview with author, January 17, 2020; Michael Simmons, interview with author, January 31, 2020.

22. "Dormitory Racism at Temple Charged," *Philadelphia Tribune*, May 18, 1968, 5.

23. Michael Simmons, interview with Veterans of Hope, May 18, 2001, tape A-4, Emory University; Michael Simmons, interview with author, January 17, 2020; W. E. B. Du Bois, *Black Reconstruction in America* (New York: Free Press, 1998).

24. R. Early, "Editorial," *Maji Maji* 2, no. 7 (May 1968): 5.

25. Michael Simmons, "Another View on the Role of the Black Artist," *Maji Maji* 3, no. 2 (January 1969): 3–4.

26. Kalam id-Din, interview with author, August 5, 2020; G.H.S. "Editorial," *Maji Maji* 4, no. 1 (September 1969): 2; "Related Readings," *Maji Maji*, 4, no. 1 (September 1969): 17.

27. John Brantley Wilder, "Black Students Make Demands at Temple U.," *Philadelphia Tribune*, March 29, 1969, 1, 32.

28. James Garrett, interview with author, July 7, 2020; Kalam id-Din, interview with author, August 5, 2020; Martha Biondi, *The Black Revolution on Campus* (Berkeley: University of California Press, 2012), 43–78.

29. Lyons, *People of This Generation*, 203; Kalam id-Din, interview with author, August 5, 2020; Len Lear, "Students Dispute Temple U Claim That 2,037 Negroes Are Enrolled," *Philadelphia Tribune*, July 16, 1968, 24; "Negro Named Head of Temple's Recruitment Program," *Philadelphia Tribune*, August 29, 1969, 20.

30. Michael Simmons, interview with author, February 11, 2019; *Michael W. Simmons v. United States of America*, Case No. 25371 (February 23, 1968), 122–123, box 48, folder 11, Howard Moore Papers, Emory University; Duane Riner, "Draft Melee Jury Sees NCO Pick 7," *Atlanta Constitution*, September 12, 1967, 8.

11. PRISON AND OTHER METAPHYSICS

1. John Braxton, interview with author, July 8, 2020; Paul Beach, interview with author, July 16, 2020; Michael Simmons, interviews with author, February 12, 2019, and January 29, 2021.

2. Zoharah Simmons and Michael Simmons, interview with author, January 24, 2020; NWRO quoted in Felicia Kornbluh, *The Battle for Welfare Rights: Politics and Poverty in Modern America* (Philadelphia: University of Pennsylvania Press, 2007), 143.

3. Zoharah Simmons, interview with author, May 21, 2021; Dina Portnoy, interview with author, June 2, 2019; David Rudovsky, interview with author, April 12, 2019.

4. Michael Simmons, letter to Rebecca Chapman, November 8, 1970; Michael Simmons, interview with author, February 11, 2019; Zoharah Simmons and Michael Simmons, interview with author, January 29, 2021; Michael Simmons, interview with author, April 12, 2012.

5. Paul Beach, interview with author, July 16, 2020; Michael Simmons, interview with author, February 11, 2019.

6. "Prison Struggle, 1970–1971," *War Behind the Walls*, 14–15. (This publication was a one-off newspaper produced by the Red Family and printed by People's Press in September 1971. It is archived in the Prison Newspapers collection at the Freedom Archives.)

7. Michael Simmons, interview with author, February 11, 2019; "50% of Inmates Working at Allenwood," *Daily Item* (Sunbury, PA), August 20, 1970,

5; "End Allenwood Strike, Study Inmate Requests," *Daily Item* (Sunbury, PA), August 22, 1970, 7.

8. Zoharah Simmons and Michael Simmons, interviews with author, January 24, 2020, January 29, 2021; Zoharah Simmons, interview with author, May 21, 2021; Aishah Simmons, interview with author, May 12, 2021.

9. Michael Simmons, interview with author, February 11, 2019; Gaye Walton-Price and Tom Ficklin, interview with author, February 12, 2021.

10. John Braxton, interview with author, July 8, 2020; Rachelle Patterson, "Acton Man Says Beliefs Got Him into Prison Rift," *Boston Globe*, August 15, 1971, 63; Glen Maynard, "Protestors Mass Outside Allenwood," *Daily Item* (Sunbury, PA), July 31, 1971, 1.

11. Michael Simmons, interview with author, February 11, 2019; Adrian McCray, interview with author, July 15, 2020; Braxton, interview with author, July 8, 2020.

12. Michael Simmons, interview with author, February 12, 2021; Maynard, "Protesters Mass Outside Allenwood," 1; Glen Maynard, "Discipline at U.S. Pen Challenged," *Daily Item* (Sunbury, PA), September 30, 1971, 25.

13. Michael Simmons, interviews with author, February 11, 2019, and February 12, 2021; Michael Simmons, interview with Veterans of Hope, May 18, 2001, tape A-5, Emory University.

14. Glen Maynard, "Legislator Seeks Explanation of Incidents at Federal Pen," *Daily Item* (Sunbury, PA), August 5, 1971, 19; Zoharah Simmons, interview with author, May 21, 2021.

15. US Census Bureau, "Chapter B: General Population Characteristics: Pennsylvania," in *1970 Census of Population Vol. 1, Part 40, Pennsylvania—Section 1* (Washington, DC: US Government Printing Office, 1973), 121; Gaye Walton-Price and Tom Ficklin, interview with author, February 12, 2021.

16. Zoharah Simmons, interview with author, October 2, 2020; Lana Dalberg, *Birthing God: Women's Experience of the Divine* (Woodstock, VT: SkyLight Paths, 2013), 219–227.

17. George Jackson, *Soledad Brother: The Prison Letters of George Jackson* (Chicago: Lawrence Hill Books, 1994), 26–27.

18. Jackson, *Soledad Brother*, 266; Michael Simmons, interview with author, April 12, 2012.

19. Heather Ann Thompson, *Blood in the Water: The Attica Prison Uprising of 1971 and Its Legacy* (New York: Pantheon, 2016), 78–79.

20. *John Braxton et al. v. Norman Carlson and Noah Alldredge*, 483 F.2nd 933, No. 72-1491 (August 27, 1973); David Rudovsky, interview with author, April 12, 2019.

21. Hazrat Inayat Khan, *The Mysticism of Sound and Music* (Boston: Shambhala Publications, 1991), 167; Michael Simmons and Zoharah Simmons, interview with author, January 29, 2021.

22. Khan, *Mysticism of Sound and Music*, 190; Zoharah Simmons, interview with author, October 2, 2020; Zoharah Simmons, interview with Veterans of Hope, June 25, 1998, series 1, box 14, Emory University; Hazrat Inayat Khan, *Spiritual Dimensions of Psychology* (New Lebanon, NY: Omega Publications, 1991), 20.

23. Zoharah Simmons, interview with author, October 2, 2020; Merin Shobhana Xavier, *Sacred Spaces and Transnational Networks in American Sufism: Bawa Muhaiyaddeen and Contemporary Shrine Cultures* (London: Bloomsbury Academic, 2018), 43–44; Mohamed Mauroff, "The Culture and Experience of Luminous and Liminal Komunesam" (PhD diss., University of Pennsylvania, Philadelphia, 1976).

12. FRIENDS AND COMRADES

1. Michael Simmons, interviews with author, February 11, 2019, and February 12, 2021; Menika Dirkson, "Safe Streets, Inc.: The 'Hustle' to End Black Gang Violence in Philadelphia, 1969–1976," Arlen Specter Center Research Fellowship, Paper 2, https://jdc.jefferson.edu/ascps_fellowship/2.

2. "Former Temple Student Appointed by Friends Unit," *Philadelphia Tribune*, October 10, 1972, 28; Gerald Jonas, *On Doing Good* (New York: Scribner, 1971); Gregory A. Barnes, *A Centennial History of the American Friends Service Committee* (Philadelphia: Friends Press, 2016).

3. "Third World Coalition Position Paper on Self-Determination," January 26, 1972, 1, CRD (Community Relations Division) TWC 1972, folder: General Administration, TWC: Administration, Background Materials 1972, American Friends Service Committee Papers, Philadelphia; Ed Nakawatase, interview with author, March 24, 2019.

4. Cal Winslow, "Overview: The Rebellion from Below, 1965–1981," and Kim Moody, "Understanding the Rank-and-File Rebellion in the Long 1970s," in Aaron Brenner, Robert Brenner, and Cal Winslow, eds., *Rebel Rank and File: Labor Militancy and Revolt from Below During the Long 1970s* (New York: Verson, 2010), 1–36, 105–148.

5. Trevor Griffey, "From Jobs to Power: The United Construction Workers Association and Title VII Community Organizing in the 1970s," in *Black Power at Work*, ed. David Goldberg and Trevor Griffey (Ithaca, NY: Cornell University Press, 2010), 161–188.

6. Michael Woo, interview with author, July 14, 2020; Michael Fox, interview with author, July 24, 2020; American Friends Service Committee, Northwest Regional Office, "An Issue Whose Time Has Come: Minority Employment in the Seattle Construction Industry" (memo), February 5, 1970, https://depts.washington.edu/civilr/images/ucwa/idea.pdf; Michael Schulze-Oechtering, "Blurring the Boundaries of Struggle: The United Construction Workers Association (UCWA) and Relational Resistance in Seattle's Third World Left" (PhD diss., University of California, Berkeley, 2016), 71–113.

7. Michael Simmons, interviews with author, February 11, 2019, and March 31, 2021; Michael Woo, interview with author, July 14, 2020; Trevor Griffey, "Black Power's Labor Politics: The United Construction Workers Association and Title VII Law in the 1970s" (PhD diss., University of Washington, 2011), 366.

8. Nancy MacLean, *Freedom Is Not Enough: The Opening of the American Workplace* (New York: Russell Sage Foundation, 2006); Griffey, "Black Power's Labor Politics," 345–406; Michael Simmons, "Report of UCWA/AFSC Southern Employment Project, May–December 1973," folder: Southwest Workers Federation, and AFSC, "Proposal to the Equal Employment Opportunity Commission," March 1973, folder: Committees and Organizations: AFSC/UCWA Contract, both in box CRD 1973, American Friends Service Committee Papers.

9. Michael Simmons, interview with Trevor Griffey, September 16, 2007.

10. Michael Simmons, transcript of speech at Bishop College, December 8, 1973, tape 1, box 12, folder 36, Tyree Scott Papers, Labor Archives of Washington, University of Washington, Seattle; Griffey, "Black Power's Labor Politics," 367–392.

11. Griffey, "Black Power's Labor Politics," 384–385, 400; Fox, interview with author, July 24, 2020; Michael Simmons, "In Search of a Left Agenda: A Personal Journey" (unpublished essay in author's files).

12. Michael Simmons, "Report of UCWA/AFSC Southern Employment Project, May–December 1973," 5.

13. Elizabeth (Betita) Martinez (née Sutherland), interview by Loretta Ross, March 3, 2006, Voices of Feminism Oral History Collection, Sophia Smith Collection, Smith College, Northampton, MA.

14. Rosemary Cubas, "Staff Report to TWC: December–January," February 1, 1973, 3, box: TWC 1973, folder: TWC Reports, Staff Reports, AFSC.

15. Third World Coalition, "TWC 2nd Annual Meeting September 18–23, 1973," November 9, 1973, box: TWC, 1973, folder: TWC Administration, Annual Meeting, AFSC; Michael Simmons, interview with author, February 12, 2021.

16. Michael Simmons, interview with author, February 12, 2019; Domingo Gonzalez, interview with author, October 17, 2021.

17. Michael Simmons, interview with author, March 24, 2021; Nico Slate, *Colored Cosmopolitanism: The Shared Struggle for Freedom in the United States and India* (Cambridge, MA: Harvard University Press, 2012).

18. Michael Simmons, interviews with author, March 24 and March 31, 2021; Sally Richardson, "India Travel/Seminar" (memo), January 28, 1974, 2–3, box: TWC, 1974, folder: TWC Trips, India Travel Seminar, AFSC.

19. Michael Simmons, interviews with author, March 24 and March 31, 2021; T. S. Sandaram, "The TWC Indian Odyssey," June 5, 1974, box TWC 1974, folder: TWC Trips, India Travel Seminar, AFSC.

20. "India Trip" (press release), May 23, 1974, 1, box: TWC 1974, folder: Trips, India Travel Seminar, AFSC.

21. Michael Simmons, interview with author, March 25, 2021; Michael Woo, interview with author, July 14, 2020; James E. Bristol, "Report on Seminar on Angola, Havana, Cuba, February 26–29, 1976," African Activist Archive, https://africanactivist.msu.edu/document_metadata.php?objectid =210-808-770.

13. WATCHING OVER

1. M. R. Bawa Muhaiyaddeen, *The Tree That Fell to the West: Autobiography of a Sufi* (Philadelphia: Bawa Muhaiyaddeen Fellowship, 2003), 71.

2. Zoharah Simmons, interviews with author, October 2, 2020, and May 28, 2021; Gaye Walton-Price, interview with author, February 12, 2021; Aishah Simmons, interview with author, May 12, 2021.

3. Elizabeth Hinton, *From the War on Poverty to the War on Crime* (Cambridge, MA: Harvard University Press, 2016), 180–191; Lombardo, *Blue-Collar Conservatism*, 147–153.

4. Michael "Cetewayo" Tabor, "Capitalism Plus Dope Equals Genocide," https://www.marxists.org/history/usa/workers/black-panthers/1970/dope .htm; Thomas A. Johnson, "Unanswered Questions Still Surround H. Rap Brown," *New York Times*, October 25, 1971, 16; James Forman Jr., *Locking Up Our Own: Crime and Punishment in Black America* (New York: Farrar, Straus, & Giroux, 2017), 25–33.

5. Betty Medsger, *The Burglary: The Discovery of J. Edgar Hoover's Secret FBI* (New York: Vintage, 2014).

6. AFSC press release, December 23, 1975, box: Govt Surv & Cit Rts, 1975, folder: Publicity, News Releases, AFSC; and Wallace T. Collett and Louis W. Schneider, memo, November 14, 1975, 2, box: Govt Surv/Cit Rts, 1975,

folder: Admin/Background for Program, 1970–1975, AFSC; AFSC, "Proposal for an AFSC Program on 'Government Surveillance and Citizens' Rights,'" box: Gov Surv/Cit Rts, 1975, folder: Admin/Proposal, AFSC.

7. AFSC, *Freedom for All Americans: 1976* (Philadelphia: AFSC, 1976), 17–18.

8. Zoharah Simmons, conversation with Susan Rosenblum, tape 5 transcript, July 11, 1976, 21, folder: Regional Offices: Midwest, General Administration 1976, AFSC; Ken Lawrence, "Proposed Action Against Secret Police in Mississippi," box: Gov Surv/Cit Rts 1976, folder: Regional Office: Southeastern, AFSC.

9. Zoharah Simmons, letter, March 19, 1976, 1, box: Gov Surv/Cit Rts, folder: Comms & Orgs: ACLU, AFSC.

10. Frank Donner, *Protectors of Privilege: Red Squads and Police Repression in Urban America* (Berkeley: University of California Press, 1990), 221–237.

11. Aishah Simmons, interview with author, May 12, 2021; Zoharah Simmons, interview with author, June 11, 2021; Harry Amana, "Groups Say Cops Abused 227 People; Will Oppose LEAA Funding to City," *Philadelphia Tribune*, January 28, 1975, 13.

12. Richard Kent Evans, *MOVE: An American Religion* (New York: Oxford University Press, 2020), 67–85; Linn Washington, "MOVE Says Mth.-Old Baby Killed in Clash with Police," *Philadelphia Tribune*, March 30, 1976, 1.

13. Christopher Capozzola, "'It Makes You Want to Believe in the Country': Celebrating the Bicentennial in an Age of Limits," in *America in the 70s*, ed. Beth Bailey and David Farber (Lawrence: University Press of Kansas, 2004), 29–49; "Demonstrate! For Jobs, Equality, Freedom, Independence, Peace," *The Organizer*, June–July 1976, 11.

14. Len Tinker, memo, December 31, 1976, box: Gov Surv/Cit Rts 1976, folder: Regional Offices: Dayton, Cleveland, AFSC; Zoharah Simmons, "Report on Field Trip for Program on Government Surveillance and Citizens' Rights, July 7–August 5, 1976, AFSC Staff Meeting, September 21, 1976," box: Gov Surv/Cit Rts 1976, folder: Trips. Field Trip to the Regions, AFSC.

15. Zoharah Simmons, interview with Rudolph Schware transcript, tape 9B and tape 10, July 14, 1976, box: Gov Surv/Cit Rts 1976, folder: North Central-Denver, AFSC.

16. Zoharah Simmons, transcript of Seattle visit, July 16, 1976, tapes 11, 17, box: Gov Surv/Cit Rts 1976, folder: Pacific NW-Seattle-Z Simmons Trip, AFSC.

17. Simmons, "Report on Field Trip," 5; American Friends Service Committee, *The Police Threat to Political Liberty* (Philadelphia: American Friends Service Committee, 1979), 25–35.

18. Simmons, "Report on Field Trip," 7–8; AFSC, *Police Threat to Political Liberty*, 80–95.

19. Zoharah Simmons, interview with author, May 28, 2021.

20. Simmons, "Report on Field Trip," 10.

21. Zoharah Simmons, interviews with author, June 11 and 18, 2021; Michael Simmons, "Affirmative Action Committee," October 7, 1976, box: Community Relations Division 1976, folder: Evolution of Affirmative Action Plan, AFSC; Third World Coalition, memo re: Surveillance/Rights Task Force, March 23, 1977, and John Sullivan and Muriel Lewis, memo re: Surveillance/Rights Task Force, March 25, 1977, box: Gov Surv/Cit Rts 1977, folder: Administration: Board Task Force, AFSC; Domingo Gonzalez, interview with author, October 17, 2021.

22. Zoharah Simmons, memo to Board Task Force on Surveillance, May 20, 1977, box: Gov Surv/Cit Rts 1977, folder: Campaign to Stop Government Spying, AFSC; Zoharah Simmons, transcript of Seattle visit, tapes 14, 20, July 16, 1976, box: Gov Surv/Cit Rts 1976, folder: Pacific NW-Seattle- Z, Simmons Trip, AFSC; Campaign to Stop Government Spying, "Member Organizations," box: Gov Surv/Cit Rts 1977, folder: Campaign to Stop Government Spying, AFSC.

23. Zoharah Simmons, memo to AFSC Board Executive Committee, August 12, 1977, box: Gov Surv/Cit Rts 1977, folder: Citizens Commission to Investigate the FBI, AFSC; Zoharah Simmons, interview with author, June 18, 2021; Kenneth E. Tilsen, "Goals and Objectives in Combatting Police Repression," *Guild Practitioner* 34, no. 3 (Summer 1977): 65–81.

14. ALL OF US

1. Michael Simmons, "Proposed Trip to South Africa," memo to David Sogge, November 8, 1977, box: PED Southern Africa 1977, folder: Second Visit to South Africa—Background and Deliberations, AFSC; Michael Simmons, interview with Klancy Miller, December 2, 1991, AFSC Oral History Interview no. 509.

2. Rosemari Mealy-Whitehorne, memo to Third World Coalition, December 11, 1975, box: TWC 1976, folder: Administrative Review, AFSC; Michael Simmons, "Southern Africa Task Force Evaluation," box: TWC 1977, folder: Self-Evaluation, AFSC; Daniel R. Magaziner, *The Law and the Prophets: Black Consciousness in South Africa, 1968–1977* (Athens: Ohio University Press, 2010); Steven Mufson, *Fighting Years: Black Resistance and the Struggle for a New South Africa* (Boston: Beacon Press, 1990).

3. James T. Campbell, *Middle Passages: African American Journeys to Africa, 1787–2005* (New York: Penguin, 2006), 329–334.

4. "An AFSC Southern Africa Committee Statement to Clarify the AFSC International Division," November 4, 1977, box: PED Southern Africa 1977, folder: Exploration and Development, AFSC.

5. Michael Simmons, "Perspectives on Bill Sutherland's Trip in the South," memo to Peace Education and International Divisions, December 3, 1975, box: TWC 1976, folder: Evolution of Affirmative Action Plan, AFSC; David Sogge, interview with author, July 20, 2021.

6. "Secretaries United," May 25, 1976, box: NWP 1976, folder: Committee Materials, AFSC; Mary Norris, "Report from the Racism-Sexism Task Group on Past Activities, and Some Questions for the Future," May 11, 1977, box: NWP 1976, folder: Committee Materials, AFSC.

7. Transcript of Tony Henry's report to the Board of Directors, April 24, 1976, box: TWC 1976, folder: Administration Review, AFSC.

8. General Consultive Group, Seminar on Racism, December 13–14, 1976, 15–19, box: TWC 1976, folder: Racism, Seminar on, AFSC.

9. Affirmative Action Planning Committee, draft, May 1977, box: NWP 1976, folder: Committee Materials, AFSC; Vinton Deming, "AFSC Affirmative Action: A Conversation with Tony Henry," *Friends Journal*, April 1992, 22–24.

10. Zoharah Simmons, interview with author, June 18, 2021.

11. Michael Simmons, "Southern Africa Proposal," November 8, 1977, African Activist Archive, and Michael Simmons, memo, October 10, 1977, box: PED Southern Africa 1977, folder: ID/PED Cooperative Planning, AFSC.

12. James E. Bristol, *Nonviolence Not First for Export* (Philadelphia: American Friends Service Committee, circa 1972), 12; David Sogge, interview with author, July 20, 2021.

13. David Sogge, interview with author, July 20, 2021; David Sogge, "Quaker Origins and AFSC's Troubled World," circa 1978, in author's files.

14. Board ad hoc committee on Southern Africa Study Tour prospectus, May 13, 1977, 3, box: PED Southern Africa 1977, folder: Board Ad Hoc Committee, AFSC.

15. H. W. van der Merwe, "Report Back to Cape Town Monthly Meeting," August 20, 1977, box: PED Southern Africa 1977, folder: Correspondence—van der Merwe/AFSC, AFSC.

16. Michael Simmons, memo to David Sogge, November 8, 1977, box: PED Southern Africa 1977, folder: Background & Deliberations, AFSC; David Sogge, interview with author, July 20, 2021.

17. Lyle Tatum, letter to Pat Hunt, January 20, 1978, and Michael Simmons, letter to Lyle Tatum, February 9, 1978, box: PED Southern Africa 1978, folder: Buethelezi, Sipho Speaking Tour, AFSC.

18. Guenter Lewy, *Peace and Revolution: The Moral Crisis of American Pacifism* (Grand Rapids, MI: W. B. Eerdmans, 1988), 228–229; David L. Hostetter, *Movement Matters: American Antiapartheid Activism and the Rise of Multicultural Politics* (New York: Routledge, 2006), 55.

19. Ray Holton, "The Siege Is On," *Philadelphia Inquirer*, March 17, 1978, 1, 4.

20. Jonathan Neumann, "Philadelphia Police: 'Toughest in the World,'" *Washington Post*, August 14, 1979; Jonathan Neumann and William K. Marimow, "The Homicide Files: How Phila. Detectives Compel Murder 'Confessions,'" *Philadelphia Inquirer*, April 23, 1977.

21. Evans, *MOVE: An American Religion*, 98–138, passim.

22. Ron Whitehorne, interview with author, April 10, 2019; Ron Whitehorne, "MOVE Blockade Ends," *The Organizer*, May 1978, 1.

23. Jessica Ann Levy, "Black Power in the Boardroom: Corporate America, the Sullivan Principles, and the Anti-Apartheid Struggle," *Enterprise & Society* 21, no. 1 (March 2020): 170–209; Andrew Young, address to UN Conference, May 19, 1977, box: PED Southern Africa 1977, folder: UN Conference, AFSC.

24. Tyree Scott, "My Brothers and I, the Buffalo Soldiers" (unpublished essay, March 1975, in author's files, courtesy of Trevor Griffey); *Southern Africa Summer Newsletter* 1, 7, box: PED Southern Africa 1978, folder: Publicity, AFSC; Michael Simmons, interview with author, March 25, 2021.

25. *Southern Africa Summer Newsletter*, box: PED Southern Africa 1978, folder: Publicity, AFSC; Michael Simmons, interview with author, March 25, 2021.

26. "Southern Africa Summer Project" (flyer), box: PED Southern Africa 1978, folder: Publicity, AFSC; Michael Simmons, interview with Klancy Miller, December 2, 1991, AFSC Oral History Interview no. 509.

27. Hostetter, *Movement Matters*, 55; J. A. Livingston, "Quakers Unload Shares to Aid South African Blacks," *Philadelphia Inquirer*, August 16, 1978, 8C; Ron Young, Ginny Hill, and Michael Simmons, memo to AFSC Executive Committee, June 8, 1978, and AFSC, "Why United States Corporations Should Withdraw from South Africa," May 1978, both in box: PED Southern Africa 1978, folder: Divestment, AFSC.

28. Zoharah Simmons, interview with author, March 25, 2021; Michael Boyette and Randi Boyette, *Let It Burn: MOVE, the Philadelphia Police Department, and the Confrontation That Changed a City* (San Diego: Endpapers Press, 1989), 111–131.

29. Laurence Stern, "Rizzo's 'Reform,'" *Washington Post*, October 30, 1978; "Every Dog Has His Day," *The Organizer*, December 1978, 1; Acel Moore and Mike Leary, "How Blacks Answered Rizzo, Then Split Tickets," *Philadelphia Inquirer*, November 9, 1978, 1; Thad Mathis, interview with author, April 10, 2019.

30. Tony Henry, "A Report to the Nationwide Affirmative Action Task Force on the Resignations and Termination of Four Third World Staff Members," May 17, 1979, box: TWC 1979, folder: Personnel Department, AFSC; Zoharah Simmons, "Luncheon Presentation," *Third World Coalition Update*, July 1979, 8–10.

31. Michael Simmons, interview with author, March 24, 2021; Michael Simmons, "Conference Held . . . National Minority Marxist-Leninists," *The Organizer*, October 1979, https://www.marxists.org/history/erol/ncm-6/oc-nat-min-conf.htm; Tyree Scott, "Conference Presentation: Speech on Party Building," June 1979, Encyclopedia of Anti-Revisionism On-Line, https://www.marxists.org/history/erol/ncm-6/min-conf-pb.htm; Nobuo N., "Evaluation of Minorities Conference," Encyclopedia of Anti-Revisionism On-Line, https://www.marxists.org/history/erol/ncm-6/nobuo-conf.htm.

32. Paul Thomas Chamberlin, *The Cold War's Killing Fields: Rethinking the Long Peace* (New York: Harper, 2018), 298–357.

33. Zoharah Simmons, interview with author, June 18, 2021; Zoharah Simmons, "Cambodian Diary," box: ID Asia 1979, folder: Kampuchea Field Trips, AFSC; Press Briefings, "Delegation Visit to Vietnam and Kampuchea," Bangkok, September 21, 1979, box: ID Asia 1979, folder: Vietnam & Kamp., AFSC; "The Talk of the Town: Notes and Comment," *New Yorker*, November 5, 1979, 39–40; Zoharah Simmons, interview with author, August 27, 2021.

15. THERE MUST BE SOMETHING WE CAN DO

1. Zoharah Simmons, interviews with author, August 20 and August 27, 2021; "Talk of the Town," *New Yorker*, November 5, 1979, 39–40; Rosemary Kendrick, "Missionary Blames Cambodia's Plight on US," *Capital Times* (Madison, WI), December 8, 1979, 19.

2. Michael Simmons, interviews with author, February 10, 2019, and September 2, 2021; Zoharah Simmons, interview with author, August 27, 2021; Mitchell Freedman, "A Tragic Souvenir of Vietnam," *Newsday*, March 3, 1979, 6.

3. Zoharah Simmons, interview with author, August 27, 2021; Aishah Simmons, interview with author, September 15, 2021.

4. John F. Bauman, "W. Wilson Goode: The Black Mayor as Urban Entrepreneur," *Journal of Negro History* 77, no. 3 (1992): 141–158.

5. Max Elbaum, *Revolution in the Air: Sixties Radicals Turn to Lenin, Mao, and Che* (New York: Verso, 2002), 240; "Principles of Unity of the Organizing Committee for an Ideological Center," adopted February 11, 1978, *OC Bulletin 2* (n.p.: OCIC, March 1979), 37–39; Ron Whitehorne, interview with author, April 10, 2019; Keith Forsyth, interview with author, August 7, 2021.

6. "Second National OCIC Conference, September 1–3, 1979, Conference Transcripts and Resolutions," 11, 84, 88, 94, https://www.marxists.org/history/erol/ncm-6/oc-2nd.pdf (Steering Committee Resolution included as an appendix in the meeting transcript, 2); Michael Simmons, interviews with author, March 31 and September 2, 2021.

7. Zoharah Simmons, interview with author, August 27, 2021; Zoharah Simmons, "Love WITH Accountability: A Mother's Lament," in Simmons, *Love WITH Accountability*, 23–29; Robin D. Stone, *No Secrets, No Lies: How Black Families Can Heal from Sexual Abuse* (New York: Roadway Books, 2004), 60–72; Michael Simmons, interview with author, September 17, 2021.

8. Gerald R. Gill, *Meanness Mania: The Changed Mood* (Washington, DC: Howard University Press, 1980); "Report to the Philadelphia Black Political Convention from the Delegates to the National Black Political Convention in New Orleans, Louisiana, August 21–24, 1980," Butch Cottman private collection; Chuck Stone, "A Black Political Party Is Born," *Philadelphia Daily News*, November 20, 1980, 2; Thad Mathis, "Position Statement from the Pennsylvania Delegation to the National Black Political Convention," 1, box 42, folder: NBP Convention August 1980, Manning Marable Papers, Columbia University; David Stein, "Containing Keynesianism in an Age of Civil Rights: Jim Crow Monetary Policy and the Struggle for Guaranteed Jobs, 1956–1979," in *Beyond the New Deal Order: US Politics from the Great Depression to the Great Recession*, ed. Gary Gerstle, Nelson Lichtenstein, and Alice O'Connor (Philadelphia: University of Pennsylvania Press, 2019), 124–142.

9. Butch Cottman, interview with author, April 11, 2019; Thad Mathis, interview with author, April 10, 2019; Sylvia Wright, interview with author, March 25, 2019; Michael Simmons, interview with author, March 24, 2021; John Malachi and Jim Griffin, "Black Political Convention," in Philadelphia Worker Organizing Committee, *Independent Political Action: A Marxist-Leninist Perspective* (Oakland, CA: Inkworks Press, circa 1979), 43.

10. Ron Daniels, statement, November 20, 1980, box 41, folder: Misc. NBIPP materials, Manning Marable Papers, Columbia University; Manning Marable, letter, October 27, 1980, box 41, folder: National Black Political Party

and Marable Coverage, 1980, Marable Papers, Columbia University; Kathleen Belew, *Bring the War Home: The White Power Movement and Paramilitary America* (Cambridge, MA: Harvard University Press, 2018), 55–76.

11. Manning Marable, "Occasional Paper Number XI: Toward Independent Black Politics" (Dayton, OH: Black Research Associates, 1981); and "Report to the Philadelphia Black Political Convention"; and Barbara A. Sizemore, "We Have Seen the Enemy! Is He Us?" box 42, folder: NBP Convention August 1980, Marable Papers, Columbia University; Benjamin F. Chavis, "Substitute Motion," box 42, folder: Black Convention Movement 1980, Marable Papers, Columbia University; Zoharah Simmons, interview with author, July 16, 2021; Ron Daniels, interview with author, April 18, 2019.

12. "Black Party Founding Convention" (flyer), box 41, folder: Press Releases—Founding Convention, Marable Papers, Columbia University; Sylvia Wright, interview with author, March 25, 2019.

13. Zoharah Simmons, interview with author, August 20, 2021; Kathy Flewellen, "The National Black Independent Political Party: Will History Repeat?" *Freedomways* 21, no. 2 (1981): 101.

14. Nan Bailey, "1,500 Blacks Launch Independent Party," *The Militant*, December 5, 1980, 4; Rhonda Miller, "Black Political Party Organized," *Washington Informer*, November 25, 1980, 1; Ron Daniels, interview with author, April 18, 2019.

15. "Charter of the National Black Independent Political Party," in *The National Black Independent Political Party*, ed. Nan Bailey, Malik Miah, and Mac Warren (New York: Pathfinder Press, 1981), 15–32; Sylvia Wright, interview with author, March 25, 2019; Zoharah Simmons, interview with author, August 20, 2021; "New Political Direction Needed," *Philadelphia Tribune*, January 2, 1981, 6.

16. Michael Simmons, interview with author, September 2, 2021; Keith Forsyth, interview with author, April 7, 2021; Dina Portnoy, interview with author, June 2, 2019; Ron Whitehorne, interview with author, April 10, 2019; Clay Newlin, "A Brief Statement on the Struggle Against Racism," August 1, 1978, https://www.marxists.org/history/erol/ncm-6/oc-racism.pdf.

17. Michael Simmons, interview with author, March 31, 2021; "An Open Letter to the Party Building Movement," October 1, 1980, 3, Brad Duncan private collection; see also Dave Forrest, "What Happened to the OCIC?" July 1981, box 13, folder 45, and Planning Committee, letter to Kai, June 11, 1980, box 13, folder 53, Tyree Scott Papers, Labor Archives of Washington, University of Washington.

18. "From the Staff," *The Organizer*, July 1981, 2; Organizing Committee for an Ideological Center, *Racism in the Communist Movement* (n.p.: December

1980); Michael Simmons, "Accommodation to Racism and the Communist Movement," *The Organizer*, August 1971, 13.

19. Michael Simmons, interview with author, March 31, 2021; Dina Portnoy, interview with author, June 2, 2019.

20. Zoharah Simmons, interview with author, August 20, 2021; Zoharah Simmons, letter to Elsa Brown et al., April 29, 1981, box 43, folder: NBIPP/Pittsburgh meeting June 1981, Marable Papers, Columbia University.

21. "'Black Party' Has No Answer to Reagan Racism," *Workers Vanguard*, December 12, 1980, 11–12; Nan Bailey, Malik Miah, and Mac Warren, eds., *The National Black Independent Political Party* (New York: Pathfinder Press, 1981); Ron Daniels, "Beyond the Chicago NPC: Some Suggestions for the Further Development and Building of the National Black Independent Political Party," box 42, folder: NBIPP-First Party Congress, Marable Papers, Columbia University; Daniels, interview with author, April 18, 2019; Wright, interview with author, March 25, 2019; Butch Cottman, interview with author, April 11, 2019; Zoharah Simmons, interview with author, August 20, 2021.

22. Zoharah Simmons, memo to NPOC and CRC members, January 7, 1981, box 41, folder: NBIPP material 1980–81, Marable Papers, Columbia University; Zoharah Simmons, memo to National Party Organizing Committee, June 10, 1981, box 43, folder: NBIPP/Pittsburgh June 1981, Marable Papers, Columbia University.

23. Michael Simmons, interview with author, April 1, 2021; Ronnie Henry, "Demand Justice for Journalist," *Daily World*, December 22, 1981; "Solidarity Day Set for Jamal," *Philadelphia Tribune*, May 4, 1982, 5.

16. THE WORLD AND ITS PEOPLE

1. Keeanga-Yamahtta Taylor, *From #BlackLivesMatter to Black Liberation* (Chicago: Haymarket Books, 2016).

2. "Unemployment Rate," *Philadelphia Tribune*, June 11, 1985, 4; Michael Davis, *Prisoners of the American Dream: Politics and Economy in the History of the U.S. Working Class* (New York: Verso, 2018); Lily Geismer, *Left Behind: The Democrats' Failed Attempt to Solve Inequality* (New York: PublicAffairs, 2022).

3. Michael Simmons, interview with author, April 1, 2021; David Sogge, interview with author, July 12, 2021; David Remnick, *Lenin's Tomb: The Last Days of the Soviet Empire* (New York: Vintage, 1994), 244.

4. Michael Simmons, interview with author, September 17, 2021; David Sogge, interview with author, July 12, 2021.

5. Michael Simmons, Oral History Interview no. 509, December 2, 1991, AFSC Third World Coalition, AFSC.

6. John Feffer, interview with author, August 24, 2020; Michael Simmons, "Speech from Alternative Security Conference," New York, May 10, 1981, box ID/PED E-W 1987, folder 11809, AFSC.

7. Michael Simmons, "Report on Trip to the Soviet Union, November 1987," January 1988, 5, box ID/PED E-W 1987, folder 59359, AFSC; Michael Simmons, interview with author, April 9, 2021; Odd Arne Westad, *The Global Cold War: Third World Interventions and the Making of Our Times* (Cambridge: Cambridge University Press, 2005).

8. Zoharah Simmons, interviews with author, June 18 and October 22, 2021; Darryl Jordan, interview with author, May 9, 2019; Gregory A. Barnes, *A Centennial History of the American Friends Service Committee* (Philadelphia: Friends Press, 2016), 324–325; Asia Bennett, memo to AFSC staff, March 9, 1988, box General Administration 1988, folder: National Office-Union, AFSC.

9. Michael Simmons, interview with author, September 17, 2021; Rosemary Cubas, memo to Asia Bennett et al., "Minute Regarding Bahiya Roberts Separation from AFSC," March 24, 1989, box: TWC 1989, folder: Annual Meeting, AFSC; Darryl Jordan, interview with author, May 9, 2019.

10. John Connelly, *From Peoples into Nations: A History of Eastern Europe* (Princeton, NJ: Princeton University Press, 2020), 685–762.

11. John Feffer, interview with author, August 24, 2020; Judit Hatfaludi, interview with author, August 24, 2021.

12. John Feffer, *Out of the Margins: A Report on a Roma/African-American Exchange* (Philadelphia: AFSC, 1996), quotes are from 3, 10.

13. Michael Simmons, interview with author, September 17, 2021; Feffer, interview with author, August 24, 2020; Judit Hatfaludi, interview with author, August 24, 2021; John Feffer, "The First Roma Feminist," John Feffer (blog), May 14, 2014, https://johnfeffer.com/2014/05/14/the-first-roma-feminist/; John Feffer, "Roma and the Civil Rights Movement," John Feffer (blog), September 20, 2013, https://johnfeffer.com/2013/09/20/roma-and-the-civil-rights-movement/; Michael Simmons, interview with John Feffer, September 13, 2013, posted September 20, 2013; Willie Colón Reyes, "'You Can Go As Far As You Want,'" *AFSC Quaker Bulletin Service* 79, no. 1 (Spring 1998): 1, 7; Judit Hatfaludi, interview with author, August 24, 2021; Clarence Lusane, interview with author, September 24, 2021.

14. Anita Hill, "Opening Statement to the Senate Judiciary Committee," American Rhetoric, October 11, 1991, https://www.americanrhetoric.com/speeches/anitahillsenatejudiciarystatement.htm; Zoharah Simmons, interview

with author, October 29, 2021; "African American Women in Defense of Ourselves," *Black Scholar* 22, nos. 1–2 (1991–1992): 155.

15. Kendall Wilson, "Friends Organize Drive on Conservative Agenda," *Philadelphia Tribune*, July 7, 1995, 5A.

16. "International Contingent of Women Sponsored by AFSC Attends the Fourth World UN Conference on Women in Beijing" (press release), September 8, 1995, box: NWP 1995, folder: 2607, AFSC; Pat Clark, interview with author, March 27, 2019.

17. Zoharah Simmons, letter to Kara Newell, September 10, 1995, and Nationwide Women's Program, Supporting Paper no. 4B, January 1996, both in box: NWP 1995, folder: 2607, AFSC; Zoharah Simmons, interview with author, October 29, 2021.

18. Zoharah Simmons, report to AFSC staff on Fourth World Conference on Women, January 22, 1996, and Nationwide Women's Program, "Report of the AFSC Delegation to the Fourth NGO Forum on Women and UN Conference in Beijing, August 1995," both in box: NWP 1995, folder: 2607, AFSC; Zoharah Simmons, "Islamic Personal Status Laws and Their Contemporary Impact on Women in Jordan" (PhD diss., Temple University, 2001), 39–41; Zoharah Simmons, interview with author, October 29, 2021.

19. Zoharah Simmons, interview with author, October 2, 2020, and October 29, 2021; Zoharah Simmons, interview with Justin Dunnavant, October 25, 2001, 38–40, African American History Project, Samuel Proctor Oral History Program, University of Florida.

20. Simmons, "Islamic Personal Status Laws," 424–429; Nancy Gallagher, "Women's Human Rights on Trial in Jordan: The Triumph of Toujan al-Faisal," in *Faith and Freedom: Women's Human Rights in the Muslim World*, ed. Mahnaz Afkhami (London: I. B. Tauris, 1995), 209–231.

21. Zoharah Simmons, interview with author, November 12, 2021; Simmons, "Islamic Personal Status Laws," 409–417.

22. Zoharah Simmons, letter to Kara Newell, August 25, 1998, in Aishah Shahidah Simmons private collection.

23. Zoharah Simmons, interview with Dunnavant, October 25, 2021; Zoharah Simmons, interview with author, November 5, 2021.

24. Zoharah Simmons, interview with author, November 12, 2021; Kathy Bergen, interview with author, November 16, 2021.

25. International Quaker Working Party on Israel and Palestine, *When the Rain Returns: Toward Justice and Reconciliation in Palestine and Israel* (Philadelphia: American Friends Service Committee, 2003), 3–19.

26. Zoharah Simmons, interview with Robyn Spencer, August 18, 2018; Zoharah Simmons, interview with author, November 12, 2021.

27. International Quaker Working Party, *When the Rain Returns*, 280; Zoharah Simmons, interview with author, November 12, 2021; Kathy Bergen, interview with author, November 16, 2021; Rachel Kamel, interview with author, March 4, 2020.

28. Michael Simmons, interview with author, September 17, 2021; Michael Simmons, interview with Veterans of Hope, May 18, 2001, tape A-7; "History of Seeds for Peace," Seeds for Peace, September 6, 2014, https://seedsforpeace.causevox.com/blog/history-of-seeds-for-peace.

29. Tyree Simmons, interview with author, October 6, 2021; Robin D. G. Kelley, interview with author, October 15, 2021; "Moorea Declaration," Abolition 2000, January 25, 1997, https://www.abolition2000.org/en/resources/newsreleasesstatements/moorea-declaration/.

30. John Feffer, "Sex Trafficking Conference," n.d., in author's files; Michael Simmons, interview with author, April 16, 2021; Pat Clark, interview with author, March 27, 2019.

31. Michael Simmons, interview with Zsuzsa Beres, May 30, 2016.

EPILOGUE: MANY MOONS

1. Vicente Fernandez, interview with author, August 19, 2020.

2. Aishah Shahidah Simmons, "Introduction: Dig Up the Roots of Child Sexual Abuse," in *Love WITH Accountability* (Oakland, CA: AK Press, 2019), 18; Gwendolyn Zoharah Simmons, "Love WITH Accountability: A Mother's Lament," in *Love WITH Accountability*, 28–29; Aishah Shahidah Simmons and Zoharah Simmons, me too. Movement Survivor Healing Series: Disrupting in the Home: Unpacking Black Familial Trauma webinar, June 16, 2021. Recordings of the book launch and conference are available on Aishah's AfroLez Productions YouTube channel, https://youtube.com/afrolez.

Index

DAN BERGER is professor of comparative ethnic studies and associate dean for faculty development and scholarship in the School of Interdisciplinary Arts and Sciences at the University of Washington Bothell. He is the author or editor of several books, including *Captive Nation: Black Prison Organizing in the Civil Rights Era*, which won the 2015 James A. Rawley Prize from the Organization of American Historians. He is a founding curator of the Washington Prison History Project, a digital archive of prisoner activism and policy. He has written for *Black Perspectives*, *Boston Review*, *Dissent*, *Truthout*, the *Washington Post*, and other publications. He can be found at www.danberger.info.